D-Day General

How Dutch Cota Saved Omaha Beach on June 6, 1944

Noel F. Mehlo Jr.

STACKPOLE
BOOKS
Guilford, Connecticut

Published by Stackpole Books
An imprint of The Rowman & Littlefield Publishing Group, Inc.
4501 Forbes Blvd., Ste. 200
Lanham, MD 20706
www.rowman.com

Distributed by NATIONAL BOOK NETWORK

British Library Cataloguing in Publication Information available

Library of Congress Cataloging-in-Publication Data available

Names: Mehlo, Noel F., Jr., author.
Title: D-Day general : how Dutch Cota saved Omaha Beach on June 6, 1944 /
    Noel F. Mehlo Jr.
Description: Lanham, MD : Stackpole Books, an imprint of the Rowman &
    Littlefield Publishing Group, [2021] | Includes bibliographical
    references and index. | Summary: "On June 6, 1944, under heavy fire,
    General Norman 'Dutch' Cota landed on Omaha Beach. He was a fighter and
    his contribution to D-Day will remain his rallying of demoralized troops
    and blazing the trail toward the breakout and victory on Omaha"—
    Provided by publisher.
Identifiers: LCCN 2020046481 (print) | LCCN 2020046482 (ebook) | ISBN
    9780811739658 (cloth) | ISBN 9780811769662 (epub)
Subjects: LCSH: Cota, Norman D. (Norman Daniel), Sr., 1893–1971. |
    Operation Neptune. | World War, 1939–1945—Campaigns—France—Normandy.
    | United States. Army. Infantry Division, 29th—Biography. |
    Generals—United States—Biography. | World War, 1939–1945—Amphibious
    operations.
Classification: LCC D756.5.N6 M44 2021 (print) | LCC D756.5.N6 (ebook) |
    DDC 940.54/21421092—dc23
LC record available at https://lccn.loc.gov/2020046481
LC ebook record available at https://lccn.loc.gov/2020046482

To General Norman Daniel "Dutch" Cota and his family

To the 29th Infantry Division "Blue and Gray" and their families

To Joseph Balkoski, for a lifetime of service to honoring the memory and
history of the members of the 29th Infantry Division, past and present

To Major General John C. Raaen Jr. and Private First Class Randall Ching
of the 5th Ranger Infantry Battalion for their stalwart defense of freedom
and their sharing of knowledge with others

To Michael White, stepson of Lieutenant Jack Shea, 29th Infantry Division

To all the veterans of Omaha Beach on June 6, 1944

To the French people

To my Lord and Savior, Jesus Christ

CONTENTS

Foreword

Joseph Balkoski

I HAVE SPENT MORE THAN FORTY YEARS STUDYING THE AMERICAN World War II soldier in depth: how he lived, how he trained, how he fought, and in so many tragic cases, how he died. In my early twenties, I became fixated on the U.S. Army's 29th Infantry Division because so many division veterans—still young men when we first met—were my neighbors. As I would soon learn, the 29ers' psyches brimmed with World War II memories, but virtually none of them had yet freely expressed those memories to anyone but their wartime comrades in arms. With just a little coaxing from me, however, their remembrances of things past flowed without restraint, revealing an astounding side of the conflict of which the postwar generation—including me—knew little. To me those friendships with 29th Division veterans were so purposeful that I could not stop telling their stories: over the next four decades, I produced seven books devoted to these men—a five-volume history of the 29th Division and a two-volume set on the American role in the D-Day invasion, in which the 29th Division played a major role.

The remarkable satisfaction I achieved in bonding with hundreds of World War II 29ers over that time span was tempered by the somber realization that my circle of 29th Division friends formed just a small fraction of the more than forty thousand men who had served in the division throughout the war years. I could, of course, never befriend the 3,720 29ers who had died in battle; their stories would have to be related to me by their surviving comrades. Furthermore, by the time the 29th

Division became the focus of my attention in the late 1970s, many of the division's senior officers had already passed away.

The inexorable march of time triggered in me acute regrets that I was never able to connect with one of the 29th Division's most renowned leaders. Norman Daniel Cota—born May 30, 1893, in Massachusetts; died October 4, 1971, in Kansas—was a man who profoundly enriched the 29th in his brief nine-month period as the division's second in command. Whether on the training ground or the battlefield, every soldier who met Cota—and that group included almost everyone in the division, from private to general—reaped inspiration from him. Never in my entire professional career as a historian did I hear a 29th Division veteran utter a single negative word about him.

He was the model "soldier's general." Of all the hundreds of "Dutch" Cota stories related to me, my favorite is the one told by the late Don McCarthy of the 116th Infantry. Sometime in early 1944, at 29th Division headquarters at Abbotsfield Hall in Tavistock, England, McCarthy delivered a late-night message, after which he looked for a quiet spot to bed down for the night. He found an empty cot in a second-floor room. After falling asleep, he was gently awakened by a touch on his shoulder; when McCarthy opened his eyes, much to his astonishment, there was General Cota, who informed him that he was sleeping in his cot. McCarthy apologized profusely and sputtered what he thought was a feeble excuse. Cota interrupted McCarthy's apology and declared, "That's OK, son. You go back to sleep. You need the rest more than me."

Cota's extraordinary heroism on Omaha Beach during the momentous June 6, 1944, D-Day invasion—during which he unquestionably saved many lives—should be the stuff of American legend, but sadly it is not. In the calamitous opening phase of the assault, Cota personally witnessed the deaths of many of his 29th Division comrades—sometimes just feet away—and came close to becoming a fatality himself more than once. For the next several hours, despite the fact that he was in all probability the oldest American soldier on Omaha Beach, he almost never stayed put, dashing through gaps in barbed wire, through unswept minefields, up the steep, smoldering bluffs, across the pastures and hedgerows, all the while encouraging those around him to do something, anything, to contribute in some small way to the resolute enemy's demise.

So frequently did Dutch Cota put his life on the line to impart confidence to his beloved 29ers that in the days immediately after the invasion, a 29th Division officer, Lieutenant Colonel John Purley Cooper of the 110th Field Artillery Battalion, urged him to take fewer risks. As Cooper related to me forty years after the event, Cota responded, "Look, Cooper, I do not have a death wish, but the U.S. government paid for my education at West Point, and part of the compact was that I would die for my country if necessary. And if I have to die, it is better that it be me rather than a twenty-year-old kid who has not started out in life yet."

I documented Dutch Cota's D-Day exploits in my books *Beyond the Beachhead* (published by Stackpole in 1989) and *Omaha Beach* (published by Stackpole fifteen years later). During the research and writing of both volumes, one salient detail emerged: amid the chaos of the invasion, a large number of American servicemen discerned that Cota's behavior was remarkable. How could they fail to notice the fifty-one-year-old general who almost never took cover, who heartened much younger men not with words of reproof but with encouragement, and who repeatedly astonished witnesses with personal acts of bravery? These amazing feats were seared into the witnesses' memories. Personal accounts and official U.S. Army reports of the D-Day invasion established beyond doubt that Cota's deeds contributed significantly to turning the tide on Omaha Beach. At the close of the *Omaha Beach* book, I concluded,

> *The facts are irrefutable that for most of D-Day, Omaha Beach was a great leveler of rank. Everyone, from general to private, was in equal danger every second. . . . The U.S. Army should seriously consider upgrading the Distinguished Service Cross award for General Cota to a Medal of Honor. This is especially appropriate now, in the twenty-first century, when careful retrospect of sixty years' duration yields mounting recognition that the Omaha Beach invasion was a pivotal test of America's resolve and arguably its most decisive moment in World War II. . . . A grateful nation must remember.*

With the publication of his excellent *D-Day General: How Dutch Cota Saved Omaha Beach on June 6, 1944*, I highly commend author Noel Mehlo for grasping the magnitude of Cota's exploits on that pivotal day and advancing D-Day historiography by a considerable factor. Yes, a grateful nation must remember, and with his impressive investigatory work, Mehlo ensures that it will do exactly that.

In *D-Day General*, the reader will not only learn the inspiring minute-by-minute account of Dutch Cota's actions on Omaha Beach but also absorb the fascinating story of Cota's early life and military career, details that will lead the modern observer to the obvious conclusion that everything about Cota's upbringing fashioned a man of extraordinary selflessness. As Mehlo points out, that selflessness emerged on Omaha Beach at precisely the moment when Dutch Cota's comrades needed it most.

America is a better country because of it.

Joseph Balkoski
Baltimore, Maryland
April 2020

FOREWORD

Current and Living Former Division Commanders of the 29th Infantry Division

OUR THOUGHTS CONCERNING UPGRADING THE DISTINGUISHED SERVICE Cross (DSC) to the Medal of Honor (MOH) for then brigadier general Norman Cota are based not on specific, limited acts of bravery, which constitute typical justifications for the MOH, but on larger, more comprehensive, continuous, sequential events of great tactical leverage and high risk to himself.

Ten percent of MOHs in World War I, World War II, Korea, and Vietnam were awarded to combatants reacting to the threat posed by an enemy hand grenade. In most cases, the scenario is a hand grenade in a confined space where there are multiple (but small numbers of) friendlies, and one person attempts to cover the grenade with his body or throw it to a safe place. In the case of Brigadier General Cota, his actions on June 6 doubtless prevented thousands of casualties. One need only ask oneself, "What if Cota had not been on the beach at 0730?"

A second measure of bravery by Brigadier General Cota is the duration of his display. Notably, it was probably not above and beyond the call of duty as he viewed it. To him, he was just doing his job to inspire soldiers to success. But by the end of the light of day on D-Day, when the exchange of violence had waned somewhat, Brigadier General Cota had left his footprints in the sand for the full length of Omaha Beach, had been to the top of the bluffs into Vierville-sur-Mer and more, and was the primary engine of inspiration that caused soldiers to leave their protected places and to close with and destroy the enemy.

We are not eyewitnesses but have read 436 pages of testimony and descriptions of the interaction and cooperation between the 29th Infantry Division and the 5th Ranger Infantry Battalion soldiers who conquered Omaha and seized control of that land area between the killing fields on the beach and the high ground adjacent to Vierville. From all of this material, it is clear that Brigadier General Cota, seeing firsthand the failures of soldiers and junior leaders (most of whom had never heard a shot fired in anger or witnessed comrades being murderously slaughtered) and taking varied actions to cajole, instruct, demand, challenge, lead, and demonstrate what needed to be done to close with and destroy the enemy, directly enabled Omar Bradley's army to secure a tactical foothold against a determined, entrenched enemy uninjured by pre-assault fires. Cota landed on Dog White Beach via LCVP (Landing Craft, Vehicle, Personnel) 71 at H+1 hour to find what was left of the lead assault regiment still on the beach, behind cover, essentially leaderless, in many cases not knowing where they were or what to do.

Post-assault analysis and debriefs verified that the amphibious landing was going so badly that at one point Lieutenant General Bradley, in charge of the landing at Omaha Beach, contemplated evacuating the survivors and abandoning the attempt. Bradley's army was trained and equipped for amphibious landings but not for amphibious retrograde, which logically would have been even more of a massacre than the landing.

There is no account of any other senior leader who took broad and repeated charge of hopeless situations and personally turned these into tactical success, or inspired others to do so, thus avoiding countless casualties. These personal leadership accomplishments, conducted in the deadliest environment known to man at the time, were largely unknown at the time that Cota was recommended for the DSC. Much of the "rest of the story" of Brigadier General Cota's excellence in leadership from the front comes from the testimony mentioned previously and from the log and report maintained and written by Cota's aide-de-camp, 1st Lieutenant Jack Shea. Shea never left Cota's side during all of June 6 and constantly urged Cota, unsuccessfully, not to expose himself so fully to the dangers.

The reports filed by Lieutenant Jack Shea were not written for months after Cota was awarded the DSC; thus, the citation supporting the DSC inadequately describes the total contribution made and the magnitude of risk taken by Brigadier General Cota with complete disregard for his own safety.

Landing at H+1 hour, Cota assessed the chaos based on having made previous amphibious assaults in North Africa and in the Italian campaign and took immediate personal action to direct and accomplish a sequence of tactical successes: by H+2 hours, he had created a gap in the wire and was moving inland off the beach; by H+3 hours, he was in Vierville at the top of the exit D-1; by H+6 hours, he was clearing D-1 at the beach end; by H+7 hours, he was clearing D-3 at the beach end.

With courage and determination, inspired in great part by Cota, the soldiers managed to fight their way off the deadly beach and up the overlooking, heavily entrenched terrain via D-1 and D-3, ending the day with a defensible posture on French soil.

Until the end of time, the 29th Infantry Division and its associations and heraldry will honor the indomitable courage displayed by Brigadier General Cota on June 6, and it shall remain the model for all soldiers to aspire to, a genuine source of unit pride, and a blessing to the generations of those whose lives his actions that day influenced. The upgrade of Cota's DSC to the MOH will ensure that his deeds that day will forever be a part of American history and the definition of individual valor under fire.

What if Cota had not been on the beach at 0730?

We, the most modern-day commanders of the 29th Infantry Division, take great pride in the knowledge that we had the honor of serving in the shadow of Major General Norman Cota.

Name	Served as Commanding General (CG) 29th Infantry Division
Carroll D. Childers, MG (Ret.)	August 1996–August 1999
H. Steven Blum, LTG (Ret.)	August 1999–October 2001, April–August 2002
Daniel E. Long, MG (Ret.)	August 2002–September 2004

Name	Served as Commanding General (CG) 29th Infantry Division
Arthur H. Wyman, MG (Ret.)	September 2004–September 2007
Grant Hayden, MG (Ret.)	September 2007–January 2010
Frank Batts, MG (Ret.)	January 2010–January 2012
Charles W. Whittington Jr., MG (active)	January 2012–July 2015
Blake Ortner, MG (active)	July 2015–April 2018
John Epperly, MG (current CG)	April 2018–present

PREFACE

TOM MORRIS, THE GRANDSON OF MAJOR GENERAL NORMAN COTA, remembers his grandfather fondly. He remembers well the hushed stories and the dignitaries who often graced his grandparents' and parents' homes when he was a young man. Once he reached adulthood, the magnitude of his grandfather's service emerged from the fog, and he came to understand just how important this man was to history. Tom's father, grandfather, and uncle all served during World War II and, ultimately, on D-Day. Tom's father landed on Utah Beach, his uncle flew cover in the Army Air Corps, and then, of course, there was his grandfather, "Dutch."

Before we delve into the military career of this man, to better understand the genesis of this story, a diversion into Norman Cota's family will give some much-needed focus as to the man and hence his character.

On November 1, 1919, Norman Cota married Constance "Connie" Martha Alexander (1901–1969) in Manhattan, New York. They were wed at the Episcopal Church of the Incarnation in New York City. They had one daughter, Ann Louise Cota (1920–1996), and a son, Norman Cota Jr. (1921–1988). Ann Cota later married a man named Thomas J. Morris Jr. (1919–1990). They had four children: Dan "DJ" Morris (1941–1990), David Richard Morris (1946–2008), Constance Ann Morris (Colby; living), and Thomas "Tom" Morris (living).

Tom recalled being a self-described "snot-nosed kid," ignorant of the importance of his family's contributions to freedom until he got much older. This situation was in part due to the often-cited quiet dignity of those men whom Tom Brokaw later labeled as the "Greatest Generation." Tom's older brothers were fifteen and ten years older than he. His sister was two years older, and he now thinks of himself as the clueless one during his childhood in relation to the knowledge of his family's military heritage. Tom and his siblings had parental orders: "Never ask Dutch/ Dad/Uncle Dan about the European Theater of Operations. Be a good listener." In this vein, his mother and father ordered their kids never to ask about Europe. If Dad or Dutch talked, just listen, the kids were told. Tom saw these parental orders as what he calls "the gold standard." As is customary with the "Greatest Generation," very little was expounded upon by the aforementioned.

Dutch was not a braggart. He was very shy about publicity and was a very private man. His grandson described him as being fundamentally in line with the "Greatest Generation." Dutch would not discuss Europe in mixed company. He was very humble, quiet, very kind, and an absolute gentleman. He was insistent on teaching his grandkids, and kids in general, to say "please" and "thank you." The grandkids could call him Dutch or Granddad.

Tom recalled going to McConnell Air Force Base in Kansas almost every other Sunday for "fried chicken" night as a boy. Tom reported that when the general walked into the room, everyone would stand at attention. As a small boy, and not knowing any better, Tom remembered thinking that when his granddad walked in, everyone sure was nice to stand for him. He told me that when he expressed that sentiment to his parents, he received the knowing smiles of parents who knew better. He remembered how his dad and Dutch would toast each other over scotch, bourbon, gin, vodka, or beer to the oft-repeated quote "There's nothing like getting shot at," and this statement remains very poignant to Tom. As an adult, he came to realize that his dad, Dutch, and Uncle Dan all experienced posttraumatic stress disorder, although it was not a clinical diagnosis at the time. His dad experienced it as a result of the artillery he had been exposed to during the war. As Tom grew, he came to have the opinion that his family's veterans were all very close based on what they experienced as part of the "Greatest Generation." He holds the position that "our generation is a pathetic embarrassment compared to that generation."

As a young boy, Tom was once on a walk with his grandpa down the street. At around 2 p.m., when something triggered a memory in the general related to D-Day, he looked at his grandson and said, "I didn't think I'd see sundown." During the 1960s, it was a family affair to watch the TV show *Combat* every Tuesday night at his grandpa's house. Tom has fond memories of this experience some fifty-plus years later. During one episode, Dutch uttered his discontent in a high-decibel voice. Tom recalled his grandpa saying, "You don't shoot uphill. You're giving yourself away. Who the hell directs this show?"

Tom recalled the high praise General Cota had for war correspondent and author Cornelius Ryan for his pivotal work in recording and documenting the D-Day story in his acclaimed book *The Longest Day*. Dutch was very enthusiastic about Ryan for the detail included in his book. His extensive interview files are housed at Ohio University in Athens.

General Cota's heroism sparked patriotism throughout the remainder of his life. After the book *The Longest Day* was published, Cota received fan mail. One young man, Mike Shaw, wrote a letter to the general likely in 1962. The lad wrote that he found *The Longest Day* to be a great book and that he had done a book report on it. He wrote, "It meant a lot to me. The struggle of men in war. Out of the whole book, I enjoyed reading about you the most." This letter was retained by Dutch and now resides along with his personal papers at the Dwight D. Eisenhower Presidential Library, Museum and Boyhood Home in Kansas. It is interesting to me that, in an age before instant messaging and gratification, this young American thought so highly of the general nearly twenty years after D-Day that he took the time to seek out the retired officer and send him this note.

However, Dutch did not like executive producer Darryl F. Zanuck and his movie portrayal of the carnage on Omaha Beach; he saw it as insulting because it "trivialized the sheer brutality of Omaha Beach." He was unimpressed with and didn't care for actor Robert Mitchum owing to what the general referred to as "taboo character issues" surrounding Mitchum's personal and political life in the mid-1950s. Dutch did think Mitchum was better looking than himself, however. He disregarded the invitation to attend the 1962 debut of the film. The members of the division remember when Dutch viewed the film in Philadelphia with them: "We remember the premiere of the movie, *The Longest Day*, in Philadelphia in 1962 when he broke away from the Hollywood publicity boys on hand to 'introduce' him and passed down the line of Philadelphia 29'ers on hand. 'These are my boys,' he told the men from Hollywood. 'They know me,' he said, as he greeted each one of us by name." Tom and his sister Connie were in grade school in 1962 and were both "plucked" from school to watch a screening of the film with their parents in Wichita, Kansas. Tom thought that Dutch would likely have happily collaborated with Steven Spielberg in the first half hour of *Saving Private Ryan*.

Once Dutch was commander of the 28th Infantry Division, Ike Eisenhower asked him to represent the United States at the liberation-of-Paris parade and ceremonies. As a boy, Tom remembered Dutch discussing this event. He said that Dutch believed that General Charles de Gaulle wasn't a grateful ally. Regarding France, Tom recalled his grandfather's feelings about the Americans' reception at the general staff officer level being "Thanks for saving us—now get the hell out." The French people were a different story.

Tom recalled, "Toward the end of the war, Dad was some thirty miles from Dutch at one point. Dad grabbed three bottles of 'liberated' wine and made off on a pass to see his father-in-law with these as a gift. He caught a ride on a truck to see him. Arriving at the destination, a soldier tossed his duffel bag from the truck to the ground, shattering the bottles." Tom said that his dad told him this was the only time he cried during the war.

To Dutch, some of his worst memories centered on writing condolence letters for those soldiers under his command who were killed. This task is daunting for any commander, but for Dutch, it remained a hard topic through the course of his life. Another difficult memory was that of having to be involved as a decisionmaker in the wartime desertion case and trial of Private Edward "Eddie" Slovik from the 28th Infantry Division. Slovik acted in a manner during wartime that compelled the decisionmakers to impose the full measure of justice. Dutch hated to have to concur in the death-by-firing-squad execution order that ultimately was approved by Eisenhower himself; this would be the first time since the Civil War that an American soldier faced such a punishment. It was hard on the general. He told his family, "It was the toughest order I had to issue."

Dutch respected General George Patton but did not like him personally. Dutch told Tom that once the two officers shared a C-47 from

Europe to Washington, DC, for a briefing with General George Marshall. Dutch refused the offer of General Patton to sit with him on the flight. Tom's father really liked David Irving's book *The War between the Generals: Inside the Allied High Command*. He attested to the accuracy of this work, and it was apparent to Tom through various conversations that Dutch remained fiercely loyal to Ike for his whole life.

In 1946, General Cota and Tom's dad attended the Army versus Notre Dame football game held at Yankee Stadium in New York City. It occurred a year after the war, and the world was still in the process of rebuilding. His dad held fond memories of that game and of attending that "large event" with his father-in-law in that context.

When Tom was a kid during the 1964–1965 time frame, John Eisenhower, son of Ike, was researching a book he was authoring, *General Ike: A Personal Reminiscence*, and so he paid a visit to Wichita to interview Ike's lifelong friend Dutch. As Tom recalled, his father met him at their home at 3:30 p.m. after school. They lived near Tom's school. His father had him ride with him to the airport. They were met by John Eisenhower. Tom remembered how much he resembled the president. Tom's mom and dad took Mr. Eisenhower to Dutch and Connie's for dinner and an interview for his book. Tom and his siblings were not invited to attend. The following day, Tom returned with the visitor and his father to the airport. While at the airport a reporter approached the father and son and asked whether that was President Eisenhower. Tom's dad responded, "No, but he sure looks like him. Come on, son, let's go," and walked on. Dutch ultimately liked this book due to its accuracy.

Dutch, Tom's dad, and Tom watched the movie *Battle of the Bulge* together at the theater in 1965. The former officers were highly critical that the brutal weather conditions in December 1944 through January 1945 weren't accurately portrayed in the film.

When President Eisenhower died on April 2, 1969, Dutch and Tom's mom and dad all cried while watching the news on television. To them he was a dear friend. Dutch was very averse to attending division reunion functions after the war, and he rarely talked about the war with anyone. Tom recalled family conversations regarding what might have occurred if the Americans had actually been able to capture Hitler alive.

His dad and Dutch both believed that the individual who performed that duty would have written his own ticket to anywhere in Europe.

More than once, Dutch and Tom's dad mentioned what a privilege it would have been to be on the squad that captured Hitler alive. They continued to say over the years that whoever pulled that off would have received "red carpet" treatment in any Allied nation from here to eternity. Those soldiers would never have paid for a restaurant, hotel, or evening's entertainment for the remainder of their lives. It seems that the two officers fancied having that on their résumés, as it were, as they aged.

Tom's paternal cousin, by Tom's father's brother, is Michael Morris. His memories are formed by having grown up in a military family, as his father was a marine and two of his sisters were soldiers. He grew up studying the battlefield exploits of those in the family who served during World War II. He told me, "I personally met Dutch a few times, as I was quite close to Tom and his family when we were Kansas residents, and we'd venture over to the general's house a few times, hoping to hear personal stories of his time in the European Theater. Dutch, however, preferred to talk about anything but. He was still a fascinating storyteller, usually regaling us with stories of his prehistoric artifacts he liked to collect."

Tom's father's last military post was at Fort Leavenworth, Kansas, and he and his wife remained in Wichita after retirement. In 1964, Dutch and Connie moved from Philadelphia to Wichita to be closer to Tom's mom and dad.

Dutch's beloved Connie died of cancer in 1969. When Dutch died on October 4, 1971, Tom was fifteen years old. General Cota and his wife are buried at the United States Military Academy Post Cemetery, West Point, Orange County, New York. They are located in a plot in Section X, Row M, Grave 287 (figure P.1). To find their graves, go near the back door of the "Old Chapel." General George Armstrong Custer is about 150 yards north of them, as are other notable American patriots. General Eisenhower's son is also buried nearby, some thirty steps away.

In April 1983, Norman Cota Jr. corresponded with Jack Shea concerning a desire to craft a biography about Dutch. He wrote, "I have always regretted the fact that Dad and I never really had the opportunity

Figure P.1. Graves of Norman and Connie Cota at West Point, New York (Tom Morris).

to talk about his experiences. It seemed my life was always at a distance which I was unable to narrow or failed to." This is now known to be a pattern followed by countless World War II veterans in the decades since the war. These men did not see fit to share their experiences. They were of a different time, and their silent dignity was a loss to the rest of us in the absence of their shared experience.

To Tom Morris, recalling these snippets moment by moment provides inspiration that he described as incalculable.

CHAPTER ONE

The Dauntless

There is nothing like being shot at.
—MAJOR GENERAL NORMAN COTA (RET.)

WHAT DOES IT MEAN THAT A SOLDIER, MARINE, AIRMAN, OR SAILOR acted beyond intrepidity? What are the circumstances that would drive a normally sane individual to conduct him- or herself in what appears to be a completely reckless manner? The word "intrepidity" is the noun of the adjective "intrepid." It means fearless or dauntless, such as one would expect of an explorer. Its synonyms are "brave," "courageous," and "bold." It is derived from the Latin word *intrepidus*, meaning undaunted, fearless, or untroubled. To be dauntless means not to be overcome with fear, not to be intimidated, not to be frightened, discouraged, or dismayed. In our society, the word "courage" is often overused, but here we find the truest meaning of the word. Courage is the quality of mind or spirit that enables a person to face difficulty, danger, or pain with firmness and without fear. Courage in combat is the ability to take all necessary action actually inspired by the fear, channeled into something much more deliberate and focused. One of my favorite posters shows the famous photo of Americans landing on D-Day on Omaha Beach. It says, "Courage—Bravery doesn't mean you aren't scared, it means you go anyway."

In the United States, the highest honor that can be bestowed upon an individual is the Congressional Medal of Honor (MOH). This award is for valor in action against an enemy force while serving in the

Armed Services of the United States. The award is generally presented to its recipient by the president of the United States of America in the name of Congress.

On December 9, 1861, Iowa senator James W. Grimes introduced Senate Bill No. 82 in the United States Senate, a bill designed to "promote the efficiency of the Navy" by authorizing the production and distribution of "medals of honor." On December 21 the bill was passed, authorizing the production of two hundred such medals, "which shall be bestowed upon such petty officers, seamen, landsmen and marines as shall distinguish themselves by their gallantry in action and other seamanlike qualities during the present war [Civil War]." President Abraham Lincoln signed the bill, and the Navy MOH was born.

Two months later, on February 17, 1862, Massachusetts senator Henry Wilson introduced a similar bill, this one to authorize "the President to distribute medals to privates in the Army of the United States who shall distinguish themselves in battle." Over the following months, the wording changed slightly as the bill made its way through Congress. When Lincoln signed Senate Joint Resolution No. 82 on July 12, 1862, the Army MOH was born. It read in part,

> *Resolved by the Senate and House of Representatives of the United States of America in Congress assembled, That the President of the United States be, and he is hereby, authorized to cause two thousand "medals of honor" to be prepared with suitable emblematic devices, and to direct that the same be presented, in the name of the Congress, to such noncommissioned officers and privates as shall most distinguish themselves by their gallantry in action, and other soldier-like qualities, during the present insurrection [Civil War].*[1]

More recently, the award criteria are codified in Sections 3741, 6241, and 8741 of Title 10, United States Code (USC). The current criteria and eligibility requirements include that the medal may be awarded to a person who, while a member of the army, navy, or air force, distinguished him- or herself conspicuously by gallantry and intrepidity at the risk of his or her life above and beyond the call of duty. The action must have occurred while the recipient was engaged in an action against an enemy of the United States or in military operations involving conflict with an opposing foreign force. The MOH recommendation must contain proof beyond a reasonable doubt that the service member performed the valorous action that resulted in the MOH recommendation. The valorous action(s) performed must have been one(s) of personal bravery or self-sacrifice so conspicuous as to clearly distinguish the individual above his or her comrades and must have involved risk of life. While MOH criteria require the member to risk his or her life, there is no requirement for the member to be wounded or killed in order to meet that criterion. The Department of Defense (DoD) defines these terms for its own use. "Conspicuous" is defined as attracting attention by being unexpected, unusual, outstanding, remarkable, or striking. "Gallantry" is described as having nobility of behavior or spirit or heroic courage. "Intrepid" is defined as being bold, fearless, dauntless, very brave, and not afraid. Lastly, the DoD defines "valor" as an act or acts of heroism by an individual above what is normally expected while engaged in direct combat with an enemy of the United States or an opposing foreign or armed force, with exposure to enemy hostilities and personal risk.[2]

The first MOH was awarded on March 25, 1863, to nineteen-year-old Private Jacob Parrott of Kenton, Ohio, who served with the 33d Ohio Infantry. He was a raider on a famous incursion into the South to disrupt Confederate rail operations. He was captured and severely beaten after interrogation. After he and six other captured soldiers escaped and returned to the Union, they became the first to receive the MOH, but he had the distinction of being the very first. His citation reads,

> *The President of the United States of America, in the name of Congress, takes pleasure in presenting the Medal of Honor to Private Jacob Parrott, United States Army, for extraordinary heroism on April, 1862, while serving with Company G, 21st Ohio Infantry, in action during the Andrew's Raid in Georgia. Private Parrott was one of the 19 of 22 men (including two civilians who, by direction of General Mitchell (or Buell) penetrated nearly 200 miles south into enemy territory and captured a railroad train at Big Shanty, Georgia, in an attempt to destroy the bridges and tracks between Chattanooga and Atlanta.[3]*

The first and only woman to earn the award was Dr. Mary Edwards Walker for heroic actions during the Civil War as a battlefield surgeon. She treated men from both sides at risk to her own person and at one point became a prisoner of war. The South ultimately freed her, and she continued her lifesaving mission.[4]

Many people have at least heard of the heroic World War I exploits of Sergeant Alvin York or those of one of World War II's most decorated soldiers, Lieutenant Audie Murphy. The reader is encouraged to take some time to research the various MOH recipients awarded over the course of history. More recently, we owe honor to men like Lance Corporal William Kyle Carpenter, who volunteered to defend America against further terrorism in response to the September 11, 2001, attacks. He was awarded the MOH, and his citation reads,

For conspicuous gallantry and intrepidity at the risk of his life above and beyond the call of duty while serving as an Automatic Rifleman with Company F, 2d Battalion, 9th Marines, Regimental Combat Team 1, 1st Marine Division (Forward), 1 Marine Expeditionary Force (Forward), in Helmand Province, Afghanistan in support of Operation Enduring Freedom on 21 November 2010. Lance Corporal Carpenter was a member of a platoon-sized coalition force, comprised of two reinforced Marine squads partnered with an Afghan National Army squad. The platoon had established Patrol Base Dakota two days earlier in a small village in the Marjah District in order to disrupt enemy activity and provide security for the local Afghan population. Lance Corporal Carpenter and a fellow Marine were manning a rooftop security position on the perimeter of Patrol Base Dakota when the enemy initiated a daylight attack with hand grenades, one of which landed inside their sandbagged position. Without hesitation, and with complete disregard for his own safety, Lance Corporal Carpenter moved toward the grenade in an attempt to shield his fellow Marine from the deadly blast. When the grenade detonated, his body absorbed the brunt of the blast, severely wounding him, but saving the life of his fellow Marine. By his undaunted courage, bold fighting spirit, and unwavering devotion to duty in the face of almost certain death, Lance Corporal Carpenter reflected great credit upon himself and upheld the highest traditions of the Marine Corps and the United States Naval Service.[5]

Lance Corporal Carpenter survived his ordeal and fought just as hard to recover from his near-fatal injuries. His story is the quintessential tale of one who threw himself on top of a grenade to save the lives of those around him. This is often the measure of bravery U.S. citizens speak of and understand when they think of valor in this context.

To date 3,520 Medals of Honor have been awarded to American servicemen and one woman.

What does it now mean to you when you think of someone who distinguished him- or herself conspicuously by gallantry and intrepidity at the risk of his or her life above and beyond the call of duty? The reader should consider this question for the remainder of this book. What would you do if you were placed in the situation you are about to absorb? What measure of respect do these real-life superheroes deserve in our society? How can you effect change in your life and for those around you with the knowledge you are currently absorbing?

World War II was the costliest war in world history. Within the context of the war between the Allies and Axis powers, one day is widely known to Americans and Europeans. This was June 6, 1944, when British, American, and other Allied forces opened the western front through the invasion of Normandy, France. On this Day of Days—D-Day, as it is known—the Americans were responsible for two of the five landing beach zones. More than 130,000 Allies landed on the shores of Normandy on D-Day. The invasion force included over 6,000 landing craft, ships, and vessels, some 176,000 troops, 822 aircraft, and 18,000 airborne troops. It remains the largest amphibious invasion in world history. One of these landing zones, known as Omaha Beach, gained the moniker "Bloody Omaha" due to the extremely well-defended coast and the high casualty rate among the invading Americans. The landing on this beach was a near disaster as it almost collapsed in on itself, and the men were nearly pushed back into the English Channel. It is widely believed that the bravery of the men assaulting the beach with all their might saved the day. Twelve men earned the MOH for their actions on D-Day.

Within this context, one man, the oldest and highest-ranking man to land on western Omaha Beach, placed mission above self and rose to lead his men from the front. This man was Brigadier General Norman Daniel "Dutch" Cota. Although he was awarded the Distinguished Service Cross for his heroism on D-Day, his extreme acts of bravery have become the stuff of legend. Seventy-five years after that historic day, Dutch was finally recommended for the only proper award equal to the task of honoring his actions. It is the hope of the Cota family and of the 29th Infantry Division community that General Cota will finally receive his due.

This said, the general often quoted this chapter's epigraph in the years following the war to his grandson, Tom Morris, in a way that contextualized for the boy what it meant to be concerned about trivial matters in life. In reflecting on the European Theater of Operations, Dutch often also said that the "worst part of it all was writing the condolence letters home." To young Tom, thoughts of having the "free world" at stake, coincident with the sheer brutality of it all while under intense enemy fire, gave realism to the concept. This was further tempered by the idea that comments made by those who had yet to experience such things were feeble statements at best and continue to be.

CHAPTER TWO

From Chelsea, Massachusetts, to North Africa

I think this permanent record of a story which we have enjoyed and laughed over, and sometimes felt like weeping over, will be a record that most of us will want to have in our libraries. We have to remember that in the future we will want to keep before our children what this war was really like. It is so easy to forget; and then, for the younger generation, the heroism and the glamor remains, while the dirt, the hardships, the horror of death and the sorrow fade somewhat from their consciousness.[1]

—Eleanor Roosevelt

Norman Daniel Cota was born on May 30, 1893, in Chelsea, Massachusetts. Chelsea was an industrial town along the Mystic River, opposite East Boston and Charlestown. His parents were George and Jessie (née Mason) Cota. His father, born in 1860, was a provisioner of French Canadian decent. A provisioner is a supplier of victuals or supplies to an army. After retiring from the railroads, his father was part owner of G. W. Cota & Co., located at 85 Winnisimmet Street in Chelsea, with his brother Frank (Norman's uncle).[2] His father was a hard taskmaster to his son. His mother, born in 1861, was a kind woman and a teacher of English descent, via a long line of Americans. The Cotas lived in an apartment above the store. Norman had odd jobs as a youth, such as picking up dropped coal from coal wagons and working as a delivery boy. While his sister went away to college to follow her mother to become a teacher, Norman's father didn't see the value of education for his son. Norman came to realize his father would push him out on his own before he began high school. In thinking about his station in life and his options, he went to his mother for encouragement.[3]

Then tragedy hit as Chelsea was ravaged by a disastrous fire on April 12, 1908. Known as the Great Chelsea Fire of 1908, it destroyed the Cotas' home and business along with 350 acres (as shown in figure 2.1). Nineteen people were killed, and fifteen thousand people were left homeless.[4] This great fire undoubtedly forged the young man in ways that only tragedy can. I think that his steady disposition came from a desire not to emulate his father, the kindness of his mother, and realizations about what is important in life as a result of surviving this calamity. Plus, he had tremendous drive.

Norman left public high school at fifteen, and by 1910 he was working as a stenographer in a bathroom supply mercantile office. He graduated from Burdett College of Business and Shorthand in Boston with a degree in business in June of that year. He was an emancipated young man. He saved his money while working with the goal of attending a private school of good quality. He enrolled in the fall of 1910 at Worcester Academy, a private school located in Worcester, Massachusetts. It is

Figure 2.1. The Great Chelsea Fire of 1908 viewed from the marine hospital (*Popular Science*).

one of the country's oldest day-boarding schools, founded as an all-male institution in 1834. The academy's motto is the Greek phrase Ἐφικνοῦ τῶν Καλῶν, which translates to "Achieve the Honorable." The school moved to its current location on Worcester's Union Hill in 1869. The main building had previously served as a Civil War hospital called the Dale General Hospital.

Norman Cota was an Episcopalian Christian, a faith he kept his whole life. Early in his academic career, he was known to participate in boxing, softball, baseball, basketball, skiing, bowling, fencing, football, golf, swimming, tennis, track, and wrestling. He was captain of his football team, which gave him the nickname "Dutch." As an adult, he stood 5'8½" tall, weighed 175 pounds, and had brown hair and striking blue eyes. In June 1913, he graduated from high school having financed his own education.

During his senior year, he took the entrance exam for the United States Military Academy (USMA) at West Point, New York. He sought and earned a nomination from Congressman Ernest W. Roberts of the 7th Massachusetts Congressional District for the entering class of 1913. He reported for duty on June 14, 1913. He was assigned army serial number O-5284. Among his classmates were Matthew Ridgway, Mark Clark, and later commanding officer (CO) Charles Gerhardt. Author and historian Robert Miller wrote the book *Division Commander: A Biography of Major General Norman D. Cota*. His work largely focused on General Cota's time with the 28th Infantry Division; however, it provides insights into Cota's early life and career. He wrote that Cadet Cota took to army life immediately and fell in lifelong love with small arms while at the USMA. Cadet Cota played football with Cadet Dwight D. Eisenhower (USMA Class of 1915). They became good friends and remained so for life. He was evaluated by his superiors in 1917. Cadet Cota's attention to detail, general bearing, military appearance, and attitude toward discipline were rated as very good. He was noted for excellent habits. He was deemed active but not athletic, even though he was captain of his football team. He qualified as a sharpshooter in rifle. His superiors assessed him as having good judgment, originality, efficiency, and character. He graduated 79th out of 139 cadets on April 19, 1917.

Figure 2.2. Cadet Norman Daniel Cota, U.S. Military Academy, West Point, New York (Tom Morris).

He weighed 156 pounds upon graduation (as pictured in figure 2.2). He was now fluent in French, Spanish, and German.[5] He sought out and was accepted into the infantry branch of the army.

On May 29, 1917, now 2d Lieutenant Cota took his oath of office in Chelsea, Massachusetts.

> *I, Norman Daniel Cota, having been appointed a 2d Lieutenant of Infantry in the military service of the United States, do solemnly swear (or affirm) that I will support and defend the Constitution of the United States against all enemies foreign and domestic; that I will bear true faith and allegiance to the same; that I take this obligation freely, without any mental reservation or purpose of evasion; and that I will well and faithfully discharge the duties of the office upon which I am about to enter: So help me God.*

Thus began the career of an American officer destined to affect history. Second Lieutenant Cota reported to the 22d Infantry Regiment on April 20, 1917, with orders to Fort Jay on Governors Island in New York Harbor. Prior to 2005, the word "regiment" was omitted from unit

Figure 2.3. Unit crest of U.S. Army, 22d Infantry (U.S. Army Institute of Heraldry).

names and will be done so from this point. Therefore, the 22d Infantry Regiment correctly becomes the 22d Infantry. The 22d Infantry Cota was assigned to traces its lineage back to September 1866 in Missouri. The regimental crest is shown in figure 2.3. Prior to the spring of 1917, this regiment had served along the Mexican border in Arizona to pursue the outlaw Pancho Villa. It then stayed in Arizona to ensure border security and peace until called east for World War I.[6] The men of the 22d arrived quietly on April 2, 1917, and took station at Fort Jay. Fort Jay is a coastal star fort and a former U.S. Army post. It is the oldest existing defensive structure on the island and was named for John Jay.[7]

On Good Friday, April 6, 1917, the regiment was sent into the first combat action of the war for America. This action occurred just minutes after the United States formally declared war against Germany with the passage of a war resolution in the U.S. House of Representatives by a vote of 373–50. The secretary of the navy immediately ordered the Atlantic and Pacific fleets to mobilize for war in accordance with orders. The 22d Infantry boarded U.S. Coast Guard cutters, crossed the harbor, and seized all twenty-seven German-owned freighters, passenger ships, and shipping terminals in New York Harbor and along the Hudson River. The seized vessels included the largest passenger ship in the world at the time: the SS *Vaterland*. She was a 950-foot-long, 54,282-gross-ton vessel and the only one not completely sabotaged by the German crews before capture. The navy renamed her the USS *Leviathan*, and she served the remainder of the war as a troop transport. The captured facilities included the piers of the great North German Lloyd and Hamburg-American lines. At all American ports, the government seized over ninety-one vessels worth more than $100 million. The German personnel in New York were interned quietly and in an orderly fashion on Ellis Island without shots fired. Cota participated in this action.

The 3d Battalion served as guards on Ellis. The government realized the importance of New York as the best harbor on the East Coast. They seized control of the Hoboken docks and piers, which became the basis of the New York Port of Embarkation from which tens of thousands of troops would depart for France, with the German cruise ships serving as troop transports. The regiment not only protected New York City but also provided other homeland security, including guarding tunnels, bridges, rail lines, and other important transportation infrastructure. One battalion was later posted in Washington, DC, to protect the capital. As the weeks progressed, the regiment developed a thorough system of harbor protection, and 1st Battalion was integral to this guard duty.[8]

From April 20 to August 24, 1917, 2d Lieutenant Cota served the 22d Infantry as company commander of Company A. This situation surprised the young officer. He was promoted to first lieutenant on May 15, 2017. The approximately four hundred men were transferred and became the nucleus of the First Division, American Expeditionary Forces in France. As a result of the syphoning of the experienced officers and enlisted personnel for combat in France, he was promoted quickly to captain on August 5, 1917. The young officer was given a gift in that he had to learn his job quickly under wartime conditions, a feat that would take much longer during peacetime. He developed his cadre and got to work developing the enlisted men and noncommissioned officers under his command. Then the company began to expand from a peacetime strength of 150 men to a wartime strength of 250 men.[9] He had to establish and enforce basic-type training for the influx of civilians into the ranks under his command. The draftees often arrived at the regiment not even knowing to which company they were assigned and without any equipment or uniforms. He rose to these challenges, and the organizational skill required undoubtedly aided him in the next war. He also had to become adept at dealing with career officers, enlisted men, and draftees alike. This helped him not be so predisposed to regular army types at the expense of the rest of the men. Captain Cota remained an infantry line officer in the regiment until September 1918. While assigned to the regiment, he also served as prison officer, battalion adjutant, exchange officer, and summary court officer.

On August 25, 1918, Captain Cota was assigned to temporary duty at the USMA as a tactical officer. He was permanently assigned to the USMA Department of Tactics on September 21. He rose to the rank of major on the same day and held the rank until after World War I, when the army downsized, and he was reduced in rank to first lieutenant on August 21, 1919, as were many career officers in the service. In 1919, he found himself under the command of Brigadier General Douglas MacArthur at the USMA. The postwar years were not pleasant at the academy. Congress cut funding to the institution, and, at the same time, pressure was put on by Congress to institute changes to make West Point more competitive academically with institutions such as Harvard. The hazing of cadets came under scrutiny as a first-year cadet died in 1918. MacArthur was successful in correcting the hazing issues but ran into a brick wall with entrenched tenured professors. Through it all Cota continued his path of excellence as an officer. In July 1919, Cota's CO wrote that he was "excellent in every way, a hard-working officer and that during a time of war he would be best utilized commanding troops." This was among the first of many such observations throughout the course of his long and distinguished career. "He was conscientious in his performance of duty." Lieutenant Cota then regained the rank of captain on September 1, 1919.

Cota remained at West Point as an instructor until July 1920. Miller wrote that compared to serving as a company commander, Cota found being an instructor less interesting and challenging. From October 1 to November 20, 1920, he served as assistant quartermaster, giving him experience as a supply officer (S-4). In the army, the S-4 "performs staff and supply duties as directed by the battalion commander and is responsible for the functioning of the battalion supply system in the field and in combat, with particular reference to rations, water, ammunition, gasoline, and oil."[10] The S-4 officer prepared battalion supply plans based on regimental supply plans and battalion tactical plans. They controlled the ammunition, kitchen, and baggage necessities. They ascertained and met the needs of the companies. Duty with the quartermaster was not the most desirable for a young infantry officer, but it undoubtedly trained him in the importance of this vital arm of warfighting and preparation.

In 1919, during his time at the academy, he took every opportunity to take passes and travel south on the Hudson River to the New York City area to visit his old friends and colleagues in the 22d Infantry at Fort Jay. On one of these jaunts, while attending a tea party on Governors Island, he first encountered a beautiful brunette named Connie, a recent high school graduate with plans to attend college to study physical education and music. Her father was a practicing lawyer in Manhattan, and she lived with her folks. The two fell in love, and a short courtship led to their marriage. After their honeymoon, she joined Captain Cota at West Point, where they had abysmal vermin-infested quarters. Connie became pregnant, and daughter Ann was born on October 23, 1920. Ann was the very first baby to be born at the cadet hospital in history. Unfortunately for Dutch, he was in New York City at the Army–Notre Dame football game—a boneheaded move for any young husband. He missed the birth, and one must wonder whether he enjoyed the doghouse.

Ever mindful of his future, Captain Cota thought it important to branch out in his military career and petitioned to become a finance officer. He was transferred to the Finance Department of the War Department in October 1920 and left West Point. He undertook training in finance and then was assigned as the property auditor, 3d Corps Area, Edgewood Arsenal in Baltimore, Maryland, on December 1, 1920, remaining there until May 31, 1922. While stationed in Baltimore, Dutch and Connie were able to find an apartment off base. This would surely have been good for the couple after their early years of hardship. During his stints in finance, he spent time training in Washington, DC, at Fort Howard, Edgewood Arsenal, and Aberdeen Proving Ground in

Maryland. When Norman Cota Jr. was born in December 1921, Connie went to the U.S. Army Walter Reed General Hospital in Bethesda, Maryland, for the birth. The young family took shape as the children began to grow, and time was spent with grandparents when possible. Captain Cota was then assigned as the finance officer at Langley Field, Virginia, on June 1, 1922, and served there until July 1, 1923. An unfortunate incident occurred while he was assigned this duty that required congressional intervention to correct; at the same time, it built additional character into an already sound officer.

At approximately 9 a.m. on January 30, 1923, Captain Cota was traveling with two armed guards through Hampton, Virginia, when two armed men robbed them at gunpoint in a busy downtown area while their government vehicle was stopped at an intersection. The party had just secured the cash for the monthly base payroll disbursement. The captain and his party were abducted and held at gunpoint in the car until about noon. They were eventually tied to trees along a creek outside town, under threat of death if they tried to free themselves, as the crooks made their getaway. After the bandits made off with the loot, the robbed soldiers initiated an escape led by Captain Cota. The thieves had absconded with $42,578.46, or the sum of the base payroll funds for the month for Langley Field. After a thorough investigation, Captain Cota was found innocent of wrongdoing, but the army burdened him with repayment of the funds lost. It took Congress (H.R. 724 dated December 7, 1925) to make right the financial burden placed on the officer by the Department of the Army. The amount lost was originally assessed against Cota as per army regulation. I debated about including this episode in this book, but, on further reflection as to Cota's character, I think this event was instructive to him and greatly aided his increasing coolness under fire.

Even in light of this unfortunate event, Cota's superiors rated him well. On June 29, 1923, Captain Cota, post finance officer, was referred to by his CO at Langley Field as a "conscientious and loyal officer who has handled his work well."

Captain Cota was transferred again to the USMA on August 26, 1923, this time serving there as the finance officer, until he felt a call to return to his roots in the infantry. Captain Cota's efficiency report for

June 30, 1924, stated he was "an earnest and hardworking conscientious officer, anxious to cooperate, and with more than the average amount of judgement and common sense." The army acquiesced to Cota's request to return to the infantry and sent him to the U.S. Army Infantry School at Fort Benning, Georgia, for the Infantry Company Officers Course on September 1, 1924, where he remained until August 11, 1925. After World War I, the army realized the need to develop training specific to the various arms within the service to better equip its officers and enlisted men. Fellow USMA alums Matthew Ridgway and Mark Clark attended the class with him. Omar Bradley was enrolled in the advanced class at that time. The army developed these classes as a "postgraduate" level of education for the officers. The army learned to balance classroom tactical and strategic learning with practical training in the field. Captain Cota found himself immersed in this training and took instruction on field problems from the platoon through the battalion levels. The officers gained hands-on experience in everything from mortars to machine guns, automatic rifles, grenades, and all other manner of weapons in the arsenal. The officers were expected to learn the weapons inside and out, as well as how to lead enlisted men who knew their deadly craft and those who were learning. The postwar army took time to analyze the lessons learned from World War I and make advances in military science so that America could learn how to outfight a potential future enemy and not repeat the trench warfare of the last war. The army was coming to terms with combined arms and mechanized warfare during the 1920s and the development of airpower and what that meant on the battlefield for the infantryman. Evidence of this can be found in various records on the U.S. Army Ike Skelton Combined Arms Research Library Digital Library.

Upon graduation, Captain Cota was ordered to Schofield Barracks, Hawaii, one of the most desirable posts in all of the army (as shown in figure 2.4). He and his family sailed from New York on August 11 and arrived in San Francisco on September 8, 1925, via the Panama Canal. They had a seven-day layover before sailing on to Hawaii. Cota reported for duty and was first assigned as an infantry line officer, serving as a company commander for nine months. Cota's grandson, Tom Morris,

Figure 2.4. Housing at Schofield Barracks, Hawaii, 1925 (Library of Congress).

recalled that the family often said Hawaii was their favorite posting of Dutch's long career.

On September 25, 1920, the 35th Infantry (whose regimental crest is illustrated in figure 2.5) was assigned to duty at Schofield Barracks. In February 1921, the Hawaiian Division, also known as the "Pineapple Army" (as illustrated in figure 2.6), was established to provide land defense

Figure 2.5. Unit crest of U.S. Army, 35th Infantry (U.S. Army Institute of Heraldry).

Figure 2.6. U.S. Army Hawaiian Division
patch (U.S. Army Institute of Heraldry).

of the territory strategically located at "the crossroads of the Pacific." It
was formed from units of the old World War I 11th Infantry Division.
From July 6, 1917, until July 31, 1942, the word "infantry" was omitted
from divisional unit designations. Therefore, the 11th Infantry Division
correctly becomes 11th Division during this period. The Hawaiian Division soldiers wore the taro leaf shoulder patch, which would later pass
down to two new divisions. The Hawaiian Division was formed under the
square structure used in World War I, with two infantry brigades, consisting of two infantry regiments each, and a brigade of artillery.[11]

Cota was assigned to Headquarters, 35th Infantry, 22d Brigade.
He ultimately became the regimental plans and training officer (S-3),
serving there until May 25, 1928. The S-3 is the commander's main
assistant in coordinating and planning for battle. In summary, the S-3
has staff responsibility for planning the tactical operations, organization,
and training as directed by the commander. S-3s work closely with executive officers to accomplish missions. They write operational directives

and plans, tactical orders, field training exercises, and training schedules. They prepare courses of action and recommend actions or decisions to the regiment commander for the accomplishment of missions. They are concerned with planning, training, control, and supervision of operations. The duties also involve monitoring budgets, establishing composition of forces to support plans, and ensuring that the unit tables of organization and equipment (TO&Es) are adequate, making recommendations to the CO to address deficiencies. S-3s establish policies and standards for unit readiness and supervise unit efforts to meet them. They plan and evaluate military operations and unit readiness. It is here that Cota came into his own. His understanding of finance and logistics gained in the 1910s and into the early 1920s allowed him to see the big picture beyond the battlefield in terms of the planning and operations of the army.

Despite the idyllic surroundings, Hawaii was a very important strategic base of operations for the United States. The 35th Infantry was tasked with the defense of the islands and the important navy base there. This fact was highlighted at the outset of World War II during the attack on Pearl Harbor. The Americans were wary of their neighbors to the west in Japan. The regiment planned for the possible eventuality of conflict. This was a very real-world assignment, and Cota rose to the challenge.[12]

On December 13, 1926, Captain Cota's efficiency report stated he was a very exceptional officer, energetic, loyal, and painstaking, with a delightful personality and a very marked leadership ability. It noted he should be sent to General Staff School at once to prepare him for that work. A year later, he was noted as an officer of exceptional abilities. "He is thoroughly dependable, most efficient and with fine tactical sense and understanding." On April 15, 1928, Captain Cota's efficiency report stated, "His work of maintaining the regiment in a state of training whereby it has been able during the past year and a half to comply creditably with all the demands made upon it has been performed in an admirable manner. Has shown himself equal to emergencies. He was rated as an excellent officer, qualified for high command."

Throughout this time, the Cota family grew close as the young children came of school age. Dutch became friendly with various fellow officers, including Omar Bradley, and he came to know others, like George

Patton. When it was time to depart, Dutch and his family sailed back to the U.S. mainland, ultimately arriving in New York City, with transit through the Panama Canal.

From here he was assigned back to Fort Benning for the one-year Infantry School Advanced Course (1928–1929). Fort Benning had changed as Colonel George C. Marshall, future chief of staff of the U.S. Army during World War II, arrived and implemented what he saw as needed improvements to the army training doctrine. He eliminated burdensome regulations and paperwork and began to transform the army to preposition itself to train vast numbers of raw civilian recruits, should the need exist in a future war. The new doctrines included four basic departments of tactics, logistics, weapons, and military history and publications. Marshall wanted officers who were skilled in the tactics of modern warfare and could communicate effectively to superiors and subordinates alike. He wanted officers who understood the dynamics of leadership. Captain Cota excelled in this environment and graduated at the top of his class. This achievement opened doors that positioned him for his next assignment.

He moved on to Fort Leavenworth, Kansas, for the Command and General Staff School (C&GS), a two-year course, in 1930 and 1931. The C&GS was a well-established school intended to train senior officers in the management of divisions and corps in battle. It was a must for promotion from captain to the field-grade officer ranks of major, lieutenant colonel, and colonel. Cota's class was the first to follow a two-year curriculum instead of the previous one-year one. The students were given what seemed an overwhelming workload. They were given case studies and theoretical problems pitting teams of students against each other in simulated combat. Cota found the course challenging and highly stimulating, even though he spent long hours in study while in attendance. He graduated in June 1931 and then went for a one-month Chemical Warfare Field Officers Course. After World War I, the United States— like many other nations—grappled with the prospect of readiness as a result of the Axis and Allied use of chemical weapons during the Great War. Cota and other officers were trained to learn the hazards of this type of warfare on the battlefield as well as advanced mortar techniques. The army developed a policy that came into being as a result of a letter between the army chief of staff, General Douglas MacArthur, and Secretary of State Henry L. Stimson on June 28, 1932. This letter stated,

> *In the matter of chemical warfare, the War Department opposes any restrictions whereby the United States would refrain from all peacetime preparation or manufacture of gases, means of launching gases, or defensive gas material. No provision that would require the disposal or destruction of any existing installation of our Chemical Warfare Service or of any stocks of chemical warfare material should be incorporated in an agreement. Furthermore, the existence of a War Department agency engaged in experimentation and manufacture of chemical warfare materials, and in training for unforeseen contingencies is deemed essential to our national defense.*

After his training was complete, Captain Cota was assigned to Fort Benning for four years as an instructor. Dutch's family took on-post residence in the newly completed Rainbow Hill officers housing located southeast of the intersection of Marne and Lumpkin Roads. He was neighbors with Omar Bradley, who ended up being Cota's boss at the weapons section. Major Bradley reported to Lieutenant Colonel George C. Marshall Jr. Dutch also became very close with Bradley. Captain Cota received his efficiency report on June 15, 1932, while on duty as an instructor in musketry and rifle company weapons at the Fort Benning Infantry School. This report, covering July 1, 1931, to June 15, 1932, stated that his performance was excellent. Bradley indicated that Cota was well qualified for duty and that he was an officer of sound judgment who should go far. Marshall concurred, with a provisional statement that he would rate Cota as underqualified for a battalion in peace and brigade staff in war. Cota was promoted to major on November 1, 1932 (as shown in figure 2.7). Shortly after his promotion, the Great Depression resulted in a reduction of military salaries. He remained an instructor at the Infantry School until May 21, 1933.

Major Cota was then assigned to duty at Fort Barrancas, Florida, as part of the Civilian Conservation Corps (CCC). The CCC was an

Figure 2.7. Major Norman Cota
(Tom Morris).

organization formed as part of President Franklin Roosevelt's New Deal. It worked to provide opportunities to Americans and to counter the unemployment of the Great Depression. The CCC was established in 1933 by an act of Congress and included men as young as sixteen as well as World War I veterans and skilled laborers. The federal government employed millions for the work associated with this organization. The CCC performed conservation and engineering projects across the nation. Though civilian in nature, it was military in fashion, with structure, discipline, and training standards. The enlistees underwent medical physicals and inoculations, followed by basic training for five days at military posts like Fort Dix, New Jersey, to become acclimated to the rigorous discipline and routines required to deliver their mission.

Men were assigned and transferred to a company, which in turn reported to a subdistrict, which reported to a district headquarters. These districts were associated with army corps commands and were led by high-ranking regular military officers. The CCC used military equipment and army uniforms. The living quarters were military-style open-bay barracks. They were led by active-duty military officers, from lieutenants to colonels, from the army, navy, or marines. Many of the higher-ranking officers assigned to the CCC had fought in World War I and would fight again in World War II, as Cota would. The civilians lived by military discipline, following standards such as lights out, marching, formations, and kitchen patrol duty.

The CCC was, however, a civilian organization. It had civilian leaders to augment the military leadership. The CCC enlistees were provided tutoring and ministering. They learned a wide variety of academic and vocational subjects and had instruction from the various federal agencies involved such as Agriculture, Forestry, or Interior. Today, many of the structures, buildings, and bridges built by the CCC remain throughout the United States, if one knows where to look.[13]

Fort Barrancas, Florida, was the home of the Supply Company, District G, Fourth Corps Area. It is located southwest of Pensacola and just to the immediate southeast of Naval Air Station Florida along the coast. When this CCC organization was officially put together in spring 1933, it originally comprised thirty young men who desired a new life and opportunities to earn a living made possible by the CCC. These young men were selected based on aptitude and physical abilities. They were assigned key positions in connection with the district CCC program. The unit was run like a military unit, and each man was assigned a specific job as clerk, typist, messenger, operator, pharmacist, hospital orderly, and so forth. As the unit progressed, demand increased for clerical and utility work, so new members were added. The strength rose to eighty-six and then higher later. Major Cota became the first CO from May 21 to August 19, 1933. He saw the experience as an opportunity to lead young men and boys on their way to becoming men and to provide valuable training to young men who someday might join the military. His experiences thus far were teaching him the value of total leadership, not of arrogance or exclusivity. Even today in military circles, some USMA graduates think themselves better than those around them, particularly fellow officers who gained their commissions through the Officer Candidate School or the Reserve Officers Training Corps (ROTC). In contrast to this attitude (shared by many of his peers), Dutch was honing his skills in communication, management, and leadership, despite whatever adversity might present itself.

Cota was then again reassigned to be a weapons instructor at the Infantry School at Fort Benning on August 19, 1933, through June 1935. Upon the end of his time there, he sought to find his way to the Army War College. He knew that attendance there was critically important to finding his way further up the chain of command into the general officer ranks, and he worked hard to achieve his goal. On June 30, Major Cota's efficiency report stated that he was superior: "An energetic Officer, brimmed full of enthusiasm, loyal, practical, excellent judgement. Plenty of force and thinks for himself. Has a pleasing personality and is capable of original work." He was noted for his preparation of training schedules and small arms firing. His efficiency report stated, "This officer is fully competent to organize and conduct a small arms school." This glowing report was prepared by Colonel Charles Weeks, who at the time had known Cota for ten years. Dutch found that he was assigned to the next class, set to begin in July 1935, and he and his family relocated to Chevy Chase, Maryland, on the northwest edge of Washington, DC. The War College at the time was located at Fort Humphreys, the present-day Fort Lesley J. McNair, at the confluence of the Potomac and Anacostia Rivers in the nation's capital. The Army War College prepared and mentored the general staff in the academic studies of war. The curriculum included responsible command, historical studies, and the effects of social, political, and economic factors on national defense. Army applicants had to have previously completed the C&GS. They also had to have obtained the required Professional Military Education for officers with the rank of major. During his time in Washington, Cota and Connie had an invitation to the White House as one of the many social functions that comes with being an officer.

From the War College, Cota was assigned to the 26th Infantry, located at Plattsburgh Barracks, New York, on March 6, 1936. This historic regiment was assigned to the 1st Division, "The Big Red One," during World War I, and after the war it remained attached to the 1st Division as one of three infantry divisions and one cavalry division authorized to remain at full peacetime strength. The 1st Division was assigned to the Second Corps Area. The post was situated on the west side of Lake Champlain, about one mile from the village of Plattsburgh, New York. On July 1, 1936, Major Cota's efficiency report stated that he was "a well-balanced officer of steady disposition. A good team worker, works thoroughly, methodically and accurately. Open-minded, appreciating the views of others. He takes a definite stand and holds to his convictions. Views problems from all angles. Produces practical ideas. Prompt and clean-cut in decision, with good judgment and firmness." He took command of 2d Battalion from July 25 to August 13, 1936. In his early time with the regiment, he served for a bit as the supply officer (S-4). Major Cota then spent from August 14 to September 12, 1936, running the rifle instruction at Camp Perry, Ohio. He then returned to Plattsburgh Barracks until his reassignment in July 1938.

The drumbeats of war began to take shape when the Japanese Empire attacked China on July 7, 1937. The Japanese initiated hostilities with a clash with Chinese near Peiping in North China. Although the U.S. civilian populace held an isolationist opinion, the military clearly realized the danger around America in the world.

Major Cota continued to excel as an officer. On June 30, Colonel Thomas L. Crystal, 26th Infantry, rated him as "truly superior." He wrote that Cota was "an officer of fine character with outstanding military ability. A serious student of the military well qualified to plan for and to effect the best results. Most dependable and a distinct asset to any commander as well as giving every indication of inherent command ability. He had served the unit as Regimental Supply Officer, Summary Court and Investigating Officer, and Plans and Training Officer." Accolades continued to pour in concerning Cota's performance and demeanor, as he was responsible for training active-duty, reserve, and National Guard soldiers alike as the various units activated and trained with the 26th Infantry. One example of praise came in a letter to Cota's superiors from the 389th Infantry, part of the New York Army National Guard.

HEADQUARTERS 389TH INFANTRY
Plattsburg Barracks, N.Y.

August 14, 1937

Colonel Thomas L. Crystal
Commanding 26th Infantry
Plattsburgh Barracks, N.Y.

Dear Colonel Crystal:
 The active duty training period of this command draws to a close and we return to an inactive duty status for another fifty weeks.
 We do not feel that justice would be done by us to various principal instructors of your command without a word of comment from the regimental commander before departing.
 Through you, the officers of the 389th Infantry, as a unanimous body, wish to express to Major Norman D. Cota, 26th Infantry, the satisfaction they feel for the superior quality of instructions, lectures and demonstrations planned and executed under his direction, despite greatly reduced personnel.
 The thought through this command is that due to the detailed military knowledge of Major Cota and his clean cut, plain and painstaking methods, every officer present leaves this camp with a better understanding of the subjects covered than has been the case in any previous camp.

       Very sincerely yours,

       Franklin A. Loomis,
       Colonel, 389th Infantry,
       Commanding

On June 30, 1938, Colonel T. L. Crystal, CO, 26th Infantry, wrote Cota a commendation. In it is a notation of outstanding performance. It states,

You occupied key positions S-3 and S-4 in the Regimental and Post organizations, as well as other important duties, and in addition assisted me as a most valuable intelligent, understanding and able advisor. You are aware of our close relations: of my confidence and trust in you, and the high regard I have in your ability, judgment and loyalty. I know of no other officer more and very few as capable generally, and particularly in the duties of S-3 as yourself. I wish to emphasize your own marked ability in all tactical and field work, as an instructor and as one of the most able Regimental staff officers I have known. You likewise have demonstrated outstanding command ability. . . . Your efforts here have entered largely into my success I have had in this command. For all these things please accept my thanks and appreciation.

In his final efficiency report from the 26th Infantry, Major Cota was noted as "the best S-3 I know. A keen analytical student, staff officer and commander. Outstanding as an instructor in training; in tactical operations. Honest and direct, devoid of pretense or sham. Loyal, willing, most industrious and cheerful. Participates in all activities with profit to them. Utterly Dependable."

On September 15, 1938, Major Cota was ordered to report back to the Command and General Staff School as an instructor at Fort Leavenworth, Kansas. By this time, young Norman Cota Jr. had decided on a course to follow his father's example to serve, and decisions were made to place him in a private boarding school with hopes to enable him to enter the USMA, which he ultimately did. Young Ann, the older of the two children, traveled to attend the University of Kansas at Lawrence. While there, she met and married Thomas Morris, an ROTC cadet.

German troops marched into neighboring Austria on March 12, 1938, and they annexed the German-speaking nation for the Third Reich. Adolf Hitler's Germany then invaded Poland at 4:45 a.m. on September 1, 1939. A force on the order of 1.5 million German troops marched on Poland all along its 1,750-mile border with German-controlled territory. The German Luftwaffe bombed Polish airfields, and German warships and U-boats attacked Polish naval forces in the Baltic Sea at the same time.

As the war in Europe and in the Pacific escalated and nations fell, the U.S. military entered into the final years of careful peace, but with an anticipation of war. The officers and enlisted men of the armed forces became increasingly aware of the perils now all around them and made final preparations as best they could under "peacetime" conditions. The utter ferocity and speed with which the Germans and Japanese conquered their opponents alarmed the military all the way up to the top, to President Roosevelt.

On June 30, 1940, Major Cota's efficiency report from the assistant commandant of the Command and General Staff School stated he was an "excellent officer. An energetic, sincere, unassuming, enthusiastic and willing officer of high value to the Service." Cota was promoted to lieutenant colonel, infantry, C&GS, Fort Leavenworth, Kansas, on July 1, 1940. He remained at Leavenworth until October 30, 1940, when he received his next set of orders. This excellent officer and growing master tactician was to be sent to where his expertise was most needed at the moment: "The Big Red One" (whose unit patch is shown in figure 2.8).

The War Department issued Special Orders No. 257 on October 30, 1940, approved by Army Chief of Staff George C. Marshall. The War Department relieved Lieutenant Colonel Cota from assignment and duty as an instructor at the C&GS and assigned him to the 1st Division, Fort Hamilton, New York. He was ordered to proceed to that station and to report to the commanding general for assignment. Colonel T. L. Crystal, General Staff Corps, chief of staff of Headquarters, 1st Division, Fort Hamilton, New York, issued Special Orders No. 230 on November 15, 1940. These orders assigned Cota to the 18th Infantry at Fort Hamilton and then further attached him for temporary duty

Figure 2.8. U.S. Army, 1st Infantry Division, insignia (U.S. Army Institute of Heraldry).

with the 16th Infantry, Fort Jay. He became the executive officer of the regiment until March 1941.

"The Big Red One" was constituted on May 24, 1917, as part of the regular army. It was organized on June 8 at Fort Jay. Its men were the first to deploy to Europe, and then on October 23, 1917, they fired the first American shell at the Germans. They fought hard, and their combat operations ended with the November 11, 1918, armistice. The division was at Sedan, France, representing the farthest American penetration of the war. It was the first unit to cross the Rhine into occupied Germany. Just before World War II, on January 8, 1940, the 1st Division had adopted a new peacetime TO&E in preparation for war. This included the new army "triangularization" structure of a division composed of three regiments and other assigned units. The thought behind the new structure was to have two of the regiments in combat at a time, while the third stood in reserve to the frontline forces, allowing for swifter and more fluid movement on the battlefield. The World War I model of a division was to have a square structure consisting of four regiments in two brigades. The authorized strength of this structure was 9,057 officers and enlisted men. The 1st Division reorganized again on November 1, 1940, adding more units such as a reconnaissance troop and two field artillery regiments, with a total authorized strength of 15,245 soldiers.[14]

The army brass decided that they wanted to bring the entire division together as one unified organization in order to fully train and prepare the men for what might come next. The War Department decided that Fort Devens, Massachusetts, would fit the bill in terms of the needs of the full division. Fort Devens was a sizable post forty miles west of Boston. The post was large enough to house the entire division. On February 5, 1941, Lieutenant Colonel Cota was detailed as a member of the General Staff Corps and assigned to general staff with troops assigned to Headquarters, 1st Division, at Fort Devens (as seen in figure 2.9). Lieutenant Colonel Cota's February 21 efficiency report from the 16th Infantry, covering from November 18, 1940, to February 16, 1941, rated him as an "exceptionally capable, energetic and efficient officer. He is alert, observant, and ready and willing to act should occasion demand. He has plenty of force." On March 11, 1941,

Figure 2.9. U.S. Army, Fort Devens, Massachusetts (U.S. Army).

Lieutenant Colonel Cota, General Staff Corps, serving as the assistant chief of staff, intelligence (G-2), Headquarters, 1st Division, was rated by his superior and ranked by order of aptitude and qualifications. He was rated as best suited for operations (G-3), followed by command (G-2), supply (G-4), and lastly personnel (G-1) duty.

Lieutenant Colonel Cota arrived in familiar surroundings with officers he had known through the course of his career. He came to understand that the 1st Division was to develop plans and train as a unit capable of amphibious warfare and landings. Just before he arrived, approximately one thousand soldiers of the division staged landings on the island of Culebra in the Caribbean, twenty miles east of Puerto Rico. The division also trained at Cape Cod in Buzzards Bay. These soldiers gained experience and a reputation as a competent landing force by the end of the year.

On July 12, 1941, Lieutenant Colonel Cota went on a one-week temporary duty to the new United States Marine Corps (USMC),

Marine Barracks, New River, North Carolina. The USMC stationed the 1st Marine Division, later to fight in the Pacific, at this newly developing post, which began construction in early 1941. The German threat, increasing mobilization, and space limitations at Parris Island and Quantico all underscored the need for one large East Coast marine base that could serve as an amphibious warfare training center for approximately fifteen thousand men. Furthermore, at that time the Army-Navy Joint Board (predecessor of the Joint Chiefs of Staff) still assumed that joint marine corps and army amphibious forces would be needed if the United States were called upon to liberate its European allies. Cota went to confer with the marines to enable more efficient planning of future 1st Division training and operations in amphibious warfare. Cota then traveled to Washington, DC, for training and briefings before returning to Fort Devens.[15]

On July 12, 1941, Lieutenant Colonel Cota's efficiency report from the 16th Infantry, covering the period from March 26 to June 30, 1941, rated him as a superior officer, "a dignified officer of character and ability. He performs all his duties well and is thoroughly reliable in all matters. Has an excellent reasoning mind and commendable force and judgement. He is cooperative and has a pleasing personality."

On August 15, Lieutenant Colonel Cota became the assistant chief of staff (G-3) for the 1st Division. Four days later, the division moved to the larger two-hundred-thousand-acre Camp Edwards, Massachusetts, for a monthlong field training. After completing this training, the division returned to Fort Devens until being deployed to the First Army maneuvers at Monroe, North Carolina, on September 29, 1941.

The first Carolina Maneuvers were designed to produce a head-on encounter battle between two very different military forces. The First Army, under the command of General Hugh Aloysius Drum, formed the Blue Army with a traditional infantry orientation of eight infantry divisions and six regimental-size antitank groups led by a traditionally minded commander. The 1st Division was assigned to the blue forces. General Oscar Griswold commanded the Red Army and assembled his reinforced IV Corps on the west bank of the Catawba-Wateree River. His command included two infantry divisions, one motorized division, and two armored divisions of the I Armored Corps. The forces engaged, and the battle took many turns, some expected and others unexpected. The 1st Division did all right for the most part, according to later army analysis, but there was room for improvement. The first phase of the Carolina exercise went on for six days. On the fifth day, the 1st, 26th, and 29th Divisions outflanked the red forces and caused chaos in the ranks (as illustrated in figure 2.10).

During phase two of the maneuvers, on November 27, the 1st Division exploited a weakness in the Red Army lines and captured the nearby town of Lancaster, well ahead of its intended objectives deep within red territory. This action cut off the Red Army escape route and placed the 1st Division only thirty miles from Camden, the key to the whole of the Red Army defenses. These exercises are detailed in Christopher R. Gabel's *The U.S. Army GHQ Maneuvers of 1941.* The maneuvers revealed

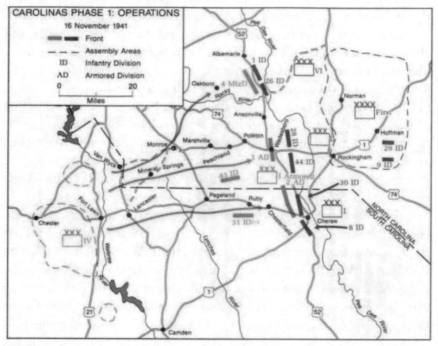

Figure 2.10. Early Carolina Maneuvers operations, November 16, 1941 (U.S. Army, Center of Military History [CMH]).

a disturbing deficiency in the training of individuals and small units. The army issued a remedial training designed to be progressive, beginning with the rudiments of basic training and carrying through to the training of regiments. Particular emphasis was placed on battalion training with more live firing of weapons, small arms, and artillery, both on the range and in the field under combat conditions, as illustrated in figure 2.11; the final engagements are shown in figure 2.12.[16]

The army analysis of the exercise stated,

Put simply, small units behaved as if they did not know how to protect themselves from enemy action or how to bring effective force of their own to bear upon the enemy. Maneuver troops showed little regard for defensive tactics and did little to avoid hostile fire. Secure in the knowledge that only blanks were being discharged, soldiers would maneuver openly in the face

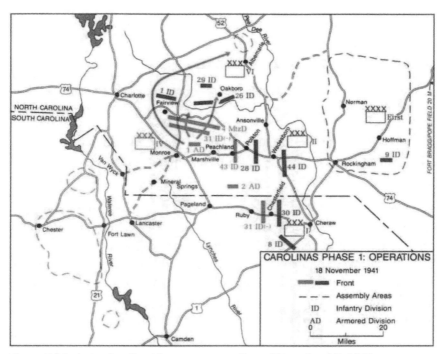

Figure 2.11. Later Carolina Maneuvers operations, November 18, 1941 (U.S. Army, CMH).

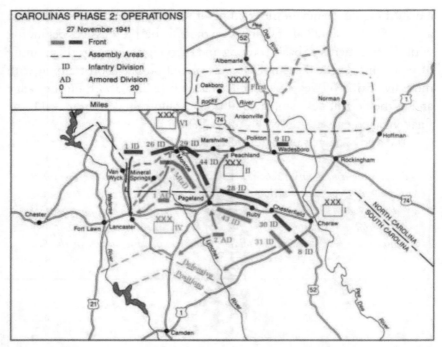

Figure 2.12. Final engagements, Carolina Maneuvers operations, November 27, 1941 (U.S. Army, CMH).

of small-arms fire rather than utilize cover. They often ignored artillery fire and sometimes stood in the open to watch air attacks that would have killed them in real war.

Cota, as the S-3, was intimately involved in the planning and operations of the division as it performed in these maneuvers, providing him with valuable training and learning for his coming years.

Dutch was promoted to colonel on December 6, 1941. The very next day, Japan attacked Pearl Harbor, and America was at war. On December 17, Colonel Cota reported to the Army War College for training and what were likely classified briefings due to the onset of hostilities.

The army had been considering development of training for selected units for amphibious operations and to develop amphibious warfare doctrine. This situation was drastically affected by the U.S. entry into World

War II. After Pearl Harbor, the army decided to partner with the marines to expand its amphibious training program. The resulting Joint Training Forces, composed of an army and a marine division with a partly integrated joint staff under a marine general officer, were established under navy command in each of the Atlantic and Pacific fleets. The 1st Marine Division and the U.S. Army's 1st Division were organized as the First Joint Training Force in June 1941 and conducted large-scale landing operations near Camp Lejeune, North Carolina, in July, with follow-on exercises in August.[17] Shortly after this, the 1st Marine Division was reassigned to the Pacific theater. The First Joint Training Force planned a subsequent, even larger landing operation for December 1941 that was postponed until January 1942. The landings were changed from New River, North Carolina, to Cape Henry, Virginia, at the mouth of the Chesapeake Bay in response to German U-boat activity off the coasts of Florida, Georgia, and the Carolinas. On December 26, Cota traveled from Fort Devens to the marine training center at Quantico, Virginia. He had orders to report to the commanding general (CG), Amphibious Force, Atlantic Fleet, USMC. The 1st Division was to engage in combined operations training with the marine corps and navy. As the S-3, Cota was to go there first to plan for the exercises.

The 1st Division reported to Cape Henry in January 1942.[18] They trained with the navy to deliver soldiers in landing craft to correct beach landing zones, improve air and naval gunfire support, and coordinate efforts between landing infantry and tanks during leading waves of an assault. Interestingly, the opposing force ashore was none other than the 116th Infantry of the 29th Division, which Cota would ultimately lead on D-Day as the assistant division commander. The landing operation demonstrated how incompetent the entire U.S. armed forces were in the execution of amphibious operations, as none of them performed at their best. The army only sent half of the 1st Division and the marines only a couple of battalions to participate in the exercises. The navy failed to provide adequate or suitable landing craft or transport and combat vessels to support and accomplish the landings. There were insufficient aircraft to bombard the shore, and the naval aviators were untrained in cooperation with ground troops. As a result, the navy failed to deliver the landing troops on the designated beaches. This all confirmed the joint amphibious force's lack of readiness for combat. Brigadier General Howland M. Smith, USMC, commanded the landing operation and rated the ship-to-shore movement of the operation as a tactical failure. The performance highlighted severe deficiencies in the command-and-control structure of the amphibious-assault landing. The command-and-control problems identified during this period reappeared during Operation Torch (the November 1942 invasion of North Africa) and ultimately on D-Day on Omaha Beach. As a result of these exercises, the army decided to develop its own amphibious training center. Through all of this, Colonel Cota was learning and analyzing the problems associated with invasion from the sea.[19]

Up to this point, based on the amount of training undertaken and the nature of the unit, the army considered the 1st Division the best of what it had to offer in terms of amphibious troops. The January exercises showed a distinct need for additional training and maneuvers. The division moved in its entirety to Camp Blanding in northern Florida, arriving by train on February 21. Division command was turned over to Major General Donald C. Cubbison, and the division was refurbished and given new equipment. Cota developed a cyst behind his right ear in March 1942, which he had to have removed surgically. This incident didn't stop him, and he returned to full duty in short order. Colonel Cota's efficiency report covering July 1, 1941, to May 18, 1942, said he was a superior officer: "He was called an exceptionally sound tactician, capable of prolonged and excellent work. High character and devoted to his duty, which always has the right-of-way. I know of no better General Staff Officer. Should be promoted to Brigadier General without further delay. In comparing this officer with all officers of his grade, I would place him among the upper third." This praise was offered by Major General Cubbison, CG, 1st Division. The division trained again and again, conducting amphibious landings along the Florida coast. It improved upon the mistakes of January and refined coordination and cooperation with the navy and marines.

The division traveled to Fort Benning, Georgia, around May 21. From there, it was sent to Indiantown Gap Military Reservation, Pennsylvania, on June 21, 1942, for final preparation for wartime overseas deployment. The division command transferred to Major General Terry Allen ("Terrible Terry"), a distinguished World War I veteran. Brigadier General Theodore Roosevelt Jr. also arrived as the new assistant division commander. This change of command resulted in some shake-up in the division. The new generals looked over the available officers and selected Colonel Cota, moving him from his role as assistant G-3 and putting him in place as chief of staff. They wanted an officer capable of handling a large volume of work who was extremely dependable. On June 30, 1942, Major General Allen, CG, 1st Division, again rated Cota as superior, noting, "An exceptionally sound officer of very sound judgement and thoroughly reliable. Has sound tactical judgement and is an exceptionally well informed infantry officer. Urgently recommend for higher command." The skill with which Cota was handling the S-3 matters of the division was drawing note as he readied his men for war.

Dutch found himself in charge of moving the division's fourteen thousand men and equipment from Florida to Indiantown Gap Military Reservation, near Harrisburg, Pennsylvania, on July 23 to prepare for the move overseas and then for another move to the New York Port of Embarkation and departure for Great Britain. There was very little precedent for moving an entire army division three times stateside and then immediately overseas in short order. He analyzed the situation, with all of the complexities of moving this amount of men and material, put his staff to work, and made it happen. The division departed New York aboard the HMS *Queen Mary* on August 1 and arrived at the Firth of Clyde on August 8, 1942, outpacing any and all U-boats. On August 1, U.S. Army divisions were officially redesignated as infantry divisions, and the 1st Division became the 1st Infantry Division.

General Allen wrote up a recommendation for the promotion of Colonel Cota to brigadier general on August 7. He said Cota had "outstanding professional qualifications, sound judgement, indefatigable energy and natural assets of leadership. He accomplishes the maximum results with the minimum amount of friction. He is forceful and aggressive, but is also level-headed and even-tempered." Allen went on to say that he "full well understood the great loss to the 1st Infantry Division that would occur with the promotion." Upon receipt of the promotion recommendation, Major General Mark W. Clark of the U.S. Army heartily concurred on August 11, 1942.

The division took up residence in Tidworth Barracks, fifty miles southwest of London, and got to work preparing for battle. The 1st Infantry Division was the first U.S. division to arrive in England. The only orders given to "The Big Red One" were to step up their training and get the division fully equipped and prepared for combat. Colonel Cota's mission was to carry out these orders. To this point, he served as the G-2, G-3, and now the chief of staff in the division. He traveled on August 26 to Glasgow, Scotland, with Generals Allen and Roosevelt and Lieutenant Colonel Eymer for briefings and training pertaining to the upcoming invasion of North Africa.

During World War II, the Norfolk House, at 31 St James's Square, Westminster, served as offices for the Supreme Headquarters Allied Expeditionary Force under Lieutenant General Dwight D. Eisenhower and various other senior officers from a variety of Allied armed forces. Colonel Cota was summoned there on September 3 to be briefed on the overall plan and subsequently to begin planning for the 1st Infantry Division's part in Operation Torch, the Allied invasion of North Africa with a landing in Morocco. Among the long list of officers in attendance was Dutch's old USMA classmate Major General Mark Clark, now the CO of II Corps. Cota and his fellow 1st Infantry Division officers discovered much planning had already taken place upon their arrival. Torch would be a three-pronged assault with a Western Task Force under General Patton, a Center Task Force, and an Eastern Task Force. The 1st Infantry Division was assigned to the Center Task Force under the new II Corps commander, Lieutenant General Lloyd Ralston Fredendall, alongside the 1st Ranger Infantry Battalion under Lieutenant Colonel William Darby, Combat Command B of the 1st Armored Division, and one battalion of the 503d Parachute Regiment. The Eastern Task Force was made up of the 34th Infantry Division and British forces. The entire operation was under the command of General Eisenhower. This was the first use of U.S. Rangers since the Civil War. Colonel Cota became very familiar with the Rangers during this battle and the ones to come. He became a fan of their capabilities and skill. This respect for Rangers later culminated in his selection of Colonel James Earl Rudder, former CO of the 2d Ranger Infantry Battalion, as CO of the 109th Infantry, 28th Infantry Division, later in the war. He really liked Rudder a lot.

The Center Task Force had the British navy serve as the naval force. Detailed planning for this assault began in earnest on September 4. The objective was the city of Oran, Morocco, with its two hundred thousand inhabitants. This was the second-largest city in French North Africa, with formidable two-thousand-foot mountains to both the east and the west overlooking its crescent-shaped and sheltered bay. The enemy were the Vichy French, loyal to the Nazis. The challenge for General Allen and Colonel Cota was to devise a plan to take Oran, minimize civilian casualties, and take vital ports and airfields intact. They decided on a pincer assault of Oran. Next, the three task forces would all land simultaneously to maximize chances of overwhelming success. Lastly, the assault was scheduled to happen at night to confuse the enemy force. At the conclusion of the conference, Allen ordered Cota to spend the next six weeks in detailed planning for the battle at Norfolk House.

In the operations plan, the general assumptions for the invasion were that Erwin Rommel's forces in North Africa were sufficiently engaged to the east, which would prevent him from effectively opposing Allied landing efforts in Morocco and Algiers. Spain was expected to remain neutral. The Luftwaffe was engaged on the Russian front and not up to the defense of this area. The last assumption was that the French troops in North Africa would resist to the maximum at the beginning of the operation. The plan called for the maximum use of American troops early in the invasion to lessen the will of the French to fight. The mission of the Oran Task Force was to secure the Port of Oran and adjacent airfields and to establish and maintain communications between Oran and Casablanca. They were also ordered to establish and maintain communications between Oran and Orleansville. The orders called for rapid movement and successful accomplishment of objectives to limit the enemy's ability to employ airborne troops against the Allied efforts.[20]

The plan came together in that the 26th Infantry under the command of Brigadier General Roosevelt would land west of Oran and head east.

Colonel Darby's Rangers would spearhead the eastern pincer, knock out the coastal defense guns, and move west. The 18th Infantry was to land to the left (south) of the Rangers and the 16th Infantry to the Ranger's left. The plan called for Combat Command B to land once the eastern beachhead was secure and drive on Oran. The airborne troops were to drop in on the airfields. It is said that Cota learned a great deal about liaising with our British allies during these weeks, a skill set he would rely on in the years to come. He worked out plans for thirty-four British naval transport vessels and their part in loading and invasion.

As a result of Colonel Cota's efforts, Major General Allen again recommended Cota for a brigadier general promotion on October 23, 1942. He said of Cota,

> *He has shown outstanding qualifications for higher command. He is intensely loyal, has indefatigable energy, has common sense and initiative, and has a high sense of duty. He has the happy faculty of exacting the utmost from his subordinates, in such a way that they like it. The movement of the 1st Infantry Division overseas, its various movements in England and Scotland, the maintaining of several Divisional Headquarters groups, the conduct of an intensive training program and the re-equipment and supply of the Division, have all been coordinated by Colonel Cota with the utmost efficiency.*

To describe the complex invasion in simplified terms, after the planning was done, a dress rehearsal occurred on October 18; then the men departed on October 26 for Africa. Aboard ship, Cota and Bob Roberts, the division operations officer, briefed all officers on the plans with instructions to relay details of the assault to every man in the division to ensure success. The invasion fleet entered the Mediterranean and, on the night of November 7, made a sharp turn to the south and headed directly for its objective. At 12:55 a.m. the Rangers were landed, and the first waves of the 1st Infantry Division followed (as illustrated in figure 2.13). On November 8, at 6 a.m., two British LCAs (Landing Craft, Assault) left the HMS *Reina del Pacifico* and made for shore. Aboard one landing craft was Major General Allen and his party, and aboard the second was Colonel Cota and his men. Once ashore, Cota headed inland a few hundred yards, established the 1st Infantry Division's very first command

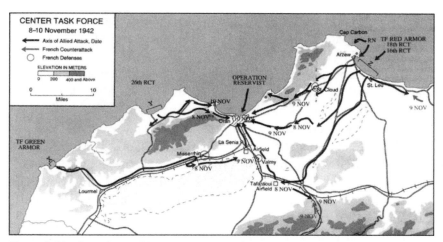

Figure 2.13. 1st Infantry Division invasion at Oran, Morocco (November 8–10, 1942) (U.S. Army, CMH).

post (CP) of the war, and set up communications. From here, the forces traveled ten miles toward Oran before becoming engaged in heavy battle with enemy forces at the town of St. Cloud, located another ten miles away. Here, the 18th Infantry's forward progress ground to a halt. General Roosevelt's forces also had an easy landing but ran into heavy opposition as they moved east. Cota found that communications were lousy, and there was insufficient telephone wire coming ashore, even though there was ample ammunition and food. General Allen declined to use artillery against the town due to the large civilian populace there. Allen visited the front and decided to do a flanking maneuver of the town to continue the advance. As the battle progressed, Cota continually assessed the situation and repeatedly moved his CP to stay as close to the front line as was practicable. The plan was successful. Both the eastern and the western groups conducted these flanking-type maneuvers, and by November 10 Oran had been captured. The casualties for the Americans at Oran numbered approximately six hundred, with ninety-four men killed in action. After the battle was over, the 1st Infantry Division was placed in reserve and provided for the overall defense of the newly acquired "real estate." Between November 10 and January 20, it remained around Oran. Several battalions and other elements of the division were parsed out to other units as needed. On January 20, the division was brought back together and moved to Guelma, approximately sixty miles east of Constantine, as Allied Force Headquarters Reserve.[21]

In December, it was time for the business of after-action analysis and personnel evaluations. Cota had left his mark on the 1st Infantry Division by enabling resounding success in combat. As the chief of staff, Cota was responsible for attending to the dead and wounded, seeing to the adequate movement of men and material, and other assigned duties. It was determined that most of the problems of the army occurred in the ship-to-shore phase of amphibious landings. The army concluded that whole idea of night landings had to be reexamined to mitigate this vulnerability in future operations.

General Eisenhower sent a message to General Marshall on December 16, 1942, recommending Cota for promotion: "Following are additional recommendations for promotion to Brigadier General: Colonel Norman D. Cota (0-5284), who is Chief of Staff, 1st Division, recommended by Allen and heartily concurred in by Fredendall. Cota was primarily responsible for the fact that troop and supply movements were maintained to an extent which permitted the Division to execute its mission. He has demonstrated qualifications of leadership, sound practical judgement and high sense of duty demonstrated in combat." General Eisenhower concurred strongly with this promotion request. The push for Cota's promotion continued. On Christmas Day, Major General Allen wrote to the commanding general, Allied Force Headquarters, regarding Cota (as seen in figure 2.14). He wrote, "This Division received a letter of commendation from General G. C. Marshall, dated August 27, 1942, through the Commanding General European Theater of Operations, because of the exemplary fashion in which its movement was conducted from the staging area in New York, through the ports of Scotland, to its station in England. I attribute this accomplishment very largely to the work of Colonel Cota as Chief of Staff." The effective invasion of Oran by the 1st Infantry Division largely had been credited by Colonel Cota's superiors to his diligence and unceasing leadership. This honor was not given lightly. Colonel Cota received his efficiency report covering the period from July 1, 1942, to December 31, 1942, on December 31.

HEADQUARTERS 1ST INFANTRY DIVISION
APO #1, U. S. Army

December 25, 1942

SUBJECT: Recommendation of Colonel Norman D. Cota, O-5264, GSC,
for promotion to Brigadier General.

TO   : Commanding General, Allied Force Headquarters.

THROUGH: Commanding General, II Corps.

1. Colonel Norman D. Cota has served under me as Chief of Staff of
the First Infantry Division since June 24, 1942.

2. This Division received a letter of commendation from General
G. C. Marshall, dated August 27, 1942, through the Commanding General,
European Theater of Operations, because of the exemplary fashion in which
its movement was conducted from the staging area in New York, through the
ports in Scotland, to its station in England. I attribute this accomplishment very largely to the work of Colonel Cota as Chief of Staff.

3. In the operations of the Center Task Force in North Africa on
November 8th - 10th, the First Infantry Division successfully accomplished
every mission assigned it. Again I attribute the success of the Division
largely to Colonel Cota, because of his skillful planning and coordination
of the multiple details involved. Because of his dependability, resourcefulness and common sense and because of the thorough confidence of all
elements of the Division in him as Chief of Staff, I was enabled to be
absent from the Division Command Post much of the time, when my presence
was needed with front line units.

4. Colonel Cota has consistently exhibited superior judgment,
ability and leadership. He is equally capable in both command and staff
functioning. He is an officer of the highest personal integrity and is
intensely loyal.

5. The promotion of commanders, who have demonstrated their ability
on the battlefield, is more readily obtained than the promotion of staff
officers under like conditions. Nevertheless, I again urgently recommend
Colonel Cota for promotion to the grade of Brigadier General, because of
his demonstrated accomplishments on the battlefield.

/s/ Terry Allen
TERRY ALLEN
Major General, U. S. Army
Commanding

A TRUE COPY:

LEONIDAS GAVALAS
Lt. Col., A.G.D.
Adjutant General

Incl #4

Figure 2.14. Christmas 1942 recommendation of Colonel Cota by Major General
Allen (Tom Morris).

General Allen rated him as superior: "He is the best Chief of Staff I have ever known. He is exceptionally capable, thoroughly dependable, absolutely loyal and has exceptionally sound tactical judgement. His personal characteristics, high moral standards and natural abilities of leadership render him exceptionally well qualified for higher command duty."

General Allen first submitted Colonel Cota for the Legion of Merit on September 24, 1942. The unrealized award recommendation spelled out the deeds that the 1st Infantry Division attributed to Cota that led to success on the battlefield. The citation reads,

> *COLONEL NORMAN D. COTA has an enviable record of long and faithful service in the United States Army. He has performed all tasks assigned to him in a meritorious manner and has thus earned for himself a reputation of being an extremely dependable and efficient officer. While serving in the capacity of division G-3, and now as Chief of Staff, he has applied himself to the work at hand with force and diligence. His ability to supervise and control the officers and men of his command makes him an example to his men and officers. His activity and determination to follow things through have enabled him to keep in touch with all units of this command. His highly developed technical skill, his thorough understanding of men and officers, provide him with a vast knowledge of his work. I have unwavering confidence in Colonel Cota, and feel sure that he deserves any honor that may be the result of his long and faithful service and complete devotion to duty.*

This award was not realized until June 4, 1944, for some reason. It was resubmitted on February 28, 1944, to General Eisenhower. This time, a more detailed description of Cota's actions specific to overseas movement, training in England, and the invasion of North Africa was included, which likely led to the awarding of the Legion of Merit:

> *General Norman D. Cota, then Colonel, as Chief of Staff of the First Infantry Division, was highly instrumental in directing and moulding untrained personnel into an effective combat team during the initial training period. He also facilitated the overseas movement from Indiantown Gap Military Reservation, Pennsylvania. Although the task was a gigantic one, no obstacle was insurmountable for him and the many problems were faced with great*

skill and efficiency. Even though he had no precedent to guide him, considering that his was one of the first divisions to leave the United States on a foreign assignment, that he lacked the fortune to draw on the experiences of any previous troop movements in the current war, he so successfully simplified and organized the various phases of the operation that the Chief of Staff, General G. C. Marshall, commended the Division for their expediency which characterized this transfer. This praise from the War Department was certainly a splendid tribute to Colonel Cota's efforts as Chief of Staff. Through his superb understanding of the technical transportation facilities involved and his infinite capacity for detail, the troop movement to Tidworth, England was made without incident.

Upon arrival in England, Colonel Cota immediately faced his most formidable task, preparing his division for its part in the forthcoming invasion. During the months of September and October, 1942, he made frequent trips to London where he cooperated with higher authorities in the important advance work, always a prelude to combat, thereby insuring the success of future projects. By his perspicacity and unflagging spirit, his personality and high degree of initiative, he secured the whole-hearted support of the General Staff and established a firm superstructure for all future activities. He executed all of these tasks with consummate mastery and military proficiency.

During this same period, he saw to it that the troops were being prepared for the Division's first combat mission. He kept in constant touch with designated leaders, supervised and directed the men in amphibious and other extensive training both in England and Scotland. In the various tactical exercises, he assured himself that the troops could cope with actual combat problems and that they could quickly capture strategically important objectives. At the same time he proceeded to re-equip and supply the Division, leaving nothing undone as days passed by and "D" Day approached. Colonel Cota accomplished this with the utmost efficiency, vigor, and force. His brilliant leadership and indefatigable spirit had produced results—The First Division was ready for any eventuality.

The First Division courageously accomplished every mission assigned it in the North African Campaign. The successful Oran invasion, November 8–11, 1942 was in large measure attributable to Colonel Cota, because of his skillful planning and consolidation of the multiple details involved. Because of his dependability and resourcefulness, the Commanding General of the Division was able to absent himself from the Command Post and to spend much time with front line units.

After the enemy's defeat in the Oran offensive, Colonel Cota worked unceasingly in preparation for the battles yet to come. It was largely through his initiatives and enterprise that the combat teams were organized and reorganized, weaknesses eliminated, and men conditioned for the strenuous Tunisian battles. Because of his exemplary leadership, the First Division continued to function well as a smooth fighting team in Tunis. During this time he exhibited qualities in both command and staff functioning, and certainly aided in the achievements of and the glory to his Division in this campaign. His efforts were rewarded. On 29 January 1943, he was assigned to [European Theater of Operations, United States Army] headquarters as Liaison Officer, and a few days later was promoted to the rank of Brigadier General.

Throughout his services as Chief of Staff, Colonel Cota was an inspiration to the officers and enlisted men of the Division. By his display of aggressive leadership, personal courage, tact, and mental alertness, he contributed to his organization's manifold successes. His loyal work was a stanchion that was depended upon. Even under most trying circumstances, he continued to discharge his duties in a highly commendable manner. His activity and determination to follow things through enabled him to keep in touch with all units of this command. His highly developed technical skill, his thorough understanding of men and officers, provided him with a vast knowledge of his work. His expert planning and execution of troop movements overseas and his supervision of training for combat greatly contributed to the success of the First Division.

The 1st Infantry Division worked in the rear until February 1943. When the division and Colonel Cota received orders for movement, however, they were to separate places. The 1st Infantry Division was on the march east for additional battle in North Africa. Colonel Cota received orders to go to England and was assigned to HQ European Theater of Operations, United States Army, for duty as chief with the Combined Operations Liaison Section on February 15, 1943; he was promoted to brigadier general on the same day. He finally had to say good-bye to the division he had faithfully served since the beginning of the war. His familiarity with many members of the division and their hard-fought experience would come to bear again in June 1944. Dutch received a final note of thanks from General Terry Allen, his division commander:

HEADQUARTERS 1ST INFANTRY DIVISION
APO #1, U.S. ARMY

February 9, 1943

My dear "Dutch,"

   I am not going to attempt to tell you how the Division misses you and how badly I personally feel over your separation from the 1st Infantry Division. We all hope that you will be back with us before long in one shape or another. Your influence in training and directing this Division will last forever. I am too damn dumb to express our real sentiments toward you.

Sincerely,

TERRY

CHAPTER THREE

A General Named Dutch

NEWLY PROMOTED BRIGADIER GENERAL COTA JOINED EUROPEAN Theater of Operations, United States Army (ETOUSA) as part of the training and operations section (S-3) and took over the American Section, Combined Operations Headquarters (COHQ), as the United States advisor on combined operations (USACO). ETOUSA was established on June 8, 1942, with the mission to conduct planning for U.S. forces to retake Europe and to exercise administrative and operational control over U.S. forces in Europe. President Franklin Roosevelt and General George Marshall decided to name General Dwight Eisenhower as the supreme commander of the Supreme Headquarters Allied Expeditionary Force on December 5, 1943. His appointment was publicly announced during a radio address by Roosevelt on December 24. (The insignia for ETOUSA is shown in figure 3.1.) The COHQ was a British command charged with overseeing combined arms operations, as well as the commando units and school.

Cota succeeded Colonel Claud Stadtman as USACO. He was assigned to work out plans for new invasions, and his amphibious-landing combat experience in Oran and previous interactions with COHQ made him a natural fit for the assignment. He was the first American with his level of experience in the organization. General Cota acted as U.S. advisor to COHQ, directed section activities in compliance with special orders of the chief of staff, and correlated assault training and planning between COHQ and ETOUSA. Two officers assigned to work with Cota included Major Lauren W. Merriam, who was made U.S. mil-

Figure 3.1. European Theater of
Operations, U.S. Army (U.S. Army
Institute of Heraldry).

itary signal officer, and Lieutenant Carl P. Miller, the U.S. intelligence
officer. These two officers were promoted with the assignment to lieutenant colonel and captain, respectively. Cota was tasked with working
out plans for new invasions.

On February 1, the 29th Provisional Ranger Battalion in training
at the commando facilities at Achnacarry, Scotland, went through an
exercise for an audience including Major General Russell Hartle, deputy
commander, ETOUSA; Major General Leonard Gerow, commanding
general (CG), 29th Infantry Division; Brigadier General Cota; Brigadier
General Ray Barker, assistant chief of staff of the G-3 ETOUSA; Brigadier General Harold Wernerm; Brigadier General R. Layceck; and others, including radio and newspaper reporters. The Rangers demonstrated
superb physical conditioning in climbing up and down cliffs, spanning
rivers, and racing through obstacle courses in bitter Scottish weather. The
Ranger battalion comprised an HQ company and four line companies
(later increased to six companies). Brigadier General Cota had previous
experience with Darby's Rangers in Africa, and he was a fan of them.

After graduation, the Rangers, under the command of Major Randolph Milholland, were assigned to the British No. 6 Commando, did additional training, and then participated in raids such as the Channel Island Raids. The commandos and Rangers took prisoners, shot up garrisons, and conducted guerilla-style assaults along the German defenses. Later that year, on October 18, 1943, the 29th Provisional Ranger Battalion was disbanded, and its members were folded back into the 29th Infantry Division, just as the 2d and 5th Ranger Infantry Battalions were established in the States. The infusion of these highly trained men added to the overall combat preparedness of the 29th Infantry Division.

On April 21, 1943, General Cota and Lieutenant Colonel Lucius P. Chase, HQ, U.S. Assault Training Center (USATC), had a conversation regarding developing a USATC conference on landing-assault doctrine. During the conversation they discussed the need to liaise with British Combined Operations Headquarters for certain assistance in connection with the success of the conference. They agreed that a sound and comprehensive doctrine did not exist in an assembled, usable form. There was a large amount of uncorrelated data from experiments, records of actual landings, and studies of landing operations to study. The function of the conference was to collect, evaluate, and assemble this data into a suitable form for use by the USATC as training doctrine. The conference would keep in mind the USATC's specific mission in the training of divisions and their subordinate units for the assault of a heavily fortified coast as a preliminary to a cross-channel invasion.

The specific assistance from COHQ at the conference involved several key points. One point of importance was a talk by General Hayden on the lessons of the Dieppe Raid. Second was a talk by the combined operations chief naval planner, probably in consultation with Commander Strauss or another U.S. naval representative, on the subject of naval support of a landing assault. Next, a talk by the combined operations expert on demolitions, in collaboration with a representative of the U.S. Army Corps of Engineers on the subject of reduction of obstacles and fortifications in a landing assault, was conducted to develop doctrine. The COHQ was requested to aid in development of scale models of landing ships and landing craft available for any mainland invasion. Due to the newness of this type of warfare at this scale, the development of a library of reports and reference materials for use by the USATC and later entities was deemed of critical importance. It was believed that COHQ had the most complete set of records at the time to develop any such library. Lastly, a collection of training films was requested to show the attendees the techniques under discussion.

The officers decided conference topics would cover tanks in a landing assault, German coastal defenses and defensive doctrine, reduction of obstacles and fortifications, airborne troops in a landing assault, chemical warfare support in a landing assault, artillery in a landing assault, air support in a landing assault, naval support in a landing assault, medical services in a landing assault, and signal communications for a landing assault. It was lastly decided that a practical field exercise would be included, placing the officers into three groups where they were expected to develop a field exercise for a division and its subordinate units, complete with an approved solution.

Brigadier General Cota reorganized his own section on April 23 and created the position of U.S. military quartermaster officer (USMQO), to which he appointed Major Gilbert W. Embury, with orders to learn detailed planning and equipment and supply in a landing operation. Major Cleaves A. Jones succeeded Major Embury in his previous billet as adjutant, and Captain Carl P. Miller became U.S. public relations officer.

On April 26, Lieutenant Colonel Lu Chase and Major McKeague visited the Combined Operations Command under the guidance of General Cota of the Combined Operations Section of the Special Staff of the European Theater of Operations (ETO). They had offices at both ETO and Whitehall. The purpose of the visit was to obtain cooperation of the Combined Operations Section in the coming conference. They asked for all available British literature, films, and models of landing craft. Several British officers were also requested to speak at the conference. The British made the well-made models available to the planners. There were only three films in existence, none of which was readily available, to some consternation. The available literature was more promising, and the British counterparts quickly added their American allies to the distribution lists. They discussed the proper location for a training school.

General Cota built consensus as to his vision surrounding training needs and style, seeing eye to eye with other top brass.

On May 6, 1943, General Cota sent a message to the USATC requesting a demonstration for twenty-five officers at Poole on Friday, May 21. In this demonstration, he wanted to see the newest methods of close fire support, including fire support from self-propelled mounts, tanks, and artillery pieces aboard LCTs (Landing Craft, Tanks). He also wanted the center to display all the various types of landing craft and support craft available at Poole to aid in better battle planning.

On May 22 and 23, Brigadier General Cota made one of numerous inspection trips across the British Isles, scouting for suitable terrain to establish a training center for American troops in landing operations. He traveled as far as Belfast and Londonderry, Northern Ireland, in a Cessna. This center would later be the site where all American and Allied forces trained to land at Normandy in numerous exercises that ultimately led to the success of D-Day.

The Assault Training Center Conference began on May 24 at ETOUSA. Brigadier General Cota attended this event as a speaker and major planner. The stated mission of the conference was to develop in detail sound doctrine applicable to landing assaults on heavily defended shores, with particular reference to a cross-channel operation. The COHQ facilities were opened for use by this group as it allowed for the use of models, motion pictures, photographs, and pamphlets. This monthlong conference was classified as "secret," and all appropriate measures were expected for security. A burn barrel was provided for even scraps of paper. The conference was opened with remarks by Lieutenant General Jacob Devers, commanding general, ETOUSA.

On May 27, Brigadier General Cota's section was realigned under the command of the G-3, ETOUSA, under Brigadier General Daniel Noce. Prior to this, Noce commanded the Engineer Amphibious School stateside. Dutch's colleagues surprised him on his fiftieth birthday with a party at the Park Lane Club in London on May 30.

The conference established the Allied approach to assault landings and allowed the command to formulate a realistic approach to the combined Overlord and Neptune Operations. The doctrines developed at the conference also formed the basis for training at the USATC and influenced planning for amphibious invasion.

For the naval support aspects of assault landings, the team studied and debated what landing craft would be available and their characteristics, capabilities, and limitations. The numbers of various types of landing craft suitable to land an infantry rifle battalion with normal combat attachments was discussed. The external limitations placed on the landing craft were analyzed, such as beach gradients, surf, tide, shingle, and runnels, as well as the limitations posed by ramp types on each craft. They then thought about the standard naval vessels that would or could be used to furnish fire support for the landing and what the operational characteristics were of each type of available naval gunfire. Other considerations included the volume, duration, effectiveness, and accuracy of the naval gunfire in addition to calibers, flat trajectory, high velocity, and limitations surrounding high-explosive ammunition. The team wanted to know how closely the leading assault wave could approach the beach that was under naval fire before the navy had to lift its fire. They studied whether the Allies could develop and use special types of craft, such as close-support gunboats, monitors, and rocket craft, to provide cover for the landings. The team wanted to know whether the naval forces could provide smoke and how its use would influence the landings. Naval fire support was studied in terms of an advance inland by leading troops and its effectiveness and ultimate range. Lastly, they worked up communications parameters for use between the various combined arms.

Another area of analysis involved air support for invading forces. They studied limitations imposed on fighter aircraft due to range and ammunition supply. One major question to answer was what level of air superiority would be expected on D-Day. Great emphasis was placed on aerial bombardment of the beaches prior to the landings. They wanted to know what specific types of aircraft could be employed. They studied how close air support would be used and how ground troops could communicate immediate needs to the aircraft. There was a desire to know whether the airpower could act as aerial artillery to augment naval gunfire. If the naval forces or assault forces employed smoke, the team studied how that would influence the efficacy of the airpower. Important consideration was given to the use of aerial observation, reconnaissance, and photographic missions before, during, and after the mission to provide effective intelligence. Lastly, they considered the time of day as related to airpower to determine the effect of light conditions, weather, and visibility.

The employment of airborne troops was given serious consideration related to the doctrine. The first task was to identify what airborne units were available to the ETO and how each unit deployed tactically and organized as glider or parachute regiments. The air transport requirements and support from other elements was studied to determine whether employment of these units would hamper other critical operational concerns of the landing assault. Naturally, the best use of each unit in conjunction with the amphibious units was evaluated in detail. Seizure of airdromes and ports and destruction of communication, command and control, and transportation centers was looked at, along with mission parameters such as isolation of beach areas from reinforcement or even attack of beach defenses from their rear. As with the other major elements, communication between the various arms and services was looked at in detail based on available equipment. A detailed look at airborne equipment and armament and logistical requirements for resupply and ammunition considerations was made. Final considerations related to the use of these assets included weather, visibility, the need for night operations, and designation of drop zones or landing areas before the aircraft arrived.

The infantry was the next major agenda item, and Brigadier General Cota was the point man on this topic for the conference. It was the infantry that would bear the major portion of the burden of the landing assault. The team considered whether any special infantry organization should be used for a landing and if such unit structure could be formed from within the standard infantry regimental combat team. The armaments of the troops were specified down to details such as to how to kit the men out with bayonets, hand grenades, and more machine guns and in what numbers. Cota and his team gave calculated opinions as to the differences between landing-assault troops or troops using normal combat tactics. How much equipment each individual man was to carry became a heavy topic, with discussion of every piece of equipment, ammunition, rations, and weapons. They looked at the value of cannon platoons and the use of mortars during the initial assault. The factors governing the loading of men into the landing craft were studied, and a doctrine developed as a result. The analysis included whether unit integrity was important and what tactical considerations existed related to debarking the landing craft, advance across the beach, and assault of the enemy defenses.

The attendees looked into the types of underwater obstacles employed both above and below the high-tide line used by the Germans and what means were needed to destroy or overcome them during an assault. The group studied types of fortifications expected, their employment within the terrain and in the battlespace based on German predilections, and their employment against an invading force. Plans were drawn up to eliminate any potential type of fortification encountered during the assault. The development of reliable reconnaissance and the time frames required to develop said information were given careful consideration. The team analyzed the use of combat engineers and the numbers of them required to accomplish the mission considered against all other factors. Cooperation between army and navy elements of combat engineer teams was planned for, and the equipment needs of both were tabulated.

The role of artillery in the landing assault was developed. The types and numbers of artillery pieces best suited for a landing assault were given close scrutiny. The question as to whether artillery was organic to an infantry division or another element needed to be decided for command and control and effectiveness. The normal infantry regimental structure utilized 75-mm pack howitzers, and other pieces such as tank destroyers often supported infantry. Whether these should be included as part of the doctrine was worked out. It was unknown at the outset whether artillery could be fired effectively from landing craft and hence whether it should be used. How artillery could be coordinated with naval fire was a concern to be detailed. The concepts of cover and ammunition delivery for artillery during the early landing-assault phases were unknown to the Allies prior to this important research and development.

The team worked on armored units (tanks) and their role in and suitability for assault landings. The means to transport them ashore and whether they could fire from the sea needed a hard look. The timing of landing the tanks ashore in the overall landing plan was looked at and maximized to the benefit of a successful landing. Amphibious tanks were researched, as was their effective combat use. The determining factor of the use of the tanks once ashore was developed by the team in terms of coastal defense reduction or breakthrough of lines and exploitation. Early in the planning phase, it was unknown what type of tank and how many should be employed during the assault down to the battalion and company levels. The beach conditions had to be given careful consideration on every invasion beach as related to the use of tanks at each site.

The agenda considered amphibious communications down to the smallest detail. Chemical warfare was considered, as was the use of landing smoke and flamethrowers. The medical requirements of the landing assault were given thought down to the company level, from the number of medics up through employment of aid stations and larger medical elements. Lastly, a detailed analysis of supply and administration was detailed in conjunction with all of the previous items.

A detailed discussion was held on May 26 regarding the German defenses and defensive strategy and capability. The men considered whether the Germans were likely to resort to the use of gas attack to defend the beaches. Considerations of German reinforcements were discussed at length, and it was widely acknowledged that they would hold armor in reserve and move it to the threatened coastal zones. The employment of the German fortifications, strongpoints, pillboxes, weapons positions, and so forth along the coast was thought out based on known intelligence at the time. The Germans' use of interlocking fields of fire and of small arms, artillery, and mortars was all understood by the conferees. Brigadier General Cota posed the question to the group, "In your study of those enemy dispositions, have you found any evidence of more organizations in the rear than you show on the maps?" Colonel Burton responded, "The evidence we have is largely photographic and indicates the strong points are on the coast or around towns. There is hardly any evidence of their being built more than four miles back from the coast. The rivers are expected to form the secondary line of defense. We know of no defensive positions behind the coastal positions, but if there are, they will not be of concrete, but wires and mines as it was in North Africa." The group discussed an average depth of defense along the coast of two thousand yards. Cota later asked, "When we head for the shore in boats, what kind of fire do you estimate will be encountered?" Colonel Zeller replied that artillery, mortars, machine guns, antitank mines, wire, physical obstacles, and actual fire of all kinds should be expected. Cota expanded his line of thought: "Will we run into a lot of flanking and hidden machine guns?" The consensus response was "Yes, the most dangerous will be the hidden machine guns." The group discussed the actual intelligence sources of these positions and the limitations of gathering this type of intelligence.

The final overall summary of the day's discussion was offered by Lieutenant Colonel Chase:

We know definitely how the Germans are defending France and the low-countries. They have distrust of defenses along the high-water mark, supported by heavy gun artillery and backed with lighter artillery in the rear. This artillery fire is reinforced by air attack. We will first encounter attack from the air while we are loading the boats and as we approach the beach we will come under more and more artillery fire. As the invasion progresses inland, obstacles of every type will be encountered and must be overcome under fire from echelon reserves. The Germans seem to rely on river lines for second line of resistance, so we will encounter demolished bridges. The problem posed by this defensive system is to get through this crust of obstacles covered by intensive fire, to come to grips with garrisons along the coast before the reserves further back can be brought up.

The conferees acknowledged that the German defensive system presented a difficult problem for an invading force to overcome.

On June 2, Brigadier General Cota delivered a daylong lecture on infantry in landing assaults, including a screening of the film *North Africa Landings, II.* The general had the whole day to highlight his views on infantry tactics and strategy to the august body. He was an eloquent speaker and opened with this statement:

Throughout my discussion on this subject, please keep constantly in mind the two means of action available to infantry: namely, FIRE and MOVEMENT, or as some people prefer to say, FIRE and MANEUVER. All infantry action on water or on land is based on the proper application of FIRE and MANEUVER to insure the accomplishment of its mission. MANEUVER is employed to advance FIRE POWER to positions where it can be used with maximum effective results.

Dutch made his case for the proper use of infantry during amphibious landings based on his experiences. Three essential phases of a landing operation were identified and detailed, including (1) securing the beachhead, (2) exploitation, and (3) maintaining and expanding the landing zone. Cota reasoned that the troops needed during these distinct phases required advanced planning and differing force compositions for each phase. He built his case for the new concept of assault divisions thought out between himself and the USATC staff before the conference. These would have a smaller size than a standard divisional structure, carry less unnecessary gear, and carry more individual weapons, such as grenades, and ammunition. The ultimate plan would be to increase mobility, thereby ensuring rapid movement during the landing and as the troops fought their way off the beaches. The concept would maximize firepower for the close-in type of combat expected in the situation. Cota laid out the importance of heavy and accurate naval gunfire—as was his experience in North Africa—during the initial landings when the infantry troops were exposed and at their most vulnerable. Whatever plans were finally made regarding the cross-channel assault, the capabilities and limitations of the individual soldier must be considered; the plans had to be as simple as possible. Cota strongly urged that the landings to be made at night to achieve maximum tactical surprise on the part of the infantry involved. He identified and laid out three factors that held up in his own experience on D-Day itself: (1) navigational errors would be common during the run to the beaches; (2) confusion would be prevalent during the landing; and (3) there would be interruptions to the landing once the first troops were ashore.[1]

Brigadier General Cota was relieved from Combined Operations Liaison Section and assigned to G-3, HQ, ETOUSA, on June 4, 1943. Major John Anderson, USMC, joined the unit on June 15. From June 8 to June 13, a weeklong problem was conducted at Woolacombe-Appledore

Harbor, where the USATC was established and later became functional in September 1943. This problem allowed Allied planners to refine and develop important strategic and tactical questions that arose from conferences, war games, and discussions. The USATC was designed to provide the combat teams of assault divisions in the United Kingdom with intensive, realistic training in the latest authoritative doctrines and under conditions closely approximating those the combat teams would encounter in landing-assault operations against the German-held coast of Western Europe. As several landing operations had been completed by this point in the war, General Cota came to several definitive conclusions related to the training, equipment, and personnel to be employed in an effective amphibious assault in the face of heavy enemy opposition, such as would be the case for Overlord. He worked on this task for many months, and the result was the creation of the Special Assault Division. He discussed this idea with his staff, and it became the model that carried through for D-Day. He gave orders to his men on June 24 to develop detailed plans for what this new type of special division would look like. General Cota and two of his officers traveled to Largs, Scotland, on June 27 to attend a senior officers conference. At this conference the means of Allied entry into northern France and the Low Countries was discussed and strategized. General Cota restated his case for a night landing at this conference, but the other officers largely disagreed with his assessment in light of the other needs of the operation. Operation Overlord was firmly under way with the conclusion of this conference.

On June 30, 1943, Brigadier General Cota's efficiency report noted him as superior, and he was recommended for command. Cota was said to render willing and generous support to the plans of his superiors regardless of his personal views in the matter. "He has a calm disposition, frank manner, and is broad-minded, tenacious and courageous."

Brigadier General Cota, Colonel Hillsinger, and Major Jones left London by plane on July 1 for a tour of Allied installations associated with Operation Husky in North Africa and the invasion of Sicily (as shown in figure 3.2). Over the week of July 7, Cota aided in planning the Sicilian invasion and took part in the operation as an observer with his former 1st Infantry Division. On July 13, at 6 a.m., the USS

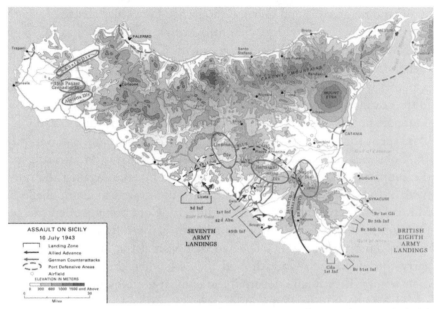

Figure 3.2. Operation Husky invasion of Sicily—Brigadier General Cota landed with 1st Infantry Division (U.S. Army, Center of Military History [CMH]).

LCI(L) 17 (Landing Craft Infantry–Large), part of Task Group 81.4 in Tunisia, embarked 182 army troops, including Brigadier General Cota and Major Jones as observers, the 17th Field Artillery, the 809th Engineer Battalion, and elements of the 15th Evacuation Hospital. They got under way at 10:03 a.m. and arrived at Gela, Sicily, at around 11 a.m. to disembark their passengers. General Cota then observed the combat operations of the invasion.

The officers departed on July 4 from Hendon, England, by Cessna and flew over several days through Prestwick, Marrakesh, and Algiers, and then on to Tunis, arriving on July 7. The officers separated, each joining a different element of the invasion. General Cota reported to Force 141, which became 15th Army Group for the Operation Husky D-Day, and he spent the next five days assisting in final planning preparations for the assault. Cota was attached to the 1st Infantry Division during the assault. He arrived ashore on July 14 from LCI(L) 17 by means of rubber boat with his party. He reported to General Geoffrey Keyes, deputy commanding general, and General Hobart R. Gay, chief of staff, Seventh Army, and then reported at Seventh Army's command post (CP) in pinewoods east of Gela, where he met with General Omar Bradley and General Keyes. He was directed to join the 1st Infantry Division and at 3 p.m. met with his old friend General Terry Allen in Gela and proceeded to the advance CP seven miles west of Gela at an Italian air force station. At 6 p.m. he met with the 26th Infantry CP near Mazzarino. On July 15, Cota spent some time visiting various divisional CPs to observe. On July 16, Cota watched the advance of the 26th Infantry on Barrafranca and the counterattack by approximately thirty enemy tanks against the right flank of the division from the CP. Major Jones moved to Campobello di Mazara to observe the Rangers. On July 17, Cota accompanied the 1st Division in its advance to a position north of Barrafranca. They visited various units through July 21, when they visited the II Corps CP. The party continued their work through July 24, when they began work on their report. They finally departed the combat zone by plane on July 25 and arrived back in England on July 31.

When General Cota, Colonel Hillsinger, and Major Jones returned from their observation of Operation Husky, they wrote a report to Combined Operations Command regarding their findings and how what was observed could influence future amphibious-landing operations. They found that Operation Husky showed great improvement in planning and execution over similar previous operations. The notes were made in the field during the actual combat conditions, and the observers were aware that a thorough after-action analysis should be made when the key commanders were no longer engaged in combat operations.

The group developed several key takeaway lessons from their observations of the invasion. Many of the participating units held previous combat experience in combined amphibious operations. These units applied lessons learned from previous operations, experiments, and tests conducted in the United Kingdom, North Africa, and the United States to great effect during the operations. During Husky, improved specialized equipment was used, especially the LCI, the LST (Landing Ship, Tank), and the six-wheel-drive amphibious DUKW-353 truck. There was greatly improved organization of shore parties (beach groups), especially where these elements had previous combined-operations experience. Based on performance, there was evidence of better training, particularly for the naval component, communications personnel, and beach maintenance personnel. Critical to the success of the operation, improved air and naval fire support were provided to the assault forces. There was also evidence of improved Ranger activities.

The assault phase was deemed highly successful, and tactical surprise was obtained. The landings were made with very few casualties despite the enemy's excellent fortifications and defensive plan. Cota's group concluded that the enemy failed to execute efficiently for several reasons, including a lack of sufficient time to fully equip and man the newly constructed defensive posts. Cota's team thought that complete surprise regarding time and place of Allied landings was achieved and that the Allied landing made on a broad front with overwhelming mass carried the battle. As for the defenders, a lack of flexibility of the enemy defensive plan led to their loss. A high degree of Allied air superiority and solid planning and execution by invading forces ultimately won the day.

Despite the astonishing success of the operation, there were still very important items to be addressed for future landings such as Overlord. The Allies had to provide for specially trained and organized, lightly equipped "assault divisions." Consideration had to be given to organization and training of additional Ranger battalions without delay, representing at least two per assault division. In the development of the assault divisions, their mission had to be confined to assault and seizure of a beachhead of sufficient depth and breadth to allow for prompt debarkation and assembly; for rapid exploitation of follow-up divisions, maintenance and defense of the beachhead and the assault divisions had to be strong in antitank weapons. For success in France, the Allies had to develop early integration within assault divisions of beach groups in order to provide proper channels of command. The Air Defense Command had to be integrated into the assault divisions. Through the USATC, the Allies had to organize standardized techniques into beach maintenance duties and incorporate into all assault divisions. They had to develop methods to teach higher echelons that well-known basic decisions must be made early, before the invasion, and could not be changed at the last moment without seriously compromising prospects of success. Small units had to be provided techniques for crossing a beach strewn with obstacles and defended by heavy enemy fire. Each infantry division had to develop and integrate a permanent air-support party as an organized part of its headquarters, and further study was recommended to develop efficient and speedy methods for close air support. Methods to provide all troops with up-to-date information as to current developments was deemed critical, as was careful planning and organization for how to handle civilian populations in the combat zone.

The officers made important observations regarding the use of Darby's Rangers during Operation Husky. Prior to the invasion, Colonel William Darby was given orders on April 15 to prepare his men for the invasion and pulled them off their North African positions at Kasserine Pass. The result of this preparation phase was the establishment of two additional Ranger battalions by breaking the 1st Ranger Infantry Battalion into thirds and rigorously training replacements to fill out the units. The end result of this was the retrofit of the 1st Ranger Infantry Battalion and creation of the 3d and 4th Ranger Infantry Battalions. Importantly, the Rangers made use of British LCAs (Landing Craft, Assault). These sat lower in the water and were quieter than the American LCVP (Landing Craft, Vehicle, Personnel) and would prove important later in 1944. The use of the Rangers was deemed important, as they quickly took the fight to the enemy as they broke through the beach and took their objective, consisting of a coastal battery. They landed lean and received their heavier equipment on Operation Husky D+1, allowing them to move quickly and succeed. The Rangers helped repel a tank counterattack on July 11, further demonstrating their value. They then took three strongpoints positioned on high ground on the road to Butera, three to four miles north-northwest of Gela. They accomplished this by conducting their mission at night and by flanking the enemy positions. The Rangers scaled cliffs to surprise the defenders and carried the day. Colonel Darby expressed interest in developing a Ranger force of considerable strength based on the British Special Service Brigade for raiding purposes. He posited that he could take the 1st, 3d, and 4th Ranger Infantry Battalions, split them, and raise the number of Ranger battalions to six. The Rangers strongly favored a six-line company over a four-line company, with company strengths of sixty-five men. They also favored replacing light machine guns with Browning Automatic Rifles at the company level and moving the light machine guns to the heavy-weapons section of headquarters. Many (but not all) of these concepts aided in the ideas leading to the formation of the 2d, 5th, and 6th Ranger Infantry Battalions later.

General Cota and his party made detailed observations of the enemy defenses in the area. They determined that the enemy had an elaborate and recently constructed defense system stretching along parts of the southern and southeastern Sicilian coast. These defenses included mutually supporting positions often created on reverse slopes. They used ingenuity in their camouflage and used natural features to their advantage.

There were many other important observations that arose during this period involving the sum of the invasion plan and its results. Included in these were important observations that had bearing on D-Day. The evidence was strong from the invasion of Sicily that it was critical to coordinate air and naval elements and provide effective communications between them and the ground forces. Bombing of beach defenses was likewise deemed critical to success. Cota's team determined that signal units should remain intact and be well supported logistically. The planners should increase the number of radio sets ashore and make sure they utilized the newest available technology. The use of combat engineers during the initial assault moves provided maximum effect in opening the landing beaches. The combat engineers were deemed important for the removal of beach debris and clutter to allow for continued free flow of men and material.

Prior operations and exercises pointed to the effective use of airborne troops in an assault landing. The assault forces should organize special platoons for pillbox destruction at the squad level using flamethrowers, Bangalore torpedoes, demolition grenades, and light machine guns for suppression fire. They should employ a battalion of medium tanks to land alongside each infantry division, as the assault landing force had to be strong in armor in initial waves. Additionally, there should be attached sufficient artillery assets to provide direct fire support at 57-mm or larger caliber, and it was acknowledged that self-propelled guns were indispensable to knock out machine-gun nests. Vehicles should be used for all ship-to-shore movement of material instead of hand loading. Special equipment should be suited for the mission, terrain, and season. The equipment should be standardized across all assault units, and the load burden lightened of individual soldiers in initial waves to maximize their mobility and to avoid their carrying equipment that would be discarded, needlessly cluttering the beach. Cota's group thought it essential to train for assault landings in the dark. Amphibious training not based on troop organization and movement on shore is wasted. This training should always provide for crossing of beaches and the advance inland.

Some final thoughts of Cota's observation party that went far in the continued planning of Overlord included that naval gunfire was deemed critical and effective because, as they stated in their report, "The navy can shoot." The communications worked, and the army-navy teams practiced for three weeks together beforehand. The establishment of beaches by color was deemed critical. This included physically setting and marking the beach landing zones with their designated color markers as soon as possible to avoid missed landings. Large-scale maps of the beach areas, including good vertical and oblique aerial photographs, were necessary for effective beach group planning. Training must be realistic with live bombs, booby traps, and wire on beaches. The training beaches must be unknown to the units using them. Initial training should occur in daylight with all subsequent training at night.

The USATC prepared a report titled *Staff Study of Assault Training Center Project on July 26, 1943*. It concluded,

> *The landing-assault against the German-held coasts of Western Europe constitutes an operation of combined arms without parallel in military history. The operation will require intimate coordination of large-scale ground, air, and naval forces, British and American. It will require specialized training on the parts of the troop units involved, to the end of welding them into effective landing-assault teams. From the military standpoint, the operation is so difficult and so important that every single preparatory step which facilitates it in any way must be taken.*

On August 5, 1943, Colonel Paul W. Thompson, commanding the new HQ, USATC, ETOUSA, submitted a report to the CG, ETOUSA, in which he had worked out the effective composition of the assault battalion based on General Cota's work and the thirty-day conference held in May. The key element of the assault battalion was identified as the assault section based on established doctrine of the War Department for assault against permanent fortifications and based on the new thirty-man assault craft, or the LCVP, widely known as the Higgins boat. With this communication, the center prepared for the impending arrival of the 29th Infantry Division for training per this new assault structure.

The assault division tables of organization were modified by General Cota on August 25 based on his observations of landing operations in Sicily. He completed this work and submitted it to the CG, ETOUSA. His idea for the new structure was for a division to assault in three groups. The force was to include Rangers to storm the beachhead, knock out enemy installations, and push inland. An air defense brigade would fend off air attack, and a shore brigade was to handle supply dumps and prepare for the heavy follow-up divisions.[2]

Robert Miller wrote his concluding thoughts regarding Cota's contribution to Combined Operations Command: "He had not only served the cause of British-American cooperation, but had added much to the understanding, doctrine, and practice of amphibious warfare."[3]

All of the training, assignments, and war fighting that Cota found himself in throughout his life to this point placed him in a unique position to affect the positive outcome of a battle yet to come. The early personal and military life of this officer, or anyone who later digs deep inside him- or herself to perform heroic acts, is worth the time to study to truly understand why. General Cota was as deeply embedded in the strategic and tactical planning as anyone for the forthcoming invasion. This includes notable officers such as Generals Bradley and Eisenhower. He developed the tactics, training, and plans for D-Day. He conceived of and established the division, regiment, and lower-echelon structure down to the individual landing craft and determined what weapons and gear each soldier carried. It was his force of personality that won him the day for these elements with his superiors involved in the planning effort. He was a fan of the Rangers and what they had to offer on this type of battlefield. He witnessed the army in action in Africa and Sicily through his own direct participation in amphibious operations ashore. He knew through the experience of his own eyes what the Germans were capable of and would prepare for Allied forces.

The World War I testimony of Sergeant Alvin York, where he simply described the facts as he saw them, not for his own glory but to save the lives of fellow soldiers, clearly provides an understanding of what it means to go beyond intrepidity. This has a common thread through all time, all cultures, and all heroes. As Sergeant York wrote of the Meuse-Argonne Offensive during the war to end all wars,

> The Germans . . . stopped us dead in our tracks. Their machine guns were up there on the heights overlooking us and well hidden, and we couldn't tell for certain where the terrible heavy fire was coming from. . . . And I'm telling you they were shooting straight. Our boys just went down like the long grass before the mowing machine at home. Our attack just faded out. . . . And there we were, lying down, about halfway across [the valley]. . . . As soon as the machine guns opened fire on me, I began to exchange shots with them. There were over thirty of them in continuous action, and all I could do was touch the Germans off just as fast as I could. I was sharp shooting. I don't think I missed a shot. It was no time to miss. . . . All the time I kept yelling at them to come down. I didn't want to kill any more than I had to. But it was they or I. And I was giving them the best I had.[4]

The stuff of men like this derives from their inner character and the environment from which they came. Nine out of ten people fail to react at all in an emergency event. In combat, it is easy to imagine that the number may be different due to training and disposition of forces; however, the logic holds true. Brigadier General Cota's stern father and kind mother molded him. Surviving the 1908 Chelsea fire as a young man shaped him, as did his lifelong military service to this point with fortitude and inner courage. His experiences in planning for divisional movement, amphibious action and landing, and the larger invasion forces for the Normandy landings themselves made him the right man at the right moment for his next duty to become the assistant division commander of the 29th Infantry Division. General Cota was relieved from ETOUSA on October 12, 1943.

CHAPTER FOUR

The Blue and the Gray

THE 29TH INFANTRY DIVISION WAS ORDERED INTO EXISTENCE FOR
World War I on July 18, 1917, and officially organized on August 25,
1917, at Camp McClellan, Alabama. It was realized during the initial
organizational period that a divisional esprit de corps must be encouraged. This was due in part to having broken up old organizational structures of the lower-echelon units. At its outset, the division was composed
of the 57th Infantry Brigade, formed by the 113th and 114th Infantry
Regiments, both from New Jersey. It also contained the 58th Infantry
Brigade, formed by the 115th Infantry Regiment of Maryland and the
116th Infantry Regiment of Virginia. It contained the Maryland 110th
Artillery Regiment, Virginia 111th Field Artillery Regiment, and New
Jersey 112th Field Artillery Regiment.

Thought was put into the fact that many of the units contained in
the division had fought in the Civil War on opposing sides. Many of the
Civil War units had themselves derived special names or distinctive designations. These units, on both sides of the Civil War, had often acquitted
themselves with honor on the battlefield, and those members and units of
that war maintained tremendous sentimental value ascribed to the honor
of their unit designations. It is believed that the chief of staff, Colonel
George S. Goodale, suggested the name of the "Blue and Gray Division."
This unit included men from both Washington, DC (the capital of the
United States), and Richmond, Virginia (the capital of the erstwhile
Confederacy). The unit trained in a Southern camp named after a famed
federal general and was under the command of a general from Maine.

This seemed appropriate to establish the heritage of this division, and the men of the unit heartily and unanimously accepted it. Major James Ulio, division adjutant, suggested the Korean symbol of life. What the 29th Division historians in the years following World War I thought was the Korean symbol of life is actually *Taegeuk*, the Korean form of the Chinese term *Taiji*, meaning "supreme ultimate." The Korean usage of *Taegeuk* commonly refers to the balance in the universe of positive cosmic forces and opposing negative cosmic forces. The division symbolically shaded its new insignia in the blue and gray of the Civil War. The symbolism relating to the concept of "a house divided against itself not being able to stand" is strong. The 29th Division was the first division to officially register its symbol with the adjutant general of the army.

The division departed for the western front in June 1918 as part of the American Expeditionary Forces and arrived in the port of Brest, a place its men would fight to liberate from the Germans in August and September 1944. During late September, they received orders to join the Meuse-Argonne Offensive as part of the French XVII Corps. The division experienced multiple raids by the Germans as it moved to the front with the French in the Alsace and assumed frontline duties. The division later moved to the citadel of Verdun and then the Meuse-Argonne battle, where it captured the Etrayes Ridge. After that, it was relieved by the 79th Division and went into reserve until the armistice. During its twenty-one days of combat, it advanced seven kilometers, took 2,148 prisoners, and destroyed over 250 machine guns or artillery pieces. The 29th Division experienced a 30 percent casualty rate, losing 170 officers and 5,691 enlisted men killed or wounded. The men of the 29th returned home in May 1919 and demobilized at Camp Dix, New Jersey; however, the division remained an active National Guard unit.[1]

Each regiment within the division has its own storied past dating back to colonial America. Others have documented these heroic military lineages, and thus we shall focus on one regiment as it is germane to General Cota on D-Day. The 116th Infantry is a long-standing infantry regiment of the Virginia Militia formerly known as the old 2d Virginia and then the Virginia National Guard. The 116th Infantry was originally formed as the Augusta County Regiment of the Virginia Militia on November 3, 1741. The regiment saw service in the French and Indian War and in Dunmore's War. On August 25, 1755, several companies of the regiment became part of the Rangers. The unit was called up for service and went through various unit designations during the Revolutionary War. It saw action in the War of 1812 and then in the Mexican-American War. On April 13, 1861, elements of the 32d, 93d, and 160th Regiments became the 5th Regiment, Virginia Volunteers. They became part of the 5th Virginia Infantry as part of the Confederate Army of the Shenandoah's 1st Brigade, later known as the Stonewall Brigade.

During the Battle of First Manassas, General Thomas J. Jackson led his troops in a stubborn defense against a determined attack by federal forces. On July 21, 1861, when the battle entered its final phase, Jackson and his men held their ground, and a general from another unit said something to the effect of "There stands Jackson like a stone wall. Rally behind the Virginians!" The name "Stonewall" came to signify the general, but also his men, later to become the 116th Infantry. After the Civil War and reconciliation, the Stonewall Brigade became the 116th Infantry. The unit then saw action during the Spanish-American War. The brigade's colors carry battle streamers for the Stonewall Brigade's actions in the Civil War, one of but a few instances in which a military unit is permitted to retain streamers for action against the United States. This heritage speaks not to the injustice or horror of slavery but purely to the heroism of those men in those engagements. The 29th Infantry Division continues to defend America to this day, proud of its heritage and of its sons and daughters, who have answered the most hallowed call of duty.

During the years between the world wars, the various National Guard regiments of the 29th Infantry Division maintained the required level of training. In the peace and prosperity of the early 1920s and then into the Great Depression, many states slashed their budgets for their National Guard units. The same thing happened in the regular army, such that by the outset of World War II the United States only had just shy of 190,000 active-duty soldiers in 1939. America was an isolationist nation, adhering to the U.S. national policy of avoiding political and economic engagement with foreign nations.

President George Washington first spoke of the concept during his farewell address. President Washington wrote, "The great rule of conduct for us, in regard to foreign nations is, in extending our commercial relations, to have with them as little political connection as possible. So far as we have already formed engagements, let them be fulfilled with perfect good faith. Here let us stop." It took shape in the nineteenth century as part of the Monroe Doctrine and continued on and off up to World War II. For the 29th Division, everything of our isolationist nature changed on December 7, 1941. The men were organized and sent to Fort Meade, Maryland. After that Christmas, the unit became determined and serious. The men became "a grim, business-like lot," according to the *Baltimore Sun* on January 29, 1942. Their morale and discipline surged, and the men often wore the uniform even off duty as a matter of pride.

The interwar division commander, General Milton A. Reckford, who assumed command in 1934, was replaced by Major General Leonard T. Gerow on March 2, 1942. Gerow was a Virginian and a graduate of the Virginia Military Institute, one of America's great schools. In February 1941, the division had a strength of 6,927 enlisted men and 656 officers. By the time Gerow took charge, the division had a strength of approximately twenty-two thousand men organized in the old square structure consisting of four regiments in two brigades. By March 1942, the division converted to the army's new triangular structure consisting of three regiments, which allowed for two on the line and one in reserve at all times. The three regiments were the 115th, 116th, and 175th Infantry. This change reduced the manpower to 15,500 men. One key for the 29th Division is that they stayed as prepared as they could during those decades, and when they participated in the army's 1941 Carolina Maneuvers and later exercises, they did so in good order. They were identified as a valuable asset to mobilize to England on the heels of the 1st Infantry Division for their part in the upcoming invasion of mainland Europe.

The division received movement orders for overseas duty and arrived at Camp Kilmer, New Jersey, on September 18, 1942. Camp Kilmer was located in Piscataway and Edison (formerly Raridan) Townships in Middlesex County, located twenty-two miles southwest of New York

City. In 1941, the War Department selected the site of the camp as the best location to serve as the New York Port of Entry due to its proximity to transportation, including rail, road, and water. It was there that the 29th Division received Colonel Charles D. Canham, a West Pointer. The division moved from Camp Kilmer to Hoboken, New Jersey, boarded the HMS *Queen Mary* and HMS *Queen Elizabeth* for deployment to England, departing on September 27, 1942. As the 29ers arrived in England, they moved to Tidworth Barracks, just slightly overlapping the time spent there by then colonel Cota and the 1st Infantry Division before they set sail for Africa. They then entered a phase of training and for a long period were the only American division in England.[2] The 29th began a grueling seven-day-a-week training program shortly after arrival, including two twenty-five-mile marches and one forty-mile march per week. The men were given forty-eight-hour passes at the end of the week, and then they repeated the process.

On December 20, 1942, the 29th Provisional Ranger Battalion was organized at Tidworth Barracks per a directive from European Theater of Operations (ETO) Headquarters. The men were volunteers from the ranks of the division. The 1st Ranger Infantry Battalion provided a cadre of three officers and fifteen enlisted men to get them trained and ready. The Rangers moved north to train with the British No. 4 Commando.

The 29th Provisional Ranger Battalion moved to the U.S. Assault Training Center (USATC) on February 26, 1943, and trained for an audience including such flag officers as Major General Russell P. Hartle, deputy commander, European Theater of Operations, United States Army (ETOUSA); Major General Leonard T. Gerow, CG, 29th Infantry Division; Brigadier General Cota, now the United States advisor on combined operations; some forty reporters; and others. The Rangers showed superb condition as they climbed up and down the cliffs, spanned rivers, and traversed obstacle courses in the bitter Scottish winter weather. The Ranger battalion was composed of Headquarters Company and four line companies and was later increased to six line companies under the command of Major Randolph Millholland. Upon graduation, the Rangers were assigned to the British No. 6 Commando for additional training and operations. They then performed some operational missions, including close-in reconnaissance and raiding activities in enemy-held territories in Norway and France.

The division began training on the Dartmoor Moor, home of the famous Dartmoor Prison. The moors were desolate, broad, and barren stretches of terrain covered with thick spongy grass, the rare prickly evergreen shrubbery, and some outcroppings of rock. The moor was notable for a cold, stinging horizontal rain driven by strong winds from the Atlantic. During the winter months, the temperatures remained in the low thirties Fahrenheit and proved a match for any personal equipment designed to keep the men warm and dry. While dealing with the rough weather and terrain, the men worked on how to attack and demolish concrete-fortified positions as part of this training.[3]

When General Gerow received a promotion in July 1943 to become the new V Corps commanding general, the division received its new CO, Major General Charles Hunter Gerhardt, who would stay with them through the war. General Gerhardt was a West Point man and a strict disciplinarian, tight on military bearing and uniform standards. He was, however, a good leader and genuinely cared about his troops, a fact that came to be so widely valued by those under his command that he gained the nickname "Uncle Charlie." According to unit historian Joe Balkoski, Gerhardt "had a simple philosophy: a division's combat efficiency reflected the skills of its senior officers." Gerhardt stated, "This war is won at the battalion level." He had little use for the petty rivalries between the regular army and National Guard. Balkoski held that "in Gerhardt's view, if a man was in the 29th Infantry Division, he was simply an American soldier, and Gerhardt didn't care how he got there."[4] One exception to this viewpoint was the officers of the division.

During July 1943, the division received an ETO order that directed it to commence preliminary amphibious-assault training. General Gerhardt and his assistant division commander, Brigadier General George M. Alexander, had to work past the lack of sufficient equipment at the outset. Their training slowly expanded beyond infantry tactics and began to include amphibious training and problems as the months passed. They soon began to assemble the proper landing craft and equipment and to teach the processes and principles of this type of warfare to the men. They taught all nonswimmers how to swim. During this period, the USATC became fully functional at Woolacombe Beach.[5] The USATC covered twenty-five square miles along ten miles of Atlantic coastline, including terrain such as beaches, cliffs, headlands, and sand dunes between Woolacombe and Appledore in southwestern England.

Beginning on September 1, the 29th Infantry Division sent its regiments through the USATC to conduct their three-week training cycle. The 116th Infantry was in fact the first unit to attend the school. Here they learned the lessons that General Cota and his colleagues had crafted into doctrine for the invasion. At this point, the men of the division had little doubt that they were training for the invasion of mainland Europe. The USATC staff calculated in 1943 that at no place along the coast of northwest France could the Germans use more than one platoon per two thousand to twenty-five hundred yards to protect beach fortifications. They deduced that the Germans would have extremely strong field defenses with concrete pillboxes, emplacements, and shelters and thinly spread defenders providing considerable automatic fire.[6] The 175th Infantry followed them to the school and later the 115th Infantry.

With the selection of Normandy as the landing area and Omaha Beach assigned to the U.S. forces, a realization came that the Americans would have to fight their way up cliffs and also take the few heavily defended valleys, or draws, that made their way inland from the beaches. These factors led to the idea of developing infantry units into thirty-man "assault sections." The assault sections were another element General Cota had a strong hand in developing. The number of men in an assault section was driven by the capacity of the landing craft, specifically the LCA and LCVP. These assault sections would have to land and attack the enemy defenses by using a variety of weapons that an infantry unit could carry. The USATC developed tactics to bring together aerial and naval bombardment and supporting fire. Pillboxes would be engaged by flat-trajectory, high-velocity naval gunfire. The Allies also developed transports capable of allowing artillery weapons to fire from aboard landing vessels. Figures 4.1 and 4.2 show the surrounds of the USATC as well as the realism of the facility. The realism came in the fact that the

Figure 4.1. 1943 US Signal Corps photo of Woolacombe Beach, USATC (National Archives and Records Administration [NARA]).

Figure 4.2. 1943 US Signal Corps photo of mock German position at USATC (NARA).

students experienced full-scale live-fire training, which even today plays a pivotal role in combat training.

The assault divisions were therefore formed simply by reducing the overhead of a normal infantry division in both men and vehicles and increasing the normal infantry firepower. While the basic divisional structure remained unchanged, the rifle companies were organized into assault teams with special equipment to deal with fortified positions. The platoons of the assault companies were split into two assault sections apiece. The two assault platoons in each company included rifle teams, a wire-cutting team, a bazooka team, a flame-throwing team, a Browning Automatic Rifle (BAR) team, a 60-mm mortar team, and a demolition team. The third platoon was similarly organized, except that it had an 81-mm instead of a 60-mm mortar and a heavy machine gun instead of a BAR. After the assault, each platoon was reorganized into a normal rifle platoon with two rifle squads and a weapons squad. The infantry assault troops were stripped to the barest combat essentials.

The assault sections were designed to attack the enemy by means of frontal assault upon a fortified position and thereby breach the enemy defenses. They were trained to provide coordinated fire and to supply the demolition team with sufficient cover to satisfy their objective. Each assault section was headed by a lieutenant, with a sergeant as second in command. A section consisted of subteams of riflemen, wire cutters, rocketeers, machine gunners, flamethrowers, and a demolition team. Each subteam was organized and equipped with the mission to ultimately advance the demolition team to the enemy structure and blow it up with explosives. Each assault team learned how to load into its landing craft LCVP or LCA in a predetermined manner to allow for a sequence of events to occur upon landing.

The assault team leader was first to exit each landing craft, and the assistant leader, a noncommissioned officer, was the last man off. Spatial separation of these two men in the landing craft maximized the chances of retaining the command structure under fire. The assistant aided the section leader and was prepared to take the section leader's place if the latter became a casualty. His mission involved staying informed of the general situation at all times, and he was particularly charged with the

Figure 4.3. 1943 USATC infantry amphibious-assault training from LCVP ashore (NARA).

responsibility of locating covering fire from open emplacements and bringing mortar fire to bear upon such enemy installations.[7] Figure 4.3 illustrates the assault team tactics in practice.

On September 12, 1943, V Corps received orders to begin planning for an assault on Normandy. General Gerhardt was briefed on this for the overall preparation of his unit in relation to the larger picture. Gerhardt provided his division with a new battle cry: "Twenty-Nine, Let's Go!" He recognized an urgent need to heighten and intensify the training of his men to bring them to peak readiness. He also realized that he needed to strengthen his division leadership. For the role of assistant division commander, he focused his attention on his old West Point classmate: Dutch. After graduation from West Point, both men returned as instructors in the 1920s. More important, though, General Cota had served in combat with the 1st Infantry Division and had a solid reputation as an expert Allied war planner of amphibious warfare for Combined Operations Headquarters. It was this experience that Gerhardt realized was critical to the success of the 29th Infantry Division in the upcoming invasion. The fact that Cota had almost total involvement in amphibious operations for over a year made him the right man for the job of assistant division commander. Cota was a known no-nonsense soldier with a strong sense of duty and a commitment to regulations and military discipline. Gerhardt requested through V Corps that General Cota join the division, and he did so on October 12.[8]

General Cota arrived at his new post along with letters of high praise from former commanders. Brigadier Godfrey Edward Wildman-Lushington, Royal Marines, CO, Combined Operations Headquarters, Whitehall, wrote on October 12 that the British appreciated Brigadier General Cota's service while attached to the command based on his sound experience and advice in planning the invasion. General Cota's final efficiency report from ETOUSA, dated October 15, 1943, rated him as superior, noting that as an officer he rendered willing and generous support to plans of his superiors regardless of his personal views in the matter and that he had an excellent theoretical and practical knowledge of landing operations.

Gerhardt's first orders to Cota were to supervise the training exercises being held on the moor. Cota immediately went to work and applied his common sense, experience, stability, and reliability to the task. The division was gathered together from all over southern England and spent several weeks together training on the moor. Cota raised the bar by use of live fire to increase the realism of the training environment and exercises. His principles of "fire and movement" quickly became the norm. During amphibious-landing problems or infantry-tactics problems, the troops of the 29th found themselves following immediately behind live rolling artillery barrages while using live ammunition of their own to hone their combat skills. If the units were not at the moor, they were at the USATC on their training cycle, only to return to the division and continue perfecting learned techniques.[9]

As General Cota worked, his love for leading troops in the field came out. His interpretation of his orders was to spend as much time away from divisional headquarters as he could. He spent his days on the moor with the men, working down to the individual squad level, getting to see their growth firsthand along with getting to know his men. "Cota's fearlessness inspired confidence," wrote Balkoski. He traveled across the moors with the men with an unlit cigar clenched in his teeth and an old-fashioned walking stick in his hand. He led his men behind the rolling artillery barrages at a distance of fifty yards in order to acclimate them to the rigors of combat and give them a faith in their artillery and in each other. Cota was known to wander through the training camps, often with a ditty on his tongue, singing as he worked. One of the notable things often heard from the assistant division commander was "If I knew the answer to this, what a hell of a smart guy I'd be." The men of the division came to love his quiet and affable nature in private, as well as his ability to act as a seasoned, crusty old squad leader in training and later in battle. He was quick to offer a pat on the back on success and rarely lost his temper on failure. Rather, he offered advice to the men to do better. General Gerhardt, a short, balding officer, impeccable in military appearance and bearing, stood in contrast to Cota, tall and stocky. Cota often dressed carelessly and was the only man in the division who could get away with it. This included Gerhardt's pet peeve: an unbuckled chin-strap. The two generals had a good working relationship and developed a singular focus on training the men for the invasion. Gerhardt worked through fear and Cota through inspiration. As the training progressed, any 29er who couldn't meet the training standards was unceremoniously run out of the division to a rear-echelon supply unit or suffered a similar fate, often an embarrassing end result for the individual soldier.[10]

The 29th Provisional Ranger Battalion ended as an organization on October 18, 1943, due to the formations of the 2d and 5th Ranger Infantry Battalions in the States. Although the 29th Provisional Rangers hated being disbanded, one benefit was that as the men folded back into their parent companies, battalions, and regiments within the division, their skill and experiences infused into the receiving units and heightened their combat effectiveness. Some experimental work was done at the USATC by the 29th Rangers. The training mission for them was to land on rocky shores inaccessible to ordinary craft and establish a small bridgehead. That experiment was so successful that an infantry company was later trained in these tactics. The ultimate aim was to train a nucleus of troops to land on an unfavorable and assumedly weakly defended coast and to then establish a strong bridgehead and neutralize enemy coastal artillery fire directed at the assault troops on the beaches. The USATC modified the concept of raiding in its usual sense and adopted these tactics for infiltration troops. These men were taught not to be hit-and-run raiders, but rather to hold on to what they seized until the main force could take over. At this point, the 29th Rangers resembled airborne units and were originally intended to be used in conjunction with them. They were set to carry enough supplies for forty-eight to seventy-two hours, counting on resupply over the beaches or by air as the situation permitted.

On October 23, Cota received special instructions directly from ETOUSA to aid in procurement of a larger training area. The brass had identified Slapton Sands on England's south coast in Devonshire, south of Torquay and about 110 miles west of Portsmouth, as a desirable location for full-scale exercises of the entire landing force. The problem was that the area was populated by British civilians. Cota was selected to work with the British subjects and to convince them to vacate their properties for an unknown duration to allow for military training operations. General Cota was cognizant of Amendment III to the United States Constitution, which holds, "No soldier shall, in time of peace be quartered in any house, without the consent of the owner, nor in time of war, but in a manner to be prescribed by law." That the Americans were involved in asking the British for their homes was ironic, as it was the British soldiers in the 1700s who took liberties with colonial (and later American) property rights during our War of Independence, which led to the creation of that important aspect of our most fundamental laws. General Cota was selected for this duty based on his experience in working well with the British during his previous assignment. He met with local officials on November 8, made a detailed reconnaissance of the area on November 10, and met with local inhabitants on November 12 and 13. During these public meetings, he discussed policing, protection of property, transportation of the residents as they moved, and the process for mitigating actual property damage. He opened his remarks with a brilliant statement to the citizens: "If it were not for the fact that I have been stationed in the United Kingdom for over a year, and have served both with and alongside your Royal Navy and British Army during this period, I fear I would not feel as much at home right now, as I actually do." He went on to discuss the nature of the training in unclassified terms and again selected his words masterfully.

> *I do know that war is destructive. Training for battle means training to destroy. I can say, however, that destruction of property will be avoided insofar as is practicable in carrying out the training missions assigned to us by the Combined Chiefs of Staff. . . . Despite all our efforts to keep destruction to a minimum we are bound to "slice" the ball on occasions in our training, and the ball will land where we hoped it would not. If we were perfect we would not need to practice. Whatever the destruction may be, however, I feel confident in saying it will be more than compensated for in the number of lives of American and British soldiers that will be saved when someday they must carry out the lessons that will be learned in this area. We admire your courage and the quiet, determined attitude you show on all occasions to go "all out" to win the present struggle. We from the United States are proud to be fighting with you for the same end.*[11]

On November 5, the 115th Regimental Combat Team (RCT), remainder of the 115th Infantry; the 110th Field Artillery Battalion, Companies A and C; and the 121st Engineer Combat Battalion, Detachment A, Military Police Platoon, and Detachment 29, Signal Company, arrived for training at the USATC. Each regiment was accompanied by one battalion of artillery and medical and engineer personnel for the training cycle. The division completed its rotation through the USATC in December.

On November 16, 1943, Admiral Louis Mountbatten, chief of combined operations, wrote of Cota, "The inclusion of United States officers on my staff at Combined Operations Headquarters during the early summer of 1942 set the model for the many combined staffs that have followed and have so successfully accomplished the difficult missions assigned to them. Many more combined staffs will follow and many more difficult missions will be accomplished successfully, due in no small degree to the part you have played on staff at Combined Operations Headquarters."

In December, after the civilians were fully evacuated, the engineers spent the following weeks modifying Slapton Sands, removing land mines and obstacles intended to hinder any invading Germans. They transformed the beach into a mock-up of the Normandy coast complete with pillboxes. The beach was somewhat protected from the surf of the channel due to its geography.

On December 9, 1943, Major General C. H. Gerhardt received Admiral Mountbatten's commendation and acknowledged his new assistant division commander by telling him that the commendation was well deserved: "Your experience as Division G-3 and Chief of Staff of the 1st Infantry Division gave you background which was invaluable to such a Combined Staff. Your services rendered while a member of this division are well up to the high standard which you have previously set." On December 31, 1943, General Gerhardt rated General Cota as superior, noting him as the third-best officer he knew—very high praise. He was described as a thoroughly competent, professional soldier, able to do and to supervise. He had an unexcelled background in amphibious operations and was highly skilled in supervision of infantry training.

By January 1944, eleven U.S. divisions were in England. The 1st Infantry Division had come back to England in November 1943, after operations in Sicily. Its men were needed to do their duty yet again. America had sent over one million of its favorite sons as part of this growing force. General Omar Bradley made the decision to pair the 1st Infantry Division with the 29th Infantry Division on Omaha Beach. He did not make this decision lightly, knowing that "The Big Red One" had "swallowed a bellyful of heroics and wanted to go home."[12] The men of the division, having survived two amphibious landings, wondered whether their luck could hold for a third. Bradley wrote,

Although I disliked subjecting the 1st to still another landing, I felt that as a commander I had no other choice. My job was to get ashore, establish a lodgment, and destroy the Germans. In accomplishment of that mission there was little room for the niceties of justice. I felt compelled to employ the best troops I had, to minimize the risks and hoist the odds in our favor any way that I could. As a result the division that deserved compassion as a reward for its previous ordeals now became the inevitable choice for our most difficult job. Whatever the injustice, it is better that war heap its burdens unfairly than that victory be jeopardized in an effort to equalize the ordeal.[13]

The entire division participated in concentration and processing for embarkation for Exercise Duck in December 1943 and January 1944. The 1st Infantry Division joined the 29th for the exercise. Due to a shortage of ships, however, the entire division was unable to mobilize and participate in the amphibious landing. The 29th Infantry Division processed 781 officers and 13,467 enlisted men as part of the exercise. In preparation for Duck, Brigadier General Cota, acting as U.S. advisor to Combined Operations Headquarters, directed section activities in compliance with special orders of the chief of staff and correlated assault training and planning between Combined Operations Headquarters and ETOUSA. Exercise Duck was designed to train and process the less certain units of V Corps (Reinforced) and other associated units in the procedures of concentration (assembly and embarkation) through to the assault on Slapton Sands to secure a designated beachhead line and cover landing of assumed follow-up forces. The V Corps tactical plan was to conduct an overseas movement under U.S. Navy control. The individual units would then land the assault force, including the 29th Infantry (Reinforced) (less 2 RCTs and other troops), from naval landing craft and, with naval and air support, assault Slapton Sands during daylight on D-Day to secure the general line, the road from Dittisham-Moreleigh. The goal was to cover the landing of the 28th Infantry Division (assumed). They were to conduct a secondary Ranger battalion assault (assumed) against Coleton Heights to contain enemy forces in the Brixham Peninsula and deny the enemy observation from Coleton Heights. (A map of Slapton Sands is shown in figure 4.4.)

The first part of the training program for Neptune was accomplished through the establishment and use of the USATC. The second part was the training phase involving many exercises geared to every aspect of the invasion. The first major exercise, known as Duck I, was held beginning on January 4, 1944, and lasted two days. From that point on, there were almost continual exercises. It could be said that Duck was the most important because the lessons learned were quickly analyzed, and improvements were made throughout the plan to lead to a successful invasion. The exercises focused on every possible nuisance from the landing operations down to supply and communications. Exercises Tiger and

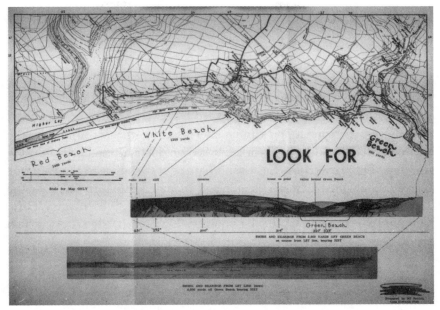

Figure 4.4. Map of Allied training area at Slapton Sands, United Kingdom (NARA).

Fabius were full-scale dress rehearsals for each of the five invasion beach-heads. The terrain of Slapton Sands was rugged and broken in many places by small ridges and drainage lines. There were no railroads, and road coverage was sparse and poor. The tide ranged from ten to fourteen feet, similar in nature to the Normandy coastline. The division continued to train hard and learn from its experiences. The men were getting what they needed to succeed through their assistant division commander.

Assumed enemy defenses included 14 pillboxes, each with at least two machine guns, and eight machine guns in open emplacements. The southern part of one beach was assumed to have been mined. Three four-gun batteries of 105 mm howitzers and one two-gun 150 mm howitzers were assumed to be behind the beach. There were anti-aircraft batteries, and one enemy airfield. Enemy capabilities included limited air, submarine and small surface-craft action, a defense at the beach line, a secondary defense along hastily prepared cliff lines, an armored attack by elements of one panzer division by H plus 3 hours, another by two tanks battalions and one armored infantry regimental combat team at H plus 8 hours, and a third by a maximum of four infantry regimental combat teams after D plus 1.[14]

Exercise Fox was held at Slapton Sands on March 9 and 10, 1944. It was the largest of the early exercises. It was delayed by V Corps to coincide with Neptune planning in an attempt to marry up elements of both. The marshalling was accomplished by XVIII District and involved entirely new personnel and camps later used for the real invasion. The entire marshalling plan was worked based on doctrine established during the three Duck exercises. The assault pattern was similar to the Neptune plan for the Omaha Beach assault and matched the 16th RCT of the 1st Infantry Division and the 116th RCT of the 29th Infantry Division, under command of the 1st Infantry Division headquarters, which reported to a headquarters group from V Corps.

Assault landings were satisfactory, and there was naval gunfire support with live ammunition. Critiques agreed, however, that the buildup and consolidation of the beachhead suffered from hasty planning and preparation. The comparatively green 5th and 6th Engineer Special Brigades fell behind their schedule, and there was considerable confusion among the assault. . . . [T]he assault suffered from lack of coordination between the Navy and the Army, and between various headquarters.[15]

Command sensed some needed improvements as a result of Fox that could be accomplished with additional focused training. On March 20, 1944, the 116th RCT returned to the USATC for a nine-day refresher course. This was the only unit to come back for a repetition of the center's training, and several interesting points were noted. The 116th RCT had kept in touch with the changes in technique, and after thorough practice and numerous exercises engaged in during the winter, they felt that practically no variations were needed or desirable. The landing exercises were planned to be in the nature of rehearsals, and to that extent they differed from previous instruction here. The weather permitted all to be made outside the estuary, and the combat training problems were very successful. Both the RCT and the USATC staff considered the modified exercises entirely worthwhile. The training center cadre noted that improvement shown by the troops in those things they had done in October was obvious and encouraging. Though the organization was slightly modified, there was no change in the thirty-man boat team.

The six Fabius exercises together constituted the greatest amphibious exercise in history. Fabius I was the rehearsal for Assault Force O: those elements of the 1st Infantry Division, the 29th Infantry Division, the Provisional Engineer Special Brigade Group, and attached units, which were to assault Omaha Beach under the command of V Corps. This force marshalled in Area D, embarked from the Portland-Weymouth area, and landed at Slapton Sands.

The Allies carried out Fabius I, II, III, and IV simultaneously at the direction of the 21st Army Group. They began on April 23 and ended May 7. The exercise for Fabius was planned in two phases: a marshalling and embarkation phase, followed by execution of the exercise. The 11th Amphibious Force moved the troops from the point of embarkation with British naval forces providing the convoys with protection from German naval attack. The Ninth Air Force provided air cover and tactical assistance. These exercises were purposefully patterned after Overlord. Fabius I included the primary elements of the 1st and 29th Infantry Divisions and attached units, including two Ranger battalions, two tank battalions, and three engineer combat battalions as assigned from the Provisional Engineer Special Brigade Group. This totaled more than twenty-five thousand troops as part of Force O. Fabius followed the same planning and formations as developed for Overlord and Neptune. The V Corps command conducted the overall planning but allowed for detailed planning down to the battalion level where appropriate. The exercise involved a simulated aerial bombing and real naval bombardment of the landing area. This was followed by landing the Duplex Drive (DD) tanks at H-Hour. DD tanks are a type of amphibious tank. After this, the troops landed per a timetable. Three Ranger companies from the 2d Ranger Infantry Battalion were to land two miles to the north of Slapton Sands at Blackpool Beach and destroy enemy artillery installations as would be done at La Pointe du Hoc. Another company was scheduled to land at the right flank of the Slapton Sands assault beach, while the remainder of the Rangers were to land with the main infantry at Slapton Sands.

These remaining Rangers were then ordered to wheel right, relieving the flanking Rangers, and then make their way to Blackpool Beach. It is important to note the Rangers' training actions. The entire 5th Ranger Infantry Battalion and the half of the 2d Ranger Infantry Battalion that landed on Omaha Beach were there by design.

In Great Britain in the spring of 1944, General Bradley made his rounds of the eleven various infantry divisions scheduled to go ashore first. While at the 29th Infantry Division, he noted the men exhibited a despondent fear of the predicted 90 percent casualty rates calculated by Allied command. His decision to pair the veteran 1st and combat-inexperienced 29th Infantry Division together was not without forethought, and General Cota was on hand to lead these men from a position of determination, skill, and experience.

Operation Neptune and its part in Overlord was set. The object of Neptune was to secure a lodgment area on the continent from which further offensive operations could be developed. It was part of a large strategic plan designed to bring about the total defeat of Germany. The mission of First United States Army (First Army) was to launch a simultaneous assault on Omaha and Utah Beaches on D-Day at H-Hour. It was tasked with capturing all assigned objectives in those respective beach zones and thereafter advancing as rapidly as the situation permitted, capturing Cherbourg with the minimum delay, and developing the Vierville-sur-Mer and Colleville-sur-Mer beachhead southward toward Saint-Lô in conformity with the advance of the Second British Army. The mission of V Corps was to assault Omaha Beach with Force O and the 2d and 5th Ranger Battalions on D-Day at H-Hour, capture assigned objectives, and thereafter advance in accordance with instructions to be issued by Headquarters, First Army.[16] The Allied invasion plan, Omaha Beach landing zones, and Omaha Beach D-Day objectives are illustrated in figures 4.5, 4.6, and 4.7.

Frank G. Oberle remembered his general once he heard of his death in 1971. His account appeared in an article in the 29th Infantry Division periodical *The Twenty-Niner* titled "General Cota Remembered."

Many of us will always remember General "Dutch" Cota as "Old Fire and Movement" from our days in England in the months of intensive amphibious infantry training before D-Day, June 6, 1944. He seemed to be every-

*where, and we saw him often. He always had some humorous remarks along
with some profound words of wisdom and sound advice on how to survive in
combat. In those days, I know that we in our Company in the 16th, whom he
visited many times on the Moors, at the Assault Training Center, and after
the Slapton Sands problems, were always impressed by the General with his
big one star on his old World War I type overseas hat, and the booming voice,
who had already survived two invasion landings in North Africa and Sicily
and who seemed more like a wise old Sergeant than "General Staff Brass."*

*Here was a man who knew what he was talking about, full of enthusi-
asm which he managed to impart to us and a man who was really interested
in each one of us. He would share chow from a borrowed mess kit, check the
head space adjustment on a machine gun, adjust the sights on a rifle, run
a boat team drill just like a platoon leader, over and over again, until it
clicked like a perfect football play and leave us a lot more tired but smarter
than when he happened to come by. Then he would walk away whistling or
humming to himself on the way to another Company with an aide running
to keep up with him.*

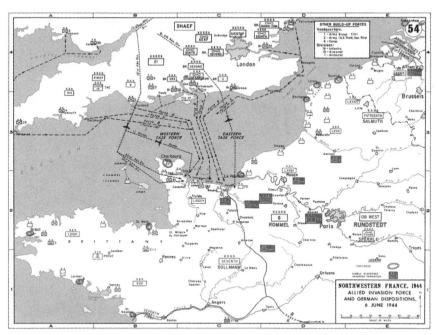

Figure 4.5. D-Day Allied invasion plan (U.S. Army, Center of Military History [CMH]).

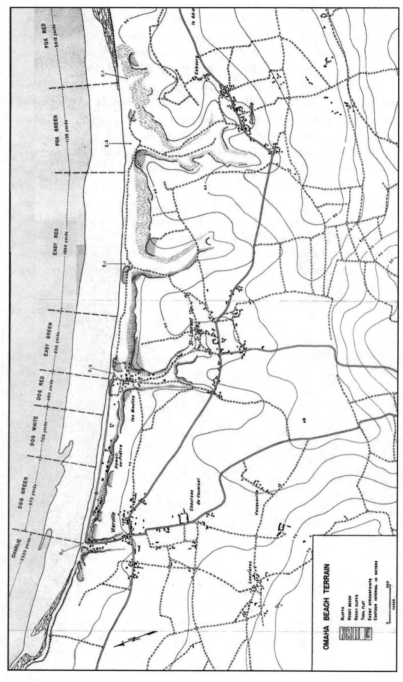

Figure 4.6. D-Day Omaha Beach terrain and landing zones (U.S. Army, CMH).

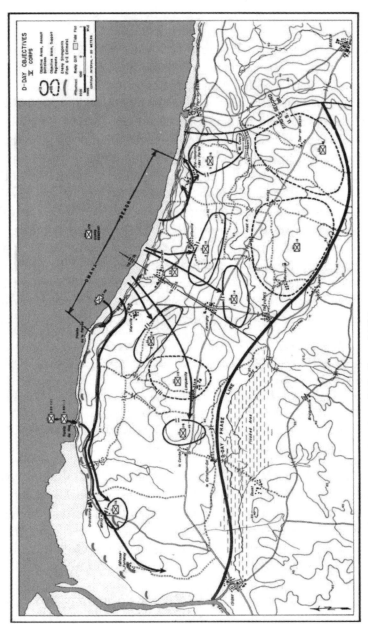

Figure 4.7. D-Day Omaha Beach objectives (U.S. Army, CMH).

So ingrained with the concept of "fire and movement" was General Cota that even his jeep was named as such, with the slogan painted on his trusty mount.

Allied planners and intelligence assets made final assessments of the present situation in Germany and of German preparations in Normandy. They surmised that the military and diplomatic reverses suffered by Germany during the past year weakened Hitler's regime and its political hold on the Hitler government both at home and on the German forces in the field. The planners assessed that if Hitler's government was to survive, the totalitarian Nazi regime must soon stop German retreats and gain victories. The Allies were unable to see any organized political opposition to Hitler based on rigid Gestapo and Nazi controls in place. They made note of the increasingly dejected feelings among German civilians due to hardship. The growing casualties on all fronts, the relentless Allied bombing, and the destruction of the German economy all were succeeding in destroying hope throughout the German military establishment. The situation in France was understood by the Germans as one in which they must hold off the Allied invasion, once it began, just long enough to seek a stalemate. In February 1944, the Allies noted fifty-three German divisions in France.

With a deadlock, the Nazis believe they can maintain their regime. To achieve stalemate in France there is one course they can take: To try to meet the British-American invasion with such force that it is either entirely repelled, or so costly in the initial stages that political pressure in Great Britain and in the United States will force a compromise with the Germans. Any effort less than full resistance would mean invasion of Germany, greater destruction to homes and industries, and, at the end, even harsher peace terms.[17]

The Germans' capabilities were studied in detail and were estimated to be led by the 709th and 716th Infantry Divisions in the assault area, with an additional offensive division located in the vicinity of Saint-Lô. American intelligence estimated that they had defense in depth along the coastal zone with ability to increase the depth of the German fortifications. The casualty estimates for D-Day were 30 percent killed in action and 70 percent wounded in action.

General Cota helped final preparations of the 29th Infantry Division for the invasion. He was known for leading his men from the front. To aid in the early organization of actions on the beach, General Gerow, Major General Clarence R. Huebner, and General Gerhardt created provisional brigade headquarters for the 1st Infantry Division to the east and the 29th Infantry Division to the west. General Cota was assigned as a member of a provisional brigade headquarters for the 29th Infantry Division, the so-called Bastard Brigade. It was in substance the advance headquarters of the 29th Infantry Division. It was scheduled to land with leading elements of the 116th RCT and ensure continuity of command until all elements of the 29th were ashore and the division's main headquarters activated. Once released from control of the 1st Infantry Division, the 115th RCT would fall under command of General Cota as well. The Bastard Brigade consisted of representatives of the 29th Infantry Division's G-2, G-3, and G-4, along with a division artillery advisor, a signal officer, a surgeon, and liaison officers from other assault-wave units (the 1st Infantry Division, 4th Infantry Division, and 29th Infantry Division's main headquarters). The members of the Bastard Brigade had operated together during both the Fox and the Fabius exercises. Once ashore, the Bastard Brigade was to hold until the command structure of V Corps and the full divisional command under Major General Gerhardt were ashore and established.

General Cota spoke to his men of the 29th Infantry Division (Provisional) Brigade Headquarters at 2 p.m. on June 5, 1944, in the aft wardroom of the USS *Charles Carroll* (APA-28), a *Crescent City*–class attack transport. General Cota addressed his staff bluntly, his final comments addressing the confusion they would all later face on the beach:

> *This is different from any of the other exercises that you've had so far. The little discrepancies that we tried to correct on Slapton Sands are going to be magnified and are going to give way to incidents that you might first view as chaotic. The air and naval bombardment and the artillery support are reassuring. But you're going to find confusion. The landing craft aren't going in on schedule and people are going to be landed in the wrong place. Some won't be landed at all. The enemy will try, and will have some success, in preventing our gaining a lodgment. But we must improvise, carry on, not lose our heads. Nor must we add to the confusion. You all must try to alleviate confusion, but in doing so, be careful not to create more. Ours is not the job of actually commanding, but of assisting. If possible always work through the commander of a group. This is necessary to avoid conflicts—duplications of both orders and efforts.*[18]

CHAPTER FIVE

German Defenses near Vierville

THE 1ST AND 29TH INFANTRY DIVISIONS AND ATTACHED AND SUP-
porting units had an appointment with destiny and the French coast.
Vierville is a French commune in the intercommunality of Trévières
in the canton of Trévières in the arrondissement of Bayeux, department of Calvados, in the Lower Normandy (Basse-Normandie) region
of France. This region is located at (latitude/longitude) 49°22'30" N,
0°54'14" W. The average elevation is 151 feet above mean sea level
(AMSL), with elevations ranging from zero to 203 feet AMSL. During
the D-Day invasion, Vierville had around 330 residents.[1] Vierville is 100
miles south of Portsmouth, England, and approximately 660 miles from
the present-day landmark Berliner Fernsehturm in downtown Berlin.
In comparative terms of distance, this number is equal to the distance
between downtown Philadelphia and downtown Chicago. This was the
distance the American and British forces needed to cover, liberating or
conquering the terrain, for victory in Europe.

When the Allied planners identified this area of Normandy as the
location of the D-Day landings, they coded nearly every detail of the
objective area with designations to enable swift and sure communication
among the Allies; this also made it harder for the Germans to understand
Allied communications without extensive effort. Normandy was selected
well in advance of the invasion due to the availability of five favorable
beachheads with sands and ample beach width to land the tens of thousands of men needed to help Overlord succeed. The Americans were given
the two western landing zones, identified as "beaches," while the British

Figure 5.1. Omaha Beach looking west from beach exit near WN 61 (Ron Knight).

and Canadians were given the eastern three beaches. Each beach in turn was divided into sectors, with identifiers such as "Charlie," "Dog Green," "Dog White," "Dog Red," and so on. The westernmost American beach on the Cherbourg Peninsula (also known as the Cotentin Peninsula) was designated Utah Beach. The eastern of the American pair was designated Omaha Beach (as previously illustrated in figure 4.6). The French called this beach La Plage d'Or, "the Golden Beach," owing to the golden color of its sands. The Omaha Beach shoreline is shown in figure 5.1, looking from east to west from a point near Colleville. It has five draws among its cliffs and bluffs, each with a road or path connecting the high ground to the beach. During the war, these geographic features were heavily defended strongpoints that served as the natural exits off Omaha Beach. The designations for these obstacles to be overcome by the Allied invaders in order for the invasion to proceed inland were, from west to east,

- Dog One (D-1) at Vierville
- Dog Three (D-3) at Les Moulins

- Easy One (E-1) at Saint-Laurent-sur-Mer (hereafter St. Laurent)
- Easy Three (E-3) at Colleville
- Fox One (F-1) at Number 5 draw[2]

As the war raged and in the years following, War Department historians prepared detailed reports of the action that resulted in publication of *Omaha Beachhead* (CMH Pub 100-11-1). This report stated, "The coast of Normandy offers only a few areas favorable for large-scale landing operations in the zone assigned to V Corps. Cliffs, reefs, and wide tidal ranges combine to present natural difficulties." The V Corps identified Omaha Beach for the assault landings in this region along a five-mile, relatively cliffless interval compared with the rest of the adjacent Normandy coastline. The Omaha Beach terrain is illustrated in figure 5.2. On the western extent of the Omaha sector, the Aure River flows north from Saint-Lô to the seaside town of Isigny-sur-Mer, where it drains into the channel. It forms a shallow estuary with reefs extending to the east to Grandcamp along the coastline. Saint-Lô lies approximately twenty miles south of Pointe du Hoc. To the east of Grandcamp, the coast is formed by one-hundred-foot cliffs running east past Pointe du Hoc to Pointe et Raz de la Percée (Pointe de la Percée).[3] In comparison, the beaches in the Utah, Gold, Sword, and Juno sectors gave way to gradual rises in elevation. The cliffs typical of the coast in the Omaha Beach sector presented themselves as either sheer cliffs or steep bluffs nearly 100–150 feet in height.

The tidal range is eighteen feet on Omaha Beach and reveals approximately three hundred yards of gently sloping, firm sand at low tide. Conversely, the high tide comes in as far as the seawall. The Germans constructed their underwater obstacles along this sometimes exposed tidal flat. Other natural features include irregular runnels parallel to shore scoured out by the tidal currents, each of which was two to four feet deep at low tide. Runnels are natural coastal features where the moving water carves channels to account for flow, and anyone who spends time at a beach has experienced them. The range in the tides in the south of England and north of France are the most challenging on Earth to cal-

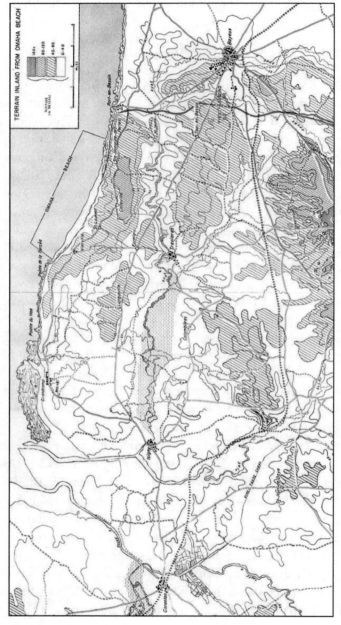

Figure 5.2. Terrain of Omaha Beach coastal area (U.S. Army, Center of Military History [CMH], Publication 100-1).

culate and complicated the planning of a successful amphibious assault based on the geography and other factors.

For the troops traveling ashore in 1944, the beach terminated at an obstacle up to eight feet in height called a shingle at the high-water mark. A shingle is a zone composed of stones worn smooth and deposited to some depth by tidal and wave action over the centuries. The shingle stones vary in size from a quarter inch to three inches in diameter, are nearly flat, and are as smooth as a glass marble. These characteristics make footing unstable and digging a hole essentially impossible as any holes refill due to gravity and the low friction of the stones. This shingle might be absent in portions of the beach in the presence of a constructed seawall. In the case of Omaha Beach, the shingle generally sloped up sharply to a height of eight feet and a width of fifteen feet and consisted mainly of heavier stones up to three inches in diameter deposited by the water. In the western portion of Omaha Beach between Vierville at Exit D-1 and St. Laurent at Exit D-3, the seawall was topped with a paved coastal roadway. The Germans placed barbed wire obstacles on the landward side of this roadway; the result was that attackers would have to expose themselves to enemy crossfire on top of the roadway as they attempted to breach the obstacle. This specific point is important to remember later in the story as relates to General Cota. Between the roadway and bluffs, the Germans demolished most of the houses or other structures that impeded line-of-sight and defensive firing along the zone or that offered any cover to the attacking forces. The bluffs overlooking the beach between D-1 and D-3 are the most abrupt on the beachhead not containing vertical cliffs.[4]

The overall beach itself is a wide, shallow, crescent-shaped feature backed by bluffs that are not vertical, as found at Pointe du Hoc, but steep and covered with mixed foliage. They can be traversed by foot soldiers, but they are taxing, and movement is considerably slowed. Five miles east from Pointe de la Percée beyond this beach, the cliffs reappear and run east to Port-en-Bessin. Omaha Beach is approximately seven thousand yards long. In 1944, the eastern two-thirds of the beach had low sand dunes acting as natural vehicular barriers. From Exit D-1 east to Exit D-3, the shingle was pushed up against a seawall four to twelve feet high. Behind the wall was a paved beach road that ran between the exits and provided access to the residents before the war. Between the seawall and the foot of the bluffs was a two-hundred-yard-wide beach flat, where the various homes stood prior to the arrival of the Germans, who either disassembled them for materials to aid in the construction of their defenses or leveled them to clear fields of observation and fire. The bluffs between Exits D-1 and D-3 average 144 feet high and represent the most abruptly steep bluffs along the entire Omaha Beach landing zone, rising sharply from the flat dominating the entire beach. The majority of the bluffs were grass covered on the western portion of the beach. The crests of the bluff were clear-cut and had been largely farmed before the war. The slopes contained many folds and irregular features, creating an uneven surface and places for troop cover once on them. To the west of Exit D-1, the bluffs merged into the previously mentioned cliff and continued as far as and beyond Pointe du Hoc. At this interface, the Germans found ample cover and siting for artillery and automatic weapons positions that would enable firing down the length of the beach from various elevations. The overall natural features of this place favored any entrenched defender based on World War II technology.

There were only four locations suitable to egress vehicles from Omaha Beach. These small, wooded valleys led south from the beaches and provided natural corridors inland. The gently rolling plain above the beaches continued to rise to 250 feet approximately 2,000 feet farther south in an undefined ridge. "Three villages, Vierville, St-Laurent, and Colleville, 500 to 1,000 yards inland, were so situated near the heads of draws and along the coastal highway as to figure inevitably in the defense of main exit routes. . . . A double track railroad from Paris (Caen) to Cherbourg runs from east to west across the high ground a few miles south of the Aure River. Cutting this line at Bayeux and Caen, and denying its use to the enemy, was a primary objective in the D-Day attack of the British Second Army."[5] The first road of importance was one running from Port-en-Bessin to Grandcamp as a fifteen-foot paved road paralleling the coast about a mile inland. The most important artery in the region was the Carentan-Isigny-Bayeux road. Another important paved road linked

Bayeux with the junction point of Saint-Lô. Farther south of the ridge, the land dropped into the Aure River valley, which runs east to west through the region. The benefit to the Allies of this valley was that there were few, very limited options for north–south traffic between the inland and the coast, with one fordable location of the river by dismounted troops at Trévières. The Germans flooded much of the valley as a line of defense, but it also hindered movement of reinforcements. These features all were V Corps tactical objectives of the assault in order to safely secure the beachhead.

Many of the small fields above the beaches were lined with hedgerows, orchards, and patches of trees. This began the famous Norman hedgerows that plagued the Allies until they fought south toward the interior in August. Normandy has historically been heavy in agricultural activity, from raising stock to growing fruit. As the centuries passed, the rocks found in the fields were stacked along the edges of the fifteen- to one-hundred-acre fields, creating dense rock- and vegetation-strewn hedges as high as ten feet. A fifteen-acre field would be approximately eight hundred feet per side to give some concept of how closely opposing forces might be separated. The farmers often installed drainage ditches along the edges of these fields, artificially increasing their height for anyone attempting to cross one. There were limited openings to the fields, usually located in corners, and this made excellent natural ambush locations for any defenders. The book *Omaha Beachhead* described fighting in these environs:

> *Fighting in country of this sort presents serious difficulties to attacking forces. Each hedgerow across the axis of advance might conceal a nest of enemy resistance, in which good positions for flat-trajectory weapons could be quickly organized, with short but usually excellent fields of fire across the nearest fields. Axial hedgerows could be utilized by defenders for delivering flanking fire. Observation would be extremely difficult for the attackers, and this might hinder the quick use of supporting heavy weapons and artillery fire. In contrast, a defending force could use prearranged fires of mortars and automatic weapons sited to cover the hedgerows leading toward any prepared positions. Split up by hedgerow walls, attacking forces were often to find difficulty in maintaining communications on their flanks and in coordinating*

the attack of units larger than a company. Fighting in this country would put a premium on initiative and aggressive leadership in small units, and armor could have only limited use.[6]

Hitler stated in his speech declaring war on the United States, on December 11, 1941, "A belt of strongpoints and gigantic fortifications runs from Kirkenes [Norway] to the Pyrenees. . . . It is my unshakable decision to make this front impregnable against every enemy." The Führer issued German Directive No. 40, Command Organization of the Coasts, on March 23, 1942. Hitler established his overall doctrines for coastal defense:

In the days to come the coasts of Europe will be seriously exposed to the danger of enemy landings. The enemy's choice of time and place for landing operations will not be based solely on strategic considerations. Reverses in other theaters of operations, obligations toward his allies, and political motives may prompt the enemy to arrive at decisions that would be unlikely to result from purely military deliberations. . . . Even enemy landing operations with limited objectives will—insofar as the enemy does establish himself on the coast at all—seriously affect our own plans in any case. They will disrupt our coastwise shipping and tie down strong Army and Luftwaffe forces which thereby would become unavailable for commitment at critical points. Particularly grave dangers will arise if the enemy succeeds in taking our airfields, or in establishing airbases in the territory that he has captured. . . . Moreover, our military installations and war industries that are in many instances located along or close to the coast, and which in part have valuable equipment, invite local raids by the enemy. . . . Special attention must be paid to British preparations for landings on the open coast, for which numerous armored landing craft suitable for the transportation of combat vehicles and heavy weapons are available. Large-scale parachute and glider operations are likewise to be expected. . . .

Recent battle experiences have taught us that in fighting for the beaches—which include coastal waters within the range of medium coastal artillery—responsibility for the preparation and execution of defensive operations must unequivocally and unreservedly be concentrated in the hands of one man (Commander in Chief West). All available forces and equipment of the several services, the organizations and formations outside of the armed forces, as well as the German civil agencies in the zone of operations will be committed by the responsible commander for the destruction of enemy transport facilities and invasion forces. That commitment must lead to the collapse of the enemy attack before, if possible, but at the latest upon the actual landing. An immediate counterattack must annihilate landed enemy forces, or throw them back into the sea. All instruments of warfare—regardless of the service, or the formation outside of the armed forces to which they might belong—are to be jointly committed toward that end.[7]

Beginning in 1943, Allied intelligence gatherers became increasingly aware that the Germans were in the process of strategically building defenses on the western front—namely, along the *Atlantikwall*. To that end, the Germans began a massive construction effort to build extensive fortifications. The Germans were well aware, as a result of World War I, that fortifications were not intended to adequately defend all points along their frontier. They developed "a military maxim of economy of force." The Germans developed their coastal fortifications as a formidable defense factor to accomplish this mission. Their desire was to employ a minimum of manpower along the coastlines, sufficient to delay any potential invaders in an effort to mobilize their much larger and highly mobile offensive forces to counterattack wherever a major attack took place. The German High Command situated armored and motorized units strategically inland within striking distance to provide swift and hard-hitting retaliation. The Luftwaffe was also well equipped to handle the task, at least in 1943, when the Allies made this assessment.[8] The loss of German air supremacy during the early years of the war ultimately cost the Germans the control of France. The war of intelligence and deception was won by the Allies well before the invasion. A prime example of this success was the German assumption that the Pas de Calais was the real target of the Allies. The Allied ruse of leading the Germans to that conclusion as a deception worked brilliantly.

The Germans relied on the sea for their outermost coastal defensive zone due to the physical parameters of the sea in a given area. They also used their industrial capacity and ability to heavily mine the nearshore environment, to install other barriers and controls, and to employ their patrol boats. At the tidal zone, or transition from sea to shore, they

Figure 5.3. Aerial photograph taken by a Royal Air Force reconnaissance plane showing the Vierville draw on June 30, 1943, noting lack of defenses in place on D-Day (National Archives and Records Administration [NARA]).

planned for vast fields of underwater steel and wooden obstacles. They conceived of various types, each with a specific role in beach defense. From the water's edge, they organized coastal defenses in depth with heavy reliance on terrain barriers, fixed strongpoints, permanent fortifications, minefields, barbed wire, weapons positions, and other fighting positions for several miles inland. This was all carefully laid out for each portion of the coastline possibly suitable as a landing site. The Germans moved civilians away from what they deemed forbidden zones, such as beach houses. In cases where the original civilian structures impeded defense, they razed them to the ground. In some limited instances, they gutted the structures and built steel-reinforced concrete fortifications inside the empty shells. This was the case at the Vierville draw (as illustrated by figure 5.3).

On the beaches, the Germans employed a variety of defenses. These included underwater stakes, booms, and barbed wire. The stakes were placed in shallow water of the tidal flat on the gently sloping beaches. The defensive strategy used embedded rows of steel stakes and wooden logs, set at an angle with the upper ends of the obstacles pointed out away from the beach, either with sharpened ends or topped with mines. The Germans interlaced barbed wire and used shorter stakes to trap landing craft and personnel. All of the tidal obstacles were intended to wreck landing craft or block them from delivering troops.

The first band of defense was a series of Element "C" gate-like structures, or "Belgian gates" (as shown in figure 5.4). These were made of reinforced iron frames with iron supports on rollers, placed about 250 yards out from the high-water line. The main support girders were ten feet high, with waterproofed Teller mines lashed to the uprights. The second line of defense comprised long log structures designed to tip an unsuspecting landing craft. These were also armed with mines and other destructive devices to harm a boat (as per figure 5.5). The tall ends of these structures pointed to shore to allow the angle of the log to tip vessels. These were located in a band generally twenty to twenty-five yards from shore. The relatively simple defense provided by these was formidable. A third band of obstructions included the hedgehogs, made of steel rails or angles welded or bolted together such that they created

Figure 5.4. German Belgian gates (NARA).

Figure 5.5. Generalfeldmarschall Erwin Rommel visits Normandy defenses in April 1944, illustrating timber groins (German Federal Archives).

six-pointed structures capable of piercing landing craft. These stood about five to six feet high and were generally placed 130 yards from shore.

Barbed wire was used liberally to inhibit movement. It was installed in dense entanglements in gullies and in cliff crevices. It was used between the beach and shingle or along the tops of cliffs. The Germans used various types of wire, including concertina fences, trip fences, electrified wire, combined fences, apron fences, and obstacles in depth. Obstacles in depth are designed so that as you move past the first ones, there are still more beyond, as if you are entering a wooded area from a field. The trees one walks past could be considered obstacles in depth.

The Germans considered camouflage, concealment, and deception very important and effective means in defense tactics. These factors were used extensively in protecting positions, men, and material from ground and aerial observation. The Germans placed many assets underground, relying on the surrounding topographic features and natural vegetation to aid in the concealment of important strongpoints and fighting positions. They used garnished nets, turf, and vegetation to conceal concrete bunkers. They covered some machine-gun nests with as much as three feet of soil.

The Germans installed gun emplacements in caves and hollows in the cliffs along the French coast. These were considerably improved with concrete as positions for both machine guns and artillery. Cave positions proved highly effective in German defensive strategy in many areas subject to Allied raids throughout the war. After smoke screens employed by either the attackers or the defenders drifted away, revealing the attackers, machine guns and artillery opened up on them from positions concealed in caves in the cliff face. The Germans sited various artillery pieces in these types of positions, including 88-mm or captured French 75-mm guns. The guns were impossible to detect even at close range until they fired.[9] The Germans placed occasional trenches, rifle pits, and machine-gun emplacements along the entire crest. "Mortar positions were sometimes included in the strongpoints but were more frequently placed behind the bluffs. About 40 rocket pits were later found, located several hundred yards inland on the high ground and each fitted to fire four 32-cm rockets."[10] Many of the firing positions were designed to cover the tidal flat, shingle, and beach flat with direct fire. Although the line of defense was not continuous, the entirety of the beach was covered by mutually supported fire from multiple positions and weapons platforms.

The system of fortifications was developed and deployed by the German army as an integrated all-around defense of mutually supporting strongpoints within the context of the surrounding terrain in a deep zone of interlocking and presighted fields of fire. This German approach followed the principle of seacoast defense by means of concentration of fire both on and beyond the beaches. The German philosophy made assumptions that the assaulting forces would attack from the seaward side and that, as a result, the attacking forces would be at their most vulnerable just before and during any attempted landings.[11]

The German organization of defensive positions was one in which a grouping method of weapons systems with overlapping fields of fire was used for maximum effectiveness. Each weapon system and position had predetermined fire coordinates and tables, marked smartly on each bastion to allow for quick ranging and accuracy. The interlocking fire approach allowed for mutual aid of the dead zones of neighboring positions to kill enemy soldiers engaged with those neighbors. "The strongpoints in turn are similarly arranged to form a deep, irregular pattern of defenses commanding all critical terrain. Minefields, wire, and other obstacles are freely used, both tactically and protectively. The complete arrangement is designed to absorb penetration, and to wear down, restrict, and impede the attack until the counterattack can be launched."[12] This structure was not an accident. The Germans made modifications in command and control in 1944 that affected the ferocity of the fighting and promoted the type of defenses to be completed that ultimately took a heavy toll on the Americans at Omaha Beach.

The art of military science is an ongoing discipline that has roots as far back as humanity itself and its desire to wage war. Sébastien le Prestre, Comte de Vauban, was born on May 4, 1633, in France and died on March 30, 1707, in Paris after dedicating fifty-two years to the art of war. He was a recognized master in siege warfare in terms of both defending places and laying siege. He was an engineer, attained the rank of *maréchal de France* in 1703, and served as the *commissaire général des fortifications* (1678–1703) for King Louis XIV. He served in the Franco-Spanish War (1635–1659), War of Devolution (1667–1668), Franco-Dutch War (1672–1678), War of the Reunions (1683–1684), Nine Years' War (1688–1697), and War of the Spanish Succession (1701–1714). Vauban was considered the expert in the field of fortifications, only rivaled by Dutchman Menno van Coehoorn. Vauban's principles served as the dominant European model of fortification for over one hundred years, and his offensive tactics lasted into the early twentieth century and beyond. He was the originator of innovations such as the bayonet, the use of siege artillery, and the development and use of combat engineers.

Vauban had the reputation of never surrendering a fort he defended and never failing to take one that he attacked over his long career. His offensive prowess led to many of his major accomplishments. He believed in defense in greater depth than did his predecessors and stressed that in both operational and tactical terms. He refined his principles as he witnessed the early development of artillery warfare. From an operational standpoint, he called for two lines of fortresses to support each other, not dissimilar to two lines of infantry formations supporting each other on the battlefield, using the warfare of the day. If an enemy broke into the first line, the second would delay the attacker until reinforcements could be brought up or would divert the direction of attack. Forcing the attacker to change direction would place his forces at the disadvantage of attacking sideways along the remaining line of the first line, thereby exposing the attacker to more concentrated firing from two fronts. Vauban believed in better defense through tactical depth of fortifications. To accomplish this task, he often developed detached forts or smaller defensive works outside his main centers of resistance. As cannons improved in the nineteenth century and beyond, the development of these clustered defensive systems, particularly in coastal defense, became the norm. In development of harbor protection, all points of approach were covered by multiple interlocking fields of artillery and mortar fire from the defensive positions in the network. This system uses the concept of enfilade fire, commonly referred to as flanking fire. It is the case where a weapon is used against the longest axis of advance of an opposing force. If the opposing force advances in a row formation, enfilade fire can strike all of the troops with relative ease. In France, the ports of Brest, Calais, and Cherbourg all have remnants of his system.

In America, Vauban principles can be seen at places such as Fort McHenry (built in 1798) in Baltimore, Maryland (as shown in figure 5.6); Fort Jay (1794) in New York Harbor; Fort Harmar (1786), at the mouth of the Muskingum River at the Ohio River in Marietta, Ohio; and Fort Duquesne (1754), at the confluence of the Ohio, Allegheny, and Monongahela Rivers in Pittsburgh, Pennsylvania. His written works published in the eighteenth century became standard references around the world, so much so that prior to World War II, American West Point cadets still studied him, as undoubtedly did the Wehrmacht's cadets and officers. The bastioned system in Europe developed during and after World War I continued to use updated Vauban principles during the interwar years. The Germans took care to implement Vauban's works into their own defensive schemes as part of *Atlantikwall* construction at these places.

In the years after fighting in World War II, Major General John C. Raaen Jr. made the connection between the German principles of mutual

Figure 5.6. Fort McHenry, Baltimore Harbor, Maryland, built with Vauban defensive strategy (National Park Service).

defense and interlocking fire, which he personally experienced, and the principles of defense established by Vauban. As he studied the defenses as part of this helping research for this book, he wrote,

> *As far as I know, nobody else has connected Vauban with the German defenses of OMAHA beach in June 1944. . . . I have known of Vauban since my cadet days. My interest in him and his concepts were ignited when two years ago (or was it three), when I took a QM II cruise to Quebec. One of the tours was to the Citadel of Quebec, a fort following the design principles of Vauban. What caught my ear was the statement by our tour guide that "any soldier within cannon range of the Citadel could be sure at least one cannon was aimed directly at him." One look at Vauban's design told you why. No cannon defended itself! Each cannon provided enfilade fire on attackers of adjacent (or even distant) walls. Some of those defensive fires were from the oblique rear, not quite as deadly but perhaps more frightening than enfilade. Think of OMAHA Beach. The Widerstandsnest (WN)s were designed to provide enfilade fire in front of adjacent WNs, trenches, and automatic weapons positions*

on the bluffs. WNs could not defend themselves. The weapons of the WNs could not be seen from the sea! The WNs contained only a few defensive Infantry troops and weapons. This whole tactical design was a linear form of Vauban's principles! Think WN 70. "A" Company of the 2nd Rangers landed in front of WN 70. They took approximately 50% casualties from positions on the bluffs, positions to the east and west of WN 70. Weakened as they were, no officers left, the non-coms took the remnants of the company straight up the bluff through WN 70, wiping it out! And they didn't even know it. To this day, nobody knows it except me and now you. This type of action was repeated all along OMAHA Dog beach and into Easy beach. Major [Sidney V.] Bingham, 2nd Bn, 116th Inf., collected stragglers at the Les Moulins exit and attacked the fortified house. Repulsed, he collected more stragglers and attacked over and over again. The WN had to try to defend itself. It abandoned its mission to provide enfilade support to adjacent units. Attacking Infantry easily overwhelmed defending Infantry on the bluffs and advanced into the bocage and attacked the WNs from the high rear ground. Others, like Don Bennett, 58th [Armored Field Artillery Battalion] did the same. Essentially, the 5th Rangers did the same. Overwhelm the unsupported troops defending the bluffs when they lost defensive enfilade fire from WN 70. (A little smoke and flame from the brush fires helped the 5th Rangers as well.)[13]

The German chain of command in Normandy fell under the supreme commander of the armed forces, Adolf Hitler. Reporting to him was the Oberkommando de Wehrmacht (OKW), or Armed Forces High Command, under Generalfeldmarschall Wilhelm Keitel. The commander in chief of the Oberbefehlshaber (OB) West, or German Army Command in the west, was Generalfeldmarschall Karl Rudolf Gerd von Rundstedt, with the mission to "prevent any hostile landing in [the area defended by his men]. The MLR [Main Line of Resistance] is the high tide line in the coast. Should the enemy land at any place, they are to be immediately thrown back into the sea." Rundstedt oversaw Army Group G and Army Group B. In autumn 1943, Army Group B was placed under the command of Generalfeldmarschall Erwin Johannes Eugen Rommel, who, due to his popularity with Hitler, maintained personal access to the Führer. Rommel in turn oversaw the LXXXVIII Corps, Fifteenth Army, and Seventh Army and had conditional tactical control over the

II Parachute Corps. The Seventh Army was in command of the units on western Omaha Beach, including the 716th Static Infantry Division and the 352d Infantry Division (Wehrmacht). The 716th Infantry Division was under the command of Generalleutnant Wilhelm Richter. The 726th Infantry Regiment (IR), with its command post at Gruchy Castle just west of Vierville, was part of the 716th.[14]

Generalleutnant Dietrich Kraiss was the commanding general of the German 352. Infanterie-Division (352d Infantry Division). He is pictured in figure 5.7. He was an experienced combat commander, having served in the invasion of Poland as a regimental commander. He then served as a regimental commander in the 20. Infanterie-Division (20th Infantry Division) during the occupation of the Netherlands and France in 1940. He served from 1941 to 1943 as a *Generalmajor* of the 168. Infanterie-Division (168th Infantry Division) during Operation Barbarossa. He earned the Knight's Cross of the Iron Cross for leadership during the Third Battle of Kharkov. He was promoted to *Generalleutnant*

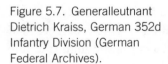

Figure 5.7. Generalleutnant Dietrich Kraiss, German 352d Infantry Division (German Federal Archives).

in October 1942. He took command of the 355. Infanterie-Division (355th Infantry Division), which was decimated in battle against the Red Army at Merefa, Ukraine. After the 355th Infantry Division was disbanded, the majority of the remaining noncommissioned and commissioned officers were reconstituted as the 352d Infantry Division in November 1943 and transferred to the western front.[15]

On December 5, 1943, Oberstleutnant Fritz Ziegelmann assumed his role as chief of staff (second in command) of the division at its headquarters in Saint-Lô. His first tasks were to review the men on hand and to determine what core of veterans remained for the newly formed division.[16]

The 352d Infantry Division included soldiers from three different combat-experienced units that had become combat ineffective through attrition on the eastern front. These were the Grenadier-Division 546, decimated at Stalingrad, and the 268th and 321st Infantry Divisions, decimated in the Kursk Offensive of 1943. Other men who had recovered from wounds received in Africa and Italy also joined the cadre of the unit. Ten percent of the overall soldiers in the division were combat veterans. In total, approximately 75 percent of all noncommissioned and commissioned officers were battle-tested veterans. All the line officers had frontline experience. To this seasoned group were added several thousand German conscripts from the training camp at Schlann, Germany. The new division was to be fully activated by January 1944 and would train in order to fight on the eastern front. The fact that this division expected to be sent to the eastern front meant that the men trained with determination, as the core of the cadre already had firsthand experience fighting the Russians. They were motivated to conduct effective fighting operations while outgunned, outnumbered, and surrounded on the field of battle.

General Rommel arrived in France on December 14. He conducted an assessment of the *Atlantikwall* and sent a report of his findings directly to Hitler. His report indicated that the defenses of the area along the Normandy coastline were inadequate. His initial assessments concluded, "I therefore consider that an attempt must be made, using every possible expedient, to beat off the enemy landing on the coast and to fight the battle in the more or less strongly fortify coastal strip. This will require the construction of a fortified and mined zone extending from the coast some five or six miles inland and defended both to the sea and to the land."[17] By 1944, as a result of the action in the Mediterranean, Rommel had a sense of the style of battle the Americans combined with the British could and would bring. Rommel and his officers knew of the supremacy of the skies and sea that the Americans created through their technological development and industrial machine. Rommel and Rundstedt disagreed vehemently regarding the placement and use of the German armor and reserve forces. Rommel wanted them up near the beaches, but he was overruled.

Within the 352d Infantry Division, there were several battalions of Eastern Europeans who had been conscripted ("volunteered") for service in the German army. These men were commanded by Germans and constituted a small fraction of the division strength at 30 percent of the total and were relegated away from the frontline positions.[18] The division continued to make do with the meager supplies that trickled in as a result of the relentless Allied air attacks and bombings. Many of the men were issued desert gear left over from North Africa.

General Kraiss arrived to take command at the beginning of January 1944. General Kraiss and Oberstleutnant Ziegelmann continued to make the best of their bad supply situation, organized the division, and managed to pull off three live-fire exercises. One exercise per regiment would have to ready the men for combat in light of the lack of ammunition. One deficiency the officers overcame was the deplorable condition and strength of their enlisted men, as made clear in February. Many of the men were malnourished and could not complete basic soldiering tasks, such as marches. When superiors turned down repeated requests for a dairy ration, Kraiss used his own funds to make local purchases of meat and dairy to strengthen his men; by March, their condition had improved. On March 1, 1944, the division had a strength of twelve thousand men ready to fight and was declared at the disposal of OKW and ready for deployment. Although Berlin proclaimed the division at full operational readiness, Kraiss and Ziegelmann wanted more training for their men and kept hard at work with them.[19] General Kraiss's headquarters was at Le Molay-Littry, eight miles south of Saint-Laurent-sur-Mer. This placed his command post some nine miles southwest of Bayeux and nine and a half miles south-southeast of Omaha Beach's Exit D-1.[20]

The Germans hence set about improving the defenses, installing Belgian gates, Czech hedgehogs, and obstruction beams (as illustrated in figure 5.8).[21] Within the context of this book, the remainder of the descriptions are focused on those German defenses and personnel emplaced in the western Omaha Beach sector that ultimately relate to the 29th Infantry Division. This zone of study is between St. Laurent at the D-3 draw east to the Vierville D-1 draw and surrounds. Two really good books for understanding the German point of view are David C. Isby's *The German Army at D-Day* and Vince Milano and Bruce Conner's *NORMANDIEFRONT: D-Day to Saint-Lo through German Eyes.*

One weakness along the Calvados coast was that between what the Allies referred to as draws, where the cliffs and bluffs overlooked the beach, the German 716th Infantry Division physically did very little to defend the crest. They put in place minefields, open trenches, and other light defensive positions but not the heavy defensive infrastructure that was abundant at the *Widerstandsnester* (WN), or strongpoints. The Germans underestimated the Allied ability to infiltrate large numbers of infantry forces up the bluffs. They assumed that the interlocking fire on the beach

Figure 5.8. German "Czech" hedgehogs (German Federal Archives).

Figure 5.9. Side view of typical bluff in vicinity of Dog Red and Dog White Sectors (U.S. Army, CMH).

would inhibit any ability to make it up the bluffs or the cliffs of Pointe du Hoc, for that matter (figure 5.9). This was found to be nowhere more critical to the assault on Omaha Beach than at Dog Red/Dog White.[22]

The static 716th Infantry Division was ill trained and poorly equipped or prepared, in the estimation of Rommel, to cover such a vast defensive sector of the Normandy coast. As a result, on March 15, he assigned the 352d the task of defending the area known to the Allies as Omaha Beach. The 716th was relocated to the area near Caen.

Rommel was having some success in his planned defenses of the coastal areas, but he had serious misgivings regarding the current state of German preparedness and the command structure. On April 23, Rommel wrote a letter to Generaloberst Alfred Jodl, stating, "The most decisive battle of the war, and the fate of the German people itself, is at stake. Failing a tight command in one single hand of all the forces available for defense, failing the early engagement of all our mobile forces in the battle for the coast, victory will be in grave doubt."[23] Rommel deduced that the invasion would occur in the rural areas of Normandy and even correctly concluded that the Omaha Beach and other Normandy landing sites looked favorable for invasion because of their similarities to the Allied landing locations at Salerno.

In a letter to his wife, dated April 27, 1944, Rommel wrote, "It looks as though the British and Americans are going to do us the favor of keeping away for a bit. This will be of immense value for our coastal defenses, for we are now growing stronger every day—at least on the ground, though the same is not true for the air. But even that will change to our advantage again some time."[24]

Rommel ordered the deployment of the 352d Artillery behind the beaches to bolster the defense of the coastal zones. Additionally, the I and III Battalions of the 726th Grenadier Regiment (GR) were transferred to the 352d Infantry Division. Rommel issued three orders to General Kraiss:

- Improve the beach defenses along each respective unit's part of the coast.

- Be responsible for building and maintaining defensive positions from the coast all the way to Saint-Lô and provide security in this area.

- Maintain the current divisional training schedule.

Kraiss responded to his orders and established two main battle lines. The first was the beach defenses along the coast. The second was a line established some ten to fifteen kilometers south of the coast. This turned out to be a mistake due to overwhelming Allied airpower and poor north–south routes to move forces. It lengthened German supply lines such that they could not resupply ammunition. The 352d was also on standing alert for movement within Europe and, as such, faced supply challenges from higher echelons. By June, the beach defenses were evaluated and a report provided to Kraiss. The report stated that only 45 percent of the bunkers were built to sustain artillery fire. Only 15 percent of these fortifications were constructed to withstand aerial bombardment. The remaining fortifications were deemed unfit to do either. Kraiss determined that he would have to rely on the readiness and quality of his troops for the invasion he knew was inevitable. Throughout the spring, he trained his men using two overall themes. His experience had shown the importance of individual training of the soldier. He knew that small groups of well-trained soldiers could inflict damage upon and hold up larger and more powerful enemy units. He also knew the value of training for the counterattack. Again, his combat experience had shown him the importance of the counterattack to retake ground or to plug gaps in battle lines. In final preparations, a failure was made by the Germans in that they did not provide enough ammunition to their coastal defenses. Many of the units simply fired their weapons until they ran out of ammo. Some German positions fired as many as ten thousand rounds on Omaha Beach on D-Day.[25]

Another impressive aspect of the 352d was its divisional intelligence-gathering ability and its commander's ability to properly weigh the intelligence data. Kraiss believed the Normandy coastline would be a major invasion objective and trained his men accordingly. On June 1, the 352d had received reports of low-flying reconnaissance aircraft. Kraiss also had reports of an increase in carrier pigeon traffic from the Normandy coast. In response, he put a bounty on pigeons. The captured messages evaluated as a result of this action revealed that the Maquis had made detailed reports to the Allies as to German positions and troop strengths. The capture and interrogation of a Maquis in Brittany resulted in a wealth of intelligence. The Allies would reportedly commence the invasion in the first week of June in Normandy. Kraiss passed this news on to Berlin, but his request that an alert be issued was denied as alarmist. This is reported in U.S. Army intelligence document MS-B-432, 352d Infantry Division, dated 1947. The German High Command of the 7th Army was scheduled to have war games for the entire first week of June, as is reported in books like *The Longest Day*. Kraiss acted skillfully on his intelligence gathering and remained at his post, using the war games as an excuse to put his men on alert on June 4. He told his subordinates of the impending invasion and that, for them, the alert was real.[26]

What the Omaha Beach sector's defenses lacked in depth, the Germans were prepared to make up for during the initial hours of the assault with artillery fire and the WN strongpoints. Two books that provide solid

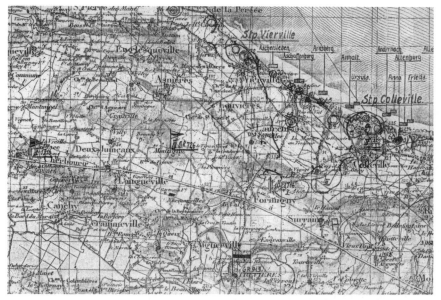

Figure 5.10. Portion of captured German map showing artillery firing solutions onto Omaha Beach between Vierville-sur-Mer and St. Laurent (NARA).

and detailed descriptions of the German defensive positions are Georges Bernage's *Omaha Beach* and Brigadier General Theodore G. Shuey's *Omaha Beach Field Guide*.

A captured German map shows that the Germans had zeroed in on the beach for artillery strikes (figure 5.10). The important fact is that the Germans were as ready as they could be, and they were waiting for the Allies, particularly at Omaha Beach, due to the command decisions of General Kraiss. For that reason, the Allies would have to pay by the inch in blood for their assault there.[27]

By D-Day, the Germans had fortified the seven-kilometer stretch of Omaha Beach from Sainte-Honorine-des-Pertes to Pointe de la Percée with fourteen WN positions numbered 60 through 73. Only WNs 63, 67, and 69 were not able to provide direct fire upon the beaches. The WNs had a massive amount of available firepower. This included but was not limited to

WN fortifications consisting of

- Two 88-mm *Panzerabwehrkanonen* (Paks)
- Fifteen mortars of various sizes
- One 76.2-mm *Feldkanone* (FK) (field gun)
- Two 80-mm mortars
- Six 75-mm FK(f)
- Six 37-mm guns
- Two 75-mm turreted guns

Four artillery batteries consisting of

- Ten 105-mm *Panzerabwehrkanone* (Pak) (antitank gun)
- Twelve 105-mm *leichte Feldhaubitze* (leFH) (light field howitzer)
- One 47-mm Pak
- Four 150-mm *schwere Feldhaubitze* (sFH)
- At least eighty-five *Maschinengewehr* 42 (MG-42) machine guns

The slit trenches, bunkers, pillboxes, mortar pits, *Nebelwerfer* (rocket launchers), and machine-gun nests were manned by men from the 916th and 726th regiments. The 726th Grenadier Regiment occupied the majority of the WNs. German unit 10/GR 726 occupied WNs 64, 65, 66, and 68. The 11/GR 726 based at Vierville occupied WNs 70, 71, 72, and 73. Stab II/GR 916 was at Formigny. The 9/GR 726 was at Gruchy near Englesqueville, 6/GR 916 was located at Formigny, and 7/GR 916 was at Surrain. The third battalion of the 726th Infantry Regiment, including the above units, was attached to the 352d Infantry Division. The total units along the beach included five infantry companies, with five additional infantry companies and four artillery batteries in support, not including the guns of Pointe du Hoc. The 352d Infantry Division also had reserve units consisting of II/IR 915 and 2/Panzerjaeger Abtl 352 (Marders) available to reinforce IR 916 at Omaha Beach.[28]

As discussed, the Germans developed methods to sight in every portion of the beach with direct and indirect fire for all locations. "Sighting

Figure 5.11. German mortar positions demonstrating German preplanning of defensive fire (NARA).

in" a location enables the user of a particular weapon to predetermine what settings to use to effectively hit a given location by mathematical formula. There is photographic evidence of firing solutions painted on walls inside the WN positions and mortar pits. The German mortar position captured by the Allies (and shown in figure 5.11) demonstrates the German artillery planning. The Germans used interlocking tunnels and other means of communications to direct the attack. Unfortunately for them, their wire-based systems became easy prey for the French Resistance and Allied forces as the battle developed.[29]

Gruchy is one kilometer to the west of Vierville. It sits at a small crossroads along the coastal highway on the way to Pointe du Hoc and is named for a manor house that sits to the south of the road. The Castle Gruchy is unseen from the roadway, as it is surrounded by forests and hedgerows. The German army established the command post of the 726th Infantry Regiment, 9th Company (9/726) at the manor under the command of Captain Grünschloss. This particular German captain was not considered a fanatical Nazi. He had been a professor of law in civilian life. He was a Bavarian, spoke fluent French, and would die on D-Day.[30]

The *Widerstandsnester*

The WNs that had a direct impact on western Omaha Beach were, from west to east, WN 74, WN 73, WN 72, WN 71, WN 70, and WN 68.[31] These German defenses must be discussed and understood to follow the battle on June 6 and 7, 1944. A description of each from west to east forms the content of the following pages.

WN 74 was located on the far western bluffs overlooking the entirety of Omaha Beach at Pointe de la Percée, as shown in figures

Figure 5.12. Aerial photo showing WN 74 (NARA).

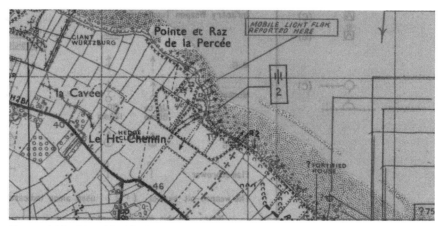

Figure 5.13. May 19, 1944, Allied intel map—WN 74 (NARA).

5.12 and 5.13. There were two bunkers, each containing a captured 76-mm Russian mountain gun of Czechoslovakian design known by the Czechs as a Skoda 75-mm M1936 mountain gun and redesignated by the Wehrmacht as the 7.62-cm GebK 307(r) (figure 5.14). This weapon

Figure 5.14. One of two Skoda 75-mm M1936 mountain guns in position at WN 74 (NARA).

had modest but effective firing characteristics. The caliber was 76.2 mm, or three inches, with a shell weight of 13.7 pounds. The weapon's elevation range was −8° to +65° with a traverse of 10°. The rate of fire was ten to fifteen rounds per minute (rpm). The muzzle velocity was 1,624 feet per second (ft/s), and the weapon had a maximum firing range of 10,720 meters (6.6 miles). These cannons were only two miles from Exit D-3. The flight time of their shells to the exit was a mere 6.4 seconds. These weapons were well camouflaged and effective killers. According to Allied defensive overlays, this WN had no less than six to ten MG-42 positions, several of them in protected concrete embrasures. The effective range of the MG-42 machine guns was 3,828 yards, with a maximum firing range of 5,140 yards, enabling them to rake Exits D-1 and D-3 with deadly fire. Mobile light flak weapons were reported here as well. The position was manned by the 9th Company of the 726th Regiment.

WN 73 was a deadly position that, along with WN 71 and WN 72, inflicted maximum carnage on the morning of D-Day due to the placement and collection of weapons available (figures 5.15 and 5.16). It had an observation post, one concrete bunker armed with a 75-mm cannon, two Tobruks for 81-mm mortars, a flak position reportedly with a 50-mm weapon, and twelve machine-gun fighting positions, two of those in concrete casemates. It had trench lines between it and WN 72 at the draw. It also contained additional concrete or underground shelters for men and material.

The Canon de 75 modèle 1897 was also known as the French 75-mm field gun (figure 5.17). This weapon was known for its rate of fire, accuracy, ability to stay on target, and lethality of ammunition against personnel. It was designed as an antipersonnel weapon system capable of firing large volumes of time-fused shrapnel shells. It had a hydraulic recoil mechanism, enabling it to remain fixed on target. The muzzle break on the end of the barrel forced expelling gases to flow backward as the shell passed, also thereby dampening the recoil. It could fire multiple kinds of ammunition, including fixed quick-firing, high-explosive, high-explosive antitank, and shrapnel shells. It had an elevation range from −11° to +18° and a traverse of 6°. Its rate of fire was one of its most impressive attributes, as a well-trained crew could

Figure 5.15. WN 73 strongpoint showing defensive positions (NARA).

Figure 5.16. Allied D-Day mapping of WN 73 strongpoint showing defensive positions noted by arrow (NARA).

Figure 5.17. French 75-mm field gun (WD 219-508 Observations on invasion of France and fall of Cherbourg, June–July 1944 [NARA]).

fire anywhere from three to thirty rpm. The shells had a muzzle velocity of sixteen hundred feet per second and had a maximum firing range of twelve thousand yards, enabling complete coverage over Omaha Beach from its high perch in WN 73. The Germans seized thousands of these French guns when they overran France in 1940 and, more important, an estimated 5.5 million shells to go with them.

WN 73 had two prepared mortar positions for the 8-cm Granatwerfer (GrW) 34 mortar (figure 5.18). This was the standard German infantry mortar throughout World War II and was accurate with a high rate of fire. The shells from the weapon weighed seven pounds, eleven ounces. The elevation was from 45° to 90° with a 10–23° traverse. The rate of fire was fifteen to twenty-five rpm. The effective firing range stood at 440–1,310 yards with a maximum firing range of 1.5 miles. Figure 5.19 illustrates German enfilade on Cota's landing location on Dog White Beach from WN 73.

These positions were not just capable of defending the D-1 exit (as demonstrated by figure 5.20). The perspective of this photo is from the beach where the 5th Ranger Infantry Battalion and General Cota landed on D-Day. The arrows denote some of the line-of-sight weapons capable of firing on a given point from their actual positions in the landscape.

Figure 5.18. German 8-cm GrW 34 mortar in position at WN 73 (NARA).

Figure 5.19. Landing location of General Cota looking west toward WNs 72–74. The
WN 73 75-mm cannon casemate is dead center in the photo (see inset) (Ron Knight).

Figure 5.20. Both casemates at WN 72 are visible (the 88-mm to the left and the 50-mm to the right) (NARA).

WN 72 was the visibly dominant feature of Exit D-1. This *Wider-standsnest* had one Type H677 casemate housing an 88-mm Pak 43/41 aimed to the east, located at the mouth of the draw on the shingle. There was a twin of this weapon positioned four miles to the east at WN 61 on the eastern edge of the beach, aimed to the west. The WN 72 casemate had protective concrete side walls designed to shelter the gun and gun port from naval gunfire. Between the bunker and the bluff, the Germans installed a massive 125-foot-long, 9-foot-high, 6-foot-thick concrete antitank wall. The casemate had separate machine-gun embrasures to allow protected MG-42 fire onto the beach. This position was constructed in the lower portion of a demolished hotel, and several elements of the former hotel were left in place to the seaward side to attempt to mask the true nature of the structure.

The Pak 43 was the most powerful antitank gun in the Wehrmacht arsenal used in significant numbers. It was very capable of firing on a very flat trajectory out to one thousand yards. The gunners were thus enabled to effectively hit targets at longer ranges with few corrections in elevation. The weapon had a maximum firing range of nine miles with a muzzle velocity of 3,707 ft/s. It was capable of handling multiple types of ammunition with exceptional penetration properties. The Pak 43 fired at a rate of six to ten rpm, with a projectile weight of sixteen pounds.

Located two hundred feet to the northwest of the 88-mm casemate was a slightly smaller double embrasure casemate constructed to house a 5-cm Pak 38 (L/60) German antitank gun capable of firing east or west due to two openings in the emplacement. The weapon is illustrated in figure 5.21. WN 72 also had multiple machine-gun and other weapons positions capable of protecting the important D-1 exit on the shoreline as well as up the bluffs.

WN 71 sat atop the southeast opening of the D-1 exit. Its main purpose was to provide supporting fire to WNs 72 and 73 in the protection of the Vierville draw (as shown in figure 5.22). The position had an observation post and was armed with two concrete double-embrasure machine-gun positions overlooking the draw and beach approaches just below the crest of the bluff. Trenches ran between all positions, enabling improvised fighting positions where needed in addition to troop protection. There were also at least three prepared open concrete machine-gun

Figure 5.21. German 5-cm Pak 38 (50-mm) (German Federal Archives).

Figure 5.22. WN 71 shown on Allied defense overlay map, May 20, 1944 (NARA).

positions with pivot points for mounted weapons. WN 71 had two 8-cm GrW 34 mortar positions similar to WN 73. The defenders could fire east as far as the D-3 exit to provide supporting interlocking fire for their neighboring positions. Most important, this series of positions at Exit D-1 made it virtually impossible to survive any landing attempt in the face of the draw.

Approximately eight hundred yards to the east of WN 71 was WN 70 along the bluff over the beach. This position enabled the Germans to provide fire support between the D-1 and D-3 exits (as illustrated in figure 5.23). The overall plateau between the exits is eighteen hundred yards long, and this position was designed to hinder any penetration of the bluff in this sector. WN 70 was fronted by minefields and barbed wire. There were two concrete 50-mm mortar pits for smaller versions of the 81-mm mortars in WNs 71 and 73. The position had one 20-mm flak gun. The German military engineers developed the 20-mm Flakvierling 38, consisting of four guns, seats, and ammunition boxes. The cannons

Figure 5.23. WN 70 overlooking western Omaha Beach.

could be shot in pairs or by fours in automatic or semiautomatic mode, reaching twenty-two hundred meters. It is unknown whether the 20-mm cannon at this position was a single, double, or quad mount weapon. There was one 75-mm field gun in an open emplacement and one 75-mm field gun in a casemate. The 75-mm artillery in the casemate was oriented to the northeast to cover the D-1 draw. The Germans built four Tobruks as machine-gun positions. One such position at the northeast corner of the 75-mm position casemate had four MG-42s.

The last WN in a direct position to affect the landings between Exits D-1 and D-3 was WN 68. This position was situated on the western side of the entrance to the Les Moulins valley. Like the positions at the D-1 draw, it was a mutually supporting position with WN 66. It had multiple machine-gun positions, French tank turrets installed on concrete casemates, and many other surprises for the invaders, such as a formidable antitank ditch and other roadblocks.

As all of the positions were developed before the landings, the German positions between Vierville and Pointe de la Percée were particularly dangerous because they could deliver enfilade fire on the majority of the landing area. Unlike Calais or certain other potential landing zones, Omaha Beach was not strongly defended by coastal batteries of heavier guns. Situated between Omaha and Utah Beaches was Pointe du Hoc, located five thousand yards to the west, where there was a battery believed to house six French 155-mm howitzers partly mounted in casemates. The Allies regarded this as the deadliest position in the American zone, as it could hit targets on both beaches. By May 13, a total of 517,000 foreshore obstacles were installed along the channel coastline. By May 20, Rommel's forces had installed 4,193,167 mines along the channel coast. On May 15, Rommel again wrote to his wife, stating, "It's quite amazing what has been achieved in the last few weeks. I'm convinced that the enemy will have a rough time of it when he attacks, and ultimately achieve no success."[32]

On May 17, before the invasion, General Rommel and General der Panzertruppe Leo Geyr von Schweppenburg had an opportunity to speak at Rommel's headquarters at La Roche Guyon; Generalleutnant Fritz Hermann Michael Bayerlein was also present at this meeting. Rommel told his subordinate,

> Our friends from the East cannot imagine what they're in for here. It's not a matter of fanatical hordes to be driven forward in masses against our line, with no regard for casualties and little recourse to tactical craft; here we are facing an enemy who applies all his native intelligence to the use of his many technical resources, who spares no expenditure of material and whose every operation goes its course as though it had been the subject of repeated rehearsal. Dash and doggedness alone no longer make a soldier, Bayerlain; he must have sufficient intelligence to enable him to get the most out of his fighting machine. And that's something these people can do, we found that out in Africa.[33]

General Rommel and Hitler spoke on May 19, and Hitler praised his efforts in fortifying the coast.[34] By the eve of battle, the 352d Infantry Division was the best trained, most prepared division in Normandy. General Kraiss went against Hitler's orders and moved his division into defensive positions above and behind Omaha Beach in the days just before the invasion. As a result of his initiative, the 352d was able to resist and delay the Allied onslaught for several weeks.[35]

The Allied intelligence efforts failed to firmly place the more experienced 352d Infantry Division in the vicinity of the Omaha Beach landing area in time to affect D-Day planning. The high command became aware of its presence in May but did not change plans in response to the realization or inform the 1st Infantry Division or the 29th Infantry Division. However, the 352d Infantry Division was near full strength, with some twelve thousand well-trained and well-equipped men. They had nearly completed their training by D-Day and were on alert and at their positions due to the actions of their commanding general. General Kraiss was charged with the defense of the section of Normandy Coast that included Omaha Beach and part of Gold Beach and did his best to prepare his men. The division had new German 105-mm and 150-mm guns. They were assigned antitank units equipped with armored vehicles. In the time given, the Germans had in fact come close to fully realizing the vision of the ideal *Atlantikwall* on Omaha Beach by June 5, 1944. The disposition of German troops was noted by captured German officers (as shown in figure 5.24).

As General Kraiss and his division waited on June 4, the day came and went without incident. He was supposed to go to Rennes to participate in war games, but because his suspicions were growing of the actual invasion, he decided to remain in Littry at the divisional headquarters. His men kept vigilant watch, making the 352d Infantry Division the only unit in Normandy on full alert. On June 5, Oberst Ernst Goth moved all other companies of the 916th Grenadier Regiment from six kilometers to within one kilometer of the beach as part of his new and stronger defensive strategy. During the day, Kraiss argued unsuccessfully with General der Artillerie Erich Marcks to place the 709th Infantry Division on his left and the 716th Infantry Division on his right on alert. These two units were slated for war games, and their superiors dismissed Kraiss as an alarmist. Throughout the day, the level of tension within the division rose as troops became anxious in their duties. Ziegelmann urged Kraiss to allow the men the afternoon or evening off. Kraiss agreed to this, with the condition that the guard be doubled on all the strongpoints and patrols.[36]

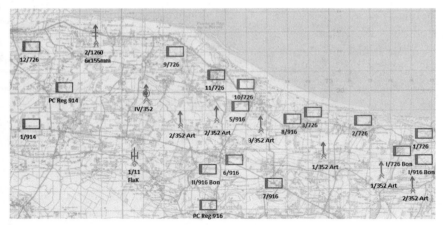

Figure 5.24. Disposition of German troops at Omaha Beach.

General der Infanterie Günther Blumentritt, OB West, reported after the war as a prisoner that his men intercepted a coded radio message between 10 p.m. and 11 p.m. on June 5 from England to the French Underground. He did not know the meaning of it, but he knew that this message deserved special attention and transmitted it to Army Group Command. The Fifteenth Army heard the message and issued an "Alert I" order. The LXXXIV Army Corps (Wehrmacht) issued a similar alert independently a little later. OB West became aware of Allied paratrooper landings between 12:15 a.m. and 3 a.m. At 6 a.m., they became aware of the aerial bombing and Allied naval bombardments of German positions and coastal areas between the Orne and Vire Rivers.

In the early morning hours near Vierville, in a tree observation post resembling a hunting platform, twenty-one-year-old Leutnant Hans Heinze peered into the darkness. He was part of the general staff of the 2d Battalion, 916th Infantry Regiment. As the darkness began to lift, he scanned through his field glasses out into the channel. On the horizon, he noted the shape of a ship's masthead appearing through the haze of the early morning mist. Soon he saw another and another, until the sea was full of them. As the minutes wore on, he witnessed the approach of an entire fleet arrayed in the waters offshore. He wrote a note to his superiors and gave it to a messenger: "Thousands of ships in front of us, the invasion is at our doorstep."

CHAPTER SIX

Western Omaha Beach, H-Hour to H+1 Hour

MAJOR JOHN SOURS, ORIGINALLY FROM ROANOKE, VIRGINIA, WAS THE 116th Infantry Regiment's supply officer (S-4) on D-Day. On July 4, 1942, Major Sours's sister wrote a letter that discussed their last visit, during which he relayed to her that "since the 29th Division was to be the first overseas, they would be the first to spearhead the invasion, and that there would be no way but that the Germans would 'mow' them down."[1]

It is reported that the opening fire on Omaha Beach was between German positions near Port-en-Bessin and the invasion fleet in the pink predawn light of June 6, 1944, between 5:30 and 5:50 a.m. Sunrise occurred at 5:58 a.m., and the first arrival of troops ashore was scheduled for 6:30 a.m., or H-Hour. General Omar Bradley planned for a massive prelanding shore bombardment in what was hailed as "the Greatest Show on Earth." The shoreline was to be bombarded from the sea and the air. The battleship USS *Texas* (BB-35) shelled multiple targets, including Pointe du Hoc with her fourteen-inch batteries between 5:50 and 6:30 a.m., ahead of the 2d Ranger Infantry Battalion's landing. She fired her 5-inch guns on the Vierville draw, or Exit D-1, from 5:50 to 6:24 a.m. The rest of the massive Allied fleet likewise let loose impressive salvos, according to those who witnessed the landing from their places aboard ship or in the air.[2]

The War Department map in figure 6.1 shows the first-wave landings on Omaha Beach and illustrates the beach sectors discussed herein. Of importance to note are the mislandings of the 116th Infantry far

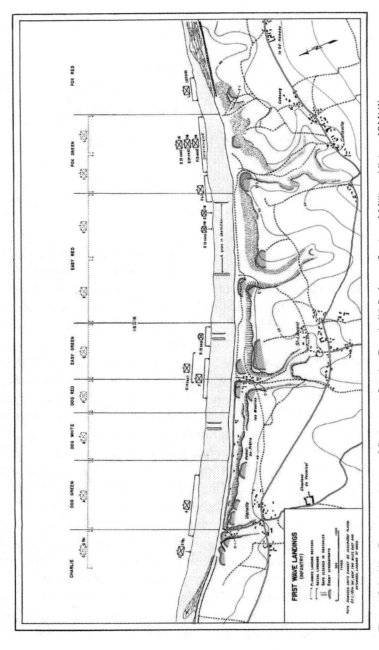

Figure 6.1. War Department map of first wave, Omaha Beach (U.S. Army, Center of Military History [CMH]).

to the east along the beach versus the intended locations along the top of the diagram. This split and separated the units and contributed to a breakdown of command and control over units at the company level. The original planned landing locations are noted in figure 6.2.

LANDING DIAGRAM, OMAHA BEACH
(SECTOR OF 116th RCT)

	EASY GREEN	DOG RED	DOG WHITE	DOG GREEN
H-5			Co C (DD) 743 Tk Bn	Co B (DD) 743 Tk Bn
H HOUR	Co A 743 Tk Bn	Co A 743 Tk Bn		
H+01	Co E 116 Inf	Co F 116 Inf	Co G 116 Inf	Co A 116 Inf
H+03	146 Engr CT	146 Engr CT / Demolitions Control Boat	146 Engr CT	146 Engr CT / Co C 2d Ranger Bn
H+30	AAAW Btry CoH HQCoE CoH 116 Inf AAAW Btry	2d Bn CoH CoF CoH 2d Bn 116 Inf AAAW Btry	AAAW Btry CoH HQCoG CoH 116 Inf AAAW Btry	Co B HQCoA Co C 116 Inf AAAW Btry
H+40	112 Engr Bn	Co D 81 Cml Wpns Bn 149 Engr Beach Bn	149 Engr Beach Bn 121 Engr Bn	HQ 1st Bn116 Co D 116 Inf 149 Beach Bn 121 Engr
H+50	Co L 116 Inf	Co I 116 Inf	Co K 116 Inf	121 Engr Bn Co C 116 Inf
H+57		HQ Co 3d Bn Co M 116 Inf		Co B 81 Cml Wpns Bn
H+60		112 Engr Bn	HQ & HQ Co 116 Inf	121 Engr Bn Co A & B 2d Ranger Bn
H+65				5th Ranger Bn
H+70	149 Engr Beach Bn	112 Engr Bn	Alt HQ & HQ Co 116 Inf	121 Engr Bn 5th Ranger Bn
H+90			58 FA Bn Armd	
H+100			6th Engr Sp Brig	
H+110	111 FA Bn (3 Btry's in DUKWS)	AT Plat 2d Bn AT Plat 3d Bn 29 Sig Bn		AT Plat Cn Co 116 Inf 1st Bn
H+120	AT Co 116 Inf 467 AAAW Bn 467 AAAW Bn	AT Co 116 Inf 467 AAAW Bn 149 Engr Beach Bn	467 AAAW Bn	467 AAAW Bn
H+150		DD Tanks	HQ Co 116 Inf 104 Med Bn	
H+180 to H+215		461 Amphibious Truck Co	Navy Salvage	
H+225	461 Amph Trk Co			

Key: LCI, LCM, LCA, DD Tank, LCT, LCVP, DUKW
Note: Plan as of 11 May

Figure 6.2. Landing diagram, Omaha Beach, from Bigot Operation Neptune Plan (National Archives and Records Administration [NARA]).

According to General der Infanterie Günther Blumentritt, OB West, on D-Day, his command was not alerted about the invasion: "In view of the uncertain situation in 1943–44, OB West and the armies ordered constant 'special attentiveness' and a rapid series of alert stages. We had no naval or aerial reconnaissance, and no information from our espionage agents. For us, the English southern coast was an impenetrable sphinx. Rumors and scattered reports did not give us specific information on the time and place of the landing. A permanent alert of the troops was not possible, since training and rest were equally important."[3]

Oberstleutnant Fritz Ziegelmann, 352d Infantry Division, was alerted to the airborne landings around midnight on June 5 into June 6. He issued an air raid warning Stage II. He then phoned all subordinate commands down to the battalion level on the 352d Infantry Division sector and alerted them accordingly.[4]

The Germans began to see the juggernaut approaching the shore. An extract from the telephone diary of the 352d Infantry Division (Coastal Defense Section Bayeux) reads,

5:32 hours: Report from 916th Grenadier Regiment: In the Bay of Colleville-Vierville, landing boats are nearing the beach. Farther on, bigger naval units have been sighted, keeping course to the west. A naval formation consisting of five men-of-war is heading toward the east; small landing boats have taken course landward. Apparently, the enemy enshrouds himself in a mantel of artificial fog.

5:52 hours: Report from the 352d Artillery Regiment: Approximately from 60–80 fast landing boats are approaching the coast near Colleville. Our own artillery cannot reach these boats. The region of Maisy is kept under fire from heavy naval artillery likewise Marcouf. The naval units on the high seas are too far away for our own artillery.

5:55 hours: Report from 916th Grenadier Regiment: Ahead of Vierville, forty-five smaller and middle-sized landing boats were observed, which opened fire on the coast.

6:20 hours: 916th Grenadier Regiment: In the Bay of Vierville, tank landing craft have been clearly observed.

On the northern end of Vierville, the Hotel du Casino overlooked Exit D-1 and Omaha Beach. It was owned by the Piprel family and was lost to the occupation at the time. The German Wehrmacht soldiers had used the hotel for rest and relaxation beginning in February 1944. On the night of June 5, 1944, an Allied bomber overflew Vierville, dropping a load of bombs along the crest of the bluff. Pierre and Fernando Piprel ventured outside at around 5 a.m. on June 6 to see the damage and to visit a local friend, aeronautical engineer Mr. Mary. The boys navigated a secret path through minefields along the bluffs to get there. Mr. Mary told the boys that this bombing was nothing out of the ordinary, and they returned home just as the sun rose. Upon reaching their home, they went to their attic bedroom. Their view of the sea was unobstructed from this perch. They recorded seeing "the multitude of black dots covering the sea beyond. My word," said Pierre, "they look like boats." The boys then went back to the home of Mr. Mary, as he owned a pair of contraband binoculars. (The Germans did not allow ownership of binoculars.) "Come Mr. Mary! Take your binoculars, we believe we see boats!" Mr. Mary had been skeptical, but, looking out to sea from an attic window, he exclaimed, "Yes! Yes! It is full of boats! It's everywhere!" The young men witnessed the armada moving closer to shore by the minute. They were perplexed as they noted the silence. They wrote, "All these vessels advancing forward, tearing the haze seems unreal. They look like ghosts." At 6 a.m. the silence ended as the naval and air bombardment commenced. They reported that Vierville was hit in the first volley, resulting in substantial damage. They referred to it as the shield launched by the Allies before the attack. The bombardment enveloped the coast. There were columns of smoke, punctuated by bursts of flames. They called it an "atmosphere of doom." In homes in Vierville, walls collapsed, electricity flickered, and tiles shattered. Power poles were sliced through and fell. It was reported that "there was no question of going outside."[5]

In WN 62, machine gunner Franz Gockel, 726th Grenadier Regiment, had a clear view of the beginning of the landings. His experience would be echoed along the length of the beach.

But that [the air bombardment] was not enough. In the grey of the morning the fleet moved closer to us, bringing more trouble. We all knew that this was the beginning of a hopeless struggle and, perhaps because we shared this feeling we would fight with much tenacity and bitterness. As if on parade an unsurveyable fleet stood before us. The sight was unique, but a horrible experience for those that would survive. With mighty flashes and deafening thunder they opened fire upon us. Salvo after salvo hit our positions. Throughout the bombardment the fleet moved closer to the shore. We watched as the fleet grew bigger. The rain of shells fell on us seemingly without end. Fountains of earth shot into the sky and fell back again. Many of the obstacles on the beach were blown apart. Everything we had seen so far indicated to us the considerable amounts of material that the Allies possessed in contrast to us, with only a few strongpoints. The anti-tank gun in our bunker was already firing at the fleet. For the rest of us the wait was still on.[6]

The result of the bombardment was unfortunate, as in the words of Major General John C. Raaen Jr. (Ret.), former company commander of Headquarters Company and a captain at the time:

The Situation at H-Hour of D-Day that faced the invading Allied Forces on OMAHA Dog Beach was far from that expected in the Invasion plan. First, the bombing of the beach fortifications was a TOTAL FAILURE. No bomb hit within a mile of the beach. Instead of destroyed German positions with bomb pock marked beaches for cover, the beach area and its defenders were unscathed. Second, OMAHA Beach was expected to have about 800 defenders in positions along the crest of the bluffs and in the fifteen Widerstandsnesten (battle positions containing automatic weapons, mortars and light artillery) that supported the Infantry defenders along the bluffs as well as defending the exits from the beach. These German troops were known to be low grade static troops, many impressed into the German Army after being captured in earlier battles. There was also one maneuver battalion in reserve. Instead, unknown to the invading forces, the 352d Infantry Division, an experienced, full strength, well trained and well rested division, had moved from its training positions near St. Lo to the beach area on June 5th. This nearly doubled the strength of the defenders to 1100 men plus increasing the reserve battalions from one to five![7]

Oberstleutnant Fritz Ziegelmann, 352d Infantry Division, reported, "At about 0600 hours, the enemy suddenly started to cover the 'landing-endangered' coastal sector around St. Laurent and the background with the fire of heavy naval artillery. Shortly after that [between 6:45 and 7 a.m.], the regimental commander who was responsible for this sector [Oberst Ernst Goth, 916th Infantry Regiment] reported the approach of a large number of enemy landing craft, some of which were also engaging with their weapons the fortified defense system."[8]

It is safe to say that the initial assault did not go as planned. There were contingencies, but between H-Hour and the time General Cota landed at nearly H+1 hour, the general's June 5 prediction of chaos had become prophecy. Many of the details of the initial assault are well documented in the works of Joe Balkoski, Stephen Ambrose, Cornelius Ryan, Major General Raaen, Robert W. Black, the U.S. Army Historical Service, and many others. What is important to know is that based on the first hour of the assault, the western portion of Omaha Beach (particularly the Charlie and Dog Sectors) later earned the moniker "Bloody Omaha."

The 743d Tank Battalion was attached to the 29th Infantry Division for the landings and scheduled to arrive ashore at H–5 (6:25 a.m.). The rough seas hindered its arrival, and the naval officer in charge ran the men closer to shore on their LCTs (Landing Craft, Tanks) than was originally scheduled. Two of the Company A tanks were swamped and lost in the surf. Company B lost seven of sixteen tanks on landing in the face of the Vierville draw (Exit D-1). The troops suffered from being swamped in addition to murderous cannon, machine-gun, antitank, artillery, and mortar fire. They lost their company commander in the initial moments. The nine remaining tanks under the command of a lieutenant began assaulting German positions at point-blank range from the water's edge. The Company C tanks landed to the east between D-1 and the St. Laurent draw (Exit D-3). They also soon attracted enemy fire.

The Omaha Beach invaders landed on a wide front of some 4.5 miles. The 116th Infantry was selected for the first wave of the 29th's landings on the western portion of the beach between D-1 and D-3. Twenty-four landing craft brought in troops of the 116th Infantry, 29th Infantry Division to the west, while twenty-four others brought the 1st Infantry Division to assault the eastern portion of Omaha. Two additional British LCAs (Landing Craft, Assault) brought Company C of the 2d Ranger

Infantry Battalion to Charlie Sector west of the Vierville draw to assault the defenses on the cliffs of Pointe de la Percée. In the first wave of the 29th's assault, Company G was supposed to land to the right of Company A but drifted east and landed on Easy Green in the face of Exit D-3 and became separated. Company F was to land on Dog Red; however, its landing craft were split in three groups between Easy Green and points farther east in the 1st Infantry Division's sector as far as Fox Green. (The area described above is visible in figure 6.3.)

As an example of the extreme carnage imposed on these Americans, Company A, 116th Infantry, landed in the face of Exit D-1 (as illustrated in figure 6.4). Within ten minutes of their landing, over 100 of the 155 men in that company alone lay dead, and the majority of the remainder were wounded. The Germans specifically targeted American officers on the beach. Among the dead of Company A were Captain Taylor Fellers, commanding officer (CO), and Lieutenant Benjamin R. Kearfott, who were cut down when the entire complement of their landing craft (LCA 1015) was destroyed by mortar fire. Among the dead were nineteen soldiers from one small town, Bedford, Virginia, who would later become known as the Bedford Boys. The German machine-gun fire placed on

Figure 6.3. Omaha Beach West, showing Exit D-1 view east (Franck Maurouard).

Figure 6.4. Allied photo of landing craft approaching Dog Green days after battle. Minus the Allied equipment ashore in this photo, this is the view facing the attackers on D-Day (NARA).

them was at a rate of twelve hundred rounds per minute from many weapons emplacements. This carnage was portrayed in the movie *Saving Private Ryan*. The destruction of Company A was so complete, so total, that no unit roster remains of what soldiers actually were loaded aboard each of the landing craft as those records were lost along with the dead in the face of Exit D-1.

Company A landed in six assault craft. The company came under enemy fire within seven or eight hundred yards of the beach. The first landing ramps dropped at 6:36 a.m. in water that was waist deep or deeper and in some areas above the heads of the men. As soon as the ramps dropped, the Germans used crisscrossed automatic machine-gun fire on the ramps of each craft, enveloping them in a sheet of lead. The carefully laid-out and rehearsed assault plan called for Company A to move in three files from the craft as the men exited the boats in a left-center-right movement. As described in a combat interview of the men conducted after the assault, "The first men tried it. They crumpled as they sprang from the ship, forward into the water. Then order was lost."[9]

Company A plodded ashore in six LCAs from their marshalling area twelve miles and two hours out before touching down at H-Hour.

Shortly after their control boat peeled off, leading them to shore at the five-mile point, Company A overtook a group of LCTs bringing the tanks of the 743d Tank Battalion, Company B, to Dog Green. The tanks were supposed to land six minutes before Company A to provide them with armor support and cover on the beach. The LCTs just couldn't keep their pace in the rough surf and fast-moving tidal currents. At 6 a.m., Lieutenant Ray Nance, Company A, peered out of a slot in the bow of his LCA and saw a pall of smoke hanging over the bluffs. Well out from shore, one of the LCAs took on water and sank. This effectively reduced the combat strength of the company by one-sixth. As the men approached the coast, the details of the D-1 draw came into focus, including the looming pillboxes of WN 72. Another LCA took a round from an antitank gun, injuring several men at around 6:25 a.m. The flotilla revved up to full speed, and the first craft hit the beach and the ramps dropped. It took over a minute for the soldiers to disembark. The men were ashore, and British sub-lieutenant Jimmy Green, LCA flotilla commander, remembered studying the bluffs above the beach. The guns were silent, and he recalled it as a "creepy silence." Captain Fellers and his men took prone positions on a slight incline 250 yards from the exit.

All along the bluff, the 352d Infantry Division lay in wait. WN 71, WN 72, and WN 73 were prepared with their interlocking fields of fire and presighted target settings. The interconnected trenches, minefields, and barbed wire, in conjunction with the massive wall, proved impassable while manned by the Germans. As Fellers ordered the advance, the Germans opened fire with no less than three MG-42s and mortars. Two dozen German riflemen were entrenched throughout the defenses. The good captain and all twenty-nine men of his boat died immediately, cut down by deadly crossfire. Less than fifty yards away, another Company A LCA touched down. Lieutenant Alfred Anderson was the first off. He and his men tried to advance ashore. The lieutenant was literally cut in half by machine-gun fire. Two American tanks made it ashore, and one of them was immediately knocked out by a direct hit. By 6:45 a.m., all five of the Company A LCAs had deposited their men and pulled away.

The utter destruction of Company A was nearly complete. The Germans fired upon the nonwounded, wounded, and dead alike. They swept the fallen with additional bullets to make sure the job was done. They felled medics and soldiers trying to help their comrades and attempting to pull them forward out of the rising tide. The snipers aimed at the forehead. They shot men in the back. It didn't matter; their orders were to hold at all costs. The bodies of the Bedford Boys lay at an interval of every ten yards.

It was at this moment that Company B landed at H+26 (6:56 a.m.). Some accounts state Company B arrived on time at 7 a.m. right on top of the carnage of Company A. All that Captain Ettore Zappacosta, Company B CO, could see were corpses. When the doors of his LCA opened, the captain was riddled with a hail of machine-gun bullets. One German up on the bluffs of Omaha was interviewed after the war. He reported that the MG-42s were so hot from use that even the triggers were hot to the touch. He said, "It was the first time I shoot at living men. . . . I don't remember exactly how it was: The only thing I know is that I went to my machine gun and I shoot, I shoot, I shoot." Company B radio operator Bob Sales witnessed his company wither around him. He recalled Private Mack Smith near a cluster of rocks. He was hit three times in the face. His eyeball lay on his cheek. Sales later found he was the only survivor of his LCA. Another landing craft was decimated as an 88-mm shell exploded it, causing fragments of men and wood to rain on the survivors. As these men made it ashore, they then faced their own appointed machine-gun fire.[10]

According to a wartime report of an interview with survivors, "It seemed to the men then that the only way to get ashore with a chance for safety was to dive head-first into the water," reported Private Howard L. Grosser. A few had jumped off, trying to follow the standard operating procedure, and had gone down in water over their heads. They were around the boat now, struggling with their equipment and trying to keep afloat. The men each had equipment akin to that illustrated in figure 6.5. In one of the boats, a third of the men were engaged in this struggle to save themselves from a quick drowning, according to Private First Class Gilbert G. Murdock. Murdock and Private First Class Leo J. Nash reported,

That many were lost before they had a chance to face the enemy. Some of them were hit in the water and wounded. Some drowned then. Others, wounded, dragged themselves ashore and upon finding the sands, lay quiet and gave themselves shots [of morphine], only to be caught and drowned within a few minutes by the on-racing tide. But some men moved safely through the bullet fire to the sands, then found that they could not hold there; they went back into the water and used it as cover of under-water obstacles. Many were shot while so doing. Those who survived kept moving shoreward with the tide and in this way finally made their landing.

Figure 6.5. Lieutenant Jack Shea's drawing of 29th Infantry Division personnel D-Day landing gear (Mike White).

The combat interview goes on to state that Company A had become inert and leaderless and almost incapable of action within seven to ten minutes of the dropping of the first ramps of the landing craft.

The report states the unit was "bereft" of officers. Lieutenant Edward N. Garing was lost when the first boat sank. All the others were dead. Lieutenant Elijah Nance was hit in the heel as he left the boat and then in the body as he reached the sands. Lieutenant Edward Tidrick was hit in the throat as he jumped from the ramp into the water. He went onto the sands and flopped down fifteen feet from Private First Class Nash. He raised up to give Nash an order. Nash saw him bleeding from the throat and heard his words: "Advance with the wire cutters!" It was a futile order, as Nash had no wire cutters, and in giving the order, Tidrick had made himself a target for just an instant. Nash saw machine-gun bullets cleave him from head to pelvis. German machine gunners along the cliff directly ahead were now firing straight down into the party. The Germans slaughtered every sergeant or above in their sights "as if to exterminate them." A medical boat team came in to the right of Tidrick's boat, and the Germans machine-gunned every man aboard, clearly going against the Geneva Conventions.

Company C of the 2d Ranger Infantry Battalion landed at 6:45 a.m. on Omaha Beach in Charlie Sector to the extreme right of the beach aboard two LCAs. Its mission was to land on the heels of 29th Infantry Division, Company A, go up the D-1 draw, and follow Company A through Vierville, and then wheel right and assault WN 73. It was well understood that the German positions in WN 73 and WN 74 were critical to the German defense of the beach as these positions gave the Germans clear views of the beach and contained critical artillery observation posts and weapons. No American could move on the beach without enemy observation from these heights. If Company A ran into trouble, the Rangers were to ascend the cliffs just below WN 73, neutralize it, and knock out the guns on Pointe et Raz de la Percée, followed by the radar station to the west, and finally link up with Lieutenant Colonel James Earl Rudder at Pointe du Hoc. Two hundred yards from shore, they had yet to receive fire, and some of the Rangers sang. As they made their way ashore, one of their two craft was struck and first blood was drawn by German mortar or artillery fire. The Rangers suffered fifteen killed or wounded.

The remaining Rangers landed under intense fire and fought their way to the base of the cliff just below the fortified house of WN 73. On the beach, 1st Sergeant Henry Golas was struck by a hail of machine-gun fire; yet he continued to charge until he was so riddled with bullets he fell, still fighting. Fellow Rangers reported that the sergeant had half of his head blown away at the base of the cliff, yet still fired his weapon. He hollered up at the Germans above to come out and fight. The witness, Ranger Donald Scribner, remembered seeing him raked across the chest three times by machine-gun fire before he fell. "He was quite a man," Scribner said of him.

The Rangers only had thirty-five men left to climb the cliffs under Captain Ralph E. Goranson. Goranson then learned of the fate of the Bedford Boys and the decision was made to climb. The Rangers ascended the cliffs and assailed the Germans, paying back the losses they experienced, and took WN 73. By nightfall, his number of combat-effective C Company Rangers was reduced to twelve men. Before the invasion, Lieutenant Colonel Rudder told Captain Goranson, "You have the toughest G-------d job on the whole beach."[11]

It was reported that the bodies floated at the edge of the water, advancing with the tide. The remaining infantrymen abandoned any attempt to move forward and simply tried to survive from that moment on. They tried to save any living comrades. The men retreated into the water, pushing the bodies of the dead and wounded ahead of them in the advancing tide. Men ashore did try to pull men from the water to keep them from drowning, "in many cases, only to have them shot out of their hands or to be hit themselves while in these exertions."[12] These would-be rescuers dropped their own personnel equipment to allow for freer movement in the surf and then cut away the equipment of the wounded in the water to keep them from drowning. Within twenty minutes of striking the beach, Company A ceased to be an assault company. "The leading hand in the rescue work, by the account of all survivors, was a first-aid man, T/5 Tom Breedin."

The six assault craft of Company B fared a little better than those of Company A. One boat landed to the right flank of the landing area at the foot of the cliffs flanking the right of the D-1 exit, near the 2d Ranger Infantry Battalion, Company C's landing position (discussed later). The twenty-eight survivors of this boat fought alongside the Rangers, assaulting Pointe et Raz de la Percée (WN 74) throughout the morning until rejoining the 29th Infantry Division at 11 p.m. near Vierville.

In the follow-on assault waves at Dog Green, Company B was scheduled to land at 7 a.m., followed by Company D at 7:10 a.m. and Company C at 7:20 a.m. Company B was supposed to come in entirely on top of Company A to support and reinforce it. The smoke and dust of battle, along with the fast currents, obscured visible landmarks. The boats landing along the flanks of Company A fared better than those that landed amid Company A. The other of the boats from Company B that mislanded would play a role in the assault of the bluffs. Company B, minus two landing craft, landed on the heels of Company A and suffered the same fate. The other craft landed to the east on Dog Red and to the right of the 2d Rangers' Company C in Charlie Sector.[13] This action was described in an interview report of Company B survivors.

Pfc Robert L. Sales was in Capt Ettore V. Zappacosta's boat. Three hundred yards out, it came under mortar fire. The boat was hit several times but the men were uninjured. About 75 yards from the beach, the ramp was dropped and enemy automatic fire then beat a tattoo all over the boat front. Zappacosta jumped from the boat and got 10 yards through the water. Sales saw him hit in [the] leg and shoulder. He yelled: "I'm hit." T/5 Kenser, a first aid man, yelled: "Try to make it in!" Zappacosta went down and they did not see him come up again. Then Kenser jumped toward him and was shot dead as he jumped. Lieutenant Tom Dallas of "C," who had come in to make a reconnaissance, also jumped out. He got to the edge of the sand and was there shot to death. Sales was fourth in line and it had come his turn. He started out with his SCR 300, tripped at the edge of the ramp and fell sprawling into the water. It probably saved his life. Man by man, all of those leaving the ramp behind him were either killed or wounded. Sales was the only one to get as far as the beach unhit, and it took him almost two hours. He had moved only 20 yards through the water and then bumped into a large floating log. At the moment, a mortar shell burst near him and knocked him groggy. He felt himself blacking out and he grabbed hold of the log.[14]

Private George Kobe, Company D, witnessed a German 88-mm shell hit the craft, blowing off the ramp and the two inner steel doors of his LCA. One of the doors hit Captain Walter O. Schilling in the head and killed him instantly as the other door smashed into his platoon sergeant, John Stinnett, blinding him in one eye.[15]

Sergeant J. Robert Slaughter served in the 29th Provisional Ranger Battalion prior to D-Day. On D-Day, he was assigned to Company D, which landed at H+40. His account of the landing in the face of Dog Green is chilling.

About 200 or 300 yards from shore we encountered artillery fire. Near misses sent water skyward, and then it rained back on us. . . . As we approached the beach the ramp was lowered. Mortar and artillery shells exploded on land and in the water. Unseen snipers concealed in the cliffs were shooting down at individuals, causing screams from those being hit. The water was turning red from the blood. The noise from artillery gunfire's explosions, the rapid-fire rattle, pr-r-r-r-r, from nearby MG-42s, and naval gunfire firing inland, was deafening. The smell of cordite was something that would forever become fixed in our minds, always associating it with death and destruction. . . . As my turn came to exit, I sat on the edge of the bucking ramp trying to time my leap on the down cycle. I sat there too long causing a bottleneck and endangering myself as well as the men that followed. The 1-inch steel ramp was going up and down in the surf, rising as much as 6 or 7 feet; I was afraid it would slam me in the head. One of the men was hit and died instantly. There were dead men in the water and there were live men as well. The Germans couldn't tell which was which. All were coming in with the tide. . . . There were dead men floating in the water and there were live men acting dead, letting the tide take them in. . . . While lying on sand behind one of the log poles, I watched a GI get shot trying to cross the beach, running from my right to left. He probably was from the craft that touched down about 50 yards to our right. An enemy gunner shot him, and he screamed for a medic. One of the aid men moved quickly to help him, and he was shot. I'll never forget seeing that medic lying next to that wounded GI and both of them screaming. They both died in minutes.[16]

The 2d Rangers, Companies A and B, were scheduled to land at Pointe du Hoc along with the entire 5th Ranger Infantry Battalion. The 5th Ranger Infantry Battalion was supposed to receive a signal to follow Lieutenant Colonel Rudder's 2d Rangers up the cliffs at Pointe du Hoc by 7 a.m. If this signal was not received, the secondary objective of these Rangers was to land at Exit D-1, carry the fight inland, and then fight westward to the Pointe. The 2d Rangers' craft sailed ahead of the 5th Rangers' craft. They landed in the face of Dog Green at 7:35 a.m. Lieutenant Robert M. Brice, Company B, 1st Platoon, was the first to land and subsequently the first to die as German machine-gun fire raked across his chest. The Rangers landed aboard British LCA craft, with a door allowing only one man to exit at a time. The Rangers reported bodies everywhere, floating in the water and on the beach. They reported that any men of the 116th not dead were pinned down on the beach. The Company B Rangers passed through the 116th casualties and made it to the rock wall. Company A landed about seventy-five yards from shore. They were savagely fired upon by the Germans, yet moved forward to the seawall. Thirty-five men of Company A and twenty-seven of Company B made it to the seawall out of companies with sixty-five men each. The survivors began to take steps to advance inland per their secondary objectives. By now it was 7:45 a.m.[17]

The other major units that landed in this maelstrom included the remainder of the 116th Infantry, 1st Battalion, including Companies B, C, and D, in addition to the Battalion Headquarters. The 2d Ranger Infantry Battalion's Companies A and B landed just east of the Vierville draw. Surviving and scattered tanks of the 743d Tank Battalion arrived on the beach throughout, along with other smaller demolitions and engineering units. The arriving units did not sense and acknowledge the danger until it was too late to abort landing atop the death and destruction.[18] This snapshot is not all inclusive of the actions in the first hour of the assault and is intended to provide a clear picture of the conditions on the beach.

At approximately 7:20 a.m., an officer informed Captain Berthier Hawks, Company C, that Dog Green was closed to further landings as they made their approach. The company swung left (east) and landed one thousand yards east of the D-1 draw, thereby sparing these men the carnage endured by their brothers. They landed on Dog White over a hundred-yard front and lost only about 20 of their 194 men.

According to Ziegelmann, "The artillery inflicted considerable loss of life upon the landing enemy by its volley fore, without having heavy casualties itself in its positions."[19] This was curtailed when the skies later cleared and Allied planes took to the air, but the damage was done.

Meanwhile, at H-Hour, to the east at the Les Moulins D-3 beach exit, Companies F and G, 2d Battalion, 116th Regimental Combat Team (RCT), landed at 6:50 a.m. after being swept eastward from their appointed landing locations by the incoming tidal currents. (The Les Moulins draw is shown in figure 6.6.) Company E was forced by the

Figure 6.6. Aerial photo of the Les Moulins D-3 exit showing the extent of the German defenses (NARA).

tide a mile to the east of D-3, touching down in the middle of the 1st Infantry Division's landing zone, and became detached from the 29th Infantry Division for the day. The men of Company G touched down so far to the east that Captain Fellers of Company A could not see them at all. Many of the 2d Battalion men of these companies were from near the Virginia–North Carolina border area. These companies were originally scheduled to land on Dog White Beach and Dog Red Beach, adjacent to and to the east of Company A, 1st Battalion. This landing was planned to extend the left flank of 1st Battalion by a mile and was designed for an amphibious assault ashore and movement abreast up the bluffs.

The naval bombardment set the grasses and other vegetation ablaze just prior to the landing. The thick smoke from these blazes shrouded the bluff and drifted eastward toward the D-3 exit and impacted WN 68. The smoke obscured the onshore landmarks from the U.S. Navy coxswains directing the landing craft, and it also obscured the men in Dog Red from German view. This geography described above pertains to the area from the middle of the draw west toward Dog White.

Private First Class John Robertson, Company F, 116th Infantry, 29th Division
Most of my boat team was seasick. I remember heaving over the side, and someone said, "Get your head down! You'll get killed!" I said: "I'm dying any-way!" So here we are, all seasick, ahead of everyone else, no bomb craters to get in, and heading straight into machine gun fire. That was my definition of Hell.

Private First Class August Bruno, Company G, 116th Infantry, 29th Division
We didn't expect any trouble on the beach and had been told not to run.

The companies each had six LCVPs to carry the men and equipment ashore. Four of the Company G LCVPs touched down in the middle of the draw and then west of the bluffs in front of WN 68. These men were shielded by the smoke of the fires of the bluffs. The 132 men of these craft experienced little trouble making their way through the tidal flat in ten to fifteen minutes to the shingle beyond and taking cover. They experienced only a few losses in their landing. The officers hesitated, trying to determine their exact location and course of action. The remaining three LCVPs of Company F landed to the right of the four Company G LCVPs and four tanks of the 743d Tank Battalion along Dog Red toward the breakwaters at the boundary of Dog Red and Dog White.

The remaining craft came ashore without the benefit of the smoke screen. Two landing craft of Company G touched down on Easy Green to the east of WN 66 and the three-story house at the beach there (as shown in figure 6.7). Three of the Company F LCVPs landed just left of the four Company G craft in the mouth of the draw.

The Germans held their fire as the men exited their craft in files of threes and traveled the four hundred yards of open beach directly in the face of the pillboxes of WN 66 and 68 and in view of WN 67 and its *Nebelwerfer* battery. Once the men were debarked, the Germans opened up as they reached the first belt of German beach defenses.

One of these two Company G LCVPs lost fourteen of its thirty-three occupants before even reaching the shingle. Fifty percent of the Company F and G men in the face of the draw were mowed down in moments in similar fashion to the Bedford Boys. According to *Omaha Beachhead*, "By 0700 Company A had been cut to pieces at the water's edge, Company F

Figure 6.7. Three-story house used as a German defensive position at WN 66 (NARA).

was disorganized by heavy losses, and of the scattered sections of Company G, those in best shape were preparing to move west along the beach to find their assigned sector." The tide was rising as this unfolded, and, as at the D-1 exit, men had to either advance or drown. The lucky ones made it to the shingle. The shingle here averaged six feet in height and was made up of well-weathered off-white stones up to three inches in diameter. The men who sheltered here found themselves safe from the machine-gun fire and had yet to experience the inevitable German mortar and artillery fire to come. A three-story house that remained to the left of the mouth of the draw was converted by the Germans into a fighting position with a concrete pillbox camouflaged into one corner of the structure at ground level. Germans used the upper floors for observation and sniping. The Americans at the seawall were a mere thirty-five feet from the structure and its surrounding trenches and fighting positions.

Private First Class Arden Earll was a mortarman, Military Occupation Specialty (MOS) 504, Company H, 2d Battalion, 116th Infantry, 29th Infantry Division. He landed just to the left of the D-3 exit. He gave an account of his company in testimony on behalf of General Cota in 2019. His unit likewise faced severe casualties. After they realized they could not complete their mission, the remaining noncoms and enlisted men considered what to do next.

Private First Class Arden Earll, mortarman, MOS 504, Company H, 2d Battalion, 116th Infantry, 29th Infantry Division

I was in a heavy weapons company (Company H). We came in at 0700. We landed at Les Moulins, at the Les Moulins draw. We were just a little bit to the left. Actually it is what is now 1st Division territory, just over the border line. I remember the aerial pictures that we saw in England, before the invasion, they showed us this picture of a three-story house. They said to our boat; that is what you'll zero in on when you go in. You men find that three-story house. We got there, it was not a house. It was a German bunker that was very well camouflaged. We didn't move out right away. Everybody just kind of hunkered down. The whole situation was not like we had been told it was going to be. We were told that the defenses, the German defenses, would be pulverized by the time we got there, and nothing to worry about. Well, the bombers missed, the big ships of the Navy, they didn't get it, they missed, and so, we landed. Well, what are you going to do? You gotta do just the best you can. The officer that I had the most to do with was Lt. Raggett [2d Lieutenant Eugene M. Raggett, 0-1305308, H Company, 116th Infantry]. I greatly respected Lt. Raggett, as he was sort of like General Cota, only he wasn't a General, he was just a Lieutenant. He got hit a little bit on D-Day, they put him on a LST, or a landing craft.

Private Rocco Russo, Company F, 116th Infantry, 29th Division
I looked to my right and saw my friend, Sgt. John Cooney, with his head cocked over, his helmet lying on the beach. He was dead. He was the first soldier whom I saw dead on Omaha Beach. He and I use to go to Mass together in England. [I] headed for the seawall, running until fired at, then hitting the beach for a short period, then running again. It did not take me long to get over to the wall, and I plopped down on the sand and rested.

Captain William Callahan, CO, Company F, attempted to establish communications with the tanks on the beach and headed to one of them to do so. In the process of trying to reach the tank, he was hit in both legs and the right hip while directing tank fire from atop one of the Sherman tanks. As he attempted to make it back to the shingle, he was hit in the face and in both hands. It took him some forty-five minutes just to advance this far. When the remaining 50 percent of surviving troops in this beach sector made it to the shingle, they were essentially combat ineffective. Company G lost many of its officers and key leaders, as well as enough men to fill two of the LCVPs, amounting to some sixty men in this first movement. The remaining men of Company G from the four western landing LCVPs decided to move to the west, away from the draw, toward their original landing location at Dog White. This movement drew additional enemy fire, and the men lost unit cohesion. Once they reached the breakwaters four hundred yards to the west, they had to stop. The men then regrouped and awaited further development. Company F lost its commanding officer, Captain Callahan, and over half its men. They hunkered, pinned down, at the shingle.

Private Rocco Russo, Company F, 116th Infantry, 29th Division
In a little while Sgt. [Francis] Ryan got to the wall and ended up close to my spot. Ryan was an older man, probably 30 years old, and I had a lot of respect

*for him. Ryan suggested that we clean our rifles, and we did just that. . . .
After the next shell came close to my position, I looked down and saw a big
chunk of bloody meat in my lap. It had hit the top part of my assault jacket
and fallen into my lap. I was shaken up and pointed it out to Ryan. He asked
if it was part of me. I told him I didn't think so, but I was so scared I wasn't
really sure. . . . Sgt. Ryan and I went snooping around and saw an area that
we thought we might be able to climb to get off the beach. We did not have
enough people to help us, so we waited until more G.I.s got up to the wall.*

German mortar and artillery fire aimed at the beach increased in fre-
quency at approximately 7:30 a.m. Toward the end of the first hour, Major
Sidney V. Bingham, CO, 2d Battalion, 116th RCT, made the determination that taking the three-story house was the first step in clearing the
beach exit. He attempted to gather men and, thinking he had fifty men at
his disposal, planned his assault over the shingle. Major Bingham had no
working radio and therefore no communications with other echelons. The
fire became so heavy that men took refuge wherever they could.

Major Sidney Bingham, CO, 2d Battalion, 116th RCT
*An impression that overcame me at this juncture was one of complete futility.
Here I was, the battalion commander, unable for the most part to influence the
situation or to do what I knew had to be done. Another impression that I had, as
I am sure others did as well, was the profound shock of seeing dead and wounded
comrades in substantial numbers—and being unable to help in any way.*

Arden Earll recounted the effect of the lack of leadership and the fear
that crept into the hearts of men as they faced this horrendous landing.

Private First Class Arden Earll, mortarman, MOS 504, Company H, 2d Battalion, 116th Infantry, 29th Infantry Division
*On the way in, over the sand, I had seen one of our troops break. He was
laying on the sand there crying for his Mama to come and take him home.
I tried, I dropped down beside him, and I told him, I said; "Your mama is
6,000 miles away. She will never be able to get here. Snap out of it. Get
out of it. You gotta go." By then I had to leave, because we had orders not to
bother with men, with people like that. So I had to leave him. I went on, I
finished up D-Day, that night, the next morning, they took us, the 116th,*

back down on the beach, and we reorganized. We had been shot up pretty bad.
They moved the 115th through us. They took up the fight and we reorganized.
Well, by that time, the bodies had washed up in the tide. There was that boy.
He was not scared anymore. I am not, I don't profess to be a great one with
religion. But right then, I realized that was an act of God. His mother could
not get him, so God came, and took him home.

As Company H worked, the men realized that the infantry company (Company F) they were intended to support with their heavy weapons had landed far to the east in the 1st Infantry Division sectors of the beach. They witnessed and participated as the Americans assaulted bunkers in the St. Laurent draw a minimum of three times, only to be repulsed each time. The navy destroyers swept in and placed heavy fire on several bunkers, silencing them. After Company H realized they couldn't help Company F, the surviving Company H men began to work to the right (west) along the shingle to the breakwaters on the western edge of Dog Red. This move would allow them to support Company G territory.

Naval historian Samuel Elliot Morrison described what the Americans faced on Omaha Beach in such a way that others have quoted him since he published his manuscript about the Normandy invasion in 1957, including General Omar Bradley, who agreed with his assessment. Morrison wrote, "Altogether, the Germans had provided the best imitation of hell for an invading force that American troops had encountered anywhere. Even the Japanese defenses of Iwo Jima, Tarawa and Peleliu are not to be compared with these. Moreover the protective works for OMAHA had hardly been touched before D-Day."[20]

By H+1 hour, the Americans of the 29th Infantry Division and attached units had landed on Omaha Beach from the western Charlie Sector eastward to the edge of Dog Red and Easy Green Beaches and beyond. They were scattered and almost leaderless. The lack of surviving commissioned and noncommissioned officers compromised effective assault capabilities at the company level down to the platoon and squad levels. The companies of the 2d Rangers and the men of Company C of the 116th RCT fared the best out of the units associated with the first wave, but the situation was indeed dire. They needed a miracle.

CHAPTER SEVEN

Cota's D-Day Landing

As a reminder, the criteria for the Medal of Honor are clear and concise. During World War II, the criteria were governed by 1918 legislation and implementing regulations. These requirements are critically important to keep in mind as Cota's actions on June 6 and 7 are considered.

> **Sixty-Fifth Congress, Sess. II., Chapter 143. 1918; Medals of Honor, Distinguished-Service Crosses, and Distinguished Service Medals**
> *That the provisions of existing law relating to the award of medals of honor to officers, noncommissioned officers, and privates of the Army be, and they hereby are, amended so that the President is authorized to present, in the name of the Congress, a medal of honor only to each person who, while an Officer or Enlisted man of the Army, shall hereafter, in action involving actual conflict with an enemy, distinguish himself conspicuously by gallantry and intrepidity at the risk of his life above and beyond the call of duty.*[1]

On the morning of June 6, 1944, the APA (Auxiliary Personnel, Attack) transport USS *Charles Carroll* (APA-28) delivered LCVPs (Landing Craft, Vehicle, Personnel) to the western approaches of Omaha Beach. Under the command of Commander Harold Woodall Biesemeier from August 13, 1942, to June 13, 1944, this ship and her crew conducted assault landings in North Africa and in Italy, including at Sicily and Salerno, while under fire. At 5 a.m., she stood eleven miles off the Normandy coast, rolling slightly in a wind-flecked channel swell, and at 5:20 a.m., her skipper gave the command "Away all boats!" This was the signal to disembark for all personnel headed ashore. The ship cleared its twenty LCVPs over its davit falls as twenty- to thirty-foot waves threatened to smash some of them against their mothership. Through the skill of the trained crew, all were launched without damage. After setting the LCVPs into the channel, the crew of the USS *Charles Carroll* swung large cargo nets over her sides, with four each to starboard and port. The soldiers aboard, who were slated as second-wave assault troops, gathered along the ship railings to climb down the nets to the waiting craft. General Cota and the Detachment 29th Division headquarters and Headquarter Company,[2] part of the 116th RCT, gathered amidships at Debarkation Station 11 and boarded LCVP 71.[3] This designation was the official reference to General Cota's landing party. His group is also referred to as the provisional brigade headquarters for the 29th Infantry Division, the Advance Division Headquarters of the 29th Infantry Division, or, commonly, "Cota's Bastard Brigade." (The USS *Charles Carroll* is shown in figure 7.1.)

J. Robert Slaughter wrote an autobiography in 1988 titled "Wartime Memories of J. Robert Slaughter and Selected Men of the 116th Infantry, 29th Division, 1941–1945" (unpublished). He provided essential details of the landing of LCVP 71 when he included a letter written by Major Robert Buckley, a surgeon with the Medical Corps, 116th Infantry. This

Figure 7.1. USS *Charles Carroll* (U.S. Navy).

January 27, 1945, correspondence was originally sent to Grace Sours (married name: Mrs. Bentley H. Strickland), the sister of Major John Sours, supply officer (S-4) with the 116th Infantry. Major Sours was one of the first men from LCVP 71 to die upon landing, and Major Buckley's letter provided an important account of these events.

Early on the morning of D-Day, after breakfast, Big John [Major Sours] and I—he had the bunk next to mine in the same stateroom—got our things together, and he finished sticking some more camouflage material in the netting of his helmet. We also helped each other make some final adjustments in our web equipment, so that all the stuff he was hanging on us would be as comfortable as we could make it. Then we went down to Col. [Charles H.] Canham's stateroom, where we were to wait until time to go over into the small landing craft. When the time came we climbed over the side of the ship and down the net, which was not any too easy that morning due to the roughness of the sea, and the load on our backs.

Looking down from the deck of the ship, that little LCVP seemed a long way down (and it was too), and with everybody standing on the same side of the little boat it was leaning way over to one side, the lower end of the net hanging into the high side when the boat bounced just right and dangling over nothing between times. The sea was slamming the little boat around like a stick of wood and kept throwing it up against the side of the APA [USS Charles Carroll]. However, all twenty-six of us made it all right, and then we moved away from the big ship, circling around a little, and headed for the shore, which we could see only as a hazy, thin line in the distance.[4]

1st Lieutenant Jack Shea, General Cota's aide-de-camp, chronicled the entire D-Day chain of events involving General Cota in a November 1, 1944, combat narrative for Headquarters, Second Information and Historical Service, to which he was assigned as of that point in the war. Much of Cota's D-Day story derives from his report. (Shea and Cota are shown in figure 7.2.) LCVP 71, crewed by an unknown ensign and Coxswain Ricardo Feliciano, and carried the first echelon of command troops ashore for the 29th Division. As an aside, Coxswain Feliciano later delivered another underappreciated D-Day hero, Colonel George A. Taylor, commanding officer (CO), 16th Regimental Combat Team (RCT), onto eastern Omaha Beach at 8:20 a.m. aboard LCVP 71.[5] At the first landing, the craft bore what was arguably the highest-ranking assemblage of officers on any craft on any unsecured beach during the assault. Aboard the craft were

Brigadier General Norman Cota, 29th Infantry Division, assistant division commander

Colonel Charles H. Canham, 116th Infantry, commander

Major Thomas D. Howie, 116th Infantry, operations officer (S-3)

Major Asbury H. Jackson, 116th Infantry, intelligence officer (S-2)

Major John Sours, 116th Infantry, supply officer (S-4)

Major Willard D. "Robert" Buckley, Medical Corps, 116th RCT, surgeon

1st Lieutenant Jack Shea, 29th Infantry Division, aide-de-camp to Brigadier General Cota

Major Mensik, 121st Engineers, S-3

2d Lieutenant Jerry I. Harless, 1st Infantry Division, liaison officer

Lieutenant Byran, 16th Infantry, liaison officer

Lieutenant Jones, 743d Tank Battalion, liaison officer

1st Lieutenant William L. Sharp, Provisional Rangers Group, liaison officer

T/5 Borst, 116th Infantry, Colonel Canham's radio operator

Private Collins, Provisional Rangers Group, Ranger radio operator

Private Donald A. Ayers, 116th Infantry, Colonel Canham's radio operator

Private George B. Namie, 116th Infantry, Colonel Canham's bodyguard

Private Abraham A. Rosen, 116th Infantry, Colonel Canham's bodyguard

Private Major, 116th Infantry, Major Jackson's radio operator

Private Grady Allen, 116th Infantry, Major Jackson's radio operator

Master Sergeant Morales, 116th Infantry, operations sergeant

T/3 C. A. Wilson, 29th Infantry Division, Brigadier General Cota's radio operator

Private First Class Greenberg, Provisional Rangers Group, Ranger radio operator

T/4 Richard N. Henritze, 1st Infantry Division, radio operator

Private George J. Musico, 1st Infantry Division, radio operator

Private First Class Blanchette, 743d Tank Battalion, radio operator

Corporal Jones, 16th Infantry, radio operator

Figure 7.2. Photo of D-Day award recipients from General Dwight Eisenhower. Brigadier General Cota in front row (closest) and Lieutenant Shea shaking hands with "Ike" (Mike White).

LCVP 71 cleared the USS *Charles Carroll* at 6:10 a.m. (H–20) for an inshore trip of eighty-five minutes. As a stiff northwest breeze aided the progress of the craft, it arrived early at 7:26 a.m. (H+56). About three miles from shore, the crew passed elements of the 111th Field Artillery Battalion, 116th RCT, with their 105-mm howitzers loaded aboard DUKW amphibious vehicles that were noted as taking on water astern due to heavy seas. The 111th Field Artillery Battalion was originally scheduled to land at 7 a.m. (H+30). It was later noted that eleven of the vehicles foundered, with great loss of life and a secondary result of less artillery support arriving ashore when it was desperately needed. They continued forward in conditions with three miles of good visibility. They then reached a point four to six hundred yards offshore, where the beach landings were directed by eight stationary British Armored Motor Launches (AMLs). The AMLs' job was to efficiently direct all landing craft into the proper mine-swept lanes by use of loud-hailers. Lieutenant Shea noted that the incoming tide was about two-thirds full, having reached the band of angled-timber groin beach obstacles. The 146th Special Underwater Demolition Battalion had yet to complete the task of blowing up these obstacles, having mislanded some two thousand yards to the east. Approximately one-third of these obstacles had Teller mines wired to the seaward face of the timbers (figure 7.3).

The U.S. Navy's 5th Engineer Special Brigade (ESB) landed in the first wave with the mission of clearing beach defenses. These men were all heroes. As General Cota approached the beach, they were furiously attempting to accomplish their own assignments under murderous fire. Their After Action Report recorded the critical beach conditions as Cota landed:

> *Army and Navy doctors and Aid men worked as they could to give emergency treatment to the wounded. A surgeon of the 16th Regimental Combat Team noticed a high proportion of casualties caused by rifle bullet wounds in the head. Wounded men, lying on the exposed sand, were frequently hit a second or third time. Officer casualties were high. Companies A, C and D of the 116th Regimental Combat Team lost all but one officer each, and the 2nd Battalion of the same regiment lost two Company Commanders on the beach. . . . The confusion of the first hour of the Invasion mounted during the period*

Figure 7.3. German timber ramp obstacles with mines (National Archives and Records Administration [NARA]).

from 0730 to 0830 hours. Landings continued, but men and vehicles could not move off the beach. . . . A majority of the units, however, piled up behind the shingle bank, where they lay in rows sometimes three deep. In many cases these units were leaderless, their officers having been killed or wounded.[6]

The solitary craft entered its landing lane at the right western edge of Dog White Beach, located approximately seven hundred meters northeast of Vierville, when it was noticed by the coxswain that the beach was under heavy enemy fire. They altered course slightly to avoid floating mines. This craft approached the shore alone and made landfall amid the breakwaters at the Dog White and Dog Red boundary. While nearing shore, Coxwain Ricardo Feliciano lost seaway and cut the throttle before beaching as they began navigating the maze of beach obstacles not previously destroyed.[7] The craft sideslipped and was swept against an angled-timber groin by the three-knot easterly crosscurrent traversing along the face of the beach. The waves were four to six feet high and thrust the LCVP into the timber obstacle multiple times. These collisions dislodged an attached Teller mine, which failed to explode. The coxswain gunned the motor and maneuvered the boat free, advancing closer to shore, and then LCVP 71 grounded on a sandbar approximately seventy-five yards from the high-water mark at 7:26 a.m. (H+56). The boat skipper dropped the ramp under heavy machine-gun, mortar, and light-cannon fire and called to the men, "Disembark!"[8]

Between the sandbar where the ramp went down and the high-water mark at the seawall was a runnel with a varying depth of three to six feet, requiring some soldiers to swim or wade ashore. Several men found themselves immersed to their armpits. As the men emerged from the runnel, many made their way to the shelter of the tanks of the 743d Tank Battalion. Lieutenant Shea's report continued:

> *Moderate small arms fire was directed at the craft as the ramp was lowered. This consisted of rifle, and judging from the sound, machine gun fire. It continued to cover the group as they made their way inland. Having landed in about two or three feet of water, it was necessary to cross a runnel (about five feet deep and thirty feet wide) which ran parallel to the high water mark. During this phase of the landing which necessitated wading through about 40 yards of water, Major John Sours, Regimental S-4, was killed. He was hit in the chest and upper body by automatic fire, fell face down in the water. His body was later recovered as it floated in the shallows.*[9]

Two other soldiers were likewise killed in these moments.[10] General Cota continued the advance through all of this, under the first of what would be many documented instances of threat to his life over the next thirty hours. Major Buckley's account regarding Major Sours continued:

Major Robert Buckley, Medical Corps, Surgeon, 116th Infantry
By the time we were about a third of the way in we were all soaking wet clear through from water splashing in great quantities over the bow and sides of the boat. No one I saw became seasick, but later I heard several of them say—and I felt the same way myself—that their throats became very dry, so much so they could hardly swallow. This was due partly to the drying effect of the seasickness-prevention capsules we'd taken for several hours prior to debarkation, but more, I think, to the excitement of the situation than to

anything else. I don't think that fear had anything to do with it, because at that early hour none of us had had time to become afraid. We were doing the very thing that we, as a chosen group, had trained so long to do, and we were fascinated, and eagerly excited about it—although, of course, we realized that any number of things might happen to us, and knew too that some things we'd never dreamed of might very well be waiting for us on the beach.

Major Sours was standing in the boat just to my right rear, and I was on the left side of the boat, second from the ramp at the front end. When we got almost in, here we thought it would be well to duck down from possible machine gun fire, we all squatted down in the boat's bottom. In a tossing small craft with a wet, slippery floor, it's no mean accomplishment to do this and keep one's balance—and many of us did fall over more than once. I remember Major Sours, two corporals (Pvt. Abraham Rosen, Security Platoon and Pvt. George B. Namie, Security Platoon) and myself trying to disentangle ourselves from a sprawled knot on the floor during the excitement of a couple of minutes—which seemed like almost a half-hour instead—when the boat became stuck against the side of a beach obstacle in the form of a large pole (the size of a telegraph pole) sticking up from the ocean's floor and carrying a Teller mine fastened loosely on its top.

Here we were, with about eighty feet of water between us and the beaches and, bouncing up and down, scraping against the side of a pole so that as the boat went up with each incoming wave, it slid up the side of the pole toward the mine, and then—after approaching to within six or eight inches of it—went down again. If a little bigger wave had come in—a perfectly good possibility—we'd have hit the mine, and the reasonable expectation is that that would've been the end of the whole business for our LCVP. Because of the high spot on the bottom of the sea the Navy crew couldn't get the boat back off the pole, so several of the men began yelling for the ramp to be let down right there.

All this time we were under fire from the beach and the high ground overlooking it (artillery, mortar, and small-arms fire), so finally the boat crew decided to lower the ramp where we were. The moment it dropped the whole boatload of men surged out into the water at once, just at H+60 minutes, exactly as scheduled. As many times as I'd done this landing business in practice, I still lost my balance in running off the side of the ramp and fell forward in about two feet of water on my hands and knees. But I got up immediately and went on towards the shore. The further I went, the deeper the water got, till finally my feet left the bottom. In addition to our inflated life-belts, we all wore on our backs gas-masks in rubber carriers, which acted as auxiliary life preservers, so there was no trouble at all keeping afloat. Across the deep stretch—about forty feet, I'd guess—I paddled along with a small piece of board I picked up from the floating debris. While doing this paddling—which worked pretty well—I looked over to my right and saw Big John coming right along too. . . .

When I got up onto the sand, where there were a lot of spider-like obstacles made of about eight-foot lengths of railroad rails crossed on each other at their centers, I flattened out on the sand behind one of them to catch my breath a little and saw Major Sours behind another off to my right, a short distance. He saw me looking, and grinning back he called over, "How're you doing, Doc?" I replied that I was doing all right and asked how he was making out, to which he answered that he was doing all right, too. We could see where machine gun bullets were peppering the water all around us, but particularly ahead, all the time we were coming in, and after we'd rested on the sand for not more than a minute or two there was an extra-heavy spattering of them in the water, in a runnel, just in front of us. This runnel was a narrow strip of water between the sandbar we were on and the beach proper, and was probably twenty feet wide where we were, and it proved to be little less than two feet deep when we ran through it. Just as this burst of machine gun fire seemed to die down I jumped up and ran across the sand, through the runnel, and up the rocky beach to a little ledge about three feet (or less) high, where a roadway running right along the beach was built up.

I think Major Sours was almost immediately behind me—I'm not sure—as he started getting up at the same time I did. Everybody ran in individually and got there the best way he could, so when I reached the little ledge I spoke of, it was hard to tell whether everybody was in or not, as we were pretty well separated. As it happened, I ran up to where Major Jackson (S-2) was, and just as he was asking if I'd seen Major Tom Howie (S-3), Major Howie ran up all hunched over, and sat down to do as we were doing, loosening our web equipment and other gear so we could get around better.

While the three of us were catching our breath, there we saw two men who seemed to need help out in the water, so with an enlisted man who was sitting next to me, I ran back out to them. The enlisted man (whom I didn't know) began helping one of them—a soldier with a wounded leg—and I went over to the other one, who was lying face down in the water about the middle of the runnel. I could tell from his uniform that he was one of our officers, and then I lifted him partly up, I saw it was Major Sours. He was already dead when I found him, and although due to the heavy fire on the beach, it was no place for any unduly extended examination, I did make absolutely sure that he wasn't either drowned or partially drowned, and there was nothing at all that could be done for him.

As best I could tell, he'd been killed by a machine gun bullet wound of the head, although at the time I did not actually see the wound. I feel sure, however, that that was what happened, and this is the reason: A few minutes later, as I was helping the enlisted man I've already mentioned with the wounded man he was trying to get into a better place on the beach, I picked up what I took to be the wounded man's helmet from where it was floating upside down in the water and put it on his head. Then we saw that it had two bullet holes in it, one where the bullet had entered on one side, and the other where it had made its exit on the other side.

We took the helmet off again, looked at the man's head and found that he had no head wound. Then, on re-examining the helmet, we saw it belonged to Major Sours and had floated down from where he had fallen in the runnel about fifteen feet away, to where we were working on this man. At that very moment, fire on that stretch of the beach became suddenly very intense—so much so that it was impossible to investigate further as to what had happened, but there is no doubt in my mind as to what caused Major Sours' death.[11]

Major Buckley relayed some personal items and concluded his letter to the family of Major Sours by saying, "I'd like to add something else here, if I may, and it is this: I just wanted her [Emma Villanna Cundiff Sours, wife of Major Sours] to know that I share the opinion of all the others in the regiment who knew Major Sours, that he was a fine man—a very fine man, who both deserved and received the respect and admiration of us all."[12]

According to official records, all officers and men interviewed about the D-Day landings reported that there was positively no evidence of friendly aerial bombardment and little evidence of naval bombardment of the beaches. There were no craters to use for cover, and the enemy beach installations remained intact.[13]

General Cota's party sought cover behind the nearest tank as the group moved across the beach under the cover of the tank that had engaged German antitank weapons to its near right front. The Duplex

Drive amphibious tanks of Company C, 743d Tank Battalion, were the first real cover available. The tanks landed at H–6, and there were an estimated eighteen tanks standing just above and advancing along with the rising tide. They all faced the bluffs and were spaced at intervals of approximately seventy to one hundred yards. This position placed them about twenty-five feet from the seawall, from which position each of them fired at enemy positions immediately in front of each tank. Lieutenant Shea noticed that two tanks were burning to the west near the Vierville exit. One, identified as Tank "C-5," was noticeably damaged from several rounds of direct 88-mm fire from the German WN 72 casemate. 1st Lieutenant Alfred H. Williams Jr., Company C, 743d Tank Battalion, and his crew managed to escape that destruction. General Cota and his men screened themselves behind a tank that was firing to its right front instead of its previously assigned target to the west: the enemy artillery positions at Pointe et Raz de la Percée (WN 74). These German strong-points were armed with two 75-mm artillery pieces situated high on the bluffs and were able to fire down the beach well beyond Dog Red.[14] The overall situation at this time is detailed in the War Department map shown in figure 7.4.

At some point during these moments, something in General Cota must have triggered his fortitude for what followed. From this moment on, he was no longer only one of many soldiers landing under fire on the beach; he rose to the occasion and led his men to a victory snatched from the jaws of imminent defeat. An official account by Headquarters, 29th Infantry Division, recounted, "Realizing that immediate steps had to be taken to move the men from the dangerous area of the beach, General Cota, exposing himself to enemy fire, went over the seawall giving encouragement, directions and orders to those about him." After observing the tanks in action, both General Cota and Colonel Canham noticed that these tanks were not firing at WN 73 and WN 74, as per operational plans, and the enemy gun positions were able to profitably employ their fire. Brigadier General Cota and Colonel Canham observed at this point that the enemy guns fired one flat trajectory shell at each landing craft just before it touched down. The Germans held fire until the point that a landing craft touched down. If they missed, they

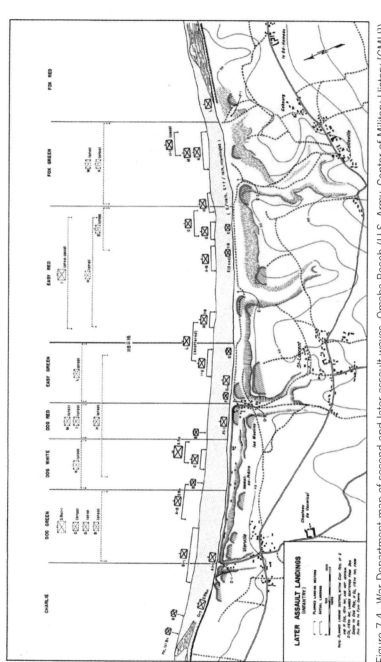

Figure 7.4. War Department map of second and later assault waves, Omaha Beach (U.S. Army, Center of Military History [CMH]).

Figure 7.5. WN 73 (75-mm casemate) above western Omaha Beach, view from west of the Vierville draw (NARA).

determined distance by line of sight, splash, and water ricochets. The German observers then adjusted fire within a three-second interval and fired a second shot that found its mark. Direct hits were achieved by no later than the third round. There were additional artillery positions at WN 73 (as discussed in chapter 5 and illustrated in figure 7.5). Cota's group suffered another casualty behind the tank from machine-gun fire, and the group advanced to the seawall approximately nine hundred yards from the Vierville exit to seek better cover. This seawall was four to five feet high and had twenty- to thirty-foot-long timber-rail breakwaters seaward at about fifty-yard intervals.[15]

A later interview with Lieutenant Joseph J. Ondre, Company A, 743d Tank Battalion, revealed that the tanks in his battalion did not disembark thirty-five hundred yards offshore as planned. Due to the heavy seas, their LCTs (Landing Craft, Tanks) brought them to within 250 yards of the shore. Other tank units that stuck with the original plan and disembarked further out in the channel foundered in the high seas with significant loss of life. In all fairness, the tanks were each

Figure 7.6. LCI 91 approaching Dog White Beach. Members of the 743d Tank Battalion and the 29th Infantry Division are visible on beach. General Cota was on the beach in this vicinity at this time, possibly in the frame of the photo (NARA).

protecting themselves from the antitank fire brought to bear on them from multiple positions that were missed during the preinvasion air and naval bombardments. By the end of D-Day, only twenty-one of fifty-one of the 743d Tank Battalion's medium tanks would survive to continue the fight. The 743d Tank Battalion's commander, Lieutenant Colonel John S. Upham, was wounded by machine-gun fire later in the morning.[16] The tanks of the 743d Tank Battalion at the boundary of Dog White and Dog Red are visible in figure 7.6.

At this point (H+60), nearly one hundred disorganized men from the Beach Brigade, 1st Battalion of the 116th RCT, Naval Aid Group men, naval fire control parties, naval beach maintenance men, 2d Rangers, and others took shelter from enemy rifle and machine-gun fire from the bluffs above. The troops were hopelessly jumbled, unled, and firmly pinned down.[17] No Americans had advanced past the seawall at the inland border of the beach. As the soldiers lay pinned down by machine-gun fire, clustered in the bays formed by the seawall and breakwaters, the enemy was beginning to bring effective mortar fire to bear on those hidden behind the wall.[18]

Sergeant Francis E. Huesser, light machine-gun squad leader, Company C, 116th Infantry, and Captain Robert J. Bedell, Company C, 116th Infantry, leader of 1st Assault Section, landed at 6:53 a.m. along with Huesser's support section right near the tank that was just twenty-five to thirty yards to the port side of where LCI(L) (Landing Craft Infantry–Large) 91 would land. Bedell arrived with Lieutenant Stanley H. Schwartz. The other six landing craft touched down to the east of Huesser's location spread out between the landing locations of LCI(L) 91 and LCI(L) 92. Company C landed approximately one thousand feet east (to the left) of its planned landing near the D-1 exit. The men of the company watched LCI(L) 91 knife into the beach and subsequently explode. They described a "tremendous blossom of orange flame and black, oily smoke." Captain Bedell saw General Cota only a minute or so after the LCI went up in flames. During an official combat interview dated March 19, 1945, conducted by Lieutenant Jack Shea, Huesser and others discussed their group's action as the first half hour of the assault led to their encounter in the minutes after Cota's landing:

> They ran forward to the little wooden seawall banked with shingle. Huddled there beneath the low timber wall. It was there that they saw General Cota for the first time, few saw Col. Canham. For he was evidently at that time working over towards the east. They said that the first time that the most of them saw Canham was when he was in the Vierville crossroads with his hand and wrist bandaged. All of them remembered seeing Cota, just after touching down on the beach. "He was waving a .45 around, and I figured if he could get up there so could I." [Captain Bedell] remarked that Cota came up to him, and prompted that "Well, Lt, we gotta get 'em off the beach. We've gotta get going."[19]

Sergeant Huesser discussed how General Cota influenced his group's actions as they blew a gap with a Bangalore torpedo. Cota "came up to us, waving that pistol around and said we had to get off the beach. That we had to get through the wire. I guess all of us figured that if he could go wandering around like that, we could, too." They snaked the pipes of the torpedo under the fencing and pulled the friction igniter. Nothing. Lieutenant Schwartz scurried over, did something to it, and took cover, and then it blew.

One critically important detail become all too apparent in the flow of events at about 7:30 a.m.: an estimated three-fourths of all radios, particularly the SCR 300s, were either destroyed by enemy fire or ruined by the salt water. The 29th Infantry Division later reported that they believed the Germans specifically targeted radiomen either purposefully or because they mistook the backpack radios for flamethrowers.[20]

Company H arrived in the vicinity of the breakwaters at approximately 7:30 a.m. Private First Class Arden Earll remembered seeing the first of the group of tanks working in this sector. The tank would go in reverse to the water's edge and gather up soldiers in need of cover. The tank would advance to the seawall and then fire a few rounds, allowing the wet soldiers to take cover at the seawall, and then reverse to do the dance all over. This approach allowed the tanks not to become stationary targets and easy picking for the Germans.

Private First Class Arden Earll, mortarman, MOS 504, Company H, 2d Battalion, 116th Infantry, 29th Infantry Division

I got there by that tank, and I had to go around it because the tide had come in by that time, and I got right behind the tank. One enemy artillery round hit out in the water. I thought to myself: "Arden, get out of here, they are after this tank." I couldn't move, I was loaded so heavy, I couldn't move very fast. The next round came in right close to the tank. It didn't hurt the tank. But I got my first Purple Heart right there. I still got part of that artillery shell in my right wrist and hand. I wasn't hurt too bad. I had seen an American panic, before, on the way in. And I started, I began to feel, and I thought, "For God's sakes Arden, you're not hurt bad. Keep Going." So I did. Our Aid-man was a hero that day. That's all we had. We didn't have any first aid, uh, hospital, or anything like that. Now, I think there was hospital ships out there, but they couldn't get in to get us off the beach, and so, a lot of the guys just laid there. I was bleeding a little bit, but I could still walk, I could still go, I carried my load. I kept going. . . . We moved to the west down the beach to the sector General Cota landed in and was working. By the time I saw General Cota, a lot of us were hunkered down. We were waiting to see what was; we knew something was wrong, but we waited for somebody to tell us what to do next, and that's when I saw General Cota. I do know that he walked up and down along the beach, quite a lot, and exposed himself to enemy fire at all times.[21]

Herb Epstein, Intelligence NCO, 5th Ranger Infantry Battalion, HQ Company

As A and B were preceding us into the beach, Colonel [Max] Schneider decided to land at the Vierville Draw because the men that preceded us in the 29th division were under murderous fire on the beach and having a hard time getting out of the boats. The fire was so intense and Colonel Schneider was observing this fire, we were in the lead boat at the time. As we got close to the shore, Schneider commanded the boat flotilla captain to swing the whole group left, parallel to the beach. So instead of landing at Dog Green according to the battle plan, we landed further to the east. As we were going parallel to the beach Schneider saw an area that wasn't too hot and ordered the flotilla commander "to get us in and get us in fast." We turned again another 90 degrees and they got us to water that wasn't very deep, at least it was reasonably dry where they landed my boat. There was a lot of artillery and mortar fire coming in and a lot of men lying on the beach.[22]

The 5th Ranger Infantry Battalion (RIB), under the command of Lieutenant Colonel Max Schneider, had the primary mission of landing at Pointe du Hoc as a follow-up force to Lieutenant Colonel James Earl Rudder and his three companies of 2d Ranger Infantry Battalion engaged there. After not receiving communications to land there, Schneider made his way to their secondary landing objective at Dog Green. As the battalion approached, the men witnessed the carnage that befell Companies A and B and the remnants of the 29th Infantry. Remaining calm and drawing on his experience as a former Darby's Ranger who fought in the Mediterranean, Schneider swung his flotilla of two waves of LCAs (Landing Craft, Assault) to the east and headed in at the breakwaters where Cota and his men were. The first wave of Rangers touched down just ahead of LCI(L) 91 and consisted of Companies B, A, E, and half of HQ, with Company B ordered to the right and the others to the left. Captain John C. Raaen Jr., CO, HQ Company, landed in the second wave along with Companies D, F, and C. Major Richard P.

Sullivan, executive officer (XO), was aboard the LCA with Raaen. Private First Class Randall Ching was a member of 2d Platoon, Company B, 5th Ranger Infantry Battalion, and was in one of the westernmost bays formed by the breakwaters. He was the only Chinese American Ranger during World War II. He was born in the States, but during the Great Depression, his family emigrated back to China. As a result, he was conscripted into the Chinese army and fought the Japanese in the late 1930s before returning to the States at the outset of U.S. involvement in the war, and he volunteered as a Ranger.

Private First Class Randall Ching, Company B, 5th Ranger Infantry Battalion
I landed on Dog White Beach with our whole 5th Ranger Battalion. It took the Rangers five minutes to get from the beach to the seawall. I watched artillery coming up to the seawall, to the left, to the right, when I was at the seawall. It walked, it come up, because the Germans got the seawall all zeroed in. And they opened up, with three shells, Boom, Boom, Boom, all over the seawall. And I thought, oh hell, this is gonna come up pretty close to me pretty soon. It just so happened, that two LCI [LCIs 91 and 92] landed, I guess from the 116th Infantry Regiment, and both ramps dropped. Both LCI had two ramps down. So the artillery, turned their attention to those LCI. LCI means Landing Craft Infantry. Each one handled one company, but there's two coming in at the same time. They hit both of them. The first one was hit, was the nearest on to me, so I saw that. They hit it with three shells. People started to jump overboard because of the fire, more or less. That is the worst part of the memory in my mind. One of the persons on the landing craft, LCI was carrying a flamethrower, and the flamethrower exploded.[23]

At 7:40 a.m. (H+70), LCI(L) 91 beached approximately eight hundred yards east of the Vierville exit on Dog White about one hundred yards west of the border of Dog Red and seventy-five feet from the water's edge. The LCI took a direct hit from the 88-mm artillery, whose range was over fifteen thousand yards, at WN 72 (figure 7.7), before her two landing ramps touched the beach. Flames worked their way from near her forward companionways aft to the stern. LCI(L) 91 was lost in a conflagration that burned for eighteen hours. Later reports indicated

Figure 7.7. View of Dog Beach from 88-mm casemate at WN 72; LCI(L) 91 visible (NARA).

that the artillery shell found its mark, striking an infantryman with a flamethrower strapped to his back. When he was hit, the fuel tank burst into a huge wave of flame. His body stiffened with convulsive reactions and catapulted off the deck, completely clearing the starboard bulkhead and plunging into the water. The burning fuel from the weapon covered the foredeck and superstructure of the ship. The passengers of the LCI immediately abandoned ship in four- to five-foot-deep water, and the crew followed shortly, realizing it was a total loss. During the conflagration, the LCI's stores of 20-mm ammunition for her Oerlikon antiaircraft guns continually exploded due the intense heat. General Cota was within a few hundred feet of this explosion (figure 7.8).[24]

A vivid account of the morning of June 6, 1944, was sent in a letter to Mr. Cornelius Ryan on June 16, 1958, in response to Ryan's plea for stories associated with D-Day so that he could incorporate them into his epic *The Longest Day*. This moving account brought forth the horrors experienced and witnessed by all on that beach.

Figure 7.8. U.S. Navy photo of LCI(L) 91 explosion on Dog White at 7:40 a.m. (U.S. Navy).

Private First Class Max D. Coleman, Company C, 5th Ranger Infantry Battalion

In your interviews with various participants of the "D" Day Operations, try to get a picture of the sky in the early dawn. I have witnessed many sunrises in my thirty-four years, but this one stayed in my mind. Apparently it was unusual not only to me, for I have asked many others about it. I am not capable of an accurate description. There was a storm of high winds, as you well know; but it was a storm with few clouds. The first rays of the sun turned the few clouds to crimson. It would have captured the imagination of any artist or poet. You may want to know about the two LSIs [LCI(L) 91 and LCI(L) 92] which had run a ground because of the storm. The sounds of the men in pain and terror as shell after shell fell on the decks could be heard above the din of other combat. Men would jump screaming into the sea only to rise as floating corpses. One man with a flame thrower on his back disintegrated into a flaming inferno.[25]

Lieutenant Colonel Harold A. Cassell, XO, 116th Infantry, was aboard LCI(L) 91 along with the alternate headquarters for the regiment. As they were on the beach in positions bracketing the vessel, Cota's men witnessed the landing as it beached and was subsequently devastated. Cassell and some fifteen men had disembarked before the blast, and the remaining survivors leapt overboard, many of them in flames. Cota's men reported that a lot of the men who did make it to shore were badly burned, including Colonel Lucius Chase, XO, 6th ESB. Once ashore, Cassell was able to raise Colonel Canham via radio and to then make physical contact with him in person.[26]

Shortly after the explosion of LCI(L) 91, with increased enemy fire, Cota and Canham conferred regarding the situation. It was decided that Cota would work to the right (west) and Canham to the left (east) along the beach to determine the most suitable exit from the beach for the troops. Canham also tried to connect with 2d Battalion, 116th Infantry, during his movements to the east. Cota and Canham speculated that the Germans would soon zero in on the large contingent of soldiers on the beach at the seawall and bring high-trajectory artillery fire down upon them. Speed was of the essence to advance and survive. While working down toward the D-3 exit, Colonel Canham was shot through the left wrist, the bullet grazing his bone; yet he continued to inspire and encourage troops huddled at the seawall. As he moved, Canham worked to organize the bulk of Company C ranged along the wall in an effort to get them to move inland and away from immediate danger on the fire-swept beach. The officers briefly rejoined each other. It was then that Cassell met with Canham and Cota on the beach. Seeing Canham's wounds, Cota ordered Cassell to take over for the colonel and ordered Canham evacuated. Canham promptly refused evacuation, carried on with his mission, and reported what he saw to the general while under heavy automatic fire.[27] Lieutenant Colonel Cassell was then sent east to reconnoiter the location of the 1st Infantry Division command post (CP) down in the vicinity of the D-3 exit. It is important to note that Cassell's interactions with General Cota were limited, and yet he and Canham provided the sole eyewitness statements associated with Cota's award recommendation for the Distinguished Service Cross.

Cota worked to the west down the beach and by some accounts made it as far as half the distance to the D-1 exit near the manor, shown as

Hamel au Prêtre on the invasion maps, below WN 70, if not farther west toward WN 72. All accounts place him calmly and tactically traversing (walking) in that direction, exhorting men to action. This amounted to a distance of between one-half and three-quarters of a mile. His journey was under full observation of no less than WN 70, WN 71, WN 72, WN 73, and WN 74, traveling in the direction of these dangers. When he turned to head back to the breakwaters, he calmly walked away from these German positions. The thought of turning one's back to this amount of active firepower is astounding.

While in the vicinity of elements of Company C, 116th Infantry, General Cota happened upon a section of seawall with a low mound of earth approximately five yards beyond it. He crawled forward to reconnoiter the firing position and then personally directed the placement of a Browning Automatic Rifle there. He told the gunner to lay down suppressive fire and shoot at any enemy movement along the bluffs. This fire was intended to cover the soldiers as they breached the wire and made their way toward the foot of the bluffs. After this, General Cota personally supervised the placement of a Bangalore torpedo in the double-apron barbed wire fence.[28] The barbed wire in this area was standard agricultural-style barbed wire, not the heavier, squarish military concertina wire expected by the men. The wire was along the inner border of the promenade, the ten-foot-wide, asphalt-surfaced road that ran parallel with the seawall along Dog Beach. This started elements of Companies C and D, 116th RCT, up the bluffs to the right of LCI(L) 91. During this action, Cota interacted with Lieutenant Colonel Robert Ploger, CO, 121st Engineer Combat Battalion, to secure the needed Bangalore torpedoes. The general acted above and beyond the call of duty in this instance alone at the risk of his life as he was under observation by the Germans.

Lieutenant Colonel Robert Ploger, commander, 121st Engineer Combat Battalion, 29th Division
While I was walking west along the beach looking for some of my engineers, I ran into General Cota. He said, "Ploger, bring me some Bangalore torpedoes so we can blow this wire." I went off to look for some. A little while later I ran into Gen. Cota again, and this time he asked me for some minefield marking tape which came in long rolls of white cloth. He wanted it to mark

*lanes through minefields beyond the wire and up the bluff. I immediately
went off on another search.*[29]

After the German success in pinning down and inflicting massive
casualties among the Americans, they increased *Nebelwerfer* and mortar
fire in the Dog White and Dog Red Sectors. The majority of the fire
landed in the sandy section of the beach; however, rounds would occa-
sionally land in the midst of the troops huddled together in the lee of
the seawall. The shrapnel from the six-barreled weapon nicknamed the
"Screaming Meemies" produced unusually large pieces, with the average
size as large as an ordinary shovel blade. Lieutenant Shea witnessed one
of these large fragments striking a man in the small of the back, almost
completely severing the upper portion of his body from his trunk. The
saving grace of these weapons was their lack of reliable targeting and the
lesser amount of overall shrapnel per shell as compared to standard mortar fire—the end result being fewer casualties per explosion. The smaller-
caliber German mortars had a higher percentage of fragmentation and
accuracy and resulted in higher casualties when they found their mark.

The medics of all units were some of the real heroes, as they were
among the most active men on the beach, treating anyone they could
save. The treatment of severe wounds was common, as casualties included
gaping head and belly wounds. Their rapid efficiency became legendary
that day. The same could be said of several chaplains ashore. The severity
of the action at Dog White/Dog Red was captured in a photo taken from
a navy vessel (figure 7.9).

The conditions on the beach were noted and recorded by German
Oberstleutnant Fritz Ziegelmann, 352d Infantry Division:

*0745 Hours—Report from the Gren Regt 916: Near Defense Work No 70,
northeast of Vierville, three tanks are rolling up the hill: three tanks penetrated into the Defense Work No. 66; the upper casemate of the Defense Work
No. 62 was put out of action by a direct hit.*[30]

The second wave of the 5th Ranger Infantry Battalion landed at 7:50
a.m. on the eastern edge of Dog White Beach, extending east into Dog
Red Beach over a 250-yard front. Major General Raaen provided testi-

Figure 7.9. Dog White and Dog Red Beaches sometime around 8 a.m.; note LCI(L) 91 and LCI(L) 92 on beach in the center left of photo with 91 clearly on fire (NARA).

mony regarding the Ranger landing on the beach in relation to General Cota. In his book *Intact*, he described that just as his landing craft was about to beach, he looked approximately fifty yards to his right and witnessed the explosion of LCI(L) 91. The resulting blast nearly capsized his LCA and threw it into a German obstacle topped with a Teller mine. He recalled looking at his watch just as his feet touched terra firma. At the time of the following account, he was a captain commanding Headquarters Company, 5th Ranger Infantry Battalion.[31] Captain Raaen made a drawing of his perspective of the landing (figure 7.10). The 5th RIB was attached to the 29th Infantry Division. The 29th Infantry Division, including the Rangers and the 116th Infantry, was in turn attached to the 1st Infantry Division, assigned to V Corps, First Army, Army Group ETOUSA, as part of Task Force O for the Normandy assault. General Cota then met with the 5th Ranger Infantry Battalion. After speaking to subordinates, he found Lieutenant Colonel Schneider, CO, and Major Sullivan, XO. He gave them a verbal order to blow similar gaps in the wire to the west and lead their troops against the enemy fortifications at Pointe et Raz de la Percée.

Major General John C. Raaen Jr., USA (Ret.), June 6, 2018, Witness Statement to Congress for Cota Medal of Honor Upgrade
My LCA 1377 (Landing Craft Assault) touched down on the east edge of Omaha Dog White Beach on June 6, 1944, at 0750 British Double

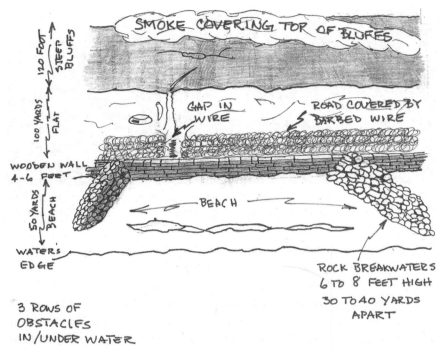

Figure 7.10. Drawing of combat landing by then captain John C. Raaen Jr., 5th Ranger Infantry Battalion (Major General John C. Raaen Jr. [Ret.]).

Daylight Time. The rest of my battalion's, the 5th Ranger Infantry Battalion, 12 boats landed to my left on Dog Red Beach. The beach was chaos. Machine gun and rifle fire poured down the beach from the enemy positions to my right. Artillery fire was concentrated on the landing craft at the water's edge. Smoke, fire, the cracking of bullets overhead, the detonation of artillery striking Landing Craft added to the chaos. The beach was littered with burning debris from materiel destroyed by enemy fire. The dead, the dying, the wounded lay everywhere.

Ranger Force C consisted of Companies A and B of the 2nd RIB, all six companies of the 5th RIB and their respective headquarters. Ranger Force C's mission was to land at Pointe du Hoc at H+15 minutes. Force C had circled, waiting to receive a signal to land for about 25 minutes. Force C was then ordered to abandon its landing by the Commander Afloat, the Commander Assault Group 0-4. Force C was now to follow its Plan B and land on Omaha Dog Green Beach (at Vierville). As Force approached D-1, the

*Vierville exit, it was waved off by Landing Control at approximately 0730.
Force C then approached a landing at the boundary between Dog White and
Dog Green. The first wave of five landing craft, Companies A and B, and
Hq elements, 2nd RIB, was met by severe fire from German Resistance Point
(Widerstandsnest 70) and other emplacements on the bluffs behind the beach.
Casualties were so high that Lt. Col. Schneider, CO, Ranger Force C, still
on the water in wave two, decided to divert the two waves of the 5th RIB's
landing craft about 1,000 yards to the east and land on Dog Red Beach.
The 5th RIB landed on Dog Red Beach over a 250 yard front. This beach
turned out to be ideal for a landing. First, there were fourteen breakwaters
providing cover against the dreadful small arms fire coming in from the
right. Second, the brush on the bluffs directly behind the beach was aflame
and the smoke and flames prevented the enemy from firing directly down on
the beach. Third, a spur or nose on the face of the bluffs prevented the enemy
to the left from firing at troops on Dog Red.*

*The situation on Dog Red Beach was desperate. The tide had reached
a point about 50 to 60 yards from the wooden seawall. No troops had left
the beach. Those who survived crossing the beach were piled on top of one
another at the base of the four foot seawall. Tides and wind from the storm
had scattered the landing craft and many had landed as far as two miles
from planned landing locations. An Infantry platoon fit into two Landing
Craft Vehicular, Personnel (LCVP). An officer in one craft, a senior non-com
in the other. Only rarely were the two platoon craft able to land near each
other. Most troops were leaderless, no idea where they were, where they were
supposed to go.*

*Two things happened to save Omaha Beach. Brig. Gen. Norman D.
Cota landed on Omaha Dog White at 0726 hours, and the 5th RIB landed
intact on the boundary of Dog White and Omaha Dog Red at 0745 hours.
(C Co., 116th Inf. also landed earlier at 0725 hours on Omaha Dog White,
also intact. This company fought alongside the 5th RIB until D + 2 when
Pointe du Hoc was relieved.)*

*I had been on the beach no more than ten minutes, checking the men
for firearms, ammunition and other equipment while awaiting orders from
battalion. Several of my men called my attention to a man about 100 yards
to my right moving along the edge of the beach. He was chewing on a cigar,
yelling and waving at the men in the dunes and at the seawall. He was
taking no action to conceal himself from the enemy who continued to pour
small arms fire. We thought him crazy or heroic. Everyone else was seeking*

cover, while this man was exposing himself not only to the enemy, but to the troops he was rallying. As he approached the bay (formed by breakwaters and the seawall) I was in, I rose to meet him. As he rounded the end of the breakwater, I saw his insignia of rank. Brigadier General! I reported to him with a hand salute. "Sir, Captain Raaen, 5th Ranger Battalion." He responded, "Raaen, Raaen. You must be Jack Raaen's son." "Yes, sir." "What's the situation here?" "Sir, the 5th Ranger Battalion has landed intact, here and over a 250 yard front. The battalion commander has just ordered the companies to proceed by platoon infiltration to our rallying points." "Where is your battalion commander?" "I'll take you to him, Sir," pointing out the location of Lt. Col. Schneider. "No! You remain here with your men." As General Cota started away, he stopped and looked around saying, "You men are Rangers. I know you won't let me down." And with that, he was off to see Schneider. During this whole conversation, General Cota never took cover nor flinched as the bullets cracked by us and artillery detonated some 50 yards away at the waterline.[32]

Captain Raaen was not alone in his witness of General Cota's actions over the next ten to twenty minutes. Several other 29ers and Rangers provided testimony in one form or another over the years. In many cases, the men providing the testimonials had no interaction with each other as they told their stories. The facts of their stories are in alignment in terms of General Cota's gallantry above and beyond the call of duty on the beach. Lieutenant Shea generated a map that illustrates many of the features mentioned by the witnesses (figure 7.11).

Major Richard P. Sullivan, executive officer, 5th Ranger Infantry Battalion
I watched the approach on an LCI [LCI(L) 91] to the beach, with troops all lined up to run down the gangway to the beach, when an artillery shell containing liquid fire (napalm?) exploded on the deck covering all with flame, causing most of the men to jump into the sea. This happened only a few yards from shore and was probably the man seen by other Rangers. He was carrying a flamethrower and took a direct hit from an artillery shell and was vaporized along with his equipment. The activities of Brigadier General Dan Cota seemed to be stupid at the time, but it was actually nothing but the sheer heroism and dedication of a professional soldier and fine officer

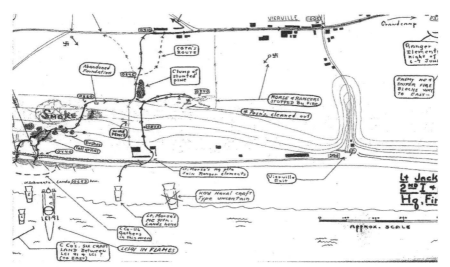

Figure 7.11. Drawing of combat landing of Brigadier General Cota and soldiers in his charge (NARA).

that prompted him to walk up and down the landing beach urging the men forward. I remember his aide-de-camp being a nervous wreck trying to get the General to stop his activities.[33]

Lieutenant Jack A. Snyder, platoon leader, Company C, 5th Ranger Infantry Battalion

Do you remember seeing or hearing anything that seems funny now, even though it did not, of course, seem amusing at the time? "Nothing funny, but something very courageous. A Brigadier General Cota, 29th Division was walking up and down the beach as if nothing was happening (Like a field inspection). He was assisting wounded and encouraging the non-wounded."[34]

T/4 Lee Brown, HQ Company, 5th Ranger Infantry Battalion

We were told to keep our heads down, but I did peak up and the "zip, zip, zip" of machine-gun fire had us ducking back down quickly. Lieutenant Colonel Schneider, and I think Captain [Hugo W.] Heffelfinger, were in my LCA—the British LCA driver did a great job getting us into the beach, I did not even step into any water—I was up onto dry beach. When the ramp went down on our LCA the lead officer off hesitated and because of that hesitation it saved many lives. The reason was because in the time of the hesitation a machine gun strafed right in front of the LCA ramp and would have cut down many of us coming right off—I was 5th, 6th or 7th off and likely would have been cut down. The officer who hesitated and didn't charge right off, like they had been told to do was Schneider. He had paused to take off his Mae West and toss it down on the beach. The delay likely saved my life. I ran all the way to the sea wall as fast as I could with my M1 rifle, there really wasn't anything to hide behind until you got there. Many men fell around me on the run in to the wall. Getting to the sea wall I looked back and saw an LCT get hit and blow up. There were bodies flying in the air—I turned to the radio man next to me and I said, "This is war!" I remember General Cota approaching us and him specifically talking to Captain John Raaen first and asking if he was Jack Raaen's son. He was then speaking with Schneider and I remember him exhorting them to lead the way on the beach. I was in awe of Cota's bravery in standing upright over them all hunkered down behind the wall and being impervious to fire. Francis "Bull" Dawson blew the barbed wire with Bangalore torpedoes nearby and then led the charge through. For the rest of the day we were combined with other companies out of necessity. I did not settle into HQ company duties; it was just fighting.[35]

1st Lieutenant Robert C. Fitzsimmons, Company B, 2d Ranger Infantry Battalion

I recall riding for a short time on an amphibious tank on the edge of the beach road looking for an exit. I had lost my helmet and rifle. When I realized the tank was drawing mortar fire each time it stopped, I got off and went in close to the cliffs. I recall seeing a Brigadier General standing up waving a pistol to show some men lying on the beach it would be best for them to move inland, not to stay on the beach.[36]

T/5 Tom Herring, Company C, 5th Ranger Infantry Battalion

Before Cota reached Schneider, a flurry of artillery fire caused him [Cota] to hit the dirt. I was lying to the left of Pfc William Stump, also C Company. Stump asked me for a match, saying his were wet. "Mine too," I said. Stump reached across my back and punched a soldier next to me and asked, "Hey, Buddy, you got a light?" As the soldier rolled onto his left side, the star on his jacket epaulet was visible to both Stump and me. Stump said—"Sorry, sir!" Cota reached into his jacket, pulled out a Zippo, flicked it, held it for Stump to light up and said, "That's OK, son, we're all here for the same reason."[37]

Herb Epstein, Intelligence NCO, HQ Company, 5th Ranger Infantry Battalion

After we left the boat, we had to run about 100 yards across the beach to the seawall. When we hit the seawall, which was roughly about 4 feet high, we laid down prone behind the wall. We were there a very short time and General Cota, the Assistant Division Commander of the 29th Division, came over to our position. I was lying on the sand next to Colonel Schneider as Cota walked up and called for him. Schneider stood up and the two were standing there while all this firing was going on and General Cota said to him, "Colonel we are counting on the Rangers to lead the way!" Schneider said, "yes sir!" and Cota walked back east. And as Schneider dropped down to the ground near me I said to him "what the hell were you doing?" And he said to me, "well he was standing and I wasn't going to be laying down here."

Anyway he got ahold of a couple of company officers and told them to get going. Using Bangalore Torpedoes, they blew the holes in the wire and we pushed forward. Elements of their platoon and headquarters went up the slope, which wasn't a cliff, but was nevertheless steep. Just about as we were going up an LCI came in behind us [LCI(L) 91]. It took a direct hit and went up in a sheet of flames about 150 feet high. We later learned it had some of the command group from the 29th Division.[38]

Private First Class Randall Ching, Company B, 5th Ranger Infantry Battalion

I remember General Cota in Normandy on Omaha Beach. He was waving a .45 pistol in his right hand. He was trying to get the men off the beach. He met with people from the 5th Rangers. He met with a Sergeant or Lieutenant. He asked them, "What outfit are you people from?" They replied, "We are from the Rangers." Cota said, "Where is your Battalion Commander?" When he met with the Battalion Commander, Cota said, "Colonel, We are getting slaughtered on the beach, You Rangers gotta lead the way, get off the beach."

That is what was said. I was only ten yards away from that. He was a big guy and pretty loud. Then the Colonel [Lieutenant Colonel Max Schneider] got our Company Commander, Captain George Whittington, and relayed the orders. Then Whittington said to B Company, "Alright you men, get four men and go find some combat engineers, and get some Bangalore torpedoes, and blow the wire and exit the beach." There was only one exit on Dog White Beach at that point. So, a few men got a Bangalore and blew an exit about 8–9 feet deep. It was two sections of torpedo, shoved under the wire and blew it. Then Company D's Captain led his men through the wire and then we [Company B] followed. Then some of the 29th infantry boys followed in with us up the hill.

I remember General Cota saying, "You Rangers have got to lead the way!" and so that is our motto. Lead the way and head out. I remember General Cota walking up and down the beach even with the danger, telling the soldiers to move it. I remember when he met with our Battalion Commander and his words were, "You Rangers have to Lead the Way. My people are getting slaughtered on the beach." Even 70 years later, I remember it that he was talking to my Battalion Commander Schneider. I remember General Cota very well. He was walking back and forth on Dog White Beach waving his .45 pistol. I landed on Dog White Beach with our whole battalion.

So finally, General Omar Bradley gave an order regarding our sector of Omaha Beach, to stop all reinforcements to the beach. That's what I heard over the radio. Until the troops on the beach now get over the top before he landed any more troops. And another thing that Captain Whittington said was, "Alright you bunch of Rangers, you're gonna die. You don't wanna die on the beach, you're gonna die inland."[39]

Staff Sergeant Donald L. Chance, Company C, 5th Ranger Infantry Battalion

In times of great crisis, people generally show either great ingenuity or self-reliance; others do incredibly stupid things. Do you remember examples of either? There appeared to be a jam up on the beach at least our section of Omaha. A four-foot sea wall barb wire fence and a steep hill. No one seemed to be moving. General Cota, a one star general of the 1st Division [29th Infantry Division] was on beach with us. He shouted "Lead the Way Rangers." This was the spark needed. The wire was blown and we stormed the heights.[40]

Captain Edward Luther, CO, Company E, 5th Ranger Infantry Battalion

Capt. [Edward] Luther of E Company was giving orders to his two platoon leaders, when an officer walked along behind his men and started urging them to get up and cross the wall. Looking over his shoulder, Luther put up a warning hand and said, "Hey Bud! Take it easy and don't get excited. This is my outfit—I'll take care of it!" The officer called out, "Well, you've got to get over that wall!" Luther hollered back, "Quit bothering my men; you'll disorganize

*them. The Colonel's over there if you want to see him, but quit bothering me."
Just then the platoon leaders started the men across the wall. A big grin came
across the officer's face, and he started walking down the beach again. As he
turned, Capt Luther saw the star on his shoulder for the first time, and took
off over the wall hoping that Gen. Cota wouldn't remember him.*[41]

**Staff Sergeant Richard N. Hathaway Jr., Company A, 5th Ranger
Infantry Battalion**
*Back on Omaha, I was lying on the shingle, attempting to gather my men
in order to breach the concertina barbed wire on top of the beach wall when
a voice behind me asked, "What outfit is this?" At the very same moment,
that German machine gun, which had given us so much trouble on the way
in, opened up. I answered the voice and said, "We're the Rangers." I got a
response of, "Well, let's get off this beach!" In a rather excited voice, I said, "We
will, as soon as I blow this f-ing wire." I then turned and noticed where the
voice came from. It was from a short stocky man with the stub of a cigar in
his mouth, wearing a field jacket with a silver star on his shoulder, the rank
of a brigadier general. It was Brigadier General Norman Cota, the Assistant
Division Commander of the Twenty-ninth Infantry Division. I couldn't
help but wonder what in hell was he doing on this beach. I turned back, still
looking for that German machine gun when I heard my Bangalore man yell,
"Fire in the hole!" The Bangalore exploded, and with Lieutenant Charles
Parker leading, we took off through the gap in the wire. I was sixth in line
as we started up the bluff.*[42]

As a result of this interaction, the Rangers' official motto was born
from General Cota's lips, under fire, at a time when their spirit and
fighting tenacity were critically needed: "Rangers, Lead the Way!" The
unit journal of the 5th Ranger Infantry Battalion recorded at 7:53 a.m.,
"VOCG [Verbal Command of Commanding General] 29th Infantry
Division 'Lead the Way Rangers.'"[43] Lieutenant Colonel Max Schneider,
CO, 5th Ranger Infantry Battalion, issued orders, the Rangers blew four
gaps into the wire along their entire front, and the men began to pour
through. General Cota himself moved to the Rangers of Company C
at 8:07 a.m. and exhorted their advance. They moved at the double and
cleared any communications trenches along the foot of the bluffs and
then began the ascent in columns. The bluffs were on fire from naval

shelling, which slowed the advance but at the same time offered a smoke screen to their movements from German eyes. The Rangers were off the beach by 8:10 a.m. LCI(L) 92 came ashore at 8:10 a.m., approximately two hundred yards to the left of the Rangers' gaps in the wire, and suffered the same fate as LCI(L) 91.

The tide was now beginning to turn at western Omaha Beach, and the Germans were starting to sense this as the Americans now began to take the heights and eliminate German positions. They were still proud and thought they would win the day.

Oberstleutnant Fritz Ziegelmann, 352d Infantry Division

Shortly after 0800—I succeeded in establishing telephone communication with the troops in WN 74 (Pointe ét Raz de La Percée). The commander, whom I knew personally, described the situation in detail: "At the water's edge at low tide near St. Laurent and Vierville, the enemy is in search of cover behind the coastal zone obstacles. A great many motor vehicles—and among these ten tanks—stand burning at the beach. The obstacle demolition squads have given up their activity. Debarkation from the landing boats has ceased; the boats keep further seawards. The fire of our strongpoints and artillery was well placed and has inflicted considerable casualties upon the enemy. A great many wounded and dead lie on the beach. Some of our strongpoints have ceased firing; they do not answer any longer when rung up on the telephone. Immediately east of this strongpoint, one group of enemy commandos has landed and attacked WN 74 from the south, but after being repelled with casualties it was withdrawn toward Gruchy..." The regimental commander [Oberst Ernst Goth of the 916th Regiment], who also had listened to this conversation, reported further that up till then we had succeeded in frustrating an enemy landing on a wide front.... Countermeasures were being taken against the weak enemy, who had infiltrated at two places. The 916th Regiment, however, had to report that the casualties on our side were successively rising in number because of the continuous fire of the naval artillery and of the landing boats, so that reinforcements had to be asked for.[44]

With the Ranger battalion on the move, General Cota turned his attention to soldiers remaining on the beach. With a gap blown in the wire in his vicinity, the first man through the wire was hit by a heavy burst of machine-gun fire and died in just minutes. Joe Balkoski tentatively identified this Stonewaller as either Private Ralph Hubbard or Private George Losey. ("Stonewaller" refers to those members of the forerunning units of the 29th Infantry Division who served under General Stonewall Jackson during the American Civil War.) As the soldier lay dying, the others could hear his pleas: "Medic, medic, I'm hit. Help me." He moaned and cried for a few minutes as life slipped away from him. Soldiers nearby heard the man call for his "mama" several times, and then it was over. This death demoralized these troops, and they stalled any advance to be made. General Cota, with a desire to urge them on, stood up and charged through the gap next. Men rallied behind him, and they crossed the road unharmed and dropped into a field of marsh grass beyond. The 29ers followed a system of shallow communications trenches until they reached taller grass beyond near the base of the bluffs. No antipersonnel mines or booby traps were discovered in the trenches as the men moved. Cota's men began the ascent on a diagonal to the right, up the bluffs, through the smoke. They reached the top of the bluffs about one hundred yards to the west of a small concrete foundation positioned twenty-five yards below the bluff. This feature of the landscape remains.

Cota remained at the foot of the bluffs and then met up again at 8:30 a.m. with Colonel Canham, who had set his first CP on the bluffs near the bottom. The radiomen tried using their SC300 radios to establish contact with the 1st Infantry Division off to the east. Their attempts were unsuccessful, as the radios were damaged. As the CP began to try to function, the Germans zeroed in on it as a target and fired five or six rounds of ranged-in two-inch mortars at the group. The fragments killed two enlisted men within three feet of the general. His radio operator, T/3 C. A. Wilson, was seriously wounded and thrown twenty to thirty feet up the bluff, while Lieutenant Shea, the general's aide, was thrown seventy-five feet down the bluff. As a result, Colonel Canham hurriedly moved the CP up the bluff.[45] The attack on the western portion of Omaha Beach was arrested and disorganized such that at 8:30 a.m., the commander of the 7th Naval Beach Battalion ordered a temporary halt of landings on Omaha in the face of the deteriorating situation.

Arden Earll's testimony about General Cota paints a profound picture of the courage and leadership he exhibited on the beach. The importance of this testimony is that it defines what it means to go from a near-catastrophic defeat to a heroic victory, as is often said of the U.S. forces that assaulted Omaha Beach west on D-Day. You can see in his words the change from hopelessness to victory in action for the American infantryman—a change that was brought on by "Dutch."

Private First Class Arden Earll, mortarman, MOS 504, Company H, 2d Battalion, 116th Infantry, 29th Infantry Division

So there the first waves were, we landed, and everybody had been told that it was going to be like a cake-walk. Just walk in, and I remember myself, when we got off of the LCVP, Sgt. Washburn was right ahead of me, and I looked around and that beach was just as flat as this tabletop, no shell craters, no nothing. We had been told we didn't need to worry about digging a fox hole, there would be so many shell craters; you could just drop into one. But there was nothing. So, why did the 29ers hunker down? Maybe I shouldn't say this, but I will. They had not been told the truth. Maybe it wasn't General Eisenhower or General Montgomery's fault, but all the preparations for before our landing had not come to pass. So the foot troops got on there; "Hey, this isn't the way it's supposed to be!" And what did they do? Right away it affected the soldiers in their heads. They hunkered down. What do we do next? And that's the reason.

General Cota directly and positively affected this battlefield condition and caused us to overcome our fear. We were all hunkered down behind the seawall, or whatever protection we could get, and Cota went along, prodding us on, to keep going. He said, "You're gonna die out here. It's better if you go inland to die." He did not seem to be scared of anything. He stood upright and just walked along. "Come on, keep going, keep going." Genera Cota had no fear for his own safety.

General Cota was exposed to enemy sniper fire, small arms fire, and everything they could throw at him, and it didn't seem to worry him at all. He just walked along, and "Come on, you've got to go!" He didn't seem to be scared of anything. He could have been shot by a sniper. He could have got hit by artillery, he could have got hit by anything. He was the only high-ranking officer I witnessed do that. Everybody else was as low as they possibly could be. So he was the only one, the only physical human target that the Germans had to shoot at. Here he was, a General, and he was the target.

He said, "If you stay here, you're gonna get killed. If you go inland, you may get killed. But let's go inland and get killed. Not stay on this Damn beach. *The tide was coming in. Don't stop. Get the hell out of here, and get em."* *I think that inspired a lot of people, a lot of the guys, to keep moving. They had a General tell them these things.*

If it hadn't have been for a few people like him, D-Day could have very well been turned into what the British went through at Dieppe. It could have very well turned into that. It very well might have been. But General Cota thought, even if he didn't do anything, or say anything, if they just saw him, walking up and down the beach, "By God, if he could do it, we could do it!" So, that is what I think. Other men also thought, "If a General can do that, we can do it." He did these actions for his entire time on the beach.

During training, the troops were notified that after all the shelling, their heads would be foggy, and they wouldn't even realize what was going on. We were told that. So, that is why you hear so much about the 29ers hunkering down. Then they pulled that, and then they found that foot troops had come up, and what our commanders had told us was not true. We were told that the enemy troops in the bunkers would not put up much of a fight. Because their heads had been shook up so bad.

When General Cota walked along the beach, just as if nothing was happening, he was just taking a walk. . . . "Get going, get going! If you stay here, you are gonna die out here! The tide is coming in. You are gonna die out here if you stay here! If you are gonna die, you might as well go inland and die." I didn't actually see him help wounded soldiers. I guess he did.

I think that did more to inspire and encourage the troops than anything else. He was walking right out there in broad sight. He could have been shot by a sniper, or anything else right away. But he, it did not seem to bother him. That he exposed himself, did more for the morale of the troops. That's really what I think.

It took courage for him to stand there in the wide open amongst all that chaos, in the midst of a lot of scared kids. General Cota probably looked like and was the age of many of their Dads. His leadership became infectious. Because when they saw the General, walking up and down and in plain sight, it inspired them to move. The General was armed only with his pistol.

Seeing General Cota gave me a lot of courage. All I could think of was, "Arden, you gotta keep going. You gotta keep going. If you're ever going to get home, there's only one way to get home, and that's to keep going." I didn't know when my time might be up. I think all of us felt that way. Our time could be up anytime, but we have to keep going.[46]

In his first hour ashore, General Cota took what was nearly a total disaster and began an arduous journey to exert command and control over the battlespace. He reinvigorated the demoralized men. His actions during that second hour saved the remaining thousand or so men on the beach who had not already fallen as honored dead or as casualties. The fact that so many men from so many different units and locations directly witnessed his actions on the beach is clear evidence of his movement up and down the beach during Cota's first hour in combat. Communications were nonexistent, and contact was yet to be established with the 1st Infantry Division or with General Charles Gerhardt afloat aboard the USS *Ancon*. General Bradley considered diverting the remaining follow-up forces to Utah Beach. But on the beach, now at the toe of the bluff, General Cota saw what had to be done. He had just missed his own death by mere feet after the mortar fire struck the advance CP. He would lead the men to Vierville and beyond. In Cota's postwar words to his grandson, "There's nothing like being shot at."

CHAPTER EIGHT

Vierville

BY 8:30 A.M., GENERAL COTA HAD SPENT SIXTY-FOUR MINUTES IN combat and traveled an estimated 1.5 miles, under direct, heavy enemy machine-gun, mortar, and artillery fire, with little to no regard for his own safety as he tactically traversed the battlefield fully visible and exposed. This distance attributed to Cota's movements was calculated and mapped based on eyewitness accounts and official records. Of importance to the men on the beach at this time, many of General Cota's predictions for D-Day came true in the first hours of the amphibious assault. This included his prophetic words to his officers aboard ship the night before the invasion. He made several hypotheses in 1943 as part of his landmark thesis "Assault Division" while he served at Combined Operations Headquarters. Among his conclusions that came to pass were the following:

- The naval gunners won't be able to see well enough to hit their targets even during daylight.
- The aerial bombardment will not effectively neutralize all enemy positions.
- The beach is going to be fouled up in any case.[1]

General Omar Bradley wrote two autobiographies after the war. He notes in each how disturbed he was as a result of the stiff defenses on Omaha Beach: "As the morning lengthened, my worries deepened over the alarming and fragmentary reports we picked up on the navy net. From these messages we could piece together only an incoherent account of sinkings, swampings, heavy enemy fire, and chaos on the beaches. By 8:30 the two assault regiments on Omaha had expected to break through the water's-edge defenses and force their way inland to where a road paralleled the coastline a mile behind the beaches. Yet by 8:30, V Corps had not yet confirmed news of the landing."[2]

The Germans had no interest in losing ground on Omaha. The men executed the German defensive plans and strategy and fought as hard as can be expected of combatant soldiers. Their machine guns, mortars, artillery, and landmines were performing largely as expected, although the Americans had placed those forces under strain. The ammunition was holding out for the moment. Oberstleutnant Fritz Ziegelmann's knowledge of the battlefield was solid, as it was partially obtained from communicating with WN 74. He was provided with a realistic assessment of the invasion. As noted in chapter 5, WN 74 had a longitudinal view of the entire beach. With proper optical equipment, individual soldiers, equipment, and units could be viewed while on the move from left (the sea) to right (the bluffs) down the entire length of the beach. The observational capacity afforded by this position and others like it was one reason the Germans were able to deliver such devastating fire on their prey. The concepts of Vauban defense, as elucidated by Major General John C. Raaen Jr., were proving effective, with few exceptions. Nowhere in the 29th Infantry Division's sectors was this fact more apparent than at the beach exits D-1 and D-3, as attackers lay dead and dying at the mercy of German fire.

Oberstleutnant Fritz Ziegelmann, assistant chief of staff, 352d Infantry Division
[Shortly after 8 a.m.] I succeeded in establishing telephone communication with the troops in WN 74 (Pointe de la Percee). The commander, whom I knew personally, described the situation in detail: "At the water's edge at low tide near St. Laurent and Vierville the enemy is in search of cover behind the coastal zone obstacles. A great many motor vehicles—and among these ten tanks—stand burning at the beach. The obstacle demolition squads have given up their activity. Debarkation from the landing boats has ceased; the

boats keep further seawards. The fire of our strongpoints and artillery was well placed and has inflicted considerable casualties upon the enemy. A great many wounded and dead lie on the beach. Some of our strongpoints have ceased firing; they do not answer any longer when rung up on the telephone. Immediately east of this strongpoint, one group of enemy commandos has landed and attacked WN 74 from the south, but after being repelled with casualties it was withdrawn toward Gruchy."[3]

By 8:30 a.m. on western Omaha Beach, the American advance was tenuous at best. The Germans remained in full control of WN 74 and from there maintained a commanding view of the developing battle. Company C of the 2d Ranger Infantry Battalion landed on Charlie Beach in two LCAs (Landing Craft, Assault) with sixty-five men at 6:30 a.m. By 8:30 a.m., they were reduced in number by half. They climbed the cliffs by 7:15 a.m. and, for the next hour and fifteen minutes, captured and neutralized large portions of WN 73. A few fortunate survivors of the 29th followed and helped them. These Rangers' actions were critical to providing relief to anyone not German. The Germans still firmly held WN 71 and WN 72 at the D-1 exit. They also held the draw. The men who landed in the face of the D-1 exit lay shattered. The men of Company A, 2d Ranger Infantry Battalion, under 1st Lieutenant Robert Edlin, assaulted the bluffs near Hamel au Prêtre. Edlin was the lone surviving officer. When they topped the bluff, they wheeled right and swept through WN 70, taking control of this vital defensive position away from previous management. They were followed up the bluffs by members of Company B, 2d Ranger Infantry Battalion, under Captain Edgar Arnold. Each of these Ranger companies was mowed in half by the defenders in the opening moves. On their heels, thirty men of Company D, 116th Regimental Combat Team (RCT), landed and ascended under 1st Lieutenant Verne Morse and joined efforts with the Rangers. The 29ers with Morse recalled the clump of scraggly pine trees near the rim of the bluff as the location of their ascent. At 8:30 a.m., this group continued the fight in the fields in the vicinity of WN 70, slowly expanding their footprint and taking ground foot by bloody foot.

Shortly after 8 a.m., as the 5th Rangers breached the wire and then ascended the bluffs, Company D led the advance to the west of their point of advance. They in fact blew four gaps in the wire and made their assault through the smoke-covered bluffs with very few casualties, clearing the beach by 8:10 a.m. On the climb, Company B passed through Company D and carried the bluff. The end result was that they made it to the top as one of the few units to maintain cohesiveness. It so happens that the author's grandfather, Staff Sergeant Herb Hull, section leader, was in this group with Randall Ching (introduced in the previous chapter).

At the D-3 exit, the 29th and 1st Infantry Divisions commingled and fought hard just to keep their slight toehold at the water's edge. The Germans still held the draw and large parts of WN 66, WN 67, and WN 68. They also held the important WN 69 in St. Laurent with weapons coverage of the entire draw. The grass fires and resultant smoke above Dog White and Dog Red and between WN 68 and WN 70 remained thick and billowing. The smoke continued to drift east along the line of advance and the face of the bluff, offering cover and concealment for Cota and those men under his influence. For those wishing to learn more about these events, there are several books that do justice to the topic, with Joe Balkoski's *Omaha Beach: D-Day, June 6, 1944,* as the quintessential research tool to gain a rich understanding of these other units and men.

General Cota joined the steady column of men ascending the bluff after his near brush with death at the advance command post (CP) when the mortar rounds struck. He and Colonel Charles Canham were separated after the mortar strike discussed in the previous chapter. As the men with General Cota reached a point just below the crest, they noticed a single American rifleman walking along the promenade directing five German prisoners with hands held high. These were the first prisoners seen by the group. When the procession down below reached a point approximately eight hundred yards east of the D-1 exit, the two leading prisoners were cut down by enemy machine-gun fire. The American dove for cover of the nearby seawall as the remaining Germans knelt down on their knees begging for mercy. The German MG-42 opened up again, striking the lead man full in the chest, and he crumpled over dead. The remaining German prisoners took cover at the seawall with their captor. The Germans' aggression against their own was a wake-up call to many of the uninitiated soldiers. Seeing this crazy event, the soldiers continued their climb.[4]

General Cota worked his way up the bluffs to the top in response to a stalling of the single file of troops. Intending to urge them on, he personally led the leading elements of the column and reached the head at about 9 a.m.[5] By 8:45 a.m., the men of Company C, 116th RCT, were the first to rim the bluff above Dog Red and Dog White. The men of Company C, 2d Rangers, were up the bluff in Charlie Sector, and a group of survivors of Companies A and B, 2d Ranger Infantry Battalion, made the climb at WN 70. Lieutenant Morse with the 2d Rangers swept west through WN 70 at 8:40 a.m., taking it. The June 16, 1944, account of General Cota's actions prepared by Headquarters, 29th Infantry Division, described his efforts during this period:

> *The attack having bogged down towards the top of the cliff, General Cota personally climbed to the top and led the leading elements of the column, crossed interlocking bands of enemy machine gun fire, and led the troops onto the St. Laurent-Vierville-sur-Mer Road, directed a hurried reconnaissance of forces and started the detachment of Rangers West toward their objective at Point de la Raz Percee and Point du Hoc. Initially this advance bogged down several times. Each time General Cota hastened to the front of the column, assisted the platoon leader in the disposition of his forces so the column could advance to the West.*[6]

As the lead men came over the rim of the bluff, they were attacked by machine-gun fire from their right and left front. Several members of Company C reported some sort of shells striking near their location as well. As expected, the heavy fire caused the column to take cover and become pinned. Cota again advanced to the very head of the column and prompted its advance. Cota said, "Now let's see what you're made of. This is how ya tell the men from the boys." The men were disorganized, and it was difficult for the general to effect a complete reorganization as at least two men were hit by machine-gun fire during the burst. One man reportedly had a portion of his right hip shot away. The report of a 1945 combat interview with Captain Robert J. Bedell and Lieutenant Morse, along with eight enlisted men, stated,

Finally, Cota asked for some "volunteers" to "go get that guy over to the left." Three Rangers said they'd go, started moving along a low hedge and ditch that ran to the south. By this route, they were able to flank the enemy machine gun from the right. The group interviewed included several men who had noted two of these three Rangers later walking along the road that led into Vierville. The Rangers told the men that one of them had been killed as they closed in on the machine gun. As proof of the success of their mission, one strode along carrying the MG 42. Several belts of German ammunition were draped around his neck and shoulders. The flanking maneuver of the three Rangers towards the machine gun fire that was hitting the column from the left front stopped as the three Rangers started towards it.[7]

The German MG-42 gunner and crew had a bad day when they were paid a visit by the Rangers, a very bad day as evidenced by the Rangers' war trophy. The Rangers didn't take too kindly to comrades being killed. That said, the Germans were well aware of Cota's men. Oberstleutnant Fritz Ziegelmann received direct reports that concerned him regarding the spaces between the D-1 and D-3 exits. As previously mentioned, the German observation of the beach was total (as illustrated by figure 8.1). The German presighting and ranging of all points is demonstrated by

Figure 8.1. Images of German mortar positions above Omaha Beach. Preselected ranges and elevations are denoted in the paintings on the walls of the positions. LCI(L)s 91 and 92 are visible on the beach near where Cota landed (NARA).

Figure 8.2. Images of German mortar positions above Omaha Beach (NARA).

the calculations, firing solutions, and targeting artwork adorning their fighting positions, as photographed after the battle was over and shown in figure 8.2. What they didn't know as of yet was that Company C of the 116th RCT and the entire 5th Ranger Infantry Battalion were largely intact and now on the offensive. They didn't know that General Cota, one of the most experienced American amphibious-landing combat leaders on D-Day, was actively leading these troops and the other survivors who joined these men as the Americans now breached their *Atlantikwall*. They didn't know that they made a huge mistake in not killing this man on the beach as he moved about fully exposed and in full view when they had ample opportunity to do so.

Oberstleutnant Fritz Ziegelmann, 352d Infantry Division (June 6, 1944), National Archives and Records Administration (NARA), Foreign Military Studies, B-Series (B-0388)
0840 Hours—Into the Artillery Regiment 352: The connection with the observation points is to be established again at the latest before the tide is

coming again, as it may be presumed that the second wave of enemy forces will try to land then. An artillery liaison detachment of the 3rd Battalion has to be held in readiness immediately with the object of supporting the attack of Task Force Meyer.

0846 Hours—Report from the Artillery Regt 352: North of St. Laurent, the Defense Works No. 65, 66, 67 and 70 have probably been taken by the enemy. Ahead of the Defense Work No. 68, strong enemy forces are landing from larger size boats, an approximate strength of 150 men.[8]

The 5th Rangers cleared the rim just after Company C, 116th RCT, did so off to their immediate right. The aforementioned Companies A and B, 2d Rangers, were three hundred yards to their west (right). The steepness of the bluff caused many Rangers to crawl. The smoke served to disorganize the movement of the men as units. A large number of Ranger units failed to maintain contact as they ascended. At the top, Captain George P. Whittington, commanding officer (CO), Company B, sought out and made contact with Lieutenant Colonel Max Schneider, who had lost contact with Cota during the ascent of all units. Whittington was tasked with sending a patrol to find Colonel Canham to receive orders, as General Cota had changed the Rangers' secondary mission objective of relieving Pointe du Hoc in favor of assisting the 116th RCT in establishing a beachhead at the moment. This patrol was from 2d Platoon, Company B, under Staff Sergeant Walter McIlwain.[9] At 8:30 a.m., a platoon of Company A, 5th Ranger Infantry Battalion, under Captain Charles "Ace" Parker lost contact with the rest of the American forces and made its way westward all the way to Pointe du Hoc by bypassing Vierville and heading west. These men were the only landward relief of Lieutenant Colonel James Earl Rudder's 2d Ranger Infantry Battalion embattled there. By 8:30 a.m., most Ranger units were up. The Americans found *Achtung Minen!* signs all along the bluff; however, only a few men fell victim to them. These heavily mined fields slowed down all units on the bluffs as they implemented proper procedures to cross such deadly obstacles. Days later, the engineers removed approximately 150 mines from the fields where Cota, his men, and the Rangers crossed on D-Day. Company D, 5th Rangers, sent a patrol along the bluff to clear any remaining Germans out of fighting positions in the trenches during this reorganization.[10]

At 8:49 a.m., the 1st Battalion of the 116th RCT was able to get a radio message to the commanding general (CG), 1st Infantry Division, that they were held up by machine-gun fire and requested fire support. At 8:59 a.m., a British officer reported to the CG, 1st Infantry Division, that Dog Green was under heavy machine-gun fire, and obstacles were not cleared.[11]

For the next half hour, the Rangers and 29ers sorted themselves out into companies, platoons, and sections to carry on the fight in the fields east of Vierville. Lieutenant Colonel Schneider's orders were to proceed as a battalion to the battalion assembly area as opposed to his earlier orders to proceed by platoon. Parker did not get those orders and proceeded to Pointe du Hoc. The survivors of Companies A and B, 2d Rangers, joined Schneider, and they were formed up as a Provisional Ranger Company with flank guard duty. Now around 9:10 a.m., the Rangers organized and moved out to the south toward the coastal road shown on Allied maps as R15H2 and currently designated by the French as Route D514 running between Vierville-sur-Mer and St. Laurent. They took on the duty of working hedgerow to hedgerow south to capture the important coastal road and protect this beachhead as ordered, facing minor opposition until they reached the road. The Germans placed machine-gun crews in nearly every field of any size to the south of the road. The Rangers split by companies and took them one by one (as illustrated in figure 8.3).

By this time, Colonel Canham had reestablished the 116th RCT CP by the scraggly clump of pine trees that bordered the north–south hedgerow some two hundred yards to the east of WN 70 above Hamel au Prêtre.[12] Canham ordered the Company B Rangers to stay with him to provide security. The Rangers declined the order in favor of their original orders to report back to their CO, Captain Whittington, and moved out to the east. The McIlwain Company B Ranger patrol headed east to Schneider, when around 9:30 a.m. a German artillery strike on the fields above the bluffs commenced.[13] This action killed and wounded many men and is clearly evidenced by an inverse image of the Allied aerial reconnaissance flight taken at 12:30 p.m. (shown in figure 8.4).

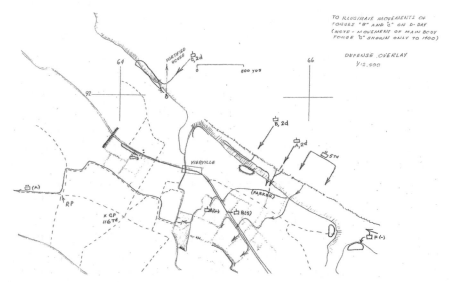

Figure 8.3. Lieutenant Colonel Charles H. Taylor map overlay of the 5th Ranger Infantry Battalion, showing its company assaults and actions (NARA).

Figure 8.4. Aerial recon photo, 12:30 p.m., showing western Omaha Beach as a reverse image highlighting artillery and similar strikes on landscape (NARA).

Note the black dots in the fields, each of which is indicative of an artillery or mortar impact in the fields. A detailed account of this artillery bombardment was recorded in Noel F. Mehlo Jr.'s *The Lost Ranger: A Soldier's Story* based on witness testimony. General Cota was in this same area during the bombardment.

> *At 0915 hours the 726th Grenadier Regiment reported to the 352d Infantry Division that WN's 65, 66, 67, 68 and 70 were in enemy hands.... By 0925 hours the 916th Grenadier Regiment requested an artillery and armored counterattack to the WN's east of St. Laurent. Around this time a call was placed by a German observer for an artillery strike in the fields southeast of WN 70. The Rangers reported this to be 88 mm artillery fire. At the same time on the southern edges of the same open fields, Captain Raaen and members of his Headquarters Company recorded taking cover due to the incoming fire. "Suddenly, I heard a low whine, not at all like the noise the artillery had been making as it passed over our heads toward the beach. No, this noise was coming straight at us. We all hit the dirt as four or five shells detonated in our field about thirty yards away." McIlwain's patrol recovered from the shelling and they assessed their wounded. S/Sgt McIlwain was wounded in the arm with shrapnel, and PFC Bernard Akers, one of S/Sgt Hull's [Browning Automatic Rifle] men, was wounded. At this point, PFC Johnson sprang into action tending to the wounded, bandaging up S/Sgt McIlwain, who at first refused to be evacuated, and PFC Akers with an unknown injury. Ranger Elmo E. Banning, T/5 was killed having been hit directly by the artillery fire.*[14]

At 9 a.m., Lieutenant Morse, along with members of the 2d Rangers and survivors of Companies A and B, 116th RCT, began to move east and met up with Colonel Canham at the scraggly pines. They deposited a few prisoners with the CP. In the meantime, Captain Bedell and his men of Company C were on the move again after their MG-42 encounter with General Cota. They moved south at the north–south hedgerow above Hamel au Prêtre, and General Cota reached the head of the column of troops. He found that they had again stalled in the face of interlocking enemy machine-gun fire from a position approximately three hundred yards south of the rim of the bluffs near Military Grid Reference System (MGRS) 649913. This position is on the northeastern edge of Vierville, north of the intersection of the coastal highway and rue du Hamel au

Prêtre, on the northeast side of Vierville along a hedgerow and trail to the western edge of WN 71. At this point, the 5th Rangers were several hundred yards to the east working south toward the coastal highway. The fire was sweeping and grazing the flat fields. Several times Cota tried to move the men by calling for an officer or NCO who was in charge, but none of the leaders seemed to be in evidence, and his exhortations were not too successful. In the face of this fire, General Cota passed through the men and personally led them in an infantry charge across the field, instructing them to fire at the hedgerows and houses as they advanced through enemy machine-gun fire. Seeing him cross the open fields finally convinced the rest of the 29ers that it could be done, and they all followed. The machine-gun fire stopped as soon as the troops advanced across the fields toward it. Several troops later recalled at least one round of artillery fire upon them as they moved. In this case, General Cota clearly went above and beyond the call of duty at the risk of his life in order to exert positive leadership on the battlefield at a critical moment in the assault.[15] Keep in mind that the German MG-42 was, and remains, one of the deadliest and most feared machine guns ever constructed (figure 8.5). It fires 7.92×57mm Mauser ammunition at a rate of twelve hundred rounds per minute (with varying capability between nine and fifteen hundred rounds per minute with different bolts) at a muzzle velocity of 2,428 feet per second. Its effective firing range is 219–2,187 yards, with a maximum firing range of 5,140 yards. There were an estimated eighty-five MG-42s on Omaha Beach. This weapon was clearly capable of cutting General Cota in half at a range of three to four hundred yards with clear lines of sight as he led this charge armed only with his trusty Colt .45 and huge stones. Lieutenant Morse followed this column with his men. A modern view of this field is shown in figure 8.6, while figure 8.7 is a wartime intelligence photo from the reverse angle.

Several Company F, 116th RCT, men from boats 4, 5, and 6 under Technical Sergeant George R. England, after the loss of their officers, advanced straight up the hill. They recalled their stoppage by the MG-42 fire and that they waited irresolutely. Private First Class Anthony Ferrara later reported that "at that stage, General Cota found them. He yelled at them 'Don't lay down now. Go on and get that machine gun!' About then,

Figure 8.5. German MG-42 (Maschinengewehr 42) (NARA).

Figure 8.6. Photo of fields crossed by the 5th Ranger Infantry Battalion and 29th Infantry Division east of Vierville (Franck Maurouard).

Figure 8.7. Aerial photo showing fields involved in Brigadier General Cota's infantry charge (NARA).

the group was joined by a party of 25–30 Rangers. The Rangers seemed to know where they were going and what to do about it: the sections from 'F' [Company] were still in a state of 'mental confusion.'"[16] This is evidence that Cota worked in and among several groups of soldiers under fire.

After this event, they turned south and worked along the margins of the fields under the cover of hedgerows. At approximately 9:10 a.m., General Cota reached the secondary road near an old gate 150 yards west of the Hamel au Prêtre road junction and about 450 yards east of the center of Vierville (MGRS 652911). Between this point and the intersection of the coastal highway three hundred yards to the west, the various platoons and sections reorganized yet again after the movement through the fields under fire. Bedell's men took point as the advance guard on the move west to Vierville. At this point, at the intersection of the two previously mentioned routes, Captain Thomas Murphy, 2d Battalion, 116th RCT, gathered up various scattered men of his battalion, and they turned east down the coastal road toward St. Laurent and the area where the 5th Rangers were killing German machine-gun crews.

Lieutenant Colonel Schneider managed to get a radio message through to the CG, 1st Infantry Division, at 9:28 a.m. that enemy gunfire on Exit D-1 and the enemy battery behind Dog Green continued to hinder the landing. At 9:30 a.m., the HMS *Prince Leopold* sent a radio message to the CG aboard the HMS *Prince Charles* that the Rangers landed safely under heavy opposition, and the beach was not cleared of obstructions. The report was that the beach was very dangerous for LCAs. At 9:41 a.m., the CG, 1st Infantry Division, reported to Center Task Group (CTG) 124.9 that gunfire on the beach exit on Dog Green hindered the landing. There was a possible battery at MGRS 649906 causing trouble. The Rangers sent a follow-up radio message at 9:47 a.m. reporting a machine gun on the right of Dog Green, left of the "Dolly," and mortar fire on Dog White coming in from the bluff. At 9:50 a.m., General Cota made one of his only radio messages to the CG, 1st Infantry Division, that the beach was fouled with too many vehicles: "Send combat troops." At 9:55 a.m., CTG 124.8 reported to Center Task Force (CTF) 124 that there were many wounded in need of immediate evacuation at Dog Red Beach. Many LCTs (Landing Craft, Tanks) were reported as standing by, unable to land and unload due to heavy shell fire on beach.[17]

By this time, the men of Company B, 5th Rangers, had knocked out the German machine-gun position and turned west along the coastal road toward Vierville. They caught up with Bedell's men and intermixed with their column. The Ranger After Action Report stated,

> *During the advance, numerous Germans, well concealed in weapons pits constructed in hedgerows, were killed. Company B advance toward Vierville-sur-Mer receiving heavy sniper and machine gun fire. Several direct hits from artillery on the rear of the battalion column caused numerous casualties. Company E attempted a penetration to the South but was halted by intense machine gun fire. An 81 mm mortar concentration fired by Company C knocked out several of these positions but they were rapidly replaced and the advance remained halted.*[18]

Troops of the 116th, 1st Battalion, mixed with elements of Ranger Group B, were strung along both sides of this road, working westward. They reached Vierville with little opposition. Lieutenant Jack Shea reported that one helmetless Ranger emerged proudly carrying a captured MG-42 as troops strung along both sides of the road in their advance west. Lieutenant Bedell's group was the first to enter Vierville at approximately 10 a.m. with Cota near the front of the column unless he needed to prompt someone. Shortly after 10 a.m., several men of Company C encountered General Cota in town, who, they reported, "was calmly twirling his pistol on his finger." He said to them, "Where the hell have you been boys?"

At that moment, the Rangers managed a radio message to the CG, 1st Infantry Division, that "tanks off Exit Dog 1 held up by crossfire from machineguns reported by Control Vessel Dog Green."

With little opposition, the soldiers reached and passed through Vierville while conducting a house-to-house search of the town. The soldiers came across ten to twelve civilians in the town who told the Americans they had escaped the air and naval bombardment while taking refuge in a shallow cellar beneath a one-story home destroyed by an American rocket barrage. The 5th Ranger journal stated, "Reaching outskirts village Vierville-sur-Mer. Sniper fire is heavy. Two MG nests located in a building, knocked out. Infiltrating through town, snipers are thinning unit rapidly. Several patrols are searching building to building while the battalion is moving cautiously." The Rangers and 29ers crossed the main intersection at the head of the Vierville Beach exit and continued west toward Pointe et Raz de la Percée.

At this point, the Company B Rangers had the lead west along the coastal highway working with Bedell's men. Light enemy machine-gun and sniper fire interrupted the advance of the column when they reached a point five hundred yards west of Vierville. The soldiers dispersed themselves along the ditches on either side of the road. General Cota again caught up with the head of the column and directed that a flank patrol be dispatched to outflank this fire. It withdrew as the Americans began to maneuver.

Company C, 116th Infantry, 29th Division, U.S. Army Historical Division, interview with various Company C soldiers, March 25, 1945
Cota had seen the column stop [west of Vierville] and was on his way to see what the delay was. "They told him that the bodies in the [ditch] had been

hit and killed by sniper fire," described Morse. "But Cota stood there with his .45 still in his hand. He told us that we had to get something off the road to maneuver against the source of the enemy fire that was holding us up. . . . It was at this point that the typical Normandy hedgerow first presented itself as a problem. Bedell and Lt. Schwartz had their men strung along the hedgerow that ran south from the farm buildings, but every move they made to cross this hedgerow and continue on toward the west was met with heavy small arms and automatic fire from a range of 200–300 yards. The enemy guns were evidently well-camouflaged, and the riflemen found it impossible to determine an enemy location by muzzle blast or smoke. The Germans were using smokeless powder."[19]

Cota moved at 10:50 a.m. right to the head of the column, now led by Captain George Whittington, a former marine and a true warrior, and his Company B Rangers. Cota wanted to determine what the holdup was and discovered that the Americans had run into a company-size prepared defense manned by the German 726th Grenadier Regiment. 1st Sergeant Avery Thornhill, Company B, 5th Ranger Infantry Battalion, was with Captain Whittington as they were held up in their westward advance. What Thornhill recounted was also witnessed by Randall Ching and separately by several men given a combat interview by Sergeant Forrest Pogue, 2d Historical Service. Cota kept his cool under machine-gun and sniper fire as he interacted with these men and spurred them to action.

1st Sergeant Avery Thornhill, Company B, 5th Ranger Infantry Battalion

We had been pinned down about 500 yd south [west] of Vierville by snipers and two men had been killed. Captain Whittington and I were in a ditch behind a hedgerow when someone bellowed out from behind to get up and start moving forward as we would never win this war on our tail. Captain Whittington and I looked around to the street and there stood Brigadier General Cota. Captain Whittington hollered to the General that there were snipers in the trees and he should take cover. He said, "there are no snipers up there" and about that time a bullet struck the ground next to the General and he turned with a passing remark, "Well, there might be one."[20]

Private First Class Randall Ching, Company B, 5th Ranger Infantry Battalion

Up above the bluffs, he met with some Rangers from my Company near Vierville where the men were held up, and the General asked "What's going on with you people over here?" He asked a Ranger. The Ranger reply was, "There is a sniper out here somewhere." Then finally a German opened up with a shot and fired at Cota and missed. Cota walked away saying, "Well guess there was a sniper up there." That was "Dutch" Cota, Brigadier General, a 1-star General, Assistant Commander of the 29th Infantry Division. I didn't see him again after D-Day. [Earlier] I saw him walking up and down the beach waving his .45 pistol in his hand while under heavy machine gun and artillery fire from up the bluff, and from the left and the right. There was direct 88 mm artillery fire coming from the right. General Cota was tall and slim with sandy hair. That took bravery. He was calm and doing his job to lead.[21]

Combat Interview of 5th Ranger Infantry Battalion

Up the road from Vierville, alone and smoking a cigar, came General Cota, who had last been seen at the top of the bluff when the Rangers were reorganizing. The General asked what was holding them up. "Snipers" said Pepper [Lieutenant Bernard Pepper, Company B]. "Sniper? There aren't any snipers here." A shot came close to the General: "Well maybe there are," and he walked off.[22]

Satisfied with the attack here, Cota turned back to the east. Whittington was the ranking officer of the Rangers and of the men of Company C and the arriving Company D of the 116th RCT. He dispersed the men into the fields and carried on the assault. He dispatched 2d Platoon, Company B, to the south to probe the German defenses. They ended up on the southern end of Vierville and were later impressed to guard Colonel Canham's CP.

Colonel Canham managed a radio message to the CG, 1st Infantry Division, that the 116th RCT had bypassed the opposition on the beach and was moving forward slowly.[23] General Cota then returned to the Vierville crossroads sometime after 11 a.m. and met with Colonel Canham, whom he had not seen or interacted with since their meeting at the first CP at the foot of the bluffs some hours earlier, when they

were mortared. They discussed the situation, decided that the 1st battalion under Lieutenant Colonel John A. Metcalf should push on as
planned, assist the Rangers in knocking out the enemy gun positions at
Pointe et Raz de la Percée, and try to reach the 2d Rangers at Pointe
du Hoc. Colonel Canham moved to the southern end of Vierville and
established his CP near the crossroads in the vicinity of Saint-André
Church of Vierville-sur-Mer (illustrated in figure 8.8). Canham desired
to gather up the 3d Battalion under Colonel Lawrence E. Meeks as
they came inland and jump them from that point to the west toward
Grandcamp on a route parallel with that of 1st Battalion.[24] Major General Raaen believed it was at this meeting that General Cota changed
the mission of the 5th Ranger Infantry Battalion in a critical battlefield
command decision that influenced the outcome of the battle at Omaha
Beach. During the research phase for the Cota Medal of Honor effort,
Raaen stated, "At 1200, in a key battlefield command decision, he
changed the mission of the 5th Ranger Infantry Battalion and held

Figure 8.8. Saint-André Church of Vierville-sur-Mer (Ikmo-ned, wiki).

them in Vierville to defend it, demonstrating true leadership under fire. This decision saved the spent 116th RCT from counterattack."[25] Whittington and the rest of the Rangers were now under Colonel Canham, with his CP in Vierville. They and the men of Companies C and D of the 116th dug in west of town.

The CTG 124.4 and CTF 124 shared many messages between 10:16 and 11:53 a.m. concerning the critical nature of the machine-gun, mortar, and artillery fire on Dog Green Beach. That situation was critical.[26]

In the four hours since he had landed, General Cota had traveled an estimated total 3.75 miles under direct, heavy enemy fire, operating at times as a platoon or even a section leader to lead men to small but important victories.

The primary mission in the opening hours of D-Day for the 121st Engineer Combat Battalion (ECB), attached to the 116th RCT, was to open the D-1 exit among other tasks. This mission was critical to allow vehicles—particularly armor and artillery—to exit the beaches and carry the fight to the Germans with heavy weaponry. Advance elements of the Battalion Headquarters landed aboard LCI(L) 91. The destruction of the vessel resulted in estimated 50 percent casualties among the engineers and 75 percent loss of their important demolition equipment. The survivors moved with Company C into Vierville, where they reorganized under the command of Major Allan Olson, executive officer, 121st ECB. He was joined by Captain Bainbridge, assistant division engineer, 254th ECB, and 1st Lieutenant John F. MacAllister, adjutant, Headquarters and Headquarters Company, 121st Engineer Battalion, and others of the engineering units.[27] The men were gathered at the Vierville crossroads around noon. MacAllister remembered feeling very lonely at that intersection.

The knowledge below is extremely important in understanding precisely how what General Cota did next was, on its own merit, worthy of the Medal of Honor all by itself.

Lieutenant (jg) Coit Coker (After Action Report, U.S. Navy Shore Fire Control Party 3, June 1944)
On the plateau was a field of grass with numerous foxholes containing Germans. It was decided about noon to bring naval fire on this field by spotting

in deflection from well to the right, crossing D-l Exit (to avoid hitting ourselves), which was then not yet clear. The destroyer McCook furnished this fire. As fire traversed the exit, McCook radioed us that a large party of Germans had emerged from the heavy concrete emplacements at the exit and were waving a white flag. We radioed to cease fire. The beach engineers took these Germans prisoner (30 in number) when fire was lifted. The total number of salvos: 4 (16 rounds). With Lt. [Donald] Vandervoort [of the 1st Battalion, 116th] spearheading, we took three more Germans prisoner by tossing hand grenades into foxholes.[28]

At 12:15 p.m., USS *Thompson* (DD 627), a Gleaves-class destroyer with five 5-inch (127-mm) Dual Purpose (DP) guns, moved to Dog Green Beach eight hundred yards off shore after a fire mission at Easy Red Beach. The landing force attempting to exit the beach was stopped by unlocated snipers or batteries. At 12:23 p.m., the *Thompson* commenced main battery fire for the demolition of all houses and structures commanding Dog Green and did so until 12:50 p.m. She expended forty-seven rounds of 5-inch projectiles with indeterminate results. She then remained on position to resume fire as needed.[29]

The USS *McCook* (DD 496), a Gleaves-class destroyer with five 5-inch (127-mm) DP guns in the vicinity of Dog Green at a distance of thirteen hundred yards, placed the D-1 exit under fire at 12:17 p.m. She moved there from the Colleville area. The targets included numerous houses and emplacements in the gulley (draw) leading from the beach toward the Vierville church. The *McCook* destroyed six houses, including one three-story one, in addition to a stone wall that hid snipers and beach gun positions. They expended 131 5-inch/38-caliber projectiles by the time they ceased fire at 12:50 p.m.[30]

The USS *Carmick* (DD 493), a Gleaves-class destroyer with five 5-inch (127-mm) DP guns, spent the morning off the D-1 exit. From H-Hour until noon, most of her targets were on Dog and Charlie Beaches. *Carmick* developed an impromptu arrangement with the American tanks whereby, whenever a tank fired upon a German target on the bluff, the destroyer opened up and let them have it. The destroyer spent the morning trying to locate the German artillery positions in the bluffs and firing upon anything suspicious. The After Action Report stated,

"Exit D-1 seemed to be particularly well protected by the Germans and in spite of frequent poundings by this and other destroyers, no troops seemed able to get through. One tank approached from the left and then seemed stopped by fire from what appeared to be a culvert or a pill box right at the edge of the sea wall. This was taken under fire and although the tank did not proceed, the fire from that particular point was no longer evident." Around noon, the *Carmick* joined the *Texas* and other destroyers to thoroughly shell all buildings at Exit D-1. The stone wall in back of the seawall road was demolished, and all buildings were leveled. (The USS *Carmick* is shown in figure 8.9.)[31]

The venerable USS *Texas* opened fire with her main guns at 12:23 p.m. and fired six high capacity (HC) rounds at Exit D-1 MGRS 645917, targeting an enemy mortar battery behind a hedge and wall. The heavy fire neutralized the battery and scattered the personnel, as reported by the foretop spot. To spot by foretop is to rely on the lookouts posted in the crow's nest in the uppermost mast of a warship. She opened up with her secondary guns and placed seven HC rounds at MGRS 664905 from 12:31 until 12:35 p.m. She closed to the point-blank range of three thousand yards to bombard the shore. The target was the D-1 exit mortar battery firing and snipers taking cover in a house (as illustrated in the navy photo in figure 8.10). The battleship scored direct hits and silenced the enemy guns.[32]

Figure 8.9. USS *Carmick* (DD 493), one of the several Gleaves-class destroyers engaged along Omaha Beach (U.S. Navy).

Figure 8.10. Image of the Vierville draw (Exit D-1), time unknown. This position fell under bombardment from 12:23 to 12:35 p.m. by the ten primary 14-inch and twenty-one secondary 5-inch gun batteries of the USS *Texas* while she was only three thousand yards from shore (USS *Texas* After Action Report) (NARA). General Cota was at the head of the draw, headed to the beach at that point, purposefully headed directly toward the naval bombardment (U.S. Navy).

The USS *Texas* (BB-35) was a *New York*–class battleship, a true dreadnought battleship and a veteran of both world wars (as shown in figure 8.11). She was launched on May 18, 1912, and served with distinction wherever she was called. She had ten Mark 12 14-inch (35.6-cm)/45-caliber guns as her primary battery weapons and six 5-inch/51-caliber guns as her secondary battery, along with miscellaneous other weapons, such as ten 3-inch/50-caliber antiaircraft guns and fourteen 20-mm (0.79-inch) Oerlikon cannons. Her 14-inch guns had chromium plating, enabling the guns to fire fifteen-hundred-pound shells, and increased the gun mount to fire at an elevation of 30° with an extended range of thirty-six thousand yards. The barrel length was 52 feet, 6 inches. The rate of fire was 1.25–1.75 rounds per minute. Her guns' muzzle velocity was 2,735 feet per second using HC shells. The velocity of the shells was 2.4 times the speed of sound. These HC shells were thin-walled bombardment projectiles, developed in World War II for blast and fragmentation

Figure 8.11. The USS *Texas* (BB-35) *New York*–class battleship (U.S. Navy).

effect against unarmored or lightly protected targets. By D-Day, the *Texas* was using HC Mark 19 shells weighing 1,125 pounds (510 kilograms) with 124.21 pounds of Explosive D (ammonium picrate). Explosive D is the standard main charge for armor-piercing bombs and projectiles and other navy projectiles.[33]

Her primary task on D-Day was to provide shore bombardment and fire support for the amphibious landings. The naval guns supplied heavy firepower in support of landing forces while they landed their own artillery support. The *Texas* turned her guns against stubborn shore installations and provided much-needed support of invading infantry throughout the landing. American naval vessels were capable of bringing fire from their various weapons to within 110 yards (100 meters) of friendly troops.[34] Specific to the *Texas*, her main guns could penetrate 11.9-inch (302-mm) steel armor at 12,000 yards; at a range of 6,500 yards, she could penetrate 19-inch (483-mm) steel armor.

As a comparative example of the destructive power of a World War II battleship, America's then newer *Iowa*-class battleships, with their 16-inch guns, were capable of firing 16-inch (406-mm) armor-piercing shells that could penetrate thirty feet (nine meters) of reinforced concrete. The USS *Iowa*, firing with a full propellant charge (six bags) of nitro powder, fired her shells at over twice the speed of sound and delivered a kinetic energy of 355.6 megajoules, or the equivalent power of a one-megawatt nuclear reactor's output over six minutes. The shell of a battleship could easily vaporize a tank and its occupants. Tank shells of the day delivered a kinetic energy of 12.5 megajoules. The battleship, any battleship, provided sheer, brute kinetic energy to its targets and victims.

For a Mark 3 16-inch naval round containing 57.5 pounds of Explosive D, the blast radius—the radius at which the blast wave itself will inflict casualties—was 193 feet. The ears are one of the body parts most vulnerable to this. The hazardous fragmentation radius is 614 feet and is defined by the radius that can reasonably be expected to inflict casualties. The maximum fragmentation radius was 3,770 feet, defined by the distance at which a person is most likely safe from injury. The shells fired by the *Texas* were more powerful, even though smaller in diameter, as they contained double the explosive weight. According to army records, the 14-inch-diameter case/shell had a maximum fragment distance equal to 5,170 feet.

When a 14-inch naval battleship shell reached its target, it created extreme amounts of force from a physics perspective. These weapons were designed to engage and destroy heavily armored enemy combatant vessels at sea with armor more than one to two feet thick. Several physical forces were unleashed by a round striking the target and detonating. The first of these is kinetic energy measured by the equation

$$E = \tfrac{1}{2}mv^2$$

where E equals energy measured in joules, m equals the mass of the object (shell) measured in pounds, and v equals the velocity of the object measured in feet per second. In the case of an HC shell fired from the *Texas*, the kinetic energy of the round was 3,802,500,000 joules. This amount can be converted to 3,802 megajoules, 3,802,500 kilojoules, 2,804,580,072 foot-pounds, or an equivalent 0.0009088 kilotons of TNT per shot. This is a big number. Today, evidence of the force and capability of this type of bombardment remains visible at Pointe du Hoc in the craters at the site.

Today's military and world community have done great work at identifying the effects of explosive blasts, weapons characteristics, and their effects on humans. Accordingly, the concept of close-in support for ground troops, developed during World War II, has matured and is still used today by ground forces. The army uses the term "danger close" when troops work around naval gunfire, artillery support, or airpower: "In a danger close situation, the fires may be crept to within minimum safe distance of friendly positions. Recommended minimum safe distance for an adjusted salvo of a 5-inch gun is 200 meters when firing parallel to the front lines, or 350 meters when not firing parallel to the front line. The ship normally advises the observer when a predicted fall of shot approaches minimum safe distance." Other elements to be concerned with include overpressure or blast overpressure. This is the shock wave or pressure exerted above normal atmospheric pressure. It can be born of a sonic boom or an explosion. In measuring overpressure, two pounds per square inch (14 kPa) can collapse residential structures, destroy brick walls, and cause injury. When the overpressure reaches four pounds per square inch (28 kPa), most buildings, except concrete buildings, collapse. Injuries and fatalities become universal among those present. When the force reaches ten pounds per square inch (69 kPa), reinforced concrete buildings are severely damaged, humans experience severe heart and lung damage, and limbs can be blown off. Fatalities are common among those present.[35]

Explosive munitions impacts can be broken into damage mechanisms and their effects—namely, primary, secondary, and tertiary. A primary effect of explosive weapons is caused by the destructive effects that radiate from the point of initiation (impact). These include blast overpressure, fragmentation, heat, and light. The blast is defined by the high-pressure wave that moves at supersonic speed, called a shock wave. The secondary fragmentation is released as a result of the exploding device and from destroyed items in the immediate vicinity of the blast. The thermal and light energy are limited to the immediate vicinity of the blast in a conventional explosion. Ground shock results from explosive energy imparted into the ground by the shock wave caused by the explosion and is what caused the ground in Vierville to heave a reported two to three feet. It poses threat to the structural integrity of buildings and can affect humans. The blast may cause injuries from the rapid compression and resulting expansion of gases in hollow organs such as the gastrointestinal tract, lungs, or ears. The blast overpressure can damage these by bruising, tearing, and puncturing the organ walls. The pressure wave can rupture the eardrum and fracture the inner ear bones.

The army established a minimum safe distance of five hundred meters when fighting around 155-mm (6-inch) naval gunfire or 5-inch gunfire. Keep in mind that multiple U.S. destroyers also engaged the D-1 exit concurrent with the *Texas* with their primary 5-inch guns, with each vessel firing approximately one hundred rounds over the half hour.[36] The United States Marine Corps defined "risk-estimate distances" for combat use and developed tables for each type of weapon used on the modern battlefield. Among these are an estimate for a Mark 83 one-thousand-pound bomb. This weapon has an approximate equivalent force to a 14-inch shell used on D-Day. The risk estimate distance is one thousand meters and a zone with a 10 percent probability-of-incapacitation distance of 475 meters.[37] The Marine Corps defined its criteria using the assumption that the soldier is lying in the prone position during the explosion. The bottom line was that anyone within 520 yards (475 meters) of the point of impact of the weapons being unleashed on the D-1 exit between 12 and 12:30 p.m. was in imminent mortal danger.

Account of the actions taken by Brigadier General Norman D. Cota on June 6, 1944—D-Day for the Invasion of Europe (dated June 16, 1944)
Returning to Vierville Sur Mere, he observed that no engineer demolition work was being done in the beach exit. He with a party of four additional men, including Major Olson, two enlisted men and another officer, made his way down to the beach through the Vierville Sur Mere beach exit. This patrol was accomplished in the fire of Heavy Naval Guns from about 800 yards offshore, since the Navy was trying to Neutralize strong cannon positions at beach level at the exit. Five prisoners were driven from the fortifications at this point by this patrol and taken to the beach.[38]

When asked by Lieutenant Shea around the noon hour at Vierville, Morse and his men stated, "Cota had been back near the crossroad, Morse evidently had seen him in passing, but met him as Cota came towards the head of the column to see what was holding it up." Lieutenant Morse recounted the naval fire that came in at about noon at Vierville. He reported that the fire came in after Colonel Canham reached the crossroad. Without the knowledge of what vessels were actually engaged, Morse stated, "The cruiser guns were battling the defenses at the mouth of the Vierville exit, and some of the heavy fragments were blasting up over the Vierville crossroads. A couple of 'overs' made the roadway heave and crack a little. The group recalled this naval fire, [and] said they had gone past the crossroads when it started to come into the area in volume."[39] Lieutenant Shea reported that the "concussion from the bursts of those guns had seemed to make the pavement of the street in VIERVILLE actually raise beneath our feet in a 'bucking' sensation, had knocked several regimental group off their feet as they passed the crossroad above the exit."

It was now shortly after 12 p.m., and no traffic had been cleared through the Vierville exit. Lieutenant Colonel Harold Cassell had made his way into Vierville toward noon and joined Cota and Colonel Canham at the crossroads. When the navy began shelling the D-1 exit, the blast of the fire knocked down several members of the CP group.[40] Canham and Cassell headed south and established the CP at the Chateau de Vaumicel. Their radios were still unable to contact outside units. Cota, Lieutenant Shea, and an SC300 radio operator left Canham and headed to the crossroads in order to head to the beach to determine the overall situation of the landing and to ascertain why no traffic had been cleared through it.

General Cota's team met with Major Olson, Lieutenant MacAllister, and Captain Bainbridge, and Cota made a remarkable decision under heavy naval fire.[41] His conscious decision without a working means of communication was to head into the zone of active naval bombardment to accomplish the mission of opening the D-1 exit. MacAllister recalled the meeting. He wrote about the event in a letter to General Robert R. Ploger in March 2000:

1st Lieutenant John MacAllister, S-1, 121st Engineer Combat Battalion, 29th Division
Sometime later, Cota (the task force commander) and an infantry rifleman came up. He said, "Good morning Lt., where's the rest of the invading army?" Then noticing the Castle on my collar his next question was "Why has the beach exit not been opened?" When I replied that I didn't know, he said "Well suppose you go find out." I started down the road to the beach and he called "wait, we'll go with you." By the time that Maj. Olson (our Bn. Executive Officer) had joined the group and we all started back to the beach. On the way down, General Cota noticed two German soldiers on the top of the cut and waving his 45 at them said "come on down here, you sons-of-bitches!" which they did, and we took them with us back to the beach. (The prisoners were shot by their own people as we moved through the beach exit to the beach.)[42]

Lieutenant Shea recorded the events in his report. Major Olson said, "I hope they cut out that firing." The valley of the draw was filled with smoke, dust from the shattered concrete, and the acrid tang of cordite from the exploded shells from Vierville to the beach. General Cota responded, "That firing probably made them duck back into their holes. But keep a sharp eye on those cliffs to your right." The patrol experienced a few scattered rounds of small arms fire, but a few dozen rounds of carbine and pistol fire, along with the overpowering show of force of the naval fire, convinced five Germans to surrender and come down from the caverns in the east wall of the draw to the north of the quarry. The surrendering troops were stripped of their weapons as they reached the road and herded before the patrol as it proceeded to the mouth of the draw. The Germans thought they could trick Cota's patrol and said they could use some help to evacuate some twelve wounded *kamerades* lying in the caverns. The general sensed a trap and declined to assist them. Shea reported that fifty-four prisoners were taken from the same cave later on.[43] Shea made a combat drawing of these events and appended it to his November 1944 report (as shown in figure 8.12). The general forced the Germans to lead his patrol the remaining distance to the tank wall at

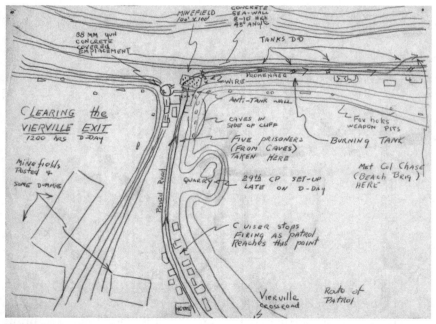

Figure 8.12. Lieutenant Jack Shea's diagram of the clearing of the Vierville exit (Mike White).

WN 72 to show him and his patrol where the mines were located. This effort was successful, as General Cota led the first U.S. forces to breach the seemingly impenetrable German defenses at the D-1 exit.

The After Action Report of the 121st ECB noted the gallantry of the action as related to MacAllister's participation in Cota's patrol, for which he was awarded a Silver Star. The 121st's unit journal noted that the patrol captured five German prisoners during the advance north to the beach. MacAllister's Silver Star citation reads,

The President of the United States of America, authorized by Act of Congress, July 9, 1918, takes pleasure in presenting the Silver Star to First Lieutenant John F. MacAllister (ASN: 0-517515), United States Army, for gallantry in action while serving with the 121st Engineer Combat Battalion, 29th Infantry Division. On 6 June 1944, during the initial assault on the beaches of Northern France, Second Lieutenant MacAllister voluntarily joined a reconnaissance party which entered, from the rear, the heavily defended beach exit at Vierville-sur-Mer to determine the enemy dispositions at that place. Although exposed to enemy observation and fire from fortified positions in the hills overlooking the beach exit, and to friendly naval gunfire which was being directed against the enemy positions at or near this beach exit, this patrol accomplished its mission, obtained much valuable information, and captured prisoners. In his active participation in this successful and hazardous reconnaissance, without regard for his own safety, Second Lieutenant MacAllister demonstrated a high degree of courage which reflected great credit on himself and the Military Service.[44]

General Cota's aide, 1st Lieutenant John "Jack" T. Shea, was also awarded the Silver Star for this event. His citation reads,

The President of the United States of America, authorized by Act of Congress, July 9, 1918, takes pleasure in presenting the Silver Star to First Lieutenant (Infantry) John T. Shea (ASN: 0-445928), United States Army, for gallantry in action while serving with the 29th Infantry Division. On 6 June 1944, during the initial assault on the beaches of Northern France, First Lieutenant Shea voluntarily joined a reconnaissance party which entered, from the rear, the heavily defended beach exit at Vierville-sur-Mer to determine the enemy dispositions at that place. Although exposed to enemy observation and fire from fortified positions in the hills overlooking the beach exit, and to friendly naval gunfire which was being directed against the enemy positions at or near this beach exit, this patrol accomplished its mission, obtained much valuable information, and captured prisoners. In his active participation in this successful and hazardous reconnaissance, without regard for his own safety, First Lieutenant Shea demonstrated a high degree of courage which reflects great credit on himself and the military service.[45]

Major Allan Olson likewise received the Silver Star for this event. His citation reads,

The President of the United States of America, authorized by Act of Congress, July 9, 1918, takes pleasure in presenting the Silver Star to Major (Corps of Engineers) Allan F. Olson (ASN: 0-329631), United States Army, for gallantry in action while serving with the 29th Infantry Division. On 6 June 1944, during the initial assault on the beaches of Northern France, Major Olson voluntarily joined a reconnaissance party which entered, from the rear, the heavily defended beach exit at Vierville-sur-Mer to determine the enemy dispositions at that place. Although exposed to enemy observation and fire from fortified positions in the hills overlooking the beach exit, and to friendly naval gunfire which was being directed against the enemy positions at or near this beach exit, this patrol accomplished its mission, obtained much valuable information, and captured prisoners. In his active participation in this successful and hazardous reconnaissance, without regard for his own safety, Major Olson demonstrated a high degree of courage which reflects great credit on himself and the military service.[46]

On reaching the mouth of the exit, the patrol rounded the corner on the rue de la Mer as it became the promenade. The present-day improved road to the beach was not yet constructed. The road taken was what is now the smaller, eastern one of the modern pair of routes. When the men made it to WN 72, they saw that the antitank wall remained in place. The wall was approximately 125 feet long, 9 feet tall, and 3 feet thick, made of concrete that, it turned out, was not steel reinforced. It was located from the southeast corner of the 88-mm bunker of WN 72 and ran to the southeast, where it tied into the toe of the bluff. There was a man-sized opening in the wall at the wingwall of the firing port of the bunker. This is the location of the present-day National Guard of the United States Monument. The wall would have been partially obscured from view out to sea. Cota's group found a fifty-square-foot minefield in their path. Based on his uniform, one of the prisoners was believed to have been a member of the static coastal defense force; he was forced to go through the minefield first, and the patrol and other prisoners followed exactly in his footsteps. Although there was barbed wire in the area, the group made it through without having to use wire cutters. Lieutenant Shea recalled the ghastly site that greeted them as they made it through to the promenade and gained full view of the miles of beach splayed before them as they began to move to the east: "Bodies of riflemen, obviously from the 116th Infantry by the insignia they wore, were spread along the base of the concrete, inclined seawall. The first body lay about forty yards east of the exit, and in any 100 yard sector from there down to Dog White Beach, there could be found 35–50 bodies. The math estimate on this adds up to approximately 1,000 dead along the beachhead." This scene is illustrated in figure 8.13. The

Figure 8.13. American dead on beach between D-1 and D-3 exits after battle (NARA).

sacrifice of the men of the 29th Infantry Division and other first-wave units came into laser focus for General Cota and his party.[47] To put this loss in some context, the 1st Battalion, 116th RCT, went in with forty-six officers on D-Day. At the end of the day, twenty-four of them were killed, wounded, or missing.[48] Company A lost nearly 90 percent of its numbers as casualties on Dog Green. It was now about 1 p.m. General Cota had at this point traveled three miles under intense enemy fire and had positively influenced and affected the outcome of the battle for Omaha Beach. He had fourteen miles to go.

CHAPTER NINE

Seventeen Miles

From *Omaha Beachhead*: "The general saw little activity on the beach flat at D-1. The only infantry nearby were the exhausted remnants of Company A, 116th."[1] At 11 a.m., the weather changed, and the sun appeared overhead through the clouds for the first time since dawn. At 11:31 a.m., General Cota made a command decision via radio message under fire to send the 115th Regimental Combat Team (RCT) in on Easy Red to reinforce the 16th Infantry and clear the high ground southwest of Easy Red.[2] Cota's efforts demonstrated the true, dire magnitude of the situation for the invaders.

> *In the early afternoon, destroyers continued their work of knocking out enemy gun emplacements along the beach front. The strongpoint guarding the Vierville draw was silenced by 1300; somewhat later, the dangerous flanking positions near Pointe de la Percee were literally blown off the face of the cliff. These actions greatly helped the situation on the beach, but by no means ended all enemy opposition. Though the most dangerous enemy guns were now neutralized and some emplacements were surrendered without a fight, there was still enough resistance to block three of the main exits. The Vierville draw, as General Cota's trip through it showed, was ready for opening, but there was not enough force at hand for systematic mopping-up of the weakened positions.[3]*

Without knowing that from the USS *Ancon* they had just witnessed the direct actions of General Cota on the beach and the influence of his leadership, Headquarters, 1st Infantry Division, recorded, "From Dog

Green Control Vessel to Gen. Huebner: We can see POWs being taken from pillbox that was blocking Exit Dog One."[4] It was General Cota's gallantry that enabled prisoners to be taken after the punishing naval barrage. What soldier in his right mind, German or American, would expect a brigadier general with a small patrol of high-ranking officers to emerge from the rear of the maw of the smoke and confusion caused by the four destroyers and USS *Texas*, literally moments after their fire lifted, and to personally capture five prisoners from WN 72 armed with a handgun? It is entirely reasonable to consider that the soldiers on the USS *Ancon* actually witnessed Cota's party through their binoculars and scopes as they recorded that message without realizing they were seeing General Cota.

General Cota realized the need to firmly establish command and control over the chaos following the landing to this point. He determined to make contact with the 1st Infantry Division to the east. He had not had word of the division and also needed to know how the 2d Battalion, 29th Infantry Division, was doing at present. He was convinced that the D-1 draw was in good hands for the time being with leaders like Colonel Charles Canham and Lieutenant Colonel Max Schneider in the fight. The Germans at WN 71, WN 72, and WN 70 were effectively neutralized. WN 74 was under fire by the navy, and Company C, 2d Rangers, was on the bluffs in that vicinity assaulting WN 73. There were still isolated German riflemen and snipers along the bluffs of Dog Green and Dog White, but the remnants of 1st Battalion of the 29ers and the 5th Rangers continued their deadly work along the bluffs here. The real fight at the moment in this sector was south and west of Vierville and was attended to appropriately. With that, Cota continued east along the promenade under fire to locate Brigadier General Willard G. Wyman, assistant division commander of the 1st Infantry Division. Figure 9.1 is a photo of the promenade taken in the following days. Before General Cota made his way to the east, the D-3 exit was as hotly contested as the D-1 exit. The D-3 exit was so well defended, in fact, that the Germans there would hold out until the next day.

Cota knew the mission. He knew the stakes. He was witness to the lack of mission success. He moved throughout the battlefield from situation to situation with a purpose. He went where he was needed most

Figure 9.1. Photo of promenade from vicinity of Dog Red looking west, showing Cota's route under fire (National Archives and Records Administration [NARA]).

at the time to effect change. Pursuant to Field Order #35, the mission of the 1st Infantry Division, less RCT 26, with RCT 116 and other troops attached, was to make the initial assault on Beach Omaha at H-Hour on D-Day with two RCTs abreast, reduce the beach defenses in its zone of action, secure the beachhead maintenance line, and secure the D-Day phase line by two hours before dark on D-Day. They were to cover the landing of the remainder of V Corps and be prepared to participate in the extension of the beachhead to the south and southwest.[5] General Cota's responsibilities stemmed from this master mission statement. By 1 p.m., by his actions, he ensured that the beachhead had at least a fighting chance of becoming secured from the utter chaos he found at 7:26 a.m. when he landed.

As he moved through the battlefield, he had the mission of the 116 RCT (Reinforced) on his mind as well, since he was the commander ashore. The 116th's mission included landing the battalion landing teams, the 116th Combat Team and one company of the 2d Ranger Battalion, simultaneously at H-Hour, D-Day, on Omaha, Easy Green, Dog Red, Dog White, and Dog Green Beaches, as well as three companies of the 2d Ranger Battalion on Baker and Charlie Beaches, with the Reserve Battalion, 116th Combat Team, and the balance of the Ranger force to follow as directed by the combat team commander. This was done. The next part of the mission was to reduce beach defenses in the 116th's zone of action, seize and secure that portion of the beachhead maintenance line in its zone of action, capture Pointe du Hoc, and seize and secure that portion of the D-Day phase line in its zone of action by two hours before dark on D-Day. Cota knew that this was at risk of failure and acted to ensure success by any means necessary. He often told his grandson in his later years that he didn't expect to survive the day on D-Day.

Subsequent to these primary missions above, the 116th RCT—and General Cota specifically—was to gain and maintain contact with the 16th Combat Team on the left and for Cota to physically report to General Wyman, to whom General Cota was subordinate on D-Day through D+1 at the D-3 St. Laurent exit. In making contact with Wyman, Cota would have means to gain and maintain contact with U.S. VII Corps on the right at the earliest possible time. Many radios were lost by this point, which hindered communications. Cota's men were then to capture Isigny, organize it for all-around defense, and protect bridges in the vicinity. The 116th RCT was to patrol to the D+1 phase line within its zone of action. These orders are further described in the Operation Neptune Operations Overlay, Annex 1, of Field Order #35.

Subordinate to Cota during D-Day was the Ranger Force, split into three groups. They were able to successfully follow their orders to this point in time. Force A under Lieutenant Colonel James Rudder, commanding officer (CO), along with 2d Ranger Battalion, Companies D, E, and F and half of Company Headquarters, landed at H-Hour, D-Day, at Pointe du Hoc and destroyed enemy installations there and in the surrounding vicinity. Rudder and his men were among the first U.S. forces to accomplish their primary D-Day objective with the destruction of the 155-mm guns they found one mile inland after the Germans relocated them to avoid preinvasion aerial bombardment. Rudder's orders called for him to be prepared to repel hostile counterattack and assist the advance of the remainder of the Ranger Force and 116th Infantry. General Cota did not know of the success or failure of Rudder's men at present. Force B, commanded by Captain Ralph Goranson, CO, landed on Charlie Beach with Company C, 2d Ranger Battalion, and scaled the cliffs to Cota's back at this moment and continued to remain actively engaged with the Germans on the bluff at WN 73 as Cota made his way through the tank wall. Goranson's men were ordered to take out WN 73 and WN 74 at Pointe et Raz de la Percée and then continue west to Rudder. Cota knew these Rangers were up the bluff but likely did not know of the carnage they suffered thus far. Force C, under Lieutenant Colonel Max Schneider, CO, along with the 5th Ranger Infantry Battalion and Companies A, B, and C and the other half of Headquarters Company, 2d Ranger Infantry Battalion, served as the force multiplier Cota relied on with Company C of the 116th RCT in Vierville and the surrounding fields. Up to the point when Cota changed their orders through Colonel Canham, Schneider and his men had the mission to pass through elements of the 116th Combat Team under cover of coastal ridges and proceed rapidly via Château d'Englesqueville to Pointe du Hoc, where they were to relieve Rudder. They were then to assist the right battalion landing team, 116th Infantry, in the reduction of the hostile fortifications along the coast between Pointe du Hoc and Isigny and in the capture of Isigny. Major General John C. Raaen Jr. contends that, among his other notable accomplishments, Cota's "decision to hold Ranger Forces B and C in the night time defenses of the beachhead, probably saved the Omaha Dog beachhead."

Cota was well aware that the right battalion landing team, 116th Combat Team, was to land at H-Hour on Beach Omaha, Dog Green, reduce the beach defenses in its zone of action, capture Vierville-sur-Mer, and assist the Ranger Force in the capture of the fortifications along the coast from the western limits of Beach Omaha, Dog Green, to Pointe du Hoc. After the capture of Pointe du Hoc, they were to join with the Rangers and reduce the hostile fortifications along the coast between Pointe du Hoc and Isigny and be prepared to seize and secure Isigny. The left battalion landing team, 116th Combat Team, was ordered to land at H-Hour on Beach Omaha, Easy Green, Dog Red, and Dog White, reduce beach defenses in its zone of action, capture Saint-Laurent-sur-Mer and the high ground (beachhead maintenance line) twenty-five hundred yards southwest of Saint-Laurent-sur-Mer, and establish company strongpoints, prepare for all-around defense, and prepare to augment the defense by use of Duplex Drive tanks and elements of the Engineer Special Brigade moving into semiprepared positions between company strongpoints. These men were then to patrol to the inundated areas on the south and to Longueville on the west.[6]

These missions all hung in the balance at this very moment. Cota knew it. Generals Wyman, Clarence Huebner, Charles Gerhardt, Leonard Gerow, and Omar Bradley all knew it. To make matters worse, most of these leaders had no full and proper lines of communications established yet to manage the battle unfolding before them. For Cota's part, he knew he had to continue to aggressively employ the "fire and movement" tactics that he had mastered and taught to the thousands of Allies who trained under him before D-Day in England. This was the only path before him as he witnessed the utter destruction on the beach shown in figures 9.2 and 9.3. He had to advance. He had to carry the fight.

There were no tanks near the tank wall at Exit D-1, and this fact concerned Cota greatly. He knew the importance of clearing the armor and vehicles off the beach as quickly as possible. The tanks, in conjunction with the engineers, were tasked by the Neptune plan with blowing up the wall and proceeding to Vierville. The nearest tanks to WN 72 were DD tanks of Company B, 743d Tank Battalion. Cota's patrol observed they were parked on the promenade at about 80-yard intervals, with the closest units 150–200 yards to the east, and at least two tanks were burning hulks. As the patrol moved to the east, it began to draw scattered German rifle fire from the bluffs above. Cota and his men ran to the tanks and then rushed from tank to tank for cover to avoid getting hit. They turned their five prisoners over to a rifleman at the first tank.[7]

The bluffs were denuded of vegetation; the acrid stink of battle, including the exhaust of diesel engines and the smell of cordite and other explosives, hung in the air. Add to this the stench of tens of thousands of dead fish and of the exposed entrails of wounded, burned, and vaporized

Figure 9.2. Scene on Omaha Beach during the afternoon of June 6, 1944 (NARA).

Figure 9.3. Wreckage of men and equipment along Omaha Beach (NARA).

men. The sounds of the battle raged all around. The water of the shore ran red with the precious blood of these honored casualties.

Private Hal Baumgarten, Company B, 116th RCT, one of the few survivors of Dog Green, became a reliable witness to the events of D-Day. During an interview for Alex Kershaw's *The Bedford Boys*,[8] he gave an account of his interaction with Cota on the beach. Baumgarten would never forget seeing Cota's rangy figure approach him that morning. It was as if he were immortal; from the outset, officers had been first to be picked off by snipers. "He was coming from the west with a major, had a pistol in one hand, and the fellows were all yelling for him to get down. He looked very similar to the actor Robert Mitchum with his slanted eyebrows. He was very, very brave." Baumgarten became a doctor after the war and produced a book, *D-Day Survivor: An Autobiography*.[9] In it, he provided additional details surrounding this event, allowing him to be placed in the story in the context of Cota's movements.

> *About 11:00 A.M. [corrected to after 1 p.m. based on other records and accounts], Brig. Gen. Norman D. Cota, with a pistol in his hand, came running up our beach from the west. He was accompanied by a major I didn't recognize [Major Allan Olson, 121st Engineer Combat Battalion (ECB)]. I couldn't talk due to my face wound, but some of the guys called to him to get down. It was reassuring to us to see this brave man on the beach, disregarding the snipers. We were advised that the only ones who were going to remain on the beach "were the dead, and those who were going to die." The call was "Twenty-nine, let's go," and we went.*

A few hours later, after a tank blew up near D-1, as he recalled, Baumgarten ascended the bluff with eleven other walking-wounded soldiers and ended up on the western outskirts of Vierville. Back on the beach remained the carnage of the dead, dying, and wounded, along with the tangled mass of wrecked German defenses, vehicles, and equipment.

General Cota's party discovered that Company B, 743d Tank Battalion, had landed on the left flank and Company C on the right flank of the 116th RCT's beach. The tanks that landed after them were the DD tanks of Company A. Four of the five officers of Company B were killed in action before leaving the beach. Captain Charles Emkha and his tank crew were hit by 88-mm fire while disembarking from the LCT (Landing Craft, Tank) 250 yards offshore. This fire caused the driver, T/4 Lockey, to lose a leg. When Lockey and Emkha tried to swim ashore, they drowned. Other tankers, including Lieutenant Gilbert Allis, the liaison field officer with 1st Battalion, 116th Infantry; 1st Lieutenant Turner; and 2d Lieutenant Hodgson, were killed on the beach by machine-gun fire.[10]

Along the base of the bluff, an aid station was established and served as the temporary waypoint of a cluster of Rangers and dozens of badly wounded and exhausted survivors of Companies A and B, 116th RCT.[11] (A representative army aid station photo from Omaha Beach is shown in figure 9.4.) Cota and his party discovered about seventy men were gathered in shelter provided by the first remaining villa, located directly east down the promenade from the exit to the south of the promenade.

Figure 9.4. Wounded soldiers, Normandy, Omaha Beach, June 6, 1944, D-Day (NARA).

These men shouted warnings of "Sniper! Sniper!" to the patrol. Lieutenant Jack Shea recorded in his report,

> *General Cota informed them that we had troops up behind the bluffs in Vierville, that they should start cleaning-up the snipers. At this point, their attention was momentarily drawn to an action on the crest of the bluffs. American riflemen were closing in on a foxhole where a single German rifleman was emplaced. As they reached a point about 30 yards away from him, he rose out of the hole and hurled a stick grenade at them. They hit the ground, waited for it to explode, then closed in and killed him.*[12]

Cota knew the destruction of the tank wall at the D-1 draw was the most important task of the moment. General Cota then released Major Olson and 1st Lieutenant John F. MacAllister and told them to find and organize some of their engineers to accomplish this vital mission. The tanks, artillery, and other vehicles had to clear off the beach and join the real fight waiting up the bluffs in the Norman fields and towns. Then Cota turned to meet Colonel Lucius Chase, CO, 6th Engineer Special Brigade, about five hundred yards east of the Vierville exit. Lieutenant Colonel Chase became CO on the morning of D-Day when Colonel Paul Thompson was wounded and evacuated. Cota asked the colonel whether he could blow up that antitank wall at the exit. Lieutenant Shea captured the conversation:

> *Col Chase responded "We can, sir, just as soon as the infantry clean out those pillboxes around there." General Cota replied that they had just come through there and to "Get to it!" Col Chase told Cota that the men had no TNT for the job. General Cota pointed to a bulldozer with 20 cases of TNT lashed to its top. "Use that," Cota responded and turned to continue down the beach to the east.*[13]

According to the After Action Report of the 121st ECB, an estimated 50 percent of the initial force of the 121st ECB became casualties, and 75 percent of their equipment was lost. Captain Holmstrup, CO, Company C, was killed exiting his landing craft. In all, they suffered two officers and thirty enlisted men killed in action, one officer and sixty-five enlisted men missing in action, and six officers and fifty-six enlisted men wounded in action. "The wall blocking the beach exit D-1 was breached with an external charge of 1100 lbs of TNT. . . . Company 'B' remained on the beach to complete opening of the beach exit and to clear the road to Vierville-sur-Mer. These missions were accomplished by 062100 B hours [June 6 at 9 p.m.]."[14] The records of the 5th Engineer Special Brigade support the evidence of the timing and importance of the destruction of the tank wall. "Germans continued to infiltrate into the town [Vierville] throughout D-Day and D+1, delaying the complete opening of Exit D-1, although tanks were able to use the road from time to time beginning at 1400."[15] The June 30, 1944, 121st Engineer Combat Battalion unit journal entry for June 6 reported that Lieutenant Colonel Robert Ploger joined the efforts at the tank wall at the D-1 draw at 2 p.m. This was after Lieutenant Colonel Chase's meeting with Cota.

The 121st ECB prepared a document titled "Unit Report No. 1— June 5–8," dated June 8, 1944. It stated that the 2d and 3d Platoons of Company C landed at H+240 minutes. Companies were reorganized, and Company B with 2d Platoon, Company C, were given the mission of clearing the D-1 beach exit. Work was halted on the beach exit because of naval fire and small arms fire from snipers located on high ground to the rear of the beach. Combat groups were sent up to get the snipers and were fired on by the navy, a base of fire was organized, and the preparation of the wall for demolition was started with 1,150 pounds of TNT used to open up a fifteen-foot-wide gap in the wall. Twenty-five yards of barbed wire were likewise blown by Bangalore torpedoes during this time.[16]

This record further documents the results of Cota's leadership of the demoralized and disorganized units as he came upon them under fire after his trip through the draw. The basic enlisted combat engineers may or may not have noticed Cota's influence on their actions as they were quite busy before he arrived. Many of the survivors here could previously do little more than remain in the cold 56°F water as the tide advanced. Cota's influencing actions were focused on exhorting the likes of Major Olson, Lieutenant Colonel Ploger, and Lieutenant Colonel Chase to take charge and to lead their men—many of whom had been there under the most murderous fire anywhere on any beach on D-Day since

6:30 a.m.—to victory in their task of clearing the antitank obstacles and opening the roads leading from the beach. With his unflinching attitude under fire, again he inspired the men around him to action, in this, the Dog Green Sector.

Shea reported that General Cota next met up with Major William Bratton, acting G-2, 29th Infantry. "The Major reported to General Cota; 'Damn it, I can't get these people to move,' he said, gesturing towards the troops on the ground. 'They just stay here on the beach.' Cota called a young infantry captain over and told him to organize the troops stalled there, ascend the bluffs in front of him and clean out the remaining riflemen. The captain saluted, hurried off to the task."[17] On June 17, Major Bratton was interviewed regarding his experience on D-Day. He recalled the perils of his landing and eventual meeting with Cota. He credited Cota with leading the scared, immobilized men to action beyond their paralyzing fear.

Major William Bratton, acting G-2, 29th Infantry
29th Division Hq, landed on the Omaha Beach in three echelons, plus a very small group headed by Brig. Gen. Cota. Cota's group preceded all the others. In fact, Cota was the first U.S. General Officer to land in France. The Advance echelon itself, headed by Maj. Sewell S. Watts (Asst G-3), was the party that Bratton came in with, and it arrived H+220 min. It was supposed to come in at the exit to Vierville; but fortunately, the coxswain brought them in at least 1 mile east of this point. It was fortunate because enemy fire in the Vierville sector was heavy at this time, and at the actual point of landing no opposition was encountered. As Bratton worked west on the beach, trying to get to where his party was supposed to have landed (they seem to have lost contact among themselves), he found hundreds of men lying down on the beach, immobilized by fear of snipers. However, Bratton continued westward and after about two hours he reached the Vierville Sector. After a while he located General Cota, and together they went eastward on the beach. As he went along, Cota organized the scared, immobilized men on the beaches.[18]

As Cota continued east on the promenade, he came to a second engineer bulldozer laden with cases of TNT. Cota went up to a group of troops huddled behind the seawall near it. "Who drives this thing?" he asked the group. No one answered. No one seemed to know. They just looked around at each other. "Well can anyone drive this damn thing?" Again there was no answer. "They need the TNT down at the exit. I just came down through the exit from the rear. Nothing but a few riflemen on the cliff, and they're being cleaned up. Hasn't anyone got guts enough to drive it down?" A red-haired soldier came out of the group and said he'd get it down there. Cota slapped him on the back and sent him off with a hearty "That's the stuff!" It was about 1:30 p.m. Lieutenant Shea wrote that the general remarked to him that he wished he had gotten that soldier's name to put him in for a citation. The 121st had its work cut out for it for sure, as noted in *Omaha Beachhead*:

> *The 121st Engineer Combat Battalion, responsible for [clearing] the D-1 exit, had experienced the usual troubles in landing; its units were scattered as far as Les Moulins, 75 percent of its equipment had been lost in landing, and personnel losses had run high. The battalion officers had spent several hours collecting their men, and salvaging explosives and equipment along the beach. The work of reorganization was made difficult by scattered fire from snipers along the bluff, and small combat patrols were used in an attempt to clean out bluff positions. One of the patrols entered the Hamel-au-Pretre strongpoint and found it wrecked by naval fire and almost abandoned. However, here and at the Vierville draw, long connecting tunnels, some of them going as far inland as the village, afforded a shelter for the enemy and made a quick clean-up of the fortifications impossible.*[19]

An official account of Cota's actions on D-Day by the 29th Infantry Division, dated June 14, 1944, stated, "There General Cota, though under constant sniper and machine gun fire from the high ground beyond the beach, progressed Eastward along the beach herding and hastily reorganizing tank units, engineer demolition units, supplies of demolitions, bulldozers, and in general directing units suffering from the initial confusion of landing under fire so that their efforts could be effectively bent toward the establishment of the beachhead."[20]

Jonathan Gawne's *Spearheading D-Day: American Special Units in Normandy* gives an account of the destruction of the tank wall that provides additional filling details. Sergeant Noel Dube, squad leader, 9th Squad, C Company, 121st ECB, was assigned to move up the draw into a field near Vierville. He originally landed far to the left of the D-1 exit and spent hours traversing the beach to his objective. When he arrived on scene, he recalled that either Major Olson or Colonel Ploger told him, "Sergeant, we need you to blow this wall. Go reconnoiter the other side and make sure it's safe to blow." He carried out his orders with Frank Wood and another man from C Company, 121st ECB, and they moved halfway up the draw to check for friendlies. They observed none but reported Germans on the bluffs above them. When they returned, they found that two bulldozers laden with ten cases of TNT each had joined the growing effort at the wall. The dozer drivers were identified as Joe Drago and Al Velleco, with one of these likely the redhead mentioned by Shea. The engineers first used Bangalore torpedoes to clear the road of the barbed wire and then used the first ten cases on the first half of the tank wall. The cases were arranged with four along the ground and three additional cases stacked high on the two end boxes for a U-shaped charge. The resulting blast cleared not only the first half of the wall but the entire thing, as it did not have reinforcing steel.[21] These additional details provided by Gawne, another independent researcher, aid in clarifying the story as the puzzle comes together. Photos of the tank wall location and results of its destruction are shown in figures 9.5 and 9.6.

Figure 9.5. WN 72 promenade area showing previous location of tank wall looking west (NARA).

Figure 9.6. WN 72 promenade area showing previous location of tank wall looking east (NARA).

Enemy artillery continued to strike the beach with regularity as of 1:30 p.m. It came at approximately ten-second intervals, and one could hear the shells whistling before taking cover and hitting the dirt. (An illustrative photo of this type of artillery fire from Utah Beach is shown in figure 9.7.) According to Shea, "Judging from the burst, the whining noise, and the craters left in the sand, it seemed that it was the fire of 155 mm or similar medium artillery." With the defenses of the D-1 draw tank wall finally breached, now maybe the armor and artillery had a chance at getting off the beach and joining the fight on western Omaha Beach. This was a critical factor to the overall success of the day. Without the opening, the armor and all other vehicles on the beach were sitting ducks for German artillery, which was still a potent and active factor.[22] At 1:41 p.m., the navy contacted Major General Huebner to report that Beaches Dog Green, White, and Red were entirely clear of opposition and ready for landing troops.[23]

From the tank wall at the D-1 exit, General Cota traveled over 1.5 miles eastward along the coastal promenade from the Vierville exit to a position beyond the Les Moulins draw while under enemy observation and fire, as the Germans still had machine guns, snipers, and riflemen at various locations along the bluff. The German artillery fire remained thick along the beach during his journey. Of importance, he traveled past the mouth of the D-3 exit, which was still under German management. He did so in the face of direct enemy fire from defensive positions at WN 66 and WN 68 at the mouth of the draw and from

Figure 9.7. D-Day photo from Utah Beach exemplifying enemy artillery strike on beaches (NARA).

WN 67 and WN 69 at the head of the draw with firing solutions at the beach. He arrived at the next location he needed to reach: the D-3 exit and the battle for Les Moulins and St. Laurent. He was now also in the vicinity of Brigadier General Wyman, and this close proximity allowed

246

him to complete one of his many important D-Day orders: namely, to make contact with the 1st Infantry Division to the left of the 116th RCT. He had now tactically traversed a total of 4.4 miles under intense enemy fire since his arrival ashore.

When Major Bratton came ashore on Easy Green Beach at H+220, he was accompanied by the remainder of the 29th Division's Advance Headquarters. This included Lieutenant Colonel William T. Terry, division transport quartermaster; Major Sewell S. Watts Jr., antitank officer; Lieutenant Colonel Stanley W. Phillips, assistant chief of staff (G-4); Major Gerald LeGrippo, surgeon; Captain Harry L. Yerby, 29th divisional artillery representative; Lieutenant Colonel Murray A. Little, assistant division signal officer; Lieutenant Hilderbrandt, Signal Company, 29th Division; Lieutenant Beatty, Headquarters Company, 29th Division; Major Stanley M. Bach, liaison officer between Cota's headquarters and the 1st Infantry Division; and various enlisted men from both the Signal Company and Division Headquarters. They touched down at a location approximately five hundred yards east of the D-3 exit concurrently with two LCTs of the 58th Armored Field Artillery Battalion (FA-Bn). The LCTs both took direct hits by enemy artillery. The Headquarters Group proceeded inland, took shelter behind a beach wall, and dug in at 9:30 a.m. when troops in this vicinity were pinned down by rifle and artillery fire. The 6th ESB and the 2d and 3d Battalions of the 116th RCT were ashore in this vicinity. Major Bach left the protected position and went to see General Wyman at 10:30 a.m. This was when Major Bratton headed west, as mentioned earlier, and Major Watts headed east, both with the intention of connecting with command elements ashore. The group came in contact with Captain Weyman K. Clark, liaison officer, 4th Infantry Division, and they discovered that the 2d Battalion up the bluff had suffered many casualties. The battle raged through the morning at the D-3 exit. At 11:30 a.m., the mortar, rifle, and machine-gun fire on the beach was so heavy that Bach wrote, "It's either get to the ridge in back of beach or be killed." Leaders such as Major Sidney V. Bingham and many others rose to the occasion as they tried again and again to vanquish their strongly entrenched German opponents. Here, too, the destroyers nearly beached at times to offer point-blank-range 5-inch naval gunnery support to the stalled advance. At noon, the beach high tide was in. The men witnessed the bodies of many dead GIs floating on the beach at the high-water mark, lashed by waves red with blood. *Omaha Beachhead* recounts,

> *Except for Company M, pinned on the beach flat near E-1 draw, most of the 3d Battalion, 116th Infantry, had reached high ground by 1000 and were starting to push south. As a result of enemy resistance in and near St-Laurent, they were to make only a half mile of progress during the rest of the day. No clear picture can be drawn of the confused fighting that took place during the morning, as a dozen or more groups, varying from one to four or five boat teams in size, worked south from the bluff toward St-Laurent, with the aim of reaching a battalion assembly area west of the village. The fields between St-Laurent and the bluffs are cut by unusually few hedgerows, and the open ground made the advancing troops more conscious of hostile fire, even when it was wild. Here and there, small enemy detachments with machine guns offered resistance from prepared and well dug-in positions, and a number of skirmishes were fought by sections of Company L and I. By noon most of Company L and several sections of I were at the edge of St-Laurent, on the northwest, where the road from Les Moulins comes into the village at the head of the draw. An enemy rocket battery in this area had been disposed of by Company I's mortar fire and a naval shell. Company K was nearby, and the battalion command group was endeavoring to bring the units together and effect a preliminary reorganization. Major Bingham had worked east on the beach from Les Moulins with a handful of men from F, H, and Headquarters of the [2d] Battalion, and this group had now come inland. Enemy resistance was stiffening. Snipers were straggling in the village, but the main trouble came from the western end of St-Laurent. Here, dug in on the high ground commanding the upper end of the draw, Germans estimated at a company in strength controlled the approaches to the main crossroad, and their machine guns had good fields of fire on all the upper draw. Two boat teams of K and a few men of I, trying to bypass the enemy resistance to the north, cut across the draw about halfway down toward Les Moulins [D-3 exit].*[24]

As Major Bratton moved back to the east now with General Cota, he noted how the general influenced all the men around him: "As he went along, Cota organized the scared, immobilized men on the beaches. When 400 or 500 stood up and got moving, the snipers held their fire. Cota then led the Advance Echelon up the St. Laurent exit and the party bivouacked [had a tactical pause] in the woods south of St. Laurent."[25] Bratton went on to characterize the German defenders: "The defensive positions on the Omaha beach were not only stronger and more numerous than our intelligence had indicated; they were manned by many more troops than were expected. In particular, elements of the 352d Division were right on the beach, in addition to the expected static troops. Local French people have since said that they never expected any force to get through Vierville, the defenses there were so thorough."

Brigadier General Cota likely saved the lives of hundreds, if not most, of these men as surely as any soldier saves the lives of a handful of other soldiers by absorbing the blast of a hand grenade with his own body. Risking his own life and safety by demonstrating personal "in-your-face" confidence, he caused them to overcome their mortal fear and follow his commands to leave their temporary shelter and move off the beach and out of the line of German machine-gun, mortar, and artillery fire. He accomplished this feat by sheer force of his will and knowledge based on having done this previously in North Africa and Sicily with "The Big Red One." Cota clearly exhibited conspicuous gallantry and intrepidity beyond valor at the risk of his own life under intense enemy fire.

Historians such as Joseph Balkoski, Stephen Ambrose, Joseph H. Ewing, and the army's official history attest to this battle through noon. At 12:15 p.m., the Germans began raking the entire length of Omaha Beach, from east to west, with heavy mortar and 88-mm fire in five-round bursts, striking a tank near the D-3 exit. At 12:30 p.m., an LCT hit mines, and then the Germans bombarded it. Two navy men flew through the air into the water, not to be seen again. For the next half hour landing craft had a hard time landing at D-3. By 1 p.m. the tide had begun to go back out. At 1:20 p.m. an LCM (Landing Craft Mechanized) took a direct hit, and men were seen trapped and burning alive aboard. At 2 p.m., the fire on the beach increased, and the Germans picked off medics with impunity. Major Bach wrote, "I've seen movies, assault training demonstrations and actual battle but nothing can approach the scenes on the beach from 1130–1400 hours—men being killed like flies from unseen gun positions—Navy can't hit em—air cover can't see em—so infantry had to dig em out."[26] Per the 1st Infantry Division G-3 journal, General Wyman radioed the navy to report that both Dog Red and Easy Green were being shelled again at 2:35 p.m.[27] Again, General Cota vectored to the danger to effect positive change as he approached from the west along the promenade. The progress between the D-3 and E-1 exits is shown in figure 9.8. Captain Robert E. Walker, S-2 Section, 116th Infantry, described the carnage in this area. He noted the devastation brought by exploding flamethrowers hit by enemy fire and the horrific outcome for the men wearing the weapons and for those around the blasts.[28]

> Everywhere I looked I could see dead and wounded. But when I moved along the beach for a few hundred yards I couldn't find a single rifle or helmet. The men had just dropped them in the boats or in the water or had thrown them away. . . . I met a Ranger lieutenant and we radioed to see how things were on other parts of the beach. The man who answered us wasn't trying to be funny. He was dead serious. He said: "The situation on the beach is normal."[29]

Major Watts made contact with General Wyman, who informed him that he had ordered ashore the 115th Infantry, set to arrive in the 1st Infantry Division sector in a few minutes to reinforce his men. Wyman ordered Watts to stay in close contact and to run a wire between their command posts. Part of General Wyman's mission was to link up with General Cota and the 29th Infantry Division ashore and to coordinate actions on the beach. Bach and Watts were the first contacts Wyman had with Cota's advance command post (CP) since landing. He wasn't about to lose contact with them. Wyman was located in a concrete dugout eight hundred yards east of the 29th Infantry Division Advance CP.[30]

General Cota arrived in the vicinity of his CP amid the heavy fire just mentioned and traversed the face of the D-3 exit from west to east under full view of the defenders above. This is the spot where the Omaha Beach D-Day monument now stands. Stopping at that spot today and looking to the east, to the south, and to the west, one will see just how

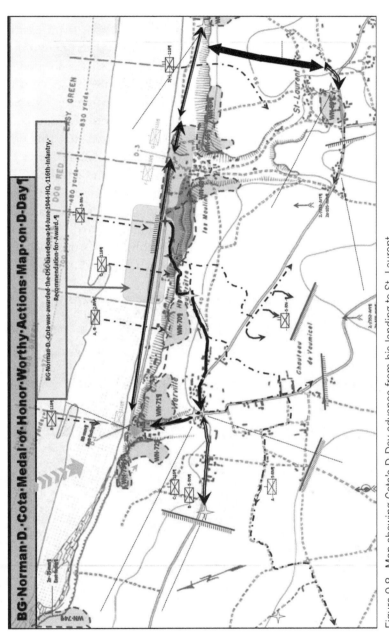

Figure 9.8. Map showing Cota's D-Day advance from his landing to St. Laurent.

exposed the men were to the full range of German weapons employed on D-Day. Cota met Captain Yerby, on the beach at a point east near Les Moulins (Military Grid Reference System [MGRS] 666907). The captain informed the general that the division CP was located at a dugout near a concrete wall near a villa (MGRS 66959045) and took him there. (This location is shown near the center of figure 9.9.) Sensing danger to the position and a lack of proper command and control from this location, General Cota immediately advised that this CP be advanced forward up the bluffs. General Cota then established a more traditional command-and-control structure to get the advance CP up and running to aid the overall mission of the combat team. Major William Bratton (G-2 of the provisional brigade staff) was dispatched to identify a suitable location for the new CP. He then made contact with the 1st Infantry Division. General Cota established his presence at the new CP. His staff included Captain Weyman K. Clark, liaison officer

Figure 9.9. D-3 exit and location of 116th RCT advance CP at approximately 1:30 p.m. (NARA).

(G-4), 4th Infantry Division, on Utah Beach; Major Gerald LeGrippo, surgeon; Lieutenant Colonel Murray Little, signal officer; Major Stanley Bach, liaison officer, 1st Infantry Division; Master Sergeant Edloe Donnaly, operations sergeant; Sergeant S. R. Chase, clerk (G-2); Corporal Neil Lyle, clerk (G-2); Sergeant Barry Cassel, artillery clerk; Corporal R. Llewelyn, clerk (G-4); Sergeant S. Zvonkorich, surgeon's clerk; and Corporal H. Neuman, clerk (G-2).

General Cota issued various orders to the men around him to begin the process of establishing proper command and control at this point. Cota instructed Captain Yerby to determine the status of the 111th Field Artillery Battalion, to assist them in any way possible, and then to report back their location, potential strength, and limits of fire. Captain Little was ordered to contact the signal facilities ashore, make contact with the 116th RCT, 1st Infantry Division, maintain communications for the brigade CP, and then report back as soon as practicable. Major LeGrippo was ordered to investigate and assist the beach medical situation, including medical evacuation, with additional orders to report back as soon as practicable. Lieutenant Colonel Phillips was ordered to investigate the situation surrounding the 29th's vehicles and those of attached units entering Transit Area 2. His orders included reporting back as to the status of vehicles and supplies on hand with special attention given to the ammunition supply.

General Cota then took Major Watts with him to meet with General Wyman. Major Watts had previously located the general's CP in a pillbox at the E-1 exit (MGRS 676700). General Cota found General Wyman sometime between 1:30 and 2 p.m. wrapped in a blanket, his clothing soaked. General Wyman likely had hypothermia and needed to warm up at the moment so he could stay in the fight. General Wyman's aide, Lieutenant Ricks, had been wounded by rifle fire. The two assistant division commanders conferred about the situation, and General Wyman reminded Cota to position the 111th Field Artillery Regiment (Self-Propelled) in such a manner as to provide fire missions for both the 29th and the 1st Infantry Divisions. The generals decided that the 29th should stay on mission. The 116th RCT was to continue west above the bluffs from Vierville to Grandcamp. The 115th RCT was to work westward on the left flank of the 116th RCT and advance generally to Longueville, keeping the inundated lands to the south on its left flank as a barrier. On D+1 at noon, the 175th Infantry Regiment would land and advance west to Isigny.[31]

At 2 p.m., per the Bigot Map Tide Table, General Cota noticed that the receding tide was about halfway out as he walked from General Wyman's CP back toward his own. He noted approximately twenty immobilized 2.5-ton trucks in the Dog Beach area alone, which he surmised had been immobilized by mines. The enemy poured fire upon these stationary stranded vehicles. Three or four of them, one loaded with ammunition, burned fiercely; it likely served as a catalyst for the German artillerymen to continue this strategy. A navy man, a survivor of a destroyed LCT, came to Cota's aide seeking direction. He said to Shea, "How in hell do you work one of these?" He was holding an old naval-craft rifle, crusted with sea grime. Cota advised him to pick up a weapon from one of the casualties. The sailor walked away, swearing loudly, as Shea recounted: "This was just the g----m thing that he had wanted to avoid by joining the Navy, fighting as a g----m foot-soldier."[32] Figure 9.10 illustrates the danger faced near the D-3 exit.

Continuing to his CP, Cota had to go from the villa on the beach where it had been, south toward the bluffs, where he passed some members of the 82d Chemical Mortar Battalion who were working to advance heavily laden handcarts through thick underbrush. For the second time since landing, Cota again ascended the bluffs between the D-3 and E-1 exits. (These bluffs are shown in figure 9.11.) In this area, he encountered large numbers of antipersonnel mines and several medics who were busy evacuating litter patients hit by mine fragments as they ascended the bluff. The lack of vegetation and poor drainage conditions on the slope caused ruts that looked and functioned like steps. Cota found that these steps contained many obvious mines, and a soldier on the alert could watch his step and advance with some ease. The mines were often given away by suspicious mounds of earth, clumps of foliage, and bits of boards covering or around them. About two-thirds up the bluff, Cota, Shea, and Cota's entourage worked their way about one hundred yards to the west, where Major Bratton had led the operations section of the CP. Soldiers,

Figure 9.10. June 6 photo of a GI killed and a vehicle destroyed by enemy artillery (NARA).

Figure 9.11. June 6 aerial photo showing area east of D-3 exit where Cota made his second accent of the bluffs (NARA).

hunkered down along the path, told the members of the group where it was safe to walk and place each step. The GIs marked mines with conventional white tape, handkerchiefs, cigarettes, and bits of K-and D-ration boxes. On the advance, they stepped on nothing but bare ground after carefully examining each foot's placement. General Cota ordered the group to move farther inland at the first opportunity. He was concerned that this geography was still too near to the beach and would undoubtedly catch some of the German artillery fire by direct observation or indirect long-range fire. Cota then observed the self-propelled guns of the 58th Armored Field Artillery Battalion at the foot of the draw. As they attempted to maneuver into battery position, the heavy vehicles bogged down in the marshy ground. A soldier informed Cota that the 116th Infantry had established a wirehead and CP at MGRS 672898. Cota moved forward to that position, arriving at approximately 3 p.m.; he there found communication officer Captain James D. Sink, Colonel Taylor, and Lieutenant Rex Gibson of the Intelligence and Reconnaissance (I&R) Platoon, establishing a CP for the second echelon of the regimental CP. This element was led by Lieutenant Colonel Harold A. Cassell, whom Cota had last seen on the beach before 9 a.m. Cassell and Major Thomas D. Howie, S-3, 3d Battalion, at this point had made their way to Canham's position near Vierville. Cota ordered Captain Sink to lay wire to Canham's position, and then Cota was on the move again.

Meanwhile, the 2d Battalion, 116th Infantry, under command of Major Sydney Bingham, had landed on Dog Red at about 9:30 a.m., as previously mentioned. Bingham and his men ultimately ascended the bluffs directly to their front in the area to the immediate left of the draw when facing it from the channel. They passed through the field at MGRS 672896, which was later to become Transit Area 2, and proceeded four hundred yards farther south. From there, they turned west in an effort to take St. Laurent-sur-Mer. Major Bingham's men were somewhat scattered during their landing. One platoon of Company H under Lieutenant Leon D. Harvey landed fourteen hundred yards farther to the east in the 1st Division sector. Major Bingham and his officers gathered the available men located near Dog Red into columns of companies, headed west, and arrived at the Vierville–St. Laurent road at MGRS 667894.

The men were stopped cold three hundred yards west of this junction by heavy enemy rifle and automatic weapon fire from German defenses associated with the protection of WN 69. Reconnaissance teams found that the enemy strongpoints were located in some farm buildings and an orchard at MGRS 662896. The Germans had direct observation and excellent fields of fire over most of the area, which contributed to the stout defense of the entire D-3 exit. This prime defensive position also prevented the attackers from passing through St. Laurent (shown in figure 9.12). General Cota, who now was back in the business of active warfighting, came to the front of the infantry column where it was halted—again placing himself in harm's way. This was at a point where two large stucco barns stood flush by the side of the road. There Cota found five dead American riflemen who had been picked off by accurate enemy shooting from WN 69. He advised Major Bingham and his 2d Battalion to contain and bypass the strongpoint. Bingham complied and chose to bypass it to the right, intending to clean out the area along the top of the bluffs as he moved to join the remainder of the regiment at Vierville followed by Lieutenant Colonel Lawrence E. Meeks, 3d Battalion. Arriving in support of the 116th RCT between 2 and 3 p.m., the first elements of the 115th Infantry, under the command of Colonel Eugene N. Slappey, CO, 115th RCT, entered the eastern limits of St. Laurent.[33]

At 3:30 p.m., General Cota met with Colonel Slappey; Slappey's executive officer (XO), Lieutenant Colonel Louis G. Smith; and Major

Figure 9.12. February 1944 reconnaissance photo of St. Laurent (NARA).

Victory P. Gillespie, the 3d Battalion CO, in a large barn to the south of the road at MGRS 66408943. This location is the present-day route de Port en Bessen (D514), located between avenue de la Libération (D517) to the west and rue de l'Église to the east. This location is illustrated by the annotated cluster of structures on Lieutenant Shea's battlefield drawing in figure 9.13. Cota ordered Slappey to reduce the enemy strongpoint WN 69 and associated German resistance in St. Laurent. By now Cota had tactically traversed, under intense enemy fire or threat of fire or through mined areas with a second ascent of the bluff under threat to his life, an additional 2.4 miles for a total of 6.8 miles so far.

Back on the beach, near the original site of the CP, Major Bach worked to get inland with his men. He recorded that at 2 p.m. machine-gun fire increased. He witnessed a man hit and another man who went to his aid being grabbed from behind and pulled into a foxhole. By 2:40 p.m., mortar fire increased in the vicinity, and more men were hit. Five

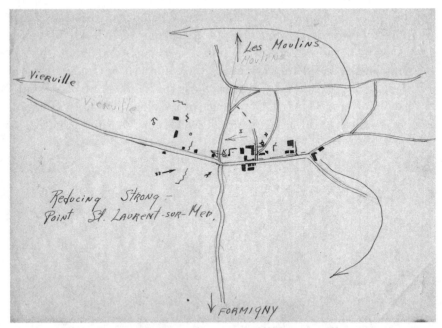

Figure 9.13. Lieutenant Jack Shea's diagram of clearing St. Laurent and Les Moulins (Mike White).

LCVPs (Landing Craft, Vehicle, Personnel) landed, and as the men debarked, mortars immediately killed five men. The remainder scrambled to safety. Bach noted snipers in a large brick house at 3 p.m. only fifty yards from the high-water mark whose fire kept men in their holes. At 3:20 p.m., a terrible explosion occurred as a 2.5-ton truck laden with gasoline was struck by enemy fire, causing a conflagration one hundred yards square and burning up anything and anyone within the radius. With mixed success, gas-covered men attempted to roll in the dirt to extinguish the flames. Many of them died. By 3:40 p.m., Bach was on the move up the bluffs by the same route previously taken by Cota. His advance was stopped by machine-gun fire for several minutes. These Germans could have fired on Cota's group earlier. When the fire lifted, Bach found himself in an open field where he saw a dead GI with no body from the waist down, just entrails and chest organs. The unfortunate soldier had stepped on one of the mines in the area—a prime example of the danger faced by Cota and his men. Continuing forward, they reached a wooded area approximately five hundred yards from the top of the bluff where they witnessed another GI in a kneeling position who had died on his knees, praying. At 4:30 p.m., Bach and his party encountered barbed wire, mines, and mortar, machine-gun, rifle, and 88-mm fire everywhere. He recalled praying several times, asking God, "Why do these things have to be forced upon men?"

Cota reached the CP at 4:50 p.m. Major Bach's testimony is good because it gives a second, unrelated perspective on the peril faced by General Cota and everyone in the vicinity of St. Laurent during the afternoon of D-Day.

At 3:30 p.m., Cota was on the move again, and he headed east in search of the 1st Infantry Division's new CP. He located it in an orchard on the eastern end of town at MGRS 669894. As he passed through town, he noted a house with a corner blown off at MGRS 66528945. The first impression was that this damage was done by enemy artillery, but later discussions revealed that naval fire in support of the movements of the 3d Battalion, 115th RCT, caused the damage. This same naval fire had wounded many men among the 2d Battalion, 116th RCT, as they moved around the north side of the village, working to mop up enemy resistance near Les Moulins. The 2d Battalion, 116th RCT, then headed west toward Vierville with the 3d Battalion, 115th RCT, to join the 1st Battalion holding Vierville along with the Provisional Ranger Group forces located there.

General Cota reported on the progress and intentions of the 116th RCT to General Wyman and then spoke with Major General Clarence Huebner, who had arrived at the CP at about 7 p.m. After this report, Cota returned to his own CP at MGRS 668894 located opposite two adjoining houses there. Cota met with Major Bratton, G-2, who was analyzing usable intelligence from some letters, booklets, and other personal belongings from a battered suitcase brought in from a nearby home. As Bratton assessed the contents, he made the important discovery of several German *Soldbuchs*, the basic German identity papers carried by all personnel and used to keep track of pay, leave, equipment issued, and other personal data. They recorded what unit a man belonged to and his former units, as well as his rank, physical attributes, military awards, and medical history. The German instructions dictated that the *Soldbuch* would always be carried by the soldier on his person in a tunic pocket; leaving the book in one's baggage or in one's quarters was not permitted.[34] This vital find indicated to Bratton that several German soldiers had shed their uniforms and credentials in an attempt to blend in with the civilian population. Bratton also remarked to Cota that in his assessment the German coastal defensive positions in this particular sector appeared to be manned in excess of 70 percent over the strength of the preinvasion estimates. This was official acknowledgment to Cota by his intelligence officer that the German 352d Infantry was in the area and actively engaged in the battle.

After his interaction with Major Bratton, Cota checked on installation of his communications at his advance CP. Satisfied with the progress, he passed down through the newly forming Transit Area 2 at MGRS 668897 in a field just north of St. Laurent. Cota wanted to inspect the flow of vehicles now arriving from the beach via the newly opened E-3 exit at MGRS 676902 and to arrange for tank support of the 115th Infantry in their efforts at WN 69. He discovered two standard M-4 Sherman tanks of the 741st Tank Battalion parked in a shelter of hedgerows along the western boundary of the transit area. In talking to the tankers, he quickly discovered that they were under the control of the 1st Infantry Division. He ordered the captain, the tanker CO, to contact the 1st Infantry Division CP on his authority for operational clearance. Once that had been completed, Cota ordered the tanks to meet Colonel Slappey at the barn where Cota had left him just east of WN 69 near the center of St. Laurent. The tanks were off to their new task, and Cota checked the state of the other vehicles at the transit area. Here Cota made yet another important battlefield decision that saved the lives of men under his command and thereby affected the battle at St. Laurent for the positive. Lieutenant Shea reported on Cota's cursory check of the transit area:

> *Drivers, having gotten their vehicles to the Transit Areas, were engaged in de-waterproofing their cars and trucks. But before they took even one smitch of the compound off they scooped shallow slit trenches in the earth for protection from artillery which continued to whirr overhead towards the beach. Stray bullets whined above the transit area, but in comparison to the beach, it was relatively quiet and about one-fourth of the personnel in the area were busily engaged in opening 10-in-one ration boxes; cooking stuff on the little gasoline stoves that they had brought with them. There seemed to be little loss of appetite even though the corpses of the first riflemen hit near the transit area were still sprawled against the hedges.*[35]

As General Cota turned south yet again toward his CP, he came across and stopped to speak with members of Battery B, 58th Armored Field Artillery Battalion. They were in the process of moving into position near a hedge located at MGRS 669895. He ensured that their firing positions enabled them to support both the 29th and the 1st Infantry Divisions per the orders of General Wyman earlier in the day.

Headquarters, 58th Armored Field Artillery Battalion, After Action Report

The heaviest casualties were among the foot parties that landed with the Infantry. The Commanding Officer and the Reconnaissance Officer were killed by machine gun fire upon hitting the beach. The firing batteries landed

*from 1200 to 1600 Hours, and proceeded to positions near shore. By 1800
Hours the Battalion, with eleven guns, reorganized and was functioning
as a unit under the command of the Executive Officer. Battery "A" moved
inland and was supporting the 115th Infantry.*[36] *[General Cota was directly
responsible for this reorganization.]*

Cota also encountered the advance party of the 110th Field Artillery
Battalion (FA-Bn) after it came ashore at 4 p.m. and ascended the bluffs
into the transit area. Before Cota's arrival, Captain Thomas F. Cadwalader
Jr., the 110th liaison officer with the 2d Battalion of the 115th, located
four self-propelled 105-mm guns belonging to the 58th Armored Field
Artillery Battalion on the northeastern edge of St. Laurent. The casualties sustained by the 58th left them without functioning headquarters,
observers, or communications. Captain Cadwalader's party laid light
field telephone wire from its guns to the 115th to improve the situation
when Lieutenant Colonel John Purley Cooper, CO, 110th FA-Bn, came
upon the scene. Cota followed shortly thereafter and met with Cooper.
The missions of these advance parties were to establish observation, to
reconnoiter positions for the remainder of the battalion scheduled to
land at about 4 p.m., and to secure fire support for the infantry from the
111th FA-Bn and the 1st Division artillery, which were supposed to land
earlier. The general announced that the 111th FA-Bn had been sunk in
the landing and that its commander, Lieutenant Colonel Thornton L.
Mullins, had been killed on the beach. General Cota directed Lieutenant
Colonel Cooper to take command of all artillery ashore in the sector of
the 29th Division because the 58th Armored had suffered heavily and
become disorganized when its commander, Lieutenant Colonel Bernard
W. McQuade, also had been killed. As senior artilleryman on the beach,
Lieutenant Colonel Cooper was to utilize the guns of any unit to support
the infantry. The situation being clarified, the 110th's commander took
appropriate action.[37] Cota assigned the 111th FA-Bn various missions in
direct support of the 115th RCT, then attempting to push inland from
the beach. Artillery fire, some direct and some requested by the battalion's
advance parties, was accomplished. Its effect was observed to heighten
the infantry's spirits.[38] Again, Cota's actions were critical, timely, and

decisive. They resulted in artillery support for troops in the battlespace in desperate need of that support.

He then checked in with his own CP and continued on to meet again with Colonel Slappey and his XO, Lieutenant Colonel Smith, in the barnyard as they supervised the assault of WN 69 and German resistance surrounding it. Slappey brought up a mortar section from Company M and placed it right in the midst of his CP in order to place fire on the Germans at a range of three hundred yards. The mortar observer stood on a barrel to peer through a gap in the wall of the barn to make corrections in elevation and deflection for the mortarmen located twenty yards behind him. As Cota observed this, one of the tanks he had ordered arrived, and a sergeant from 3d Battalion, 115th RCT, rode in the tank to help the tanker place 75-mm rounds on target. The tank passed down between the farm buildings on the narrowing road and fired a few machine-gun bursts and two rounds of 75-mm ammunition on target; then it reversed back into its starting position near the CP. The tank driver and the sergeant reported they were fired upon from their flank as they reached the crossroads at MGRS 663895. (This is the modern crossroads of D514 and D517 in St. Laurent.) They couldn't pinpoint the source of the fire and reported it to be at least a bazooka or an antitank gun. It was a high-velocity projectile fired on them from their left flank, so they withdrew to save the tank. Hearing this, Cota, near the front lines as always, ordered Slappey to establish his heavy weapon as a "base of fire" and stage a coordinated attack on WN 69 at the earliest practicable time.

Once this was done, Cota returned to his own CP at MGRS 668894 a little before dark with an estimated time of around 8 p.m. Sunset was at 10 p.m. on D-Day. Cota was greeted by 1st Lieutenant Robert Wallis, junior aide to General Gerhardt. As Wallis came ashore aboard his LCVP, he was separated from his unit and was unsure as to the location of the division CP. Cota attached Wallis to his staff temporarily until this could be sorted out.[39] Coincidentally, General Gerhardt's leading elements made it ashore and established the 29th Infantry Division CP in the Vierville quarry at 3 p.m., and Gerhardt himself arrived in late afternoon. After Cota's check-in at his CP, he turned around yet again, returned to Colonel Slappey, and urged him to press the attack on the strongpoint, directing him to do so under the cover of darkness if at all possible. At the latest, Cota expected Slappey to jump off at first light around 6 a.m. During the 9 p.m. hour, Cota checked in again at his CP and then traveled to the 1st Infantry Division CP. He reported to Huebner and then met with Major Coles, liaison officer to the 29th Infantry Division, who reported to Cota that Gerhardt had arrived and set up his CP in the Vierville quarry at MGRS 648916. Cota took this information, returned to his own CP, provided instructions to his men based on the latest intel, and discussed his intended use of the 3d Battalion, 115th RCT, to eliminate WN 69. General Cota had now traveled a total of 10.8 miles under enemy observation and, at times, intense enemy fire since he landed, while remaining in the most hotly contested portions of his part of the landing zone. Radio contact between the 29th Infantry Division CP and Cota's advance CP was established at about 10 p.m.[40]

Just before dark, General Cota set off with Lieutenant Shea and Major Coles to the west along the promenade to the D-1 exit, their objective being to contact General Gerhardt at the division CP at the Vierville quarry. They went to the beach from St. Laurent by way of the beach exit at MGRS 678901. They tactically traversed 2.2 miles one way to get there along the promenade, bringing Cota's total mileage to thirteen miles. The Germans still were able to employ snipers and observed artillery on the beach, so it was by no means a safe route of advance. General Cota arrived at the CP at 2 a.m.[41] The meeting was reported by Lieutenant Shea:

> *Maj. Gen. Gerhardt, seated on a box of C rations, met the assistant division commander there. Surrounded by his staff, they discussed the occurrences related thus far and coordinated plans for the employment of the 115th. The third battalion of this regiment was to reduce the ST. LAURENT strongpoint, while the first and second drove south from 674893 in the direction of TREVIERES. The 116th was to work along the rear of the coast defenses west of VIERVILLE exit. As a security measure the 1st Bn., 116th had been ordered to form a tight perimeter defense around VIERVILLE for the night D–D+1. The 175th, the last regiment to land, was to be through the VIERVILLE exit with the mission of pushing towards ISIGNY. Brig. Gen. William Sands, the 29th's Artillery Commander, and his aide, Lt.*

Christianson, joined Gen. Cota at the 29th CP, and were directed by Gen. Gerhardt to join Brig. Gen. Andrus, First Division's Artillery Commander to coordinate the artillery support fires. Having completed his report to the Division Commander, Gen. Cota and Gen. Sands started back towards the First Division CP.[42]

General Cota, General Sands, and Lieutenant Shea returned to the St. Laurent area much the same way Cota and Shea had previously traveled. Shea reported that on both legs of the journey, the medical aid facilities were attempting to provide the best care possible, given the brutal circumstances they faced. The dead and dying soldiers and sailors were collected from the beach and the ground at the foot of the bluffs. Those still alive were being treated at newly forming collection points. Cota and his party noted that the medics had very limited facilities and supplies with which to treat the casualties. The medical corps was subject to the same loss of men and material while attempting to make it ashore as the combat troops. They were forced to make hard triage decisions and to ration their meager supplies as best they could. One practice was to take blankets off the dead and place them over the wounded to keep them warm in the chill of the night air and try to slow the onset of shock. Some of the wounded dug their own shallow slit trenches to protect themselves from the still incoming artillery strikes on the beach and from anticipated air attacks in the darkness. Shea wrote, "Some of the wounded had died, only to tumble into the shallow 'graves' that they had dug." Cota and his companions saw a single surviving medical ambulance, illuminated only by its cat-eye headlights, methodically maneuvering along the beach, picking up any living casualties it encountered and dropping them at a common collection point near the now destroyed tank wall at WN 72 at the D-1 exit. In the protection afforded by those ruins, a small medical staff worked furiously to tend to wounds and to prep men for evacuation by sea. As Cota and company passed by the still burning hulks of LCI(L) 91 and LCI(L) 92, and possibly other vessels, the men had to take cover off the promenade behind the seawall below as the flames silhouetted them, making them easy targets for still-active infiltrating Germans who kept appearing along the crest of the bluffs in their defensive positions.

As they approached the D-3 exit, they were attacked by a dog loyal to the Germans. The valiant Nazi sympathizer was only dissuaded when Shea fired his carbine at it and frightened it. The D-3 exit remained in German hands, so in traversing across the face of it for a third time, Cota again found his luck held, and his team moved down to the E-1 exit. He had to this point traversed 15.21 miles, and it was now after 2 a.m. on D+1.

At Exit E-1, the party managed to catch a ride on one of several heavy trucks heading inland. Cota got off at the V Corps CP, now established ashore at MGRS 676893. After reporting in with General Gerow, he reported back to his own CP, while General Sands reported to the 1st Infantry Division CP. After Cota's check-in, shortly before first light, which occurred at 5:59 a.m., Cota headed back to the front lines to ascertain what progress the 115th RCT had made in the previous hours against defenses in a strongpoint at St. Laurent. He returned to the barn where he had left Colonel Slappey. General Cota jumped in and provided direction to 3d Battalion, 115th RCT, which pressed the attack supported by 81-mm mortars from MGRS 669895. This assault allowed the position to be taken, and it was discovered that the Germans had silently withdrawn many of their forces from the position. None of those men interviewed from the attacking force remembered much in the way of opposition.

The Germans still, however, held defensive positions west of the crossroads on a slight hill on the western edge of Saint-Laurent-sur-Mer. They could direct accurate and unobservable machine-gun fire to the east along the coastal highway. They kept their fire intermittent, so it was harder to trace its origin or to determine when it might occur. The corpses of five dead GIs lay along the road, three along the southern edge and two in the northern gutter. Colonel Slappey's officers determined that the Germans appeared to be employing roving rifle squads on the flanks of the American advance. This made it unsafe to stand in any open space between buildings, and yet General Cota moved with impunity through the area. Shea reported the final action for this German holdout position:

The mortars were set up in the shelter of the barnyards, screened by thick stone walls from the enemy. A thorough naval bombardment preceded the actual assault upon the position. Heavy machine guns were hand-carried to

*the forward fringe of buildings, prepared to open fire on "targets of oppor-
tunity"—i.e. any sources of fire that appeared to hold down the advance of
our troops. That was in accordance with "what the book said"—but it was
the first and most forceful lesson that demonstrated that a well-camouflaged
enemy can effectively pin down our forward assault troops and yet still
remain invisible to the close-support heavy machine guns that lay 200–300
yards in the rear. One of the riflemen suggested that a system of target-
designation be evolved between the assault squads and their close-support
weapons. He suggested that tracers, fired by members of the squad that was
pinned down, indicating the "general direction" from which the fire was
coming from, could successfully indicate to the weapons in the rear, the area
in which to distribute their fire.*

*K Company on the left, I Company on the right, with L Company
following K and ready to break through any weak-spot, advanced with the
main road as their boundary. The platoons of K, 1st platoon leading, threaded
down through the buildings and deployed into an open field. They were too
bunched up. But if they had been dispersed at wider intervals among the
buildings, it was felt that control would have been lost. Enemy mortar fire
would have surely stopped the attack but they seemed to have none at hand,
for they didn't use it.*

*Throughout the hours of darkness between D and D+1, it became
apparent that many units of both the First and 29th Divisions engaged
in minor fire fights between themselves due to the promiscuous shooting of
troops concerned. It was the opinion of both Gen. Cota and members of
the First Division's staff that much of the so-called "snipers" fire, allegedly
enemy—originated at this source. It was infrequently that enemy soldiers
were actually spotted by our infantry in this area. Upon one occasion an
enemy soldier attempted to break from a house and run in an attempted
escape in the ST. LAURENT SUR MER area. It was near Transit Area
2 and about 1900 hours on D-day. He had only run about 200 yards when
he was hit by a hail of 50-cal. fire coming from a quadruple-mount, power
turret, half-track of a light anti-aircraft battalion. He was virtually
"torn-apart" by the force of the fire.*[43]

This battle raged through sunrise and lasted until 9 a.m. Only once
Cota was satisfied that the engagement was a success did he return to
his CP. When he arrived at his CP, he had a welcome surprise in that his

trusty Jeep, nicknamed "Fire and Movement," had finally made it ashore and was waiting for him.

By 10 a.m., the sun rose high enough to sufficiently burn away any hint of the morning mist that had formed in the predawn hours. By this hour, the tide of battle began to finally change in a solid manner all along Omaha Beach. Men of the first assault battalions were finally able to take a collective deep breath as reinforcements finally began to make it ashore in earnest with fresh equipment and ammunition. The 115th and 116th and Rangers gave no ground in the darkness. As men poured ashore, the attackers slowly began to expand the bridgehead.

Continuing his gallantry on June 7, General Cota performed yet another widely known and documented act that sums up actions during this period characteristic of him as presented in this narrative. This narrative is from a witness interview conducted by Joe Balkoski with Lieutenant Colonel Cooper. This account is important because it was carried out by Joe Balkoski, the official command historian of the 29th Infantry Division (although it was conducted before his tenure) with a respected officer of the 110th FA-Bn. It demonstrates how General Cota's level of intensity and sense of urgency led him to do any job required to ensure the success of the mission—even that of a captain—at the risk of his life.

Lieutenant Colonel John Purley Cooper, CO, 110th FA-Bn
On June 7, General Cota was supervising clean-up efforts of the 115th Infantry Regiment near St. Laurent. In the German hedgerows a group of Americans became pinned down near a farmhouse. Brig. General Norman "Dutch" Cota, Assistant Division Commander of the 29th, came on a group of infantry pinned down by some Germans in a farmhouse. He asked the captain in command why his men were making no effort to take the building.

"Sir, the Germans are in there, shooting at us," the captain replied.

"Well, I'll tell you what, Captain," said Cota, unbuckling two grenades from his jacket. "You and your men start shooting at them. I'll take a squad of men and you and your men watch carefully. I'll show you how to take a house with Germans in it."

Cota led his squad around a hedge to get as close as possible to the house. Suddenly, he gave a whoop and raced forward, the squad following, yelling like wild men. As they tossed grenades into the windows, Cota and another man kicked in the front door, tossed a couple of grenades inside, waited for the explosions, then dashed into the house. The surviving Germans inside were streaming out the back door, running for their lives.

Cota returned to the captain. "You've seen how to take a house," said the general, still out of breath. "Do you understand? Do you know how to do it now?"

"Yes, sir."

"Well, I won't be around to do it for you again," Cota said. "I can't do it for everybody."

Later, Lt. Colonel Cooper B. Rhodes, G-1, who witnessed the scene, suggested to Cota that he stop endangering himself. "Now look, Cooper," Cota replied. "I was a poor country boy from Pennsylvania Dutch country. I heard about West Point, and that it was free, and I went. I made a contract with the government: If they paid for my education, I would serve them. Part of my contract was to die for my country if necessary. I intend to stick to it. If I get killed, then so be it, but I don't expect to be."[44]

At 10:30 a.m., General Cota, who knew the operation plan intimately and paid attention to the smallest details, showed his effectiveness as a leader and as a humanitarian when he ordered evacuation of all French civilians from St. Laurent. They started to appear at his CP, and he set some subordinates to work to find billets and provisions for them and keep them safe as the Americans finally wiped out the German resistance in their town. These actions were recorded in the diary of the Security Group, Headquarters, 1st Infantry Division.

June 7, 1944; 0930 French civilians started to come to the CP from the town of St. Laurent–sur–Mer. 1030—General Cota suggested the evacuation of all civilians from the town. French civilians in the CP started to look for temporary billets for them. Major Pelham St. G. Bissell, III, 2nd Lt Hendrickson, and 2nd Lt Patterson with three MPs go into St. Laurent–sur–Mer to arrange for evacuation of civilians. 1115—Lieutenant Patterson returns to CP with approximately 35 civilians. 1230 Major Bissell and Lieutenant Hendrickson return to CP. They report 10 dead Germans and 2 Americans in the town. The Mayor of the town reports that there is no grain warehouse nor a bank in the town. There is a Post Office. Mayor ordered to see that all civilians in town are evacuated.

By 11 a.m., the 175th Infantry began to land en masse and pour up through the Vierville exit. The German resistance melted away from the strongpoints and was reduced to artillery strikes from mobile artillery units to the south and lone riflemen and snipers here and there until captured or killed. The sight of dead Germans became more and more common for the GIs (as shown in figure 9.14). General Cota remained under threat, as Shea reported:

One particularly arrogant, jack-booted enemy rifleman was taken from the barn 50 yards from the CP of Gen. Cota. He had been there since the first assault waves had forced him back from his foxhole on the bluff at 0800 hours on D-day—about 27 hours during which he had shot and killed seven American soldiers with his machine pistol. He fired from the left in the barn.

Figure 9.14. Dead German soldier (NARA).

Capt. Tommy Neal, liaison officer with Gen. Cota's brigade staff, expressed the opinion that our troops were not thoroughly experienced in the "crack-and thump" method of locating enemy fire. When they were shot at, they had little idea of where the enemy fire was coming from.[45]

Now with St. Laurent liberated and the Germans on the run, General Cota made the decision to move his CP and staff to join with the 29th Infantry Division CP in the quarry at the Vierville exit. Cota mounted his Jeep and, followed by his staff in two others, moved west on the coastal road to Vierville, where they drew small arms and mortar fire en route from the south along exposed portions of the road. As they were traveling at thirty-five to forty mph, the rifle fire wasn't a big concern. Four or five rounds of light mortar fire (60-mm) struck in front of and behind Cota's Jeep. "Cota remarked on the enemy's ability to rapidly put these light mortars into action, and the amazingly high degree of accuracy accomplished by them. 'They're pretty good, aren't they?'" Then they arrived at 12:30 p.m. at the Vierville crossroads, where Cota had stood twenty-four hours earlier as the USS *Texas* fired at Exit D-1.

They parked the Jeeps, and Cota walked his same route of twenty-four hours earlier to meet General Gerhardt in the quarry. Cota found his boss still seated on a box of C-rations. There were close-in security outposts posted in the foxholes (formerly occupied by the enemy) at the crest of the surrounding bluffs. Groups of Rangers and 116th riflemen continued to mop up enemy foxholes and tunnels in the immediate vicinity.

General Gerhardt; his chief of staff, Colonel Godwin Ordway; Major Paul W. Krznarich (G-2); Lieutenant Colonel William Witte (G-3); General Cota; and Major Watts then gathered to discuss the present situation. They discussed the next steps such as the capture and liberation of Isigny and Longueville, in addition to the mission objectives to relieve Pointe du Hoc, Grandcamp les Bains, and Maisy. The 29th was to be released from the 1st Infantry Division at 5 p.m. Cota was left in charge of the CP at the quarry as Gerhardt set out to the V Corps CP. Cota's amazing journey of intense frontline combat had come to an end.[46]

Oberstleutnant Fritz Ziegelmann, 352d Infantry Division (June 6, 1944)

Divisional Commander, General Kraiss to Commanding General, General Marcks: Tomorrow the Division will be able with all available forces to offer the same kind of hard resistance to the supreme enemy, as it was the case today. Because of the heavy casualties, however, new forces have to be brought up the day after tomorrow. The losses of men and material in the islands of resistance are total. By the heaviest kind of bombing and cones of concentrated fire from naval artillery, greater numbers of the guns built in at field strength were buried under rubble and had to be set free again.[47]

Oberstleutnant Fritz Ziegelmann, assistant chief of staff, 352d Infantry Division, later wrote that he had asked about the strength of reserves in May and been rebuffed: "My query, that the width of the division sector (53 kilometers) and the weaknesses of our rearward defenses made possible an infiltration through the less heavily occupied sections, and that to counter this, assault reserves were necessary behind the lines, remained unanswered." This weakness would be exploited by the 116th RCT and the 5th Ranger Infantry Battalion as they assaulted the bluffs.[48]

Per Ziegelmann, the 352d experienced approximately two hundred dead on the field of battle, five hundred wounded, and five hundred missing. He stated those losses amounted to about one-fifth of the total fighting strength of six thousand men rendered ineffective. Ziegelmann noted the Americans had a few important factors: "The enemy led his troops according to orders issued beforehand, and which remained obligatory. . . . The material employed by him was of excellent and decisive quality, which can be designated as unique and which at the end of the day had its due success in terms of the actual damage as well as the moral effect of it on the German troops. On fighting for localities, the enemy, with his submachine guns and quick-reload rifles, was superior to the German troops which had only very few of the latter. It was striking to see on the first day." He praised the Americans for good human stock, good small arms and plenty of ammunition, practical clothing and equipment, excellent maps (including panoramic maps of the field of view of the attacker), and good standardized motor vehicle accessories. Of course, the battle was far from over, and many more lives would be lost or affected during the weeks and months to come. D-Day, however, was over, and the Americans, British, Canadians, and their Allies had a tenuous foothold on the shores of Normandy, thanks in no small part to General Cota and the men of Omaha Beach.

Captain Carroll Smith, S-3, 3d Battalion, 116th Infantry, 29th Infantry Division, noted the regimental casualties for June 6. He noted a landing strength of 3,486 men, a figure that excludes attached units. The casualties he recorded were 1,030, including 390 killed in action, 43 missing in action, and 597 wounded in action, for a 30 percent casualty rate. He noted 80 officer casualties, accounting for half of all officers in the regiment. Smith wrote in a report, "The Vierville draw and Dog Sector remained under fire for the next couple of days as mobile German artillery continued to shell the area."[49]

Based on Lieutenant Shea's account and available records of other units, General Cota's route was mapped for this research effort, beginning at his landing site and concluding with his return to the 29th Infantry Division CP in the Vierville quarry at 12:40 p.m. on D+1. In all, the general traveled some seventeen miles by foot under enemy fire, intense at times, and consisting of machine-gun, mortar, artillery, rifle, and U.S. Navy fire and the threat of landmines. He climbed the bluffs under fire twice, once at Dog White/Dog Red and once to the east of the D-3 exit. He traveled an additional 4.5 miles by jeep from his final CP at St. Laurent to the quarry, coming under fire at various points on that trip. This number raises his total of travel in a thirty-hour period to 21.5 miles, all without sleep. His distance traveled on some of the world's deadliest real estate is a testament to his courage and to the protection afforded him by his maker. An interesting and unanswered question is: How many other Americans on Omaha Beach traveled that far over that period?

Unbeknownst to General Cota or the invading Allied armies ashore, their commander in chief and president was a great orator humble enough to understand that prayer was a weapon far greater than any other in his mighty arsenal of democracy. Cota was a deeply spiritual man, and this prayer would have been very much appreciated by him on the battlefield. Even those who are not religious can understand the importance of this moment in U.S. and world history. President Franklin Delano Roosevelt took to the American airwaves with the following radio address at 9:57 p.m., Eastern Time (3:57 a.m. in France):

My fellow Americans: Last night, when I spoke with you about the fall of Rome, I knew at that moment that troops of the United States and our allies were crossing the Channel in another and greater operation. It has come to pass with success thus far.

And so, in this poignant hour, I ask you to join with me in prayer:

Almighty God: Our sons, pride of our Nation, this day have set upon a mighty endeavor, a struggle to preserve our Republic, our religion, and our civilization, and to set free a suffering humanity.

Lead them straight and true; give strength to their arms, stoutness to their hearts, steadfastness in their faith.

They will need Thy blessings. Their road will be long and hard. For the enemy is strong. He may hurl back our forces. Success may not come with rushing speed, but we shall return again and again; and we know that by Thy grace, and by the righteousness of our cause, our sons will triumph.

They will be sore tried, by night and by day, without rest—until the victory is won. The darkness will be rent by noise and flame. Men's souls will be shaken with the violences of war.

For these men are lately drawn from the ways of peace. They fight not for the lust of conquest. They fight to end conquest. They fight to liberate. They fight to let justice arise, and tolerance and good will among all Thy people. They yearn but for the end of battle, for their return to the haven of home.

Some will never return. Embrace these, Father, and receive them, Thy heroic servants, into Thy kingdom.

And for us at home—fathers, mothers, children, wives, sisters, and brothers of brave men overseas—whose thoughts and prayers are ever with them—help us, Almighty God, to rededicate ourselves in renewed faith in Thee in this hour of great sacrifice.

Many people have urged that I call the Nation into a single day of special prayer. But because the road is long and the desire is great, I ask that our people devote themselves in a continuance of prayer. As we rise to each new day, and again when each day is spent, let words of prayer be on our lips, invoking Thy help to our efforts.

Give us strength, too—strength in our daily tasks, to redouble the contributions we make in the physical and the material support of our armed forces.

And let our hearts be stout, to wait out the long travail, to bear sorrows that may come, to impart our courage unto our sons wheresoever they may be.

And, O Lord, give us Faith. Give us Faith in Thee; Faith in our sons; Faith in each other; Faith in our united crusade. Let not the keenness of our spirit ever be dulled. Let not the impacts of temporary events, of temporal matters of but fleeting moment let not these deter us in our unconquerable purpose.

With Thy blessing, we shall prevail over the unholy forces of our enemy. Help us to conquer the apostles of greed and racial arrogancies. Lead us to the saving of our country, and with our sister Nations into a world unity that will spell a sure peace a peace invulnerable to the schemings of unworthy men. And a peace that will let all of men live in freedom, reaping the just rewards of their honest toil.

Thy will be done, Almighty God.

Amen.[50]

Brigadier General Norman Daniel "Dutch" Cota, assistant division commander, 29th Infantry Division, had completed his unrelenting 17-mile journey by foot and additional 4.5 miles by Jeep. Brigadier General Cota accomplished all of his assigned missions except for the planned depth of penetration into France. He was fifty-one years old. It is doubted by our research team that many other men on Omaha Beach traveled anywhere near that distance under those conditions and during that time. Most infantrymen traveled approximately two miles from the time they touched dry ground over the course that first twenty-four- to thirty-hour period. Thousands of men survived D-Day because of his willingness to sacrifice his life for theirs and because of his actions above and beyond the call of duty.

CHAPTER TEN

Beyond Intrepidity

As discussed in chapter 1, the Medal of Honor (MOH) may be awarded to a person who, while a member of the army, navy, or air force, has distinguished him- or herself conspicuously by gallantry and intrepidity at the risk of his or her life above and beyond the call of duty. The action must have occurred while the individual was engaged in an action against an enemy of the United States or in military operations involving conflict with an opposing foreign force. The MOH recommendation must contain proof beyond a reasonable doubt that the member performed the valorous action that resulted in the MOH recommendation. The valorous action(s) performed must have entailed personal bravery or self-sacrifice so conspicuous as to clearly distinguish the individual from his or her comrades and must have involved risk of life.

General Cota faced off with death on the field of battle. He punched death in the mouth, smiled, threw him to the ground, and trampled on his face as he marched through him and urged his men onward to victory, all while he chewed on a stogie and waved his Colt .45 in the air. Death was simply in his way. Upon hearing of the general's passing in 1971, Frank G. Oberle of the 29th Infantry Division wrote, "We had the additional privilege of seeing the General several times in battle after D-Day and before St. Lo. He was absolutely fearless in battle and often right in the thick of things."[1]

By all accounts his actions were characterized by witnesses, from the lowest private to fellow officers, as legendary. He knew exactly what was going to happen on D-Day. He saw the battlespace in his mind well before it ever happened and even predicted it to those around him on the eve of battle aboard ship. The fact that he helped develop the doctrine and methods used to wage this war gave him a perspective shared by few in the whole of the army. His battlefield experience had hardened him, and his inner courage, dating back to his childhood and the Chelsea fire and his other experiences, came out in full view on Bloody Omaha. He was well known as a fearless soldier and leader before D-Day. On D-Day, he cemented that reputation.

In 1943, Cota wrote a thesis regarding the development of the proposed Assault Division for Combined Operations Headquarters (COHQ). Some of his thoughts were regarded as too radical at the time, particularly his idea for nighttime assault based on his experiences in North Africa in 1942. He made several observations that in effect became prophecies for D-Day. He said the planners should choose darkness "because the naval fire won't be able to see well enough to hit their targets even during daylight." This was proven on the field of battle. Interestingly, the American warfighter of today is often known as a nighttime warrior, and our forces are said to "own the night." He predicted, "The aerial bombardment will not effectively neutralize all the enemy positions." This was proven. He told COHQ, "The beach is going to be fouled up in any case. Darkness will not substantially alter the percentage of accuracy in beaching—not enough to off-set the handicaps of a daylight assault." Again, this was proven. Regarding landing men during daylight, he said, "It will aid us in no way except to light up the whole scene, providing the enemy with better targets." Based on the results in the face of the D-1 exit, this was proven. Lastly, he predicted, and it was proven, that "psychologically, the enemy will not be as well prepared to fight us during the hours of darkness." Those airborne troops who began the fight under the cover of darkness benefited from that darkness.[2] He knew what would happen on D-Day. Instead of letting these events unfold as an unwitting participant, he acted beyond intrepidity.

General Cota was later awarded the Distinguished Service Cross (DSC) for his actions on the beach as described in chapter 6. On June 14, he was nominated for the DSC. Orders were cut for his receipt of the award on July 1, and he received the award on July 7 (as illustrated

Figure 10.1. Photo of Brigadier General Cota and Colonel Charles D. Canham receiving their DSCs.

in figure 10.1). One very important thing to notice in this particular picture is just how conspicuously General Cota's rank is visible on his helmet, epaulet, and collar, in addition to the clear general officer uniform standards he wore. For context, by June 14, the battle was still raging for the Normandy hedgerows. On June 12, General Cota personally led an infantry reconnaissance in force with the Company E, 29th Infantry Division, of German positions near the Vire River near the town of Montmartin-en-Graignes. He continued to lead in combat from the front with his troops for his entire time in the division. Based on the evidence on hand at the time of this award, the DSC was the minimum for him to be awarded for his actions as presented to the decisionmakers.

The Distinguished Service Cross was awarded to Brigadier General Norman D. Cota, 29th Infantry Division, per Headquarters, First United States Army, General Orders No. 31, July 1, 1944. His citation read,

Brigadier General Norman D. Cota (05284), 29th Infantry Division, United States Army. For extraordinary heroism in action against the enemy on 6 June 1944 near Vierville sur le Mer, France. General Cota landed on the beach shortly after the first assault wave of troops had landed. At

this time the beach was under heavy enemy rifle, machine gun, mortar and artillery fire. Numerous casualties had been suffered, the attack was arrested and disorganization was in process. With complete disregard for his own safety General Cota moved up and down the fire swept beach reorganizing units and coordinating their action. Under his leadership a vigorous attack was launched that successfully overran the enemy positions and cleared the beaches. The outstanding courage and superb leadership displayed by General Cota reflect great credit on himself and were in keeping with the highest traditions of the Armed Services.[3]

The recommendation for the award, dated June 14, 1944, was based on extraordinary heroism. The detailed description of the event on the award recommendation reads as follows:

The 116th Regimental Combat Team, 29th Infantry Division, landed on the shore of France near Vierville Sur-Mere on June 6, 1944. The enemy beach defenses were manned by a stubborn and determined enemy who were making every effort to push back into the sea those troops already landed. Brigadier General Norman D. Cota, Assistant Commanding General, 29th Infantry Division, landed shortly after H-Hour. At the time, the beach was under heavy artillery, mortar, and machine gun fire, with our men receiving numerous casualties. The attack, at the time, was arrested and the units were becoming more disorganized as follow-up troops were brought ashore and dropped in the midst of the first waves. With apparent utter disregard for his own personal safety, General Cota moved up and down the fire-swept beaches and led the men forward by his own personal leadership. His perseverance, coolness under heavy fire at a time when so many men were falling were an inspiration to those who witnessed it. They moved as a man to launch a superb attack against the beach fortifications that broke the stalemate and cleared the beaches. General Cota never faltered in this recovery of a threatened major loss to an heroic victory.[4]

The nature of the terrain was exposed beach with no cover, and the enemy occupied barren cliffs in the immediate vicinity. The enemy enjoyed excellent morale and was rated a strong force. The weather was cloudy.

Colonel Charles Canham's affidavit of Cota's actions stated that he personally witnessed the heroic action of Brigadier General Cota, "who by force of personal leadership was instrumental in assisting the troops across the fire swept beaches to a position of safety. His presence, his apparent utter disregard for his own safety, his coolness under heavy machine gun and artillery fire were an inspiration to those who witnessed it."[5]

Lieutenant Colonel Harold A. Cassell, executive officer, 116th Infantry Regiment, stated,

General Cota was on the beach at a time when the enemy was directing his heaviest machine gun and artillery fire on the men then holding only a ten yard strip of beach. The attack was bogged down at the time and our force was suffering numerous casualties from the almost demoralizing fire of the enemy. With utter disregard for his own safety, General Cota moved across the beach, exhorting men and officers alike and assisting their movement across the beach. His presence, courage, and coolness under fire impressed the men and inspired them to break the deadlock and overcome the beach defenders.[6]

One important consideration for the general now is the plethora of documentation and firsthand accounts of friend and foe regarding the assault landings collected in the months and years following this action. The full account of his continued acts of bravery dwarfs what was known at the time of his DSC award on July 7, 1944.

General Cota clearly distinguished himself on D-Day conspicuously by gallantry and intrepidity at the risk of his own life and above the call of duty. He enjoined the assault landing on Omaha Beach and engaged a stubborn, well-trained, and determined enemy during the largest seaborne invasion in world history. Armed only with his automatic Colt .45 pistol, he waded ashore amid the thousands of troops ashore between the D-1 and D-3 beach exits at a time when the Germans threatened the American forces with a crushing defeat that could have pushed them back into the sea. He was not intimidated by the obvious show of German force. He indicated no fear and instilled his stalwart courage into the men around him, driving them to action through his effective leadership at a time when that was needed most. He was dauntless in his movements and actions.

General Cota landed on Dog White Beach at 7:26 a.m., just shy of one hour after the first assault wave of troops had landed on western Omaha Beach in the 116th Infantry's appointed landing zones, so he witnessed the utter carnage and failing nature of the first wave of the assault landing. As he landed, the 29th Infantry Division and attached units had experienced catastrophic casualties on the order of twelve hundred men on western Omaha Beach, including the near total loss of Company A, 116th Regimental Combat Team (RCT), in the face of the tremendous enemy fire at the Vierville draw. When he arrived, he personally took command of the chaos on western Omaha Beach and led U.S. forces to victory off the beach, saving countless lives. He led by example: not hiding or shrinking from heavy enemy fire but walking among the troops to encourage movement. He personally reconnoitered over the seawall and directed placement of automatic fire upon the enemy. To keep his men from falling into despair and further chaos, he personally led elements of Companies C and D, 116th RCT, through a hole in a span of wire after the first two men through were killed.

He reasserted command and control over the beach assault and ascension of bluffs between beach exits D-1 and D-3 per the Overlord plan upon realizing the devastating losses to the officer corps on the beach. When he realized the gift that was the intact landing of the 5th Ranger Infantry Battalion, he collaborated with commander of the Rangers and exhorted, "Rangers, lead the way!" at the seawall. General Cota then congealed command elements of the 29th Division in establishment of a command post at the base of the bluff exposed to enemy artillery fire. After a mortar shell exploded three feet from him and killed two others, he carried the fight up the bluff, undeterred, near the head of the column. His actions and route are fully illustrated in figure 10.2.

He personally led men constantly forward on the bluffs, roads, and hedgerows around Vierville. Up on the bluff, when stalled by a German position, he personally led an infantry charge of a German MG-42 machine-gun position across an open, three- to four-hundred-yard field. He exposed himself to German sniper fire on at least one occasion while seeking to advance the troops of the 29th Division and Rangers. Cota personally led units through Vierville, capturing the important crossroads village.

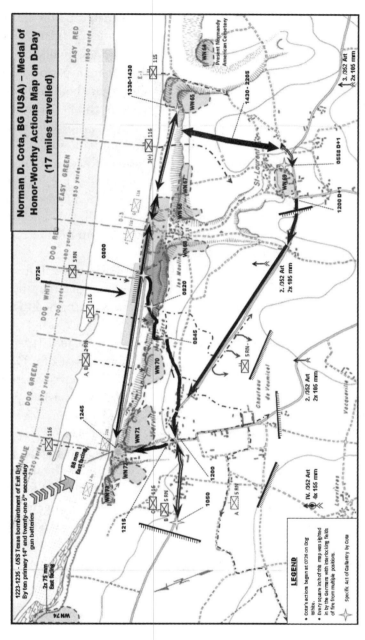

Figure 10.2. Map showing Brigadier General Cota's full seventeen-mile journey from 7:26 a.m. on D-Day to noon on D+1 (map by the author based on War Department, Historical Division, *Omaha Beachhead (6 June–13 June 1944)*, American Forces in Action Series, CMH Pub 100-11-1 [GPO: Washington, DC, September 1945], Map No. 11, "Omaha Beach Terrain").

Understanding the importance of opening the beach exits for armor, Cota personally ensured that Omaha Beach Exit D-1 was finally neutralized and opened as an egress point for men and vehicles while under fire. To accomplish this task, he personally led a six-man patrol down Vierville draw to the beach during a 14-inch main battery bombardment from USS *Texas* and four destroyers, thereby opening the D-1 exit. He personally captured five German prisoners from German fortified positions in WN 72. He saw to the destruction of the antitank wall at WN 72. General Cota led efforts to neutralize all German forces in the area and linked up with the 1st Infantry Division while under fire between D-1 and D-3. While on Exit D-3, he led four to five hundred men off the beach. He next continued leading at the D-3 exit, directly affecting combat actions of the 115th RCT and helping to clear up the Germans and open that exit by the next morning.

His DSC was approved by the 29th Infantry Division on June 14, 1944, and then approved by the 1st Infantry Division and then by V Corps on June 17, 1944. The 29th Infantry Division was attached to the 1st Infantry Division from May 17, 1944, through June 7, 1944. The First United States Army provided the final approval on July 1, 1944. Facts in evidence in support of Cota's gallantry beyond that of a DSC began to appear almost immediately after Cota's DSC recommendation was approved. On June 16, Headquarters, 29th Infantry Division, prepared a report titled *The Following Is an Account of the Actions Taken by Brig. Gen. Norman D. Cota on June 6, 1944—D-Day for the Invasion of Europe.* This report, on its own merit, justifies and supports almost the entirety of the story contained in chapters 7–9 of this book. It summarized and described the basis for General Cota's consideration for the MOH. It is odd that this report was not included in the complete official records for Cota's DSC at the National Archives. This report and all of the records uncovered by the research team constitute new and substantive evidence in support of the award of the MOH to this hero. The text of this report follows:

General Cota was landed in an LCVP at approximately H+57 minutes on Dog White Beach, with the Regimental Headquarters of the 116th Infan-

try, the right assault regiment of the First Division Assault Forces. Because of a rough sea, General Cota's LCVP breached on the beach after "hanging up" on a beach obstacle to which a Tellermine was attached. The subsequent battering the sea gave the boat loosened the Tellermine from the obstacle, but it failed to explode. The boat was under heavy machine gun fire, mortar, and light cannon fire. Three persons, including Regimental S-4 Major John Sours, were instantly killed as they endeavored to reach the beach when the ramp of the LCVP was lowered. Although the leading elements of the assault had been on the beach for approximately an hour, none had progressed farther than the seawall at the inland border of the beach. Rangers, Special Engineer Task Force men, Landing Assault Battalion, Beach Maintenance men and Naval personnel, were clustered under the wall, pinned down by machine gun fire, and the enemy was beginning to bring effective mortar fire to bear on those hidden behind the wall. Realizing that immediate steps had to be taken to move the men from the dangerous area of the beach, General Cota, exposing himself to enemy fire, went over the seawall giving encouragement, directions and orders to those about him. He personally supervised the placing of a [Browning Automatic Rifle] and brought fire to bear on some of the enemy positions on the cliff that faced them. Finding a belt of barbed wire inside the seawall, General Cota personally supervised placing a Bangalore torpedo for blowing the wire and was one of the first three men to go through the wire. At the head of a mixed column of troops he threaded his way to the foot of the high ground beyond the beach and started the troops up the high ground where they could bring effective fire to bear on the enemy positions.

At that point General Cota narrowly escaped death. Six mortar shells (probably of 50mm caliber) fell into a group of officers, NCO's and radio operators to whom he was giving instructions. It scattered the group, killed three, wounded two, but the General was unharmed.

The attack having bogged down towards the top of the cliff, General Cota personally climbed to the top and lead [sic] the leading elements of the column, crossed interlocking bands of enemy machine gun fire, and led the troops onto the St. Laurent-Vierville-sur-Mer Road, directed a hurried reconnaissance of forces and started the detachment of Rangers West toward their objective at Point de la Raz Percee and Point du Hoc. Initially this advance bogged down several times. Each time General Cota hastened to the front of the column, he assisted the platoon leader in the disposition of his forces so the column could advance to the West.

Returning to Vierville Sur Mere, he observed that no engineer demolition work was being done in the beach exit. He with a party of four additional men, including Major Olson, two enlisted men and another officer, made his way down to the beach through the Vierville Sur Mere beach exit. This patrol was accomplished in the fire of Heavy Naval Guns from about 800 yards offshore, since the Navy was trying to Neutralize strong cannon positions at beach level at the exit. Five prisoners were driven from the fortifications at this point by this patrol and taken to the beach. There General Cota, though under constant sniper and machine gun fire from the high ground beyond the beach, progressed Eastward along the beach herding and reorganizing hastily tank units, engineer demolition units, supplies of demolitions, bulldozers, and in general directing units suffering from the initial confusion of landing under fire as that their efforts could be effectively bent toward the establishment of the beachhead.

Throughout the remainder of D-Day, D+1 and D+2, General Cota, with complete disregard for his personal safety, did make every human effort to make a success of the operation. Frequently he was brought under intense sniper and machine gun fire, mortar fire, and took many chances as he personally supervised house clearing and street fighting activities in the villages of St. Laurent Sur Mere and Vierville Sur Mere.

Performing the tasks of a squad leader, platoon leader, company commander and general organizer of things military during the initial phases of this invasion, General Cota did, by his example and actions, inject into the situation an element of inspiration that was vital to the success of the operation.[7]

General Omar Bradley wrote two autobiographies after the war. In *A General's Life: An Autobiography*, he wrote that he considered the 352d Infantry, which supported the 716th Infantry, as "first line." The general referred to the bombardment experienced by the early assault troops as "a hurricane of enemy machine-gun, mortar and artillery fire" and said that "for several hours, the beach and the water just beyond was a bloody chaos." He elaborated about the critical nature of the battle and Cota's gallantry:

Omaha Beach, however, was a nightmare. Even now it brings pain to recall what happened there on June 6, 1944. I have returned many times to honor the valiant men who died on that beach. They should never be forgotten. Nor should those who lived to carry the day by the slimmest of margins. Every man who set foot on Omaha Beach that day was a hero. . . .

Omaha Beach remained a bloodbath for too long. Six hours after the landings we held only ten yards of beach. Not until the principal commanders got ashore did the men begin to move toward the cover of the seawall and bluffs. These gallant officers were Brigadier General Norman D. Cota, assistant division commander of the 29th (a good friend and onetime member of my weapons section at Fort Benning); Colonel Charles D. W. Canham, commanding the 116th Infantry; and Colonel George A. Taylor, commanding the 16th Infantry. Cota was a fearless example to every man on the beach as he calmly strode about giving sensible orders. Taylor shouted to his men, "They're killing us here! Let's move inland and get killed!" Cota yelled, "Two kinds of people are staying on this beach, the dead and those who are going to die. Now let's get the hell out of here." Men who were able dashed for the seawall through murderous fire. Hundreds more soldiers of the 18th and 115th Infantry came behind, disgorging from the landing craft. Everywhere courage and valor were commonplace. Slowly, almost imperceptibly, our foothold increased.[8]

Bradley wrote that communications with the forces on Omaha Beach were thin to nonexistent. From the few messages that did make it through, he had the impression that "our forces had suffered an irreversible catastrophe." He thought there was little hope that the Americans could force the beachhead. "Privately, I considered evacuating the beachhead and directing the follow-up troops to Utah Beach or the British beaches." Bradley later remarked to Field Marshal Bernard Law Montgomery, commander in chief, 21st Army Group, "Someday I'll tell Eisenhower just how close it was those first hours." He agonized over the withdrawal decision and prayed the men could hang on. It wasn't until 1:30 p.m. that Major General Charles Hunter Gerhardt informed him that the 116th RCT had made it above the bluffs. He sent his chief of staff, Bill Kean, ashore for a firsthand look, and it was based on his report that Bradley finally let go of his thoughts of abandoning the Omaha landings. Bradley wrote, "I often agonized over assigning green troops to spearhead the Omaha Beach assault: [Major General Leonard] Gerow and his V Corps headquarters, Gerhardt and his 29th Division. That is why I made the decision to add elements of [Major General Clarence R.] Huebner's battle-hardened Big Red One. As in the Sicily assault, the Big Red One once more bore the brunt of the enemy fury. But I thanked God the division was there."⁹

In his second autobiography, *Omar N. Bradley: A Soldier's Story*, he wrote of his inner fears and observations in an expansion of his previous work.

> *As the morning lengthened, my worries deepened over the alarming and fragmentary reports we picked up on the navy net. From these messages we could piece together only an incoherent account of sinkings, swampings, heavy enemy fire, and chaos on the beaches. By 8:30 the two assault regiments on Omaha had expected to break through the water's-edge defenses and force their way inland to where a road paralleled the coast line a mile behind the beaches. Yet by 8:30, V Corps had not yet confirmed news of the landing. . . . Aboard the Ancon, Gerow and Huebner clung to their radios as helplessly as I. There was little else they could do. For at the moment they had no more control than I of the battle on the beaches. . . .*
>
> *When V Corps reported at noon that the situation was "still critical" on all four beach exits, I reluctantly contemplated the diversion of Omaha follow-up forces to Utah and the British beaches. . . .*
>
> *With the Omaha landing falling hours and hours behind schedule, we faced an imminent crisis on the follow-up force. There was due to arrive at noon in the transport area off Omaha Beach a force of 25,000 troops and 4,400 more vehicles to be landed on the second tide. However, only a portion of the assault force of 34,000 troops and 3,300 vehicles had as yet gotten ashore. Unless we moved both forces ashore on D day, the whole intricate schedule of build-up would be thrown off balance. Whatever the improvisation, our build-up would have to be maintained if we were to withstand an enemy counteroffensive. Despite the setbacks we had suffered as the result of bad weather and ineffective bombing, I was shaken to find that we had gone against Omaha with so thin a margin of safety. At the time of sailing we had thought ourselves cushioned against such reversals as these.*
>
> *Not until noon did a radio from Gerow offer a clue to the trouble we had run into on Omaha Beach. Instead of the rag-tag static troops we had expected to find there, the assault had run head-on into one of Rommel's tough field divisions.*

In planning the assault, originally we had counted upon a thin enemy crust of two static divisions between Caen and Cherbourg. Rommel was known to have concentrated his better reserves behind the beach. Among them was the 352d Division which had been assembled at St.-Lo.[10]

Allied Supreme Commander Dwight D. Eisenhower prepared a report concerning the conduct of the war in the European theater on May 8, 1945, called *The Supreme Commander to the Combined Chiefs of Staff on the Operations in Europe of the Allied Expeditionary Force, 6 June 1944 to 8 May 1945*. In this report, he discussed the critical nature of the landings and called out the actions of the 29th Infantry Division as those of "extreme gallantry."

It was in the St-Laurent-sur-Mer sector, on Omaha beach, where the American V Corps assault was launched, that the greatest difficulties were experienced. Not only were the surf conditions worse than elsewhere, causing heavy losses to amphibious tanks and landing craft among the mined obstacles, but the leading formations—the 116th Infantry of the 29th Division at Vierville and the 16th Infantry of the 1st Division at Colleville-sur-Mer—had the misfortune to encounter at the beach the additional strength of a German division, the 352d Infantry, which had recently reinforced the coastal garrison. Against the defense offered in this sector, where the air bombing had been largely ineffective, the naval guns were hampered by the configuration of the ground which made observation difficult and were able to make little impression. Exhausted and disorganized at the edge of the pounding breakers, the Americans were at first pinned to the beaches but, despite a murderous fire from the German field guns along the cliffs, with extreme gallantry, they worked their way through the enemy positions. The cost was heavy; before the beaches were cleared some 800 men of the 116th had fallen and a third of the 16th were lost, but by their unflinching courage they turned what might have been a catastrophe into a glorious victory.[11]

On September 26, 1944, Lieutenant Jack Shea wrote a memorandum to his superiors at Headquarters, Second Information and Historical Service, regarding the events of D-Day. He said, "Inasmuch as it was Gen. Cota's duty to be with different regiments of the division during 'critical' phases of the attack, I had an opportunity to observe much of the preparation, execution and ultimate result of the 'key-actions' within the division. During any attack, Cota was always with the regiment that had the role of 'Main effort.'"[12]

The consideration regarding valorous acts in combat in part takes into account in the actions of others around the affected individuals as a measure of the intensity of the conflict. On D-Day, the heroism on Omaha Beach was beyond measure for the thousands of young men who landed in the face of what stood before them. The DSC citations for several of the officers who served in the immediate vicinity of General Cota reveal quite a story in and of itself in terms of the combat extremes experienced by those men on that beach.

Lieutenant Colonel Max Schneider was the 5th Ranger Infantry Battalion commanding officer (CO). He was one of the most experienced officers on western Omaha Beach. He served as one of Darby's Rangers in the 1st Ranger Infantry Battalion in North Africa and then in Sicily and mainland Italy. He was very observant of the conditions on the beach as his men approached Dog Green and ordered his flotilla to take a hard left at the last moment to avoid, for his men, the carnage that befell the Bedford Boys and the 2d Rangers. His leadership and decisions in the landing of these Rangers helped carry the day up the bluffs. It was to him that General Cota proclaimed, "Lead the way, Rangers!"

The President of the United States of America, authorized by Act of Congress, July 9, 1918, takes pleasure in presenting the Distinguished Service Cross to Lieutenant Colonel (Infantry) Max Ferguson Schneider (ASN: 0-384849), United States Army, for extraordinary heroism in connection with military operations against an armed enemy while serving as Commanding Officer of the 5th Ranger Infantry Battalion, in action against enemy forces on 6 June 1944, at Normandy, France. In the initial landings in the invasion of France, Lieutenant Colonel Schneider led the 5th Ranger Infantry Battalion ashore at "H" hour on D-Day in the face of extremely heavy enemy rifle, machine gun, mortar, artillery, and rocket fire. Upon reaching the beach Lieutenant Colonel Schneider reorganized his unit. During this reorganization, he repeatedly exposed himself to enemy fire. He then led his battalion in the assault on the enemy beach positions, and having accomplished this mission led them up a steep incline to assault the enemy gun emplacements on the top of the hill. The destruction of these enemy positions opened one of the vital beach exits, thereby permitting the troops and equipment which had been pinned down to move inland from the beach, with the result that reinforcements could be landed from the sea. Lieutenant Colonel Schneider's leadership, personal bravery and zealous devotion to duty set an inspiring example to his command and exemplify the highest traditions of the military forces of the United States and reflect great credit upon himself and the United States Army.[13]

Colonel Charles Draper William Canham was the CO of the 116th Infantry. He was very heroic and was wounded on the beach during the opening hour of combat ashore. He successfully led his men inland and established the regimental command post in Vierville, where he orchestrated the battle for his men and provided for the defense of Vierville. He was with Cota intermittently on the beach, at the base of the bluffs, and then met with Cota near noon at the center of Vierville. He did not witness the full width and breadth of Cota's actions. Canham's actions are very valorous in their own right.

The President of the United States of America, authorized by Act of Congress, July 9, 1918, takes pleasure in presenting the Distinguished Service Cross to Colonel (Infantry) Charles Draper William Canham, United States Army, for extraordinary heroism in connection with military operations against an armed enemy while serving as Commanding Officer, 116th Infantry Regiment, 29th Infantry Division, in action against enemy forces on 6 June 1944, at Normandy, France. Colonel Canham landed on the beach shortly after the assault wave of troops had landed. At the time, the enemy fire was at its heaviest and had completely arrested the attack. Though wounded shortly after landing, Colonel Canham, with utter disregard for his own safety, continued to expose himself to the enemy fire in his efforts to reorganize the men. His personal bravery and determination so inspired and heartened the men that they were able to break through the enemy positions. Colonel Canham's outstanding leadership, gallantry and zealous devotion to duty exemplify the highest traditions of the military forces of the United States and reflect great credit upon himself, the 29th Infantry Division, and the United States Army.[14]

Major Richard P. Sullivan was the executive officer of the 5th Ranger Infantry Battalion on D-Day. He was with the unit from its inception and would lead the battalion from shortly after D-Day through the end of the war. He was an astute leader and warrior and led his men from the front.

The President of the United States of America, authorized by Act of Congress, July 9, 1918, takes pleasure in presenting the Distinguished Service Cross to Major Richard P. Sullivan (ASN: 0-399856), United States Army, for extraordinary heroism in connection with military operations against an armed enemy while serving with the 5th Ranger Infantry Battalion, in action against enemy forces during the period 6 to 10 June 1944, in France. Completely disregarding his own safety, Major Sullivan personally directed a successful landing operation and led his men across the beach covered with machine gun, artillery and rocket fire. After reorganizing his men he immediately resumed his duties as Battalion Executive Officer and was placed in command of two Ranger companies which fought their way inland against fierce opposition to join and relieve the Ranger detachment on Pointe du Hoc. After laying communications through the enemy lines under cover of darkness, Major Sullivan directed the Rangers' progress across country to Grandcamp and Maisy. In cooperation with United States Infantry an attack was begun on the Maisy battery. When certain elements were temporarily halted by artillery fire Major Sullivan, who had been wounded at Maisy, calmly and courageously rallied his officers and men, ordered a renewal of the attack, and instead of bypassing the resistance, advanced over heavily mined terrain to capture the Maisy battery with a loss of only fifteen men. Eighty-six prisoners and several large caliber artillery pieces in concrete bunkers were taken. Attacks by Major Sullivan's command contributed greatly to the success of the entire Corps operations. By his intrepid direction, heroic leadership and superior professional ability, Major Sullivan set an inspiring example to his command. His gallant leadership, personal bravery and zealous devotion to duty exemplify the highest traditions of the military forces of the United States and reflect great credit upon himself and the United States Army.[15]

Captain Ralph E. Goranson was the company commander of Company C, 2d Ranger Infantry Battalion. It was his men who took a shellacking on Charlie Sector, yet climbed the bluffs at under half strength and began taking the fight to the enemy at WN 73 after also witnessing the fate that befell the Bedford Boys.

The President of the United States of America, authorized by Act of Congress, July 9, 1918, takes pleasure in presenting the Distinguished Service Cross to Captain (Infantry) Ralph E. Goranson (ASN: 0-1299035), United States Army, for extraordinary heroism in connection with military operations against an armed enemy while serving as Commanding Officer of Company C, 2d Ranger Infantry Battalion, in action against enemy forces on 6 and 7 June 1944, at Vierville-sur-Mer, France. Captain Goranson landed with his Ranger company at "H" hour on D-Day with the initial assault wave in the invasion of France, in the face of heavy automatic enfilading fire from three different directions and mortar and artillery fire from cliffs overlooking the beach. In spite of extremely heavy casualties, Captain Goranson calmly and courageously reorganized his company and led them in a successful assault upon the enemy positions. He then led his company in an advance to force a junction with the main body of the assault. Though it took ten hours of the heaviest kind of fighting to reach the main body, his men, inspired by his outstanding leadership, continuously advanced until the mission was accomplished. Captain Goranson's heroic actions, personal bravery and zealous devotion to duty exemplify the highest traditions of the military forces of the United States and reflect great credit upon himself, his unit, and the United States Army.[16]

Lieutenant Colonel James Earl Rudder led his Rangers against the German positions at Pointe du Hoc. He served as the overall Provisional Ranger Group commander on D-Day. His men's numbers were cut in half accomplishing their mission.

The President of the United States of America, authorized by Act of Congress, July 9, 1918, takes pleasure in presenting the Distinguished Service Cross to Lieutenant Colonel (Infantry) James Earl Rudder (ASN: 0-294916), United States Army, for extraordinary heroism in connection with military operations against an armed enemy while serving with the 2d Ranger Infantry Battalion, in action against enemy forces on 6 June 1944, at Normandy, France. Lieutenant Colonel Rudder, commanding Force "A" of the Rangers, landed on the beach with his unit which was immediately subjected to heavy rifle, machine gun, mortar and artillery fire. Devastating fire was also directed from the cliffs overlooking the beach. Completely disregarding his own safety, Lieutenant Colonel Rudder immediately scaled the cliffs in order to better direct the attack. By his determined leadership and dauntlessness he inspired his men so that they successfully withstood three enemy counterattacks. Though wounded again he still refused to be evacuated. Lieutenant Colonel Rudder's heroic leadership, personal bravery and zealous devotion to duty exemplify the highest traditions of the military forces of the United States and reflect great credit upon himself and the United States Army.[17]

Captain George P. Whittington was the Company B commander, 5th Ranger Infantry Battalion (my grandfather's unit). He was a fierce warrior and had served for five years in China as a U.S. marine before joining the army and ultimately the Rangers. He was a tough man, having been the fleet boxing champion and served along the Yangtze River to guard U.S. shipping interests from Japanese aggression. Company B knocked out several enemy positions up the bluffs. He was with Cota on the western edge of Vierville when Cota, leading from the front, was nearly shot in the head by a sniper while rallying the men to battle, as recorded by Private First Class Randall Ching in his testimony and in the testimonies and records of others.

The President of the United States of America, authorized by Act of Congress, July 9, 1918, takes pleasure in presenting the Distinguished Service Cross to Captain (Cavalry) George P. Whittington, Jr. (ASN: 0-403921), United States Army, for extraordinary heroism in connection with military operations against an armed enemy while serving as Commanding Officer of Company B, 5th Ranger Infantry Battalion, in action against enemy forces on 6 June 1944, in France. Captain Whittington commanded a Ranger company which landed on the coast of France at "H" hour. The landing was made on the beach against heavy rifle, machine gun, mortar, artillery and rocket fire of the enemy. Despite this fire, he personally supervised the breaching of hostile barbed wire and obstacles by the use of Bangalores. He then led his company and the remainder of his battalion through the gap created. He then directed the scaling of a 100-foot cliff by his company. When he reached the top of the cliff he crawled under enemy machine gun fire and destroyed the enemy position. Captain Whittington's bravery, aggressiveness and inspired leadership exemplify the highest traditions of the military forces of the United States and reflect great credit upon himself, his unit, and the United States Army.[18]

1st Lieutenant Joseph R. Lacy was the Provisional Ranger Group chaplain and served on a completely different plane of existence during the invasion. He remained on the beach and saved as many men as he could.

> *The President of the United States of America, authorized by Act of Congress, July 9, 1918, takes pleasure in presenting the Distinguished Service Cross to First Lieutenant (Chaplain) Joseph R. Lacy (ASN: 0-525094), United States Army, for extraordinary heroism in connection with military operations against an armed enemy while serving as a Chaplain with the 5th Ranger Infantry Battalion, in action against enemy forces on 6 June 1944, in France. In the invasion of France, Chaplain Lacy landed on the beach with one of the leading assault units. Numerous casualties had been inflicted by the heavy rifle, mortar, artillery and rocket fire of the enemy. With complete disregard for his own safety, he moved about the beach, continually exposed to enemy fire, and assisted wounded men from the water's edge to the comparative safety of a nearby sea wall, and at the same time inspired the men to similar disregard for the enemy fire. Chaplain Lacy's heroic and dauntless actions exemplify the highest traditions of the military forces of the United States and reflect great credit upon himself, his unit, and the United States Army.*[19]

1st Lieutenant Charles H. "Ace" Parker was commander of Company A, 5th Ranger Infantry Battalion. He and twenty-three of his men were credited with making their way through the gap on the beach and up the bluff and then making the four-mile journey in enemy-held territory from Omaha Beach to Pointe du Hoc, the only force of men able to reinforce the beleaguered Lieutenant Colonel Rudder. Ace remembered the moment when General Cota approached the Rangers and his men, and he saw Lieutenant Colonel Schneider stand up and snap a salute to the general under fire as he inspired the men and gave orders. According to Ace's biography, "Cota came up strolling down the beach and said, 'Lead the Way Rangers, my men are green.' Parker thought to himself, 'Well, we were inexperienced too.' Cota inquired, 'What unit are you?' and stated, 'We have to get off this beach now.' He was moving along from group to group. Cota was an old timer, someone to greatly admire."[20] The inspiration of General Cota, in addition to the extreme proficiency of the Rangers and their moxie, enabled these men to be some of the few on all of Omaha Beach to fully accomplish their primary D-Day objectives.

*The President of the United States of America, authorized by Act of Congress, July 9, 1918, takes pleasure in presenting the Distinguished Service Cross to First Lieutenant (Infantry) Charles H. Parker (ASN: 0-1290298), United States Army, for extraordinary heroism in connection with military operations against an armed enemy while Commanding a Company of the 5th Ranger Infantry Battalion, in action against enemy forces on 6, 7, and 8 June 1944, in France. In the invasion of France First Lieutenant Parker led his company up the beach against heavy enemy rifle, machine gun and artillery fire. Once past the beach he reorganized and continued inland. During this advance numerous groups of enemy resistance were encountered. Through his personal bravery and sound leadership this resistance was overcome, and his company succeeded in capturing *******, the Battalion objective. The following morning First Lieutenant Parker led a patrol through enemy-held territory in an effort to establish contact with the balance of the Battalion. First Lieutenant Parker's superior, personal valor and zealous devotion to duty exemplify the highest traditions of the military forces of the United States and reflect great credit upon himself, his unit, and the United States Army.*[21]

Company K landed on Easy Green to the left of WN 67 in a relatively tight group. The company organized in several small groups along with their fellow companies as assault sections, acting independently as per their training. By 9 a.m., they, along with Companies I and M, were up past the bluff. Company K was slow in its forward progress, took sporadic machine-gun fire while crossing the beach and tidal flat, and lost fifteen to twenty men before reaching the top. The company was then pinned down in the open fields by machine-gun fire and shelling. Two boat teams of K and a few men of I, trying to bypass the enemy resistance to the north, cut across the draw about halfway down toward Les Moulins. Making their way across country, this group found its way to the coastal highway, sighted the 5th Rangers ahead, and tailed them into Vierville. On the way, the Company K group was attacked by a small enemy party from the flank and lost several men to surprise machine-gun fire. Eventually, the K group reached regimental headquarters and was used as its security detachment for that night.[22] These men did not interact directly with Cota, but his training and leadership prepared them.

The President of the United States of America, authorized by Act of Congress, July 9, 1918, takes pleasure in presenting the Distinguished Service Cross to Second Lieutenant (Infantry) Leonard Alton Anker (ASN: 0-529110), United States Army, for extraordinary heroism in connection with military operations against an armed enemy while serving as Platoon Leader in an Infantry Company K of the 116th Infantry Regiment, 29th Infantry Division, in action against enemy forces on 6 June 1944, at Normandy, France. At the time of the landing of Second Lieutenant Anker's platoon, the beach was under withering fire from enemy artillery, automatic weapons and small arms. After proceeding about 200 yards, all troops in the vicinity of Second Lieutenant Anker were pinned down by the devastating fire. Second Lieutenant Anker located an enemy machine gun that was inflicting heavy casualties. With complete disregard for his own safety, Second Lieutenant Anker, aided by an enlisted man whom he inspired to action by his own gallantry, fearlessly charged and destroyed the enemy strongpoint with hand grenades, killing 16 and capturing 5 of the enemy. Second Lieutenant Anker's intrepid actions, personal bravery and zealous devotion to duty exemplify the highest traditions of the military forces of the United States and reflect great credit upon himself, the 29th Infantry Division, and the United States Army.[23]

Private First Class Alexander W. Barber was one of the Ranger medics on the beach on D-Day. His actions, like those of medics across all five beaches, were tremendous. It is unknown what interaction he had with General Cota, and based on the job he did, his attentions were elsewhere. The courage under fire of these men was and remains something to behold.

The President of the United States of America, authorized by Act of Congress, July 9, 1918, takes pleasure in presenting the Distinguished Service Cross to Private First Class Alexander W. Barber (ASN: 33575048), United States Army, for extraordinary heroism in connection with military operations against an armed enemy while serving as a Medical Aidman with Headquarters and Headquarters Company, 5th Ranger Infantry Battalion, in action against enemy forces on 6 June 1944, in France. Private First Class Barber landed with his medical unit on the coast of France at a time when the beach was under heavy enemy rifle, machine gun and artillery fire. Numerous casualties had already been inflicted by this devastating fire. In spite of this heavy fire, Private First Class Barber constantly exposed himself to the direct fire of the enemy as he went along the beach administering aid to the wounded. On one occasion he took a horse and cart into the middle of an artillery barrage to bring out three men who had been wounded. Private First Class Barber's intrepid actions, personal bravery and zealous devotion to duty exemplify the highest traditions of the military forces of the United States and reflect great credit upon himself, his unit, and the United States Army.[24]

The 29th Infantry Division's 2d Battalion Headquarters and Headquarters Company came in on Dog Red at 7 a.m. As the men landed, they had to take refuge behind tanks ashore due to heavy fire, only to realize that the tanks themselves were primary targets for the German gunners. Major Sidney V. Bingham Jr., battalion commander, was one of the first to reach the shingle. He set to work in an effort to revive the leaderless sections of Company F already ashore. These men had no working radio for nearly an hour. He attempted unsuccessfully to organize an assault of the D-3 exit. He managed to gather approximately fifty men of Company F and move them forward to a prominent three-story home on the northeastern corner of the mouth of the draw. From this position, the men took cover in a well-developed German trench system. The major gathered a ten-man party and attempted an assault of the bluff but was repulsed. When he returned to the house, he gathered men from the F, H, and Headquarters Companies of the 2d Battalion and moved them inland to the east of the draw.[25] These men passed through the fields later to become Transit Area 2, moved four hundred yards farther south, and turned west to Saint-Laurent-sur-Mer. They were held up at Military Grid Reference System 667894 some three hundred yards west of the junction with the Vierville–St. Laurent road and prevented from passing through the village. General Cota came to the front of the column at a point where two large stucco barns stood flush by the roadside. He and Lieutenant Shea witnessed five dead riflemen along the road, having been picked off by fire from a nearby strongpoint. Cota advised Bingham to contain the strongpoint and bypass it. Major Bingham bypassed the *Widerstandsnest* to the right and moved along the top of the bluffs as he and his men moved to join the remainder of the regiment in Vierville.[26]

The President of the United States of America, authorized by Act of Congress, July 9, 1918, takes pleasure in presenting the Distinguished Service Cross to Major (Infantry) Sidney Vincent Bingham, Jr. (ASN: 0-23267), United States Army, for extraordinary heroism in connection with military operations against an armed enemy while serving as Commanding Officer, 1st Battalion, 116th Infantry Regiment, 29th Infantry Division, (Hq Co, 2Bn) in action against enemy forces on 6 June 1944, at Normandy, France. When his battalion was pinned down on the beach by the heavy and intense enemy fire, Major Bingham gathered together five of his men and personally led them across the beach and up a cliff in an attempt to seek out an enemy machine gun that had been inflicting heavy casualties on his unit. Though unable to reach the machine gun, he was, nevertheless, able to discover its location. He returned to the fire-swept beach and organized a flank and rear attack which succeeded in taking the enemy position, thereby permitting his unit to advance. Major Bingham's superior leadership, personal bravery and zealous devotion to duty exemplify the highest traditions of the military forces of the United States and reflect great credit upon himself, the 29th Infantry Division, and the United States Army.[27]

The 3d Battalion of the 116th RCT was scheduled to land between 7:20 and 7:30 a.m., behind the 2d Battalion, on Dog White, Dog Red, and Easy Green. Five to ten minutes later, the entire battalion came in to the east of Les Moulins, with some elements on the edge of Easy Red. Company L came in midway between the draws, its craft rather scattered, and enemy fire was so light and ineffective that some of the troops had been several minutes on the open sand before they became aware of machine-gun fire. Here and there, small enemy detachments with machine guns offered resistance from prepared and well-dug-in positions, and a number of skirmishes were fought by sections of Companies L and I. By noon most of Company L and several sections of Company I were at the edge of St. Laurent, on the northwest, where the road from Les Moulins comes into the village at the head of the draw. The rest of the battalion was held at the crossroad all afternoon. Several attempts to advance were stopped by machine-gun fire, from positions which the men were unable to locate. Company L suffered most of its casualties for the day in these actions.

The President of the United States of America, authorized by Act of Congress, July 9, 1918, takes pleasure in presenting the Distinguished Service Cross to Technical Sergeant L. M. Armstrong (ASN: 20365625), United States Army, for extraordinary heroism in connection with military operations against an armed enemy while serving with Company L, 3d Battalion, 116th Infantry Regiment, 29th Infantry Division, in action against enemy forces on 6 June 1944, at Normandy, France. Technical Sergeant Armstrong came in on the initial wave of infantry that waded ashore from landing craft in the face of extremely heavy enemy fire. Despite severe casualties, he fearlessly stepped to the head of his men and, with complete disregard for his own safety, set an example and shouted encouragement to the others to follow him. Technical Sergeant Armstrong's gallant actions, personal bravery and zealous devotion to duty exemplify the highest traditions of the military forces of the United States and reflect great credit upon himself, the 29th Infantry Division, and the United States Army.[28]

This is just a sampling of the heroism that surrounded General Cota that day. He led these men and inspired their actions through his direct leadership and courage along his amazing seventeen-mile journey: his seventeen-mile, one-man, all-out assault on Hitler's *Atlantikwall.* There are many other examples from within the ranks of the Rangers and the 29th Infantry Division of men who rose up and conducted warfare upon the enemy, resulting in the award of the DSC. The instances of Silver Stars and Bronze Stars were very numerous on the beaches that day as well. In 1947, the army decided that all men who made the assault landing earned the Bronze Star by the nature of the event and ferocity of the day.

Among the records contained in Cota's Military Personnel Record File was a copy of documentation of an award of the Distinguished Service Order (British) on behalf of the king of England, signed by Field Marshal Montgomery in recognition of the D-Day heroics of General Cota (see figure 10.3). The citation for this award stated,

In the face of heavy enemy rifle, machine gun, and artillery fire he personally led the Division in the assault and continued in the forefront of the fight until the Division had moved inland to capture its objective. The courage and outstanding leadership of Brigadier General Cota were an inspiring example to his men, and were in keeping with the highest traditions of the Armed Forces of the United States.[29]

Figure 10.3. General Cota receives the DSC and British Distinguished Service Order on July 7, 1944 (National Archives and Records Administration).

A second item of importance in Cota's records was a December 6, 1945, recommendation for award prepared by Major General Charles H. Gerhardt, commanding general, 29th Infantry Division (attached). In this report, General Gerhardt, some sixteen months after then major general Cota had left his command, asserted his acknowledgment of Cota's accomplishments, heroics, and importance on D-Day. His words, those of General Cota's immediate superior officer on June 6, 1944, bear testimony, as proof beyond a reasonable doubt, that he performed valorous action and demonstrated a level of personal bravery, at the risk of his own life, so conspicuous as to clearly distinguish him above his comrades. The report states,

> *It is a matter of record in the history of V Corps that General Cota was the first General Officer to land on Omaha Beach, swimming and wading ashore at 0730B hours, 6 June 1944 and daringly led the troops inland from the fire swept beach. There followed a period when, as the Division Commander's*

personal representative in the field, he was on hand at every critical action from the storming of the high ground along Omaha Beach through the bitter hedgerow actions that followed and culminating in the siege and capture of St. Lo by Task Force "C" which he commanded. This vital and difficult action over hilly terrain against a fiercely resisting enemy, determined to exact the greatest possible number of casualties as the price of victory, paved the way for the Normandy breakthrough and climaxed General Cota's record with the Division. His performance in the field as a combat commander, as a tactician, and as a courageous leader were unsurpassed, and his conduct under fire on Omaha Beach on D-Day has become legend among the troops of the Division. The effects of his training program upon this command were manifested again and again in the hard months that followed his departure from the Division, and the outstanding results achieved can be traced directly to his efforts during the training phase. It can be stated without reservation that his contribution to the 29th Infantry Division and through it to the United States Government was prodigious.[30]

To Major General Carroll D. Childers, this is sure proof that General Gerhardt regarded Cota as a senior officer with no peer. This compliment by Gerhardt surely speaks to one of the key requirements for the award: specifically, that the action be so conspicuous as to clearly distinguish the individual above his or her comrades. On a day of heroism in the extreme, calling out one man for prodigious contributions and unsurpassed leadership and courage on the field of battle was amazing. Indicating that the actions of this same man under fire had become the stuff of legend breaks the mold.

Reporter Don Whitehead made a case for the general's nature in the face of battle in August 1944. He wrote the following on July 29, 1944, for the Associated Press, and it appeared in the *Twenty-Niner*, *Stars and Stripes*, and major U.S. newspapers:

When Brig. General Norman D. Cota sings to himself then the boys of the 29th Division know everything is moving along smoothly. But when the general doesn't sing, there's something wrong. Right now the general is singing. This tall soldier from Chelsea, Mass., is one of the ruggedest characters in the United States Army. He led the task force which drove into St. Lo on July 18, and he was right in the front of his column, directing operations. He usually is found around the front lines where the fighting is roughest, and he moves with complete disregard for his own safety, finding out for himself what is going on and cheering up his men with his good humor. When he led his task force into St. Lo he was wounded slightly in the arm by shrapnel. But he refused to leave for the rear until his troops had accomplished the mission of occupying the city.[31]

Joseph H. Ewing wrote about Cota and his dauntless nature in his unit history of the division, *29, Let's GO! A History of the 29th Infantry Division in World War II.*

Brig. General Norman "Dutch" Cota was a rare soldier. He seemed to be always up near the fighting. Stories about General Cota on D-Day have become almost legendary in the Division. Throughout the fighting in the hedgerows to St. Lo he was continually along the front-line foxholes. He went into St. Lo with his Task Force Charlie and walked the streets of the town while infantry was still mopping up resistance. Men in the rifle companies would see his tall, lean ambling figure moving about in the hedgerows, defiant of personal danger. Lois Azrael, Baltimore News Post war correspondent, wrote:

"He fills his canteen with water and his pockets with cigars and sets out in a jeep for whatever front is most critical. . . . After pausing at the unit's Command Post to discuss the situation and suggest tactics to the unit staff officers he sets out afoot for the places where the trouble is the toughest."

As much a part of his battle equipment as his helmet were his cane and his cigar. He was never without them. He was forever singing under his breath queer toneless tunes for which he made up his own words. Most of them were meaningless, but they must have helped him for he mumbled and sang them—more than ever when things were tough. A person couldn't always make out the words, but sometimes they were intelligible. On one occasion while he was walking through artillery fire the words of one of his "songs" came very clear. He was singing: "If I knew the answer to this what a hell of a smart guy I'd be!"

General Cota had an unruffled attitude about enemy shellfire. He almost dared it to hit him. He often scorned the foxhole and slit trench. Once an 88 mm shell burst near him. Men all about him hurried for cover. One man, calling to him, suggested that it would be healthy for him to get into a hole.

"Why?" Dutch Cota replied. "It's landed already, hasn't it?"[32]

Historian David Irving wrote his narrative about the generals involved in the D-Day invasion in *The War between the Generals: Inside the Allied High Command*. On the morning of D-Day, Irving wrote, "The politician-generals, the manager-generals, and the planning generals had done their work. Now the battle's triumph or defeat devolved on the combat commanders, who would put their lives on the line along with their men. One such was an American brigadier named Norman D. Cota." The author contended that one thing alone saved the day on Omaha Beach. That was the "generalship, particularly the bravery and cool headedness of one man. Norman Cota, an expert in amphibious assaults and infantry warfare, had decided that he probably would die that day anyhow, and that if he survived he would be a hero, but either way he would put his mission first." Omaha Beach took its place with the Battles of Saratoga (American Revolution), the Alamo (Texas's war for independence from Mexico), Gettysburg (American Civil War), and Château-Thierry (World War I) as an intensive display of American fortitude and determination. The author wrote that Cota provided both fire and heart that finally got the troops off the beach. In addition to his citations, he earned "a hell of a bawling out" from Bradley for getting too far out in front of his men. His men in turn wrote that they would "go through hell for him." Irving concluded his thoughts about General Cota by writing, "Norman Cota penetrated inland on this day, D-day, to a point the American front line as a whole would not reach until two days later. He would get a Silver Star and the Distinguished Service Cross from the Americans, the Distinguished Service Order, the second highest British medal, from Montgomery, and a 'hell of a bawling out' too from the army commander, Bradley, for getting too far out in front. His men had proved what one of them wrote a few days later, that they would 'go through hell for him.'"[33]

On June 25, 1969, the Honorable William B. Spong Jr. of Virginia rose on the floor of the U.S. Senate and read extension remarks made by Dr. Forrest Pogue, executive director of the George C. Marshall Research Library at Lexington, Virginia, on the twenty-fifth anniversary of D-Day. This remains part of the *Congressional Record*, Extensions of Remarks, pp. 17418–423, dated Wednesday, June 25, 1969.

Amidst all the gloomy summaries, there were many bright spots. On the 116th Infantry front, the assistant division commander, Brigadier General Norman D. Cota, and the regimental commander, Col. C. D. W. Canham, had set to work shortly after coming ashore around 0730 to organize the attack. Shortly afterwards Canham was wounded but he returned to the task after receiving first aid. According to the accounts of the soldiers, General Cota was everywhere that morning. His activities in rallying the men and working to clear the exits from the beaches made him a legendary figure.[34]

The research team for the MOH nomination application included Major General John C. Raaen Jr. (Ret.). He offered very candid and strong considerations for the group to weigh in preparing the package. He stated in an email,

The situation that faced the invading Allied Forces at H-Hour of D-Day on Omaha Dog Beach was far from that expected in the Invasion plan. First, the bombing of the beach fortifications was a TOTAL failure. No bomb hit within a mile of the beach. Instead of destroyed German positions with bomb pock-marked beaches for cover, the beach area and its defenders were unscathed. Second, Omaha Beach was expected to have about 800 defenders in positions along the crest of the bluffs and in the fifteen Widerstands-nesten *(battle positions containing automatic weapons, mortars and light artillery) that supported the Infantry defenders along the bluffs as well as defending the exits from the beach. These German troops were known to be low grade static troops, many impressed into the German Army after being captured in earlier battles. There was also one maneuver battalion in reserve. Instead, unknown to the invading forces, the 352d Infantry Division, an experienced, full strength, well trained and well rested division, had moved from its training positions near St. Lo to the beach area on June 5th. This nearly doubled the strength of the defenders to 1100 men plus increasing the reserve battalions from one to five!*

Major General John C. Raaen, Jr (ret)
June 30, 2018

Private First Class Arden Earll's moving testimony on behalf of General Cota concluded with what is perhaps the most compelling argument for how Brigadier General Cota affected not just this one soldier but thousands of men on Bloody Omaha, on D-Day, and beyond.

Private First Class Arden Earll, mortarman, MOS 504, Company H, 2d Battalion, 116th Infantry, 29th Infantry Division
Seeing the General with that type of courage he was expressing through his leadership gave me and those around me the courage to keep going. If anybody needed any courage, just seeing him just walk up there in broad sight, exposing himself, it encouraged the troops. Had he not done that, it might have been just a heck of a lot worse. So as you can see, in my own opinion, General Cota saved D-Day for all of us. If he hadn't have done what he did, and the troops would have really spooked out, we might have lost D-Day altogether, but for a few people like General Cota. He never thought of himself or his own safety, or anything like that, I don't think. He deserves the Medal of Honor.[35]

During World War II, the 29th Infantry Division lost 3,887 killed in action, 15,541 wounded in action, 347 missing in action, and 845 taken prisoners of war, in addition to 8,665 noncombat casualties, during 242 days of combat. This amounted to over 200 percent of the division's normal strength. How could one look upon the actions of this humble man, a true warrior and leader of men during one of the most important military operations in U.S. military history, and not come to the conclusion that General Norman Cota is worthy of our nation's highest honor, the Congressional Medal of Honor?

In conclusion, the case for General Cota's deserving the Medal of Honor is solid and the evidence overwhelming. Brigadier General Cota landed in the midst of the most critical sector of Omaha Beach in terms of the possibility of failure within the overall invasion on D-Day. The Germans inflicted thousands of casualties and threatened to push the 29th Infantry Division and supporting units back into the sea. His conspicuous leadership, gallantry, and intrepid demeanor clearly demonstrate a level of valor not just for a single event at a moment in time but also for his complete set of actions for well over a twenty-four-hour period.

CHAPTER ELEVEN

A Dream Realized

IN HIS 1983 AUTOBIOGRAPHY, *A GENERAL'S LIFE*, OMAR BRADLEY WROTE, "Omaha Beach . . . was a nightmare. Even now it brings pain to recall what really happened there on June 6, 1944. I have returned many times to honor the valiant men who died on that beach. They should never be forgotten. Nor should those who lived to carry the day by the slimmest of margins. Every man who set foot on Omaha Beach that day was a hero."[1]

Tom Morris grew up in a family of heroes, and that has greatly influenced his life. There was Dutch, of course, but also his own father, Thomas J. Morris Jr., who served as the company commander of Company I, 358th Infantry Regiment, 90th Infantry Division, on D+2 at Utah Beach. Tom's uncle Dan (Norman D. Cota Jr.) was a U.S. Army Air Corps fighter pilot and served in theater "flying over all of 'em." Tom refers to these men as heroes of magnificent proportion. Growing up, he never thought much about his grandfather's pivotal role in the D-Day operations. He often refers to himself as a "snot-nosed kid," unaware of the magnitude of Dutch's service. He remembers attending Sunday evening fried chicken dinners at the Officers Club at McConnell Air Force Base as a youngster and telling his own mother how everyone must sure like his grandfather because they all got to their feet when he entered the room. His mother would just smile at her son, knowing the real reason for the display of military courtesy exhibited. Tom remembers his parents' orders: "Never ask Dutch, Dad, or Uncle Dan about the European Theater of Operations [ETO]. Be a good listener." He soundly remembers that, as is customary with the "Greatest Generation," very little was expounded upon by his family. As Tom aged, he came to realize what he calls "the learning curve" of the ETO during the war, with all of its horrors. He remembers his dad telling him while he was growing up, "Don't ever lose a deal because you were 'outworked.'" "The harder you work, the luckier you get." "Tommy, are they shooting at you? No? Then it's not that bad, now is it?"

Dutch never sought the Medal of Honor (MOH) for himself. What was shared with family about D-Day were Dutch's words: "I didn't think I'd see sundown." When he passed away in 1971, two years after his beloved Connie, the military was not the most important thing on his mind; rather, it was his family. In 1965, Dutch, Connie, and Tom's parents traveled to Normandy. They retraced Dutch's and Uncle Jim's wartime journeys from "Normandy through the road to Berlin" in 1944 and 1945. Tom remembers family discussions that centered on his father and grandfather having returned to "Normandy going East to Berlin" in the years following the war.

He distinctly remembers how they couldn't return to the States fast enough, owing to the memories the visit sparked. When asked whether they ever desired to return to Europe, they couldn't say "HELL NO!" fast enough.

Tom's first experience in Normandy was on Sunday, August 28, 1994. He drove from Paris and arrived at the American Cemetery at Omaha Beach, Colleville, on Sunday at 4:30 p.m. The closing time of the cemetery was 5 p.m. He found himself walking over the hallowed grounds in overwhelmed astonishment at what he was seeing, his field of vision full of some of the more than ninety-three hundred graves of the honored dead (as illustrated in figure 11.1). He remembers distinctly how each of the gravestones faced westward, toward home. He remembered the giant American flag standing sentinel over our warriors. As he meandered through the graves, the cemetery's uniformed superintendent, Hans Hooker, yelled out to him that the facility would close shortly. Tom described himself as a "naïve tourist and punk," and so he walked right up to Hans to say hi, not knowing him at all at the time. Hans asked, "Do you know anyone buried here? Do you know anyone who landed in Normandy?" Tom told Hans, "This is the first time I've been here. I'm

Figure 11.1. American Cemetery at Colleville (Ron Knight).

General Cota's grandson." Hans asked, "What hotel are you staying at?" Tom told him, "I have no hotel yet," and Hans courteously offered the Cemetery Barracks. This arrangement lasted for three days. Hans effectively acted as Tom's personal tour guide as Tom explored the sites, and the two became friends.

That Sunday evening, Hans took Tom to the Restaurant L'Omaha on Omaha Beach, near the Vierville exit. After a couple beers, Hans later directed Tom to a plaque erected along the D517, the boulevard de Cauvigny, about 440 feet southwest from the 88-mm casemate of WN 72 along the western retaining wall on the road leading to Vierville. The plaque states,

5TH RANGER BN

On D-Day, 6 June 1944, the Fifth U.S. Army Ranger Battalion Landed on Omaha Beach near Vierville-Sur-Mer under Intense Enemy Fire. Responding to the Brigadier General Cota's Historic Order, "Lead the Way

309

Rangers" the Fifth Ranger Battalion with A, B, And C Companies of the Ranger Battalion, Advanced against Strongly Defended Enemy Fortifications Manned by General Rommel's Toughest Troops. The Ranger Breakthrough Opened the Beach Allowing Troops of the 29th Infantry Division to Pour Through and Thus Paved the Way for the Liberation of France.

Dedicated to Our Fallen by the Ranger Battalions Assoc. WW II, the Citizens of Normandy and the 5th Ranger Battalion. 6 June 1984

Seeing his grandfather's name etched in bronze on this hallowed battlefield moved him to tears. Tom says he will never forget how reading those words made him feel. On the next day, August 29, 1994, he drove west to Sainte-Mère-Église, Saint-Lô, Carentan, Periers, Vire, and Bayeux to explore the places where he knew his family had served. He recalled getting lost along the way near Carentan and that the hedgerows remained the dominant feature in the area. He thought to himself, "What if these centuries-old buildings and roads could talk?" The citizens of Normandy provided Tom with the utmost in superior hospitality during his trip. As he moved west and stopped at Periers, a town liberated by his own father, he found a roster of liberators posted in town. It displayed the name "Captain Thomas J. Morris, Jr." Again, Tom shed tears as he had overwhelming feelings of humility, gratitude, appreciation, patriotism, and admiration for the work ethic of his kin. He can't help but recall his father's words: "Tommy, are they shooting at you? No? Then it's not that bad, now is it?" The memories and thoughts burned into his mind will dominate Tom's thoughts about his family from here to eternity.

He found himself in Normandy again on the sixtieth anniversary of D-Day in June 2004. Tom's first thought that his grandfather's exploits on D-Day warranted the MOH occurred as he attended the anniversary celebration. It was here that he first met Joe Balkoski, and he vividly recalled how Joe "graphically educated" him regarding Dutch and his role on D-Day. The first thing Balkoski did when they met was to pull out a copy of his book and hand it to Tom. He told him to flip to pages 359–61, and Tom then read his description of the argument for an upgrade of Cota's Distinguished Service Cross (DSC) to the MOH. The two men discussed the merits of General Cota's service and case for the MOH. Joseph Balkoski spent thirty-four years as the military historian for the famed 29th Infantry Division. Tom and Joe became friends. Tom considers Joe a great guy, a great friend, and a great author. In his book *Omaha Beach*, Balkoski gave perhaps the first scholarly account of the rationale for a potential upgrade of Cota's DSC to the MOH. Tom found this case moving and compelling, and this chance meeting planted the seeds of a worthy effort that would mature over sixteen years. Tom described the effort to seek an upgrade to a MOH as a "ship with no sails" until 2017. Joe Balkoski's 2004 case argued,

> *The Medal of Honor is the highest military decoration that may be awarded to members of the armed forces of the United States. The U.S. Army's version of the Medal of Honor was established in 1862 by Congressional resolution, later approved by President Lincoln, to recognize soldiers who "shall most distinguish themselves by their gallantry in action, and other soldier-like qualities." In recognition of their valor on Omaha Beach on June 6, 1944, the U.S. Army awarded Medals of Honor to three soldiers, all from the 1st Infantry Division. Two of these awards were posthumous. . . .*
>
> *One can only speculate as to why, in a battle of such intensity and significance as Omaha Beach, only three applications for decorations resulted in Medals of Honor—all in the 1st Infantry Division. According to the officer boards examining each appeal, perhaps only those three actions satisfied the clearly stated requirements for "conspicuous gallantry and intrepidity at risk of life above and beyond the call of duty." However, the battle-hardened 1st Infantry Division, which had fought in two major campaigns in the Mediterranean theater prior to D-Day, was presumably much more familiar and adept with the process by which military decorations were applied for and awarded than units new to combat. Once the Omaha invasion was over, the Fighting First's staffs knew exactly what to do to gain official recognition of its soldiers' extraordinary courage on D-Day, and they jumped to the task with celerity and professionalism. The result was three Medals of Honor and fifty-three DSCs for June 6 alone. The 1st Division's fifty-three D-Day DSCs amount to slightly more than 1 percent of all U.S. Army DSCs awarded throughout World War II.*
>
> *In comparison, most of the other outfits that participated in the Omaha invasion filed far fewer appeals for decorations. For example, the Fighting First's partner in the Omaha assault, the 29th Division, received no Medals of Honor and about half the number of DSCs (twenty-seven) as the 1st*

Division for its D-Day actions, despite the fact the 1st and 29th contributed roughly equal numbers of men to the invasion. Indeed, this pattern continued until the end of the war in Europe: In the European theater of operations (ETO), the army granted the 1st Division roughly 4,300 decorations of Silver Star or higher, while the 29th Division was accorded only 877—this despite the fact that the 29th suffered about 5,000 more casualties in the ETO than the 1st and was in action for roughly the same time period. And yet there is one person in the 29th Division whose actions on Omaha Beach were so worthy of the Medal of Honor that it is astonishing that he was never even considered for it. Dozens of eyewitness accounts . . . establish beyond any doubt that Brig. Gen. Norman D. Cota, the 29th's assistant division commander, repeatedly performed extraordinary feats of valor that were instrumental in rescuing the seemingly unsolvable and deadly situation faced by first-wave assault troops on the western sector of Omaha Beach at about 8:00 A.M. on D-Day. Cota's exploits in encouraging the troops to leave the beach and move up the bluffs, which ultimately led to the capture of Vierville and the opening of the Vierville draw, surely fulfilled the Medal of Honor requirements for "conspicuous gallantry and intrepidity at risk of life above and beyond the call of duty." In spite of overwhelming evidence corroborating Cota's performance, however, he was awarded not the Medal of Honor, but the DSC.

Officer boards established to evaluate petitions for decorations in Normandy may have maintained an unspoken understanding that senior officers of colonel rank and above should be considered for awards no higher than the DSC, limiting Medals of Honor to officers and men whose duties required them to be present more or less continuously in the front lines. Such a theory would also account for the army's failure to grant a Medal of Honor to the 16th Infantry's CO, Col. George Taylor, who performed acts of heroism on D-Day almost identical to Cota's on an adjacent beach sector, with equally beneficial results. The only exception to the senior officer rule on D-Day was Brig. Gen. Theodore Roosevelt, Jr., the 4th Infantry Division's assistant division commander and son of the former president, who was granted the Medal of Honor in September 1944 for his D-Day actions on Utah Beach. The award was posthumous, as Roosevelt had died of a heart attack in July.

The facts are irrefutable that for most of D-Day, Omaha Beach was a great leveler of rank. Everyone, from general to private, was in equal danger every second; there was no such thing as a secure command post anywhere on the beach where colonels and generals could calmly deliberate their next moves, with runners rushing in and out bearing dispatches to and from the distant front. By necessity, Cota and Taylor fought all day on Omaha Beach not as a conventional general and colonel, but as de facto platoon leaders or company commanders—positions typically held by young officers half the ages of the two older men. Cota's and Taylor's extraordinary actions on D-Day, by any measure, contributed mightily to the invasion's ultimate success.

The U.S. Army should seriously consider upgrading the DSC awards for General Cota and Colonel Taylor to Medals of Honor. This is especially appropriate now, in the twenty-first century, when careful retrospect of sixty years' duration yields mounting recognition that the Omaha Beach invasion was a pivotal test of America's resolve and arguably its most decisive moment in World War II. Cota's and Taylor's remarkable accomplishments on Omaha Beach on June 6, 1944, are critical reminders that military leadership—well timed, expertly and courageously applied—is the key to success in war. Today their actions are worthy of far broader recognition and gratitude, for without them the end result of the Omaha invasion might have been much different.

A grateful nation must remember.[2]

As the ember of Tom's desire to see this mission through smoldered and slowly transitioned from a glowing ember into a small and growing flame over time, he found moral support within the small ranks of his family. The Cota family is not terribly large in number. Tom's mother and her brother, his uncle Dan Cota, were the only offspring of Dutch and Connie, and both are now deceased. To this day, very few of the Cota grandchildren and great-grandchildren survive. The living family includes Tom's son, Tommy, who deeply appreciates all of this history. Tom's sister, Connie, is also interested in her grandfather's service. He has a first cousin, Barbara, the only child of his uncle Dan Cota. Barbara has a son, Philippe, who has a keen appreciation of this legacy. Tom has nieces, Kathy and Amy, and a nephew, Jim, along with their families, all of whom are equally appreciative. (The aforementioned are all children of his deceased brother, Dan Morris.) Sister Connie's son is Wyatt Colby, who shares the same feelings as the rest of his family.

Unbeknownst to the living heirs of General Cota, a soldier, Al Dogan, who served under Major General Cota in the 28th Infantry Division after D-Day and befriended Cota's second wife and widow, wrote a letter to President Ronald Reagan on May 15, 1984, with a request to consider Cota for the MOH. Congressman Elwood H. "Bud" Hillis of Indiana responded to him on August 27, 1984. This time frame corresponds with President Reagan's famous "Boys of Pointe du Hoc" speech given on the fortieth anniversary of D-Day in France. It is unknown whether President Reagan actually saw this correspondence or if it was read by an aide or if any appreciable discussion or action was taken on behalf of Cota as a result of these correspondences. (Copies of these letters are in appendix I.)

The experience of meeting Joe Balkoski and his emotional response to walking the ground covered by his grandfather created in Tom a desire to see an upgrade to his grandfather's DSC. He then slowly started to think with Joe about how to make it a reality. They enlisted the aid of Michael White, stepson of Lieutenant Jack Shea, in mid-2017. In March 2017, Balkoski highly recommended contacting Major General John C. Raaen Jr. and inviting him to join the growing research team. Major General Raaen enthusiastically embraced the project and brought additional resources to bear in the form of contacts at the National World War II Museum in New Orleans. In 2018, Major General Raaen suggested bringing me onto the project.

Tom placed a cold call to my home in March 2018 and asked me to consider joining the group. I received this call on the day before a planned family vacation to Florida with my wife and kids. Tom got back with me in April upon our return, at which point we had a proper introduction and time to discuss what he had in mind. Upon hearing that Major General Raaen had suggested my involvement, I heartily agreed; I deeply respect the general. I got to work evaluating the facts and details provided by the other members of the team and then began to research the law and regulatory environment of the Medal of Honor.

I found that we needed to satisfy the requirements as outlined in the following:

- Title 10, United States Code § 1130
- 10 U.S.C. § 357—Decorations and Awards (2006)

- 32 CFR 578.4—Medal of Honor
- AR 600-8-22, Section II, U.S. Army Individual Decorations— Authority and Criteria, 3-8. Medal of Honor (June 25, 2015)
- *DoD Manual 1348.33.* Vol. 1: *Manual of Military Decorations and Awards: Medal of Honor (MOH)*

The team then prepared an outline based on the Department of Defense criteria. This process allowed us to identify gaps in information held by the team. From there, we created a narrative based upon an aggregation of the various military primary-source documentation and filled in by other sources. It quickly became clear to the team, after evaluation of the original DSC award recommendation for General Cota, that his actions transcended the scope of the original award. The original DSC clearly focused on his actions on the beach, at the seawall, and below the bluffs. The two original witnesses, Colonel Charles D. Canham and Lieutenant Colonel Harold A. Cassell, clearly focused their testimony on the action on the beach. Missing from the DSC considerations were the actions to lead men up the bluffs, to take charge of the assault above the bluffs, and particularly to lead the charge against a machine-gun position firing on the men. Cota's leadership of the Rangers at various points and his nearly getting killed by sniper fire west of Vierville demonstrated just how exposed he was. The DSC did not cover in any way his critical leadership in taking Exit D-1 at the Vierville draw in the face of 14-inch battleship fire as he took charge of and led a small patrol down the draw, capturing prisoners as he went. Nor did it cover his leadership in the destruction of the massive antitank wall at WN 72 or his continued leadership as he walked the length of the beach to the D-3 exit and his subsequent actions into D+1.

We took all of this information and, in preparing the application recommendation, narratively and visually demonstrated evidence of his actions through text, maps, photos, and drawings. We compiled and identified key pieces of evidence for any reviewers of the package. Considering the seventy-four years since D-Day, the regulations dictated that we solicit congressional support to champion the project. We sought this aid out by contacting senators and House representatives in Kansas, Florida, Ohio, California, Maryland, and Massachusetts and key members of the Armed Service Committees in both congressional houses. We finalized the requisite paperwork and letters to the congressional delegations on the weekend of July 4, 2018. Tom Morris flew to Ohio, and together, with the assistance of the entire Mehlo family, we produced and collated over forty of the 450-page application packages and sent them off via FedEx to the respective offices.

In August, Tom Morris received a call from the office of Kansas senator Pat Roberts, as the senator enthusiastically stepped up to champion this effort on behalf of Congress. He built a bipartisan team from both houses and provided the required support needed for the application package. Of note, the entire congressional delegation of Kansas signed on. The signers of the congressional request letter included Senator Pat Roberts (KS), Senator Jerry Moran (KS), Congresswoman Lynn Jenkins (KS), Congressman Kevin Yoder (KS), Congressman Ron Estes (KS), Congressman Roger Marshall (KS), and Congressman Darren Soto (FL). (A copy of this letter is in appendix II.)

Senator Roberts assigned his crackerjack staff to the project, including Lauren Stockwell, Gilda Lintz, and John Stout. They prepared all of the required documentation for final compilation and submission to the army. They made contact with Secretary of the Army Mark Esper in August 2018 and got the long evaluation process started.

As we waited, additional support came from Antoine de Bellaigue, mayor of Vierville-sur-Mer, and Jean-Marc LeFranc, chairman, Comité du Débarquement (French D-Day Commemoration Committee). Retired senator Bob Dole of Kansas heard of the efforts and wrote a letter of support, as did Kansas governor Jeff Colyer, MD, on behalf of the state of Kansas. (Copies of these correspondences are in appendix III.)

French D-Day Commemoration Committee chairman Jean-Marc LeFranc wrote,

> *We have come to understand from some of our American contacts that your office leads efforts for the process of consideration of an upgrade of the Distinguished Service Cross of General Norman D. Cota for exceptional valor*

he exhibited on June 6, 1944 at Omaha beach and Vierville sur Mer to the Congressional Medal of Honor.

On behalf of the board and members of the "Comite du Debarquement," founded in 1945 and representative of all the French towns and people included in the 5 landing beaches, we offer this heartfelt letter of support for these efforts.

The exploits of General Cota and the 29th Infantry Division are well known here, as the efforts of these men ended the tyrannical rule of the German Nazi regime here. Along with your American soldiers, many of our citizens paid a heavy toll for liberty during the war. Seventy-five years later, our town and the surrounding areas still bear witness to the ferocity of that day. Several thousand graves and other memorials to the liberating forces are scattered throughout our region. From the General's heroic breakout on the beach, and his utterance of the American Ranger slogan "Rangers Lead the Way!" to liberation of our fair town, he exemplified courage, and we fully support your efforts to honor him and his men. If we can be of any assistance in your efforts, please let us know.

Jean-Marc LeFranc
Chairman
Former member of the French Parliament
Legion of Honor
Ranger Hall of Fame Inductee

Retired senator and World War II veteran Bob Dole reached out to Secretary of the Army Mark Esper on August 10, 2018, with this letter:

Dear Secretary Esper,

I am writing to respectfully request that the Army review the heroic actions of Brigadier General Norman Cota to posthumously bestow upon him the Medal of Honor.

General Cota's tremendous valor on D-Day is well documented. His steady and strategic leadership—undaunted by surrounding enemy fire—is widely believed to have been instrumental in the ultimate outcome and success of the D-Day landings on Omaha Beach.

Upon reviewing his impressive record of service, I believe the actions and achievements of this true American hero certainly deserve careful consideration with respect to the Medal of Honor criteria.

I appreciate your time and consideration of this matter. Thanks for all you continue to do on behalf of our nation's finest service branch.

God Bless America.
Signed—Bob Dole

On August 21, 2018, Kansas governor Jeff Colyer, MD, sent a letter of support as governor to augment the 100 percent congressional support for the upgrade of General Cota's DSC. He wrote,

Dear Senator Roberts:

As Governor of the State of Kansas, I endorse the consideration of an upgrade of Major General Norman Daniel "Dutch" Cota's previously earned United States Army Distinguished Service Cross to a posthumously earned Congressional Medal of Honor. Major General Cota honorably served our nation during both World Wars.

The courage and leadership Major General Cota displayed throughout his military career certainly marks him as an American hero. His extraordinary selfless acts on Omaha Beach reflects a man of outstanding character, one committed to a life that protects the lives of others. It is with great honor that I stand with the family of Major General Cota asking for consideration to further honor the Major General with the Congressional Medal of Honor.

Signed—Jeff Colyer, M.D., Governor

The mayor of Vierville offered a similar letter to that of the chairman of the French D-Day Commemoration Committee to Senator Roberts:

Dear Senator Roberts,

We have come to understand from some of our American contacts that your office leads efforts for the process of consideration of an upgrade of the Distinguished Service Cross of General Norman D. Cota for exceptional valor he exhibited on June 6, 1944 at Vierville-sur-Mer to the Congressional Medal of Honor.

On behalf of the citizens of Vierville-sur-Mer, in the department of Calvados of the French region of Basse-Normandie, we offer this heartfelt letter of support for these efforts.

The exploits of General Cota and the 29th Infantry Division are well known here, as the efforts of these men ended the tyrannical rule of the German Nazi regime here. Along with your American soldiers, many of our citizens paid a heavy toll for liberty during the war. Seventy-five years later, our town and the surrounding areas still bear witness to the ferocity of that day. Several thousand graves and other memorials to the liberating forces are scattered throughout our region. From the General's heroic breakout on the beach, and his utterance of the American Ranger slogan "Rangers Lead the Way!" to liberation of our fair town, he exemplified courage, and we fully support your efforts to honor him and his men. If we can be of any assistance in your efforts, please let us know.

Signed—Antoine de Bellaigue, Mayor of Vierville-sur-Mer

During the fall of 2018, Major General John Epperly, commanding general, 29th Infantry Division, made his administrative staff available to the senator's office and to the research team to ensure that the required DA Form 838, "Recommendation for Award," was filled out in accordance with Army Regulation 600-8-22 and all other army requirements. Several officers and enlisted personnel in the 29th Infantry Division and the Virginia National Guard command structure aided the effort.

The various offices involved had many points of communication, including calls, meetings, letters, and emails. In the fall of 2018, the army forwarded the package to the Army Human Resources Command for evaluation. This part of the process took a long time, as the office had to conduct a rigorous review in accordance with law and regulation. This work was under the command of Brigadier General Robert W. Bennett Jr., adjutant general (AG), and his staff; Colonel Michael R. Harper, AG, chief, Soldier and Service Division; and Lieutenant Colonel Kandace M. Daffin, chief, Awards and Decorations Branch, and her staff. In March 2019, the Awards and Decorations Branch office received approval to board the recommendation of the MOH for General Cota with the secretary of the army. This was the first deliberative official action taken by the army toward approval or denial per the process detailed in Army Regulation 600-8-22.

In May, the Awards and Decorations Branch issued a denial for the upgrade. Senator Roberts countered with a letter requesting reasons as to why the denial was given. The senator was never provided a substantive reason for the denial by the army. The research team went back to work and returned to the National Archives and other sources of records to further develop the award recommendation. We also sought new witness testimony and were honored to come across Arden Earll, who provided an additional one. In doing all of this work, the team found that we did in fact uncover new and substantive information that is to be prepared and sent to the 29th Infantry Division for analysis and recommendation and another submission to the Army Human Resources Command through Senator Roberts's office.

Ranger Randall Ching stated, regarding his motivation to see General Cota's possible MOH upgrade through to approval, "I wanted to ensure that General Cota receives the recognition he deserves for leading us in such a historic event. It was men like him that helped us succeed in that operation, and making his service a part of recorded history is monumental." In receiving this honor, General Cota brings honor and recognition to all the men who sacrificed and landed on Omaha Beach that day. Ching said, "This would mean a tremendous amount to all of us. In any chaotic event, people look for a leader to guide them and inspire bravery. General Cota did that for us that day and I can safely say that any soldier that interacted with him would feel the same." As the process of applying for the upgrade of Cota's DSC to the MOH unfolded, Ching formed strong opinions about him. Ching, now one of the very few remaining survivors of any unit that hit the beach that day, summed up just how deserving General Cota is of the MOH:

I firmly believe that he is extremely deserving of The Medal of Honor. General Cota not only led us Rangers, but also helped coordinate the rest of the soldiers landing on the beach as well. He did this while putting his own life at risk at the front lines and that bravery should be recognized. I offered testimony to Congress since I am one of the very few soldiers left who witnessed his leadership first hand that day. It was both an honor and even obligation to let others know what he had done. This testimony was a way I could do that. I believe that the actions and bravery of General Cota truly illustrate both the kind of man and leader he was and without a doubt, he is incredibly worthy of the Medal of Honor.[3]

Major General Raaen's personal motivation was that he has known the Cota family for years: "Dan was a classmate of mine at West Point. I'm not sure, but Dan may have been in prep school with me." Although General Raaen never met Tom Morris in person, Tom seemed sincere to him in all of their dealings. The major general stated, "I am sure he wants sincerely to have the upgrade approved to honor a man who certainly deserves it." Major General Raaen shares a very unique position on the research team. In fact, he shares a unique position within military history. He spent a lifetime as an officer in the United States Army. He is one of the few remaining officers of any unit from the D-Day invasion still alive. At ninety-seven years old, he is a gentleman and a scholar who has studied D-Day not only through his own experience but also through the longer lens of military strategy and contextual history. As a result of his many years of study on the topic, he is widely regarded as a national expert on D-Day. His book *Intact* is a must-read for anyone interested in the Ranger action on that day and on the days that followed. He told me, "When I first started writing in the 1980s, I fully believed General Cota deserved the Medal of Honor. I still feel that way."[4] He is strongly convinced that this honor for General Cota is long overdue.

The current and the living former commanding generals of the 29th Infantry Division all collaborated in the nomination process for General Cota for the MOH. They all feel very strongly about Dutch's leadership and his unsurpassed bravery during the D-Day invasion. They offered support in the form of a unanimous signing of the army award recommendation form, provided multiple written pieces required to properly submit the recommendation, and wrote the forewords to this book.

Major General Carroll D. Childers, the 15th Division commander of the 29th Infantry Division, summarized his thoughts regarding General Cota in March 2019:

The effort to get the MOH for Cota is greatly appreciated. I believe he was the key inspiration which caused the 116th Infantry Regiment to move inland from Bloody Omaha thereby saving thousands of lives on 6 June

44, and because of this success, enabled securing key terrain before further German forces could be redeployed, thus saving many more lives in the days following D-Day, and perhaps changing the perspective of General Bradley who openly admitted his thoughts of recalling the landing force. The Germans would not have been fooled by another deception plan.[5]

Brigadier General Cota performed his duty with a full understanding of the strategic and tactical requirements, the personal and mission-oriented risks, the challenges, and the mind-set of the young soldiers under his command. His battle experiences in Africa and Sicily uniquely prepared him for what he faced as a leader. Despite these considerations, he landed in the midst of one of the most critical and hotly contested sectors of Omaha Beach in terms of possibility for failure within the overall Allied invasion on D-Day. The Germans inflicted thousands of casualties, thoroughly disrupted command and control of the forces remaining and arriving on the beach, and threatened to push the 29th Infantry Division and supporting units back into the sea. He took charge of the situation and became a very active frontline participant in the victory.

Joe Balkoski contends that D-Day was the pivotal date of the twentieth century, for if D-Day had failed, what would the consequences for world history have been?

Tom Morris firmly believes that Dutch was the most valuable player on this most pivotal day of the twentieth century. He often thinks about his grandfather, at age fifty-one, leading and inspiring the men on the beach, who were teenagers and young twenty-somethings. He is moved by the murderous carnage on that beach and the actions of General Cota that day. Tom is amazed by the "grenade 101" training on D+1 at the D-3 draw, when his grandfather taught a young captain and his squad how to flush Germans from the house. These men had been trained to do it, they were just scared, and Dutch rose above that. The dauntlessness was the true lesson that day. Tom is amazed by the continual march east from there over the next eleven months. If D-Day had failed—and it nearly did—the Nazis might have been able to develop an atomic bomb, many of us wouldn't have been born, and the world might ultimately have been ruled by the most murderous regime in human history. The stakes were high regarding human freedom on that day. From Dutch praying for and

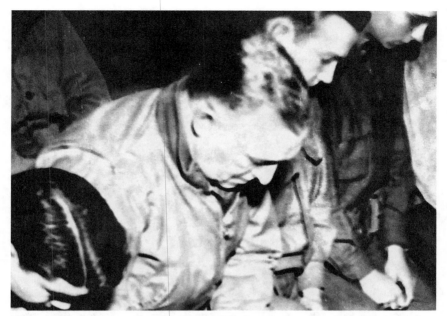

Figure 11.2. Dutch praying with his troops before Battle of the Bulge (Cota family private collection).

over his troops before his heroic actions (as seen in figure 11.2) to the honor of the British Distinguished Service Order bestowed upon him in the name of the king of England (figure 11.3) to the fact that Ike Eisenhower himself selected Dutch to help represent the American forces as part of the liberation of Paris (figure 11.4), it is clear just how important he was to history and how critically important his actions were on D-Day.

Amy Morris is Tom's niece. She first thought her great-grandpa should have earned the MOH because "the impacts of the leadership on D-Day were realized while in history class in junior high school. That was when I realized that the MOH seemed appropriate." She changed and matured in her views of his heroism over the years: "As a younger adult his leadership was always evident in the documentation read or videos displayed. As I grew into an adult as well as a mother, the word 'hero' comes more into play as you tell others your family history. My family chose to give our daughter the middle name Cota as a tribute to a hero." She has come to understand the important role he played in world

Figure 11.3. Dutch receives British Distinguished Service Order as awarded by
Field Marshal Bernard Law Montgomery (Cota family private collection).

events. "General Cota played an important role in two World Wars, as
well as was instrumental to the victory at D-Day reshaping WWII." She
acknowledged the efforts of her uncle, Thomas J. Morris III, in the effort
regarding the MOH for the general. She noted that he "has been the

Figure 11.4. Dutch was selected to represent the American forces in the parade celebrating the liberation of Paris as part of the 28th Infantry Division on August 29, 1944 (Cota family private collection).

lead on the MOH effort, and he has done tremendous work that is well–appreciated. Without his efforts, I'm afraid there would not be a potential MOH. For my immediate family, our six-year old daughter lights up when she hears how she is named after a family hero." When asked, she told me that if the effort to upgrade him to the MOH is successful, "a feeling of complete joy will overcome any other feeling." It is her strong opinion that her great-grandfather would be humble about it, as usual, if he were still alive today.

Brigadier General Theodore G. Shuey, former assistant division commander of the 29th Infantry Division, wrote in *Omaha Beach Field Guide* that after visiting the beach several days later, British field marshal Sir Bernard Law Montgomery prepared a personal report to his superior, head of the British army, Field Marshal Lord Alanbrooke. He wrote of his shock at what he saw: "If you saw Omaha Beach, you would wonder how the Americans ever got ashore."[6]

To this statement my fellow contributors and I respond by saying that the Americans got ashore and secured Omaha Beach by the hand of the Almighty God and the determination of U.S. infantry and Brigadier General Norman Daniel "Dutch" Cota.

Tom thinks that if an MOH upgrade is declined, Dutch might say, "Thanks for trying. Perpetuate what we fought for to the best of your ability. Now get on with your life, and God Bless America." If it is approved, Tom hears his grandfather in his head saying, "Thanks for trying. Perpetuate what we fought for to the best of your ability. Now get on with your life, and God Bless America." Finally, in Dutch's own actual words to his family, "How anyone lived through Normandy/ETO is a miracle of God."

Rangers, Lead the Way!
29, Let's Go!

POSTSCRIPT

Holbrook "Hobey" Bradley, a reporter embedded with the 29th Infantry Division and writing for the *Baltimore Sun* newspaper.

The tide was running in, bringing corpses still in life jackets or without—those who'd died trying to make this beach, men with the blue and gray patch of our division, many with the distinctive red one of the First. The Blue-Gray shoulder patch told us he was one of ours. He'd been hit in the left shoulder, the uniform ripped and bloody, a temporary bandage on the jagged tear which seemed to cover a quarter of his torso. The wax-like face, eyes closed, no sign of breathing will be with me until I die. Those first few hours on the beach must have been living hell. And we saw there had been no discrimination in the way the men fell, for the two bars of captains were among the plain uniforms of the privates.[7]

What if General Cota had not been there or had been killed? What kept the Germans from blowing Dutch away?

APPENDIX I

1984 Letter to President Reagan and Congressional
Response to Mr. Al Dogan for Cota MOH Upgrade

ALBERT W. DOGAN
Certified Public Accountant

May 15, 1984

President Ronald Reagan
The White House
Washington, D. C.

In re: Your upcoming trip to Normandy, France;
(D-Day + 40 years)

Dear Mr. President:

It has come to my attention through various newspaper articles that you will be traveling to Normandy, France to meet with French President, Francois Mitterrand on June 6, 1984 to commemorate the fortieth anniversary of the D-Day invasion by dedicating a memorial on Utah Beach to the honor of the American soldiers who participated in the June 6, 1944 invasion in that sector.

I have been researching for the past dozen years and more the life and war experiences of one of the greatest, unsung hero's on D-Day and in the whole European phase of World War II. His name is General Norman D. Cota who among many other major achievements was the first general to land on Omaha Beach with the first troops at the crack of dawn on June 6, 1944. Many authorities consider his personal exploits and leadership on Omaha Beach to be the difference between success and failure of the whole Omaha assault.

I hope to live long enough to do what he would not do for himself which is to honor him with a biography that will do justice to his historic World War II career not only on the Normandy Beaches but all his heroic actions before and after that day i. e. African Invasion, Invasion of Sicily, COSSACK, St. Lo, Mortain, Falais Gap, Liberation of Paris, Huertgen Forest, Battle of the Bulge, and the Liberation of Strasbourg. In each of these actions he and his various infantry units were "front and center." In the Battle of the Bulge his 28th Infantry Division held off nine German Divisions for four days in front of Bastogne to allow the 101st Airbourne Division to arrive from Paris by truck to take up defensive positions. By accomplishing this delay, the whole Hitler time schedule was so upset that the enemy surprise attack was doomed to complete failure.

Enclosed with this letter are only a few citations from published works which I would hope would help you appreciate the significant and great accomplishments of this valorous man who willingly risked his life to perform many acts of outstanding bravery in the presence of the enemy in the front lines in a most gallant manner "above and beyond the call of duty."

It appears to me that you have a unique opportunity to memorialize General Cota's heroic accomplishments and his dedication to duty by publically awarding him in the name of Congress at the 40th anniversary celebration on June 6, 1984 the Medal of Honor posthumously. If he were living, I am sure he would have accepted it only in recognition of the sacrifices of the thousands of men who served under him on D-Day and all the other battles which he gallantly led before and after the Normandy Invasion.

It is noted that Gen. Teddy Roosevelt got his Medal of Honor for the Utah Beach landing which General Omar Bradley described saying in his recent book published in 1983, "Utah Beach was a piece of cake," He went on to say, "Omaha Beach however was a nightmare. Even now it brings pain to recall what happened there on June 6, 1944. I have returned many times to honor the valiant men who died on that beach. They should never be forgotten. Nor should those who lived to carry the day by the slimmest of margins. Every man who set foot on Omaha Beach that day was a hero.(underscoring added)

It is ironic that the landing on Utah Beach which was "a piece of cake" warranted a Medal of Honor for General Roosevelt but the leadership of General Cota, who saved the day and the success of the invasion by unscrambling under merciless enemy fire the "nightmare" of the more important Omaha Beach has not been so recognized.

France, Belgium, and Luxembourg each awarded him their Croix de Guerre and the British bestowed high honors with its Distinguished Service Order.

If you want more information on General Norman D. Cota, (under whom I served in Huertgen Forest and the Battle of the Bulge but did not meet until 1971) I have collected a vast amount of data on this soldiers' soldier and would be happy to share it with you.

Respectfully yours,

Albert W. Dogan
Ex-Pvt. 15303738 AUS
"C" Co. 109th Regiment
28th Infantry Division

Enc:

ELWOOD H. "BUD" HILLIS
5TH DISTRICT, INDIANA

ROOM 2336
RAYBURN HOUSE OFFICE BUILDING
WASHINGTON, D.C. 20515
(202) 225-5037

P.O. BOX 5048
2016 SOUTH ELIZABETH STREET
KOKOMO, INDIANA 46902
(317) 457-4411

323 SOUTH ADAMS STREET
MARION, INDIANA 46952
(317) 662-7227

2 INDIANA AVENUE
VALPARAISO, INDIANA 46383
(219) 462-6499

Congress of the United States
House of Representatives
Washington, D.C. 20515

August 27, 1984

COMMITTEES:
ARMED SERVICES
SUBCOMMITTEE ON MILITARY
PERSONNEL AND COMPENSATION
SUBCOMMITTEE ON SEAPOWER AND
STRATEGIC AND CRITICAL MATERIALS
VETERANS' AFFAIRS
SUBCOMMITTEE ON OVERSIGHT AND
INVESTIGATIONS
SUBCOMMITTEE ON HOSPITALS AND
HEALTH CARE

CO-CHAIRMAN, CONGRESSIONAL
AUTOMOTIVE CAUCUS
EXECUTIVE BOARD MEMBER,
CONGRESSIONAL STEEL CAUCUS
MEMBER, THE RURAL CAUCUS

Mr. Al Dogan
1307 Forrest Park Avenue
Valparaiso, Indiana 46383

Dear Mr. Dogan:

It has been brought to my attention that you have been in touch with my district office relative to your letter addressed to President Reagan calling for special recognition for General Norman D. Cota. It is my understanding that although your correspondence was sent in May, you have not yet received a reply from the White House.

Upon contacting the White House correspondence office in your behalf, it was learned that I must be able to provide the date the letter was written (in addition to the subject material which I already have) in order for that office to determine if your letter was received. I would therefore appreciate it if you could provide me with the approximate date your letter was mailed. Upon its receipt, I will again contact the White House, and I have been assured a reply will be sent if they are able to locate your letter.

I am pleased to have this opportunity to be of assistance, and I will be looking forward to hearing from you in the near future.

With best wishes, I am

Sincerely,

Elwood H. "Bud" Hillis
Member of Congress

H:z

APPENDIX II

Congressional Request Letter for Cota DSC Upgrade to MOH

Congress of the United States
Washington, DC 20510

August 9, 2018

The Honorable Mark Esper
Secretary
Department of the Army
101 Army Pentagon
Washington, D.C. 20310

Dear Secretary Esper,

We write to respectfully request that you review the heroic actions of Brigadier General Norman "Dutch" Cota on D-day to elevate his previously awarded Distinguished Service Cross to the nation's highest military award, the Medal of Honor. On June 6th, 1944, General Cota of the 29th Infantry Division landed on Omaha beach and through his gallant leadership contributed to the success of that operation. Through historical investigations and eye-witness testimony it is believed that his actions warrant this recognition.

We request that this case be reviewed, and in accordance with Section 1130 of Title 10, U.S. Code, ask that General Cota be considered to posthumously receive the Medal of Honor.

Attached you will find declassified documents that include supporting evidence of General Cota's heroic achievements.

Please send your response to my District office, 444 SE Quincy, Room 392, Topeka, KS, 66683. Thank you for your consideration of this important matter.

Sincerely,

Pat Roberts
United States Senator

Jerry Moran
United States Senator

APPENDIX II

Lynn Jenkins
United States Representative

Kevin Yoder
United States Representative

Ron Estes
United States Representative

Roger Marshall, M.D.
United States Representative

Darren Soto
United States Representative

APPENDIX III

Letters of Support for BG Cota MOH Upgrade

D-Day General

BOB DOLE

August 10, 2018

Dear Secretary Esper,

    I am writing to respectfully request that the Army review the heroic actions of Brigadier General Norman Cota to posthumously bestow upon him the Medal of Honor.

    General Cota's tremendous valor on D-Day is well documented. His steady and strategic leadership – undaunted by surrounding enemy fire – is widely believed to have been instrumental in the ultimate outcome and success of the D-Day landings on Omaha Beach.

    Upon reviewing his impressive record of service, I believe the actions and achievements of this true American hero certainly deserve careful consideration with respect to the Medal of Honor criteria.

    I appreciate your time and consideration of this matter. Thanks for all you continue to do on behalf of our nation's finest service branch.

God Bless America,

BOB DOLE

The Honorable Mark Esper
Secretary
Department of the Army
101 Army Pentagon
Washington, D.C. 20310

STATE OF KANSAS

CAPITOL BUILDING
ROOM 241 SOUTH
TOPEKA, KS 66612

PHONE: (785) 296-3232
FAX: (785) 368-8788
GOVERNOR.KS.GOV

GOVERNOR JEFF COLYER, M.D.

August 21, 2018

The Honorable Pat Roberts
Frank Carlson Federal Office Building
444 SE Quincy – Room 392
Topeka, KS 66683

Dear Senator Roberts:

As Governor of the State of Kansas, I endorse the consideration of an upgrade of Major General Norman Daniel "Dutch" Cota's previously earned United States Army Distinguished Service Cross to a posthumously earned Congressional Medal of Honor. Major Cota honorably served our nation during both World Wars.

The courage and leadership Major General Cota displayed throughout his military career certainly marks him as an American hero. His extraordinary selfless acts on Omaha Beach reflects a man of outstanding character, one committed to a life that protects the lives of others. It is with great honor that I stand with the family of Major General Cota asking for consideration to further honor the Major with the Congressional Medal of Honor.

Sincerely,

Jeff Colyer, M.D.
Governor

République Française

MAIRIE DE VIERVILLE-SUR-MER ✠
14710

OMAHA-BEACH   CALVADOS

Antoine de Bellaigue
Maire
Vierville, France

August 12, 2018

Senator Pat Roberts
Washington, D.C. Office
109 Hart Senate Office Building
Washington, DC 20510-1605
        Attention: Ms. Lauren Stockwell

Dear Senator Roberts,

We have come to understand from some of our American contacts that your office leads efforts for the process of consideration of an upgrade of the Distinguished Service Cross of General Norman D. Cota for exceptional valor he exhibited on June 6, 1944 at Vierville-sur-Mer to the Congressional Medal of Honor.

On behalf of the citizens of Vierville-sur-Mer, in the department of Calvados of the French region of Basse-Normandie, we offer this heartfelt letter of support for these efforts.

The exploits of General Cota and the 29th Infantry Division are well known here, as the efforts of these men ended the tyrannical rule of the German Nazi regime here. Along with your American soldiers, many of our citizens paid a heavy toll for liberty during the war. Seventy-five years later, our town and the surrounding areas still bear witness to the ferocity of that day. Several thousand graves and other memorials to the liberating forces are scattered throughout our region. From the General's heroic breakout on the beach, and his utterance of the American Ranger slogan Rangers Lead the Way!, to liberation of our fair town, he exemplified courage, and we fully support your efforts to honor him and his men.

If we can be of any assistance in your efforts, please let us know. If you have any questions, please do not hesitate to contact me at 0033670271036 or at antoine.de-bellaigue@orange.fr.

Sincerely,

Antoine de Bellaigue
Maire, Vierville, France

COMITÉ DU DÉBARQUEMENT
D-DAY COMMEMORATION COMMITTEE

August 12, 2018

Senator Pat Roberts
Washington, D.C. Office
109 Hart Senate Office Building
Washington, DC 20510-1605
Attention: Ms. Lauren Stockwell

Dear Senator Roberts,

We have come to understand from some of our American contacts that your office leads efforts for the process of consideration of an upgrade of the Distinguished Service Cross of General Norman D. Cota for exceptional valor he exhibited on June 6, 1944 at Omaha beach and Vierville sur Mer to the Congressional Medal of Honor.

On behalf of the board and members of the "Comité du Debarquement", founded in 1945 and representative of all the French towns and people included in the 5 landing beaches, we offer this heartfelt letter of support for these efforts.

The exploits of General Cota and the 29th Infantry Division are well known here, as the efforts of these men ended the tyrannical rule of the German Nazi regime here. Along with your American soldiers, many of our citizens paid a heavy toll for liberty during the war. Seventy-five years later, our town and the surrounding areas still bear witness to the ferocity of that day. Several thousand graves and other memorials to the liberating forces are scattered throughout our region. From the General's heroic breakout on the beach, and his utterance of the American Ranger slogan Rangers Lead the Way!, to liberation of our fair town, he exemplified courage, and we fully support your efforts to honor him and his men.

If we can be of any assistance in your efforts, please let us know. If you have any questions, please do not hesitate to contact me at 0033673594732, email jml.debarquement@orange.fr

Sincerely,

Jean-Marc Lefranc
Chairman
Former member of the French
Parliament
Legion of Honor
Ranger Hall of Fame Inductee

4 RUE DU BIENVENU – B.P. 43402 – 14404 BAYEUX CEDEX
☎ 02 31 92 00 26 ▌ fax 02 31 22 11 35 ▌ courriel : el.debarquement@orange.fr
Association loi 1901 / N° SIRET : 432 083 954 000 11

Notes

Chapter 1. The Dauntless

1. "History," Congressional Medal of Honor Society, http://www.cmohs.org/medal-history.php (retrieved May 2, 2019).
2. Department of Defense (DoD), *DoD Manual 1348.33*, vol. 1: *Manual of Military Decorations and Awards: Medal of Honor (MOH)* (Washington, DC: U.S. Government, 2016).
3. Hall of Valor, https://valor.militarytimes.com/hero/1433.
4. "Recipients," Congressional Medal of Honor Society, http://www.cmohs.org/recipient-archive.php (retrieved May 2, 2019).
5. "Recipients," Congressional Medal of Honor Society.

Chapter 2. From Chelsea, Massachusetts, to North Africa

1. Eleanor Roosevelt, "My Day," Eleanor Roosevelt Papers Project, June 5, 1945, https://www2.gwu.edu/~erpapers/myday/displaydoc.cfm?_y=1945&_f=md000042 (retrieved May 20, 2019).
2. U.S. Census Bureau (1900–1920), U.S. Census Records, https://www.ancestry.com (retrieved May 20, 2019).
3. Robert A. Miller, *Division Commander: A Biography of Major General Norman D. Cota* (Spartanburg, SC: Reprint Company Publishers, 1989), chap. 2.
4. "Great Chelsea Fire of 1908," Wikipedia, https://en.wikipedia.org/wiki/Great_Chelsea_fire_of_1908 (retrieved February 9, 2019).
5. Miller, *Division Commander*, chap. 2.
6. "22nd Infantry Regiment (United States)," Wikipedia, https://en.wikipedia.org/wiki/22nd_Infantry_Regiment_(United_States) (retrieved February 9, 2019).
7. "Fort Jay," Wikipedia, https://en.wikipedia.org/wiki/Fort_Jay (retrieved February 9, 2019).
8. Michael Belis, "The 22nd Infantry during the World War 1917–1918," 1st Battalion 22nd Infantry, http://1-22infantry.org/history/hoboken.htm (retrieved February 9, 2019).
9. "22nd Infantry Regiment (United States)," Wikipedia.
10. War Department, *Infantry Battalion* (FM 7-20) (Washington, DC: GPO, 1944), 10.
11. 35th Infantry Regiment Association, "The 35th Infantry Regiment, Camp Travis, Texas, the 35th Infantry Regiment Assignment to the 18th Division, Aug. 20, 1918

to Nov. 8, 1919," A Walk with the 35th, http://www.cacti35th.com/history/1916-45/Camp%20Travis%20to%20Hawaii.pdf (retrieved February 9, 2019).

12. 35th Infantry Regiment Association, "The 35th Infantry Regiment, Camp Travis, Texas, the 35th Infantry Regiment Assignment to the 18th Division, Aug. 20, 1918 to Nov. 8, 1919."

13. John Justin, "James F. Justin Civilian Conservation Corps Museum," James F. Justin Museum, 2015, http://www.justinmuseum.com/famjustin/ccchis.html (retrieved February 9, 2019).

14. "1st Infantry Division (United States)," Wikipedia, https://en.wikipedia.org/wiki/1st_Infantry_Division_(United_States) (retrieved February 9, 2019).

15. "Origins of Marine Corps Base Camp Lejeune," Marine Corps Base Camp Lejeune, https://www.lejeune.marines.mil/Portals/27/Documents/EMD/Cultural-Resources/Semper%20Fidelis%20Popular%20History%20Publication/08_Chapter%202.pdf (retrieved February 9, 2019).

16. United States Army, Center of Military History, *The U.S. Army GHQ Maneuvers of 1941* (CMH Pub 70-41-1) (by Christopher R. Gabel) (Washington, DC: Department of the Army, 1992).

17. "Origins of Marine Corps Base Camp Lejeune," Marine Corps Base Camp Lejeune.

18. Cole Kingseed, *From Omaha Beach to Dawson's Ridge: The Combat Journal of Captain Joe Dawson* (Annapolis, MD: Naval Institute Press, 2013), chap. 1.

19. United States Army, Center of Military History, *The U.S. Army GHQ Maneuvers of 1941* (CMH Pub 70-41-1) (by Christopher R. Gabel) (Washington, DC: Department of the Army, 1992).

20. Scanned NARA Record 301-0.13.1: Outline of Operation Plan "TORCH" (II Army Corps), First Division Museum, September 1942, https://www.fdmuseum.org/researchers/digital-archives (retrieved January 12, 2020).

21. United States Army, Center of Military History, *The U.S. Army Campaigns of World War II: Tunisia* (CMH Pub 72-12) (by Charles R. Anderson) (Washington, DC: Department of the Army, 1996); Miller, *Division Commander*, chap. 2.

Chapter 3. A General Named Dutch

1. Miller, *Division Commander*, chap. 7; NARA, Administrative History Collection, Historical Section, ETOUSA, Combined Operations Headquarters No 87, NARA Record Group 498, Roll MP63-9_0012.

2. NARA, Administrative History Collection, Historical Section, ETOUSA, Combined Operations Headquarters No 87, NARA Record Group 498, Roll MP63-9_0012.

3. Miller, *Division Commander*, chap. 7.

4. Entry dated October 8, 1918, in Sergeant Alvin York, *Diary of Alvin York* (Pall Mall, TN: Sergeant York Patriotic Foundation, 2013).

Chapter 4. The Blue and the Gray

1. Lt. Col. John A. Cutchins and Lt. Col. George S. Stewart Jr., *History of the Twenty-Ninth Division "Blue and Gray," 1917–1919* (Philadelphia: Press of MacCalla & Co., Inc., 1921).

2. Joseph Balkoski, *Beyond the Beachhead: The 29th Infantry Division in Normandy* (Mechanicsburg, PA: Stackpole Books, 1989), chap. 3.

3. Joseph H. Ewing, *29 Let's GO! A History of the 29th Infantry Division in World War II* (Washington DC: Infantry Journal Press, 1948), 20–21.

4. Balkoski, *Beyond the Beachhead*, chap. 3.

5. Ewing, *29 Let's GO!*, 20–21.

6. Miller, *Division Commander*, chap. 8.

7. United States Army, Center of Military History, *The Corps of Engineers: The War against Germany* (CMH Pub 10-22) (by Alfred M. Beck, Abe Bortz, Charles W. Lynch, Lida Mayo, and Ralph F. Weld). United States Army in World War II: The Technical Services (Washington, DC: U.S. Army, 1985), 289–93.

8. Noel F. Mehlo Jr., *The Lost Ranger: A Soldier's Story* (Miami: YourOnlinePublicist, 2019).

9. Mehlo, *The Lost Ranger*.

10. Balkoski, *Beyond the Beachhead*, chap. 3.

11. Norman D. Cota, "Talk to the Citizens of Slapton Sands Area" (speech given to UK residents during training for D-Day that required forfeiture of property for the war effort, Slapton Sands, UK, November 12, 1943).

12. Omar Bradley, *A Soldier's Story* (New York: Holt, 1951), 236.

13. Bradley, *A Soldier's Story*, 236.

14. United States Army, *The Administrative and Logistical History of the ETO*, Part VI: *NEPTUNE: Training, Mounting, the Artificial Ports* (by Lt. Clifford L. Jones) (Washington, DC: Historical Division, United States Army Forces, March 1946), 222–35.

15. United States Army, *The Administrative and Logistical History of the ETO*, Part VI: *NEPTUNE: Training, Mounting, the Artificial Ports* (by Lt. Clifford L. Jones) (Washington, DC: Historical Division, United States Army Forces, March 1946), 222–35.

16. Headquarters, First United States Army, "Operations Plan 'NEPTUNE,' BIGOT. 25 FEB 1944; Annex I (Page No. 3) to First United States Army Operations Plan Neptune Current Estimate; 1. Political, b. Germany—Situation in France," Ike Skelton Combined Arms Research Library Digital Library, Call No. 3052, http://cgsc.contentdm.oclc.org/cdm.

17. Headquarters, First United States Army, "Operations Plan 'NEPTUNE,' BIGOT. 25 FEB 1944; Annex I (Page No. 3) to First United States Army Operations Plan Neptune Current Estimate; 1. Political, b. Germany—Situation in France," Ike Skelton Combined Arms Research Library Digital Library, Call No. 3052, http://cgsc.content dm.oclc.org/cdm.

18. Balkoski, *Beyond the Beachhead*, chap. 3; War Department, "Combat Narrative of 1st Lt Jack Shea, Aide-de-camp to Brigadier General Cota, 29th Infantry Division," November 1, 1944, 29th Infantry Division Archives, Baltimore, MD, and NARA, College Park, MD, 29d-4 (hereafter cited as Shea).

Chapter 5. German Defenses near Vierville

1. Mehlo, *The Lost Ranger*, 261.

2. Mehlo, *The Lost Ranger*, 261.

3. War Department, Historical Division, *Omaha Beachhead (6 June–13 June, 1944)* (CMH Pub 100-11-1), American Forces in Action Series (Washington, DC: GPO, 1945), 15.

4. Mehlo, *The Lost Ranger*, 261.

5. War Department, Historical Division, *Omaha Beachhead (6 June–13 June, 1944)*, 15.

6. War Department, Historical Division, *Omaha Beachhead (6 June–13 June, 1944)*, 15.

7. The Fuehrer and Supreme Commander of the Armed Forces, "Directive No. 40, Subj: Command Organization of the Coasts," March 23, 1942, https://history.army.mil/books/wwii/7-4/7-4_C.HTM.

8. Military Intelligence Service, War Department, *German Coastal Defenses*, Special Series No. 15, MIS 461 (Washington, DC: U.S. Army Military History Institute, 1943).

9. Military Intelligence Service, War Department, *German Coastal Defenses*.

10. War Department, Historical Division, *Omaha Beachhead (6 June–13 June, 1944)*, 15.

11. Military Intelligence Service, War Department, *German Coastal Defenses*.

12. Military Intelligence Service, War Department, *German Coastal Defenses*.

13. Major General John C. Raaen Jr., email to author, March 4, 2019.

14. Mehlo, *The Lost Ranger*, 261.

15. "Dietrich Kraiss," Wikipedia, https://en.wikipedia.org/wiki/Dietrich_Kraiss (retrieved March 3, 2019).

16. Vince Milano and Bruce Conner, *NORMANDIEFRONT: D-Day to Saint-Lo through German Eyes* (Stroud, Gloucestershire, UK: History Press, 2011), chap. 1.

17. Erwin Rommel, *The Rommel Papers*, ed. B. H. Liddell-Hart (New York: Da Capo Press, 1982), 455.

18. Mehlo, *The Lost Ranger*, 261.

19. Mehlo, *The Lost Ranger*, 261; Milano and Conner, *NORMANDIEFRONT*, chap. 1.

20. Mehlo, *The Lost Ranger*, 261.

21. Mehlo, *The Lost Ranger*, 261.

22. Mehlo, *The Lost Ranger*, 261; Balkoski, *Omaha Beach: D-Day, June 6, 1944*, chap. 7.

23. Rommel, *The Rommel Papers*, 455.

24. Rommel, *The Rommel Papers*, 455.

25. Mehlo, *The Lost Ranger*, 261; Milano and Conner, *NORMANDIEFRONT*, chap. 1.

26. Mehlo, *The Lost Ranger*, 261; Milano and Conner, *NORMANDIEFRONT*, chap. 1.

27. Mehlo, *The Lost Ranger*, 261.

28. Mehlo, *The Lost Ranger*, 261.

29. Mehlo, *The Lost Ranger*, 261.

30. Mehlo, *The Lost Ranger*, 261.

31. Georges Bernage, *Omaha Beach* (Saint-Martin-des-Entrées, France: Heimdal, 2002).

32. Rommel, *The Rommel Papers*, 455.

33. Rommel, *The Rommel Papers*, 467–68.

34. Rommel, *The Rommel Papers*, 455.

35. "Dietrich Kraiss," Wikipedia, https://en.wikipedia.org/wiki/Dietrich_Kraiss (retrieved March 3, 2019).

36. David C. Isby, *The German Army at D-Day: Fighting the Invasion* (London: Greenhill Books, 2004).

Chapter 6. Western Omaha Beach, H-Hour to H+1 Hour
1. John Robert Slaughter, *Omaha Beach and Beyond: The Long March of Sergeant Bob Slaughter* (Stillwater, MN: Voyageur Press, 2009).
2. Balkoski, *Omaha Beach*, chap. 5.
3. NARA, Foreign Military Studies, B-Series, MS# B-283, "Evaluation of German Command and Troops, OB West on D-Day, General der Infanterie Günther Blumentritt," March 25, 1946.
4. NARA, Foreign Military Studies, B-Series, MS# B-432, "352d Infantry Division (5 DEC 1943–6 JUN 1944), Oberstleutnant Fritz Ziegelmann, 352d Infantry Division."
5. Mehlo, *The Lost Ranger*, chap. 16.
6. Milano and Conner, *NORMANDIEFRONT*, 75.
7. Major General John C. Raaen Jr. (Ret.), 5th Ranger Infantry Battalion HQ Company Commander, email to author, June 30, 2018.
8. NARA, Foreign Military Studies, B-Series, MS# B-432, "352d Infantry Division (5 DEC 1943–6 JUN 1944), Oberstleutnant Fritz Ziegelmann, 352d Infantry Division."
9. Lieutenant Colonel S. L. A. Marshall, "Operations, 29th Infantry Division Group Critique Notes, 116-A," War Department, 1944.
10. Alex Kershaw, *The Bedford Boys: One American Town's Ultimate D-Day Sacrifice* (New York: Da Capo Press, 2004), chap. 12.
11. Balkoski, *Omaha Beach*, chap. 5; Ronald L. Lane, *Rudder's Rangers: The True Story of the 2nd United States Ranger Battalion's D-Day Combat Action* (Longwood, FL: Ranger Associates, 1979), chap. 8; Michael Green and James D. Brown, *War Stories of D-Day: Operation Overlord: June 6, 1944* (Minneapolis: Zenith Press, 2009); Robert W. Black, *The Battalion: The Dramatic Story of the 2nd Ranger Battalion in WWII* (Mechanicsburg, PA: Stackpole Books, 2006).
12. Lieutenant Colonel S. L. A. Marshall, "Operations, 29th Infantry Division Group Critique Notes, 116-A," War Department, 1944.
13. Kershaw, *The Bedford Boys*, chap. 12.
14. Lieutenant Colonel S. L. A. Marshall, "Operations, 29th Infantry Division Group Critique Notes, 116-B," War Department, 1944.
15. Balkoski, *Omaha Beach*, chap. 5.
16. J. Robert Slaughter, "Wartime Memories of J. Robert Slaughter and Selected Men of the 116th Infantry, 29th Division, 1941–1945" (unpublished manuscript, 1988).
17. Ronald L. Lane, *Rudder's Rangers*, chap. 8.
18. Balkoski, *Omaha Beach*, chap. 5.
19. NARA, Foreign Military Studies, B-Series, MS# B-432, "352d Infantry Division (5 DEC 1943–6 JUN 1944), Oberstleutnant Fritz Ziegelmann, 352d Infantry Division."
20. Samuel Elliot Morrison, *History of United States Naval Operations in World War II*, vol. 2: *The Invasion of France and Germany, 1944–1945* (Champaign: University of Illinois Press, 1957), 115.

Chapter 7. Cota's D-Day Landing
 1. Statutes at Large; July 9, 1918, ch. 143 (8th par. under "Ordinance Department") (40 Stat. 870) (1919).
 2. War Department, "Operation Neptune Plan, 1st Infantry Division Assignment Orders and Landing Tables CT 16, 18 & 116, Annex 3 to Field Order No. 5," Headquarters, CT 116, Force "O," Landing Chart, Ship and Boat Assignment Table, p. 22 of 52 (NARA 301-3.20), May 31, 1944.
 3. Shea, 29d-9.
 4. Slaughter, "Wartime Memories," chap. 6.
 5. Peter Caddick-Adams, *Sand and Steel: The D-Day Invasions and the Liberation of France* (New York: Oxford University Press, 2019), 671.
 6. War Department, "5th Engineer Special Brigade (5th ESB) After Action Report (AAR) Dated June 1944," NARA, Record Group: 498, Roll: MP63-9_0016, Series: Subject File, File Number: 120, File Name: Engineers, 5th Special Brigade, 69.
 7. Shea, 29d-9; War Department, "29th Infantry Division, ACTIONS OF CP GROUP, CT 116 FROM D-DAY TO 2400 7 JUNE (D+1) 1944," 29th Infantry Division Archives, Baltimore, MD, and NARA, College Park, MD.
 8. Shea, 29d-9; War Department, "HEADQUARTERS, 29TH INFANTRY DIVISION, A.P.O. 29, U.S. ARMY, The following is an account of the actions taken by Brig. Gen. Norman D. Cota on June 6, 1944–D-Day for the Invasion of Europe," June 16, 1944, 29th Infantry Division Archives, Baltimore, MD, and NARA, College Park, MD.
 9. Shea, 29d-9.
 10. War Department, "HEADQUARTERS, 29TH INFANTRY DIVISION, A.P.O. 29, U.S. ARMY, The following is an account of the actions taken by Brig. Gen. Norman D. Cota on June 6, 1944–D-Day for the Invasion of Europe," June 16, 1944, 29th Infantry Division Archives, Baltimore, MD, and NARA, College Park, MD.
 11. Slaughter, "Wartime Memories," chap. 6.
 12. Slaughter, "Wartime Memories," chap. 6.
 13. War Department, "29th Infantry Division, ACTIONS OF CP GROUP, CT 116 FROM D-DAY TO 2400 7 JUNE (D+1) 1944," 29th Infantry Division Archives, Baltimore, MD, and NARA, College Park, MD.
 14. Shea, 29d-9.
 15. War Department, "HEADQUARTERS, 29TH INFANTRY DIVISION, A.P.O. 29, U.S. ARMY, The following is an account of the actions taken by Brig. Gen. Norman D. Cota on June 6, 1944–D-Day for the Invasion of Europe," June 16, 1944, 29th Infantry Division Archives, Baltimore, MD, and NARA, College Park, MD.
 16. War Department, 2d Information and Historical Service, Headquarters, First U.S. Army, APO #230, Lieutenant Jack Shea, "Fragmentary Interview with Captain Joseph Ondre, Armored Section, Hq., First Army," April 4, 1945, 29th Infantry Division Archives, Baltimore, MD, and NARA, College Park, MD.
 17. Shea, 29d-9.
 18. War Department, "HEADQUARTERS, 29TH INFANTRY DIVISION, A.P.O. 29, U.S. ARMY, The following is an account of the actions taken by Brig. Gen. Norman

D. Cota on June 6, 1944–D-Day for the Invasion of Europe," June 16, 1944, 29th Infantry Division Archives, Baltimore, MD, and NARA, College Park, MD.

19. War Department, 2d Information and Historical Service, Headquarters, First U.S. Army, APO #230, Lieutenant Jack Shea, "Combat Interviews with C Co 1st BN 116th RCT, Combat Interview Notes," March 19, 1945, 29th Infantry Division Archives, Baltimore, MD, and NARA, College Park, MD.

20. War Department, "29th Infantry Division AAR, June 44; Phase 1, Landing of CT 116 on OMAHA BEACH and Reduction of Enemy Defenses, Subsequent Attack to Capture St. Laurent Sur Mer, Vierville Sur Mer," June 1944, 29th Infantry Division Archives, Baltimore, MD, and NARA, College Park, MD, p. 1.

21. Private First Class Arden Earll, MOS 504, H Company, 2d Battalion, 116th Infantry, 29th Infantry Division, interview by Eric Montgomery and subsequent sworn affidavit for Cota Medal of Honor effort, December 8, 2019.

22. Herb Epstein, intelligence NCO, 5th Ranger Infantry Battalion, HQ Company, interview by Patrick J. O'Donnell, 1997; Patrick K. O'Donnell, *Beyond Valor: World War II's Rangers and Airborne Veterans Reveal the Heart of Combat* (N.p.: Gale Group, 2001).

23. Private First Class Randall Ching, Company B, 5th Ranger Infantry Battalion, Witness Statement to Congress for Cota Medal of Honor Upgrade, June 4, 2018.

24. USCG, Commanding Officer, "USS LCI (L) 91, History: Flotilla 4 / 10, Group 29, Division 58, Subject: Operation Neptune, Participation in by USS LCI (L) 91," U.S. Coast Guard, June 10, 1944, https://www.uscg.mil/history/webcutters/LCI_91.pdf (retrieved August 2, 2014).

25. Private First Class Max D. Coleman, Company C, 5th Ranger Infantry Battalion, Mahn Center for Archives and Special Collections, Alden Library, Ohio University, Athens, Cornelius Ryan Collection, Box 10, Folder 23.

26. War Department, "29th Infantry Division, ACTIONS OF CP GROUP, CT 116 FROM D-DAY TO 2400 7 JUNE (D+1) 1944," 29th Infantry Division Archives, Baltimore, MD, and NARA, College Park, MD.

27. Shea, 29d-9.

28. Shea, 29d-9.

29. Lieutenant Colonel Robert Ploger, CO, 121st Engineer Combat Battalion, 29th Division, unpublished correspondence with Joe Balkoski, 29th Infantry Division Archives, Baltimore, MD, April 7, 2000.

30. Oberstleutnant Fritz Ziegelmann, MS# B-432, 352d Infantry Division (December 5, 1943–June 6, 1944), NARA Foreign Military Studies, B-Series (B-0388).

31. John C. Raaen Jr., *Intact: A First-Hand Account of the D-Day Invasion from a 5th Rangers Company Commander* (St. Louis: Reedy Press, LLC), chaps. 5 and 6.

32. Major General John C. Raaen Jr., USA (Ret.), CO, Company C, 5th Ranger Infantry Battalion, Witness Statement to Congress for Cota Medal of Honor Upgrade, June 6, 2018.

33. Major Richard P. Sullivan, Executive Officer, 5th Ranger Infantry Battalion, Mahn Center for Archives and Special Collections, Alden Library, Ohio University, Athens, Cornelius Ryan Collection, Box 10, Folder 54.

34. Lieutenant Jack A. Snyder, Platoon Leader, Company C, 5th Ranger Infantry Battalion, Mahn Center for Archives and Special Collections, Alden Library, Ohio University, Athens, Cornelius Ryan Collection, Box 10, Folder 51.
35. Gary Sterne, *The Cover-Up at Omaha Beach: D-Day, the US Rangers, and the Untold Story of Maisy Battery* (New York: Skyhorse, 2014), 28.
36. Robert C. Fitzsimmons, Company B, 2d Ranger Infantry Battalion, Mahn Center for Archives and Special Collections, Alden Library, Ohio University, Athens, Cornelius Ryan Collection, Box 10, Folder 26.
37. Tom Herring, T/5, 5th Ranger Infantry Battalion, Company C, Joe Balkoski Collection, unpublished manuscript, 29th Infantry Division Archives, Baltimore, MD.
38. Herb Epstein, intelligence NCO, 5th Ranger Infantry Battalion, HQ Company, interview by Patrick J. O'Donnell, 1997.
39. Ching, Medal of Honor testimony.
40. SSG Donald L. Chance, Company C, 5th Ranger Infantry Battalion, Mahn Center for Archives and Special Collections, Alden Library, Ohio University, Athens, Cornelius Ryan Collection, Box 10, Folder 22.
41. War Department, U.S. Army Historical Division, "Interview with Various 5th Rangers, July 1944, Captain Edward Luther, CO, E Company, 5th Ranger Infantry Battalion," National Archives II, College Park, MD, RG 407, Combat Interview 5th Rangers (CI); United States Army, "U.S. Army Historical Section Headquarters, European Theater of Operations, War Department Notes, Volumes 1 and 2" (by Lt. Col. Charles H. Taylor and Sgt. Forrest Pogue, historian/transcriptionist), War Department, November 11, 1944, 93 (hereafter cited as Taylor's Notes).
42. Richard N. Hathaway Jr., *Training for Bloody Omaha: Activation, Training and Combat of the 5th Ranger Infantry Battalion through 8 June 1944* (New York: Vantage Press, 2002), 38.
43. Unit Journal, 5th Ranger Infantry Battalion, September 44, NARA, College Park, MD, Record Identification, Entry: 427 WWII Operations Reports 1944–1948, File # INBN-5-0 all boxes, located in boxes 16916-16919; see file: INBN-5.0.7 4933 Jnl.
44. Oberstleutnant Fritz Ziegelmann, MS# B-432, 352d Infantry Division (December 5, 1943–June 6, 1944), NARA Foreign Military Studies, B-Series (B-0388).
45. Shea, 29d-9.
46. Earll, Medal of Honor testimony.

Chapter 8. Vierville
1. Shea, 29d-2.
2. Bradley, *A Soldier's Story*, 270.
3. Oberstleutnant Fritz Ziegelmann, assistant chief of staff, 352d Infantry Division, National Archives, RG 319, MS B-432, p. 27.
4. Shea, 29d-20.
5. War Department, "HEADQUARTERS, 29TH INFANTRY DIVISION, A.P.O. 29, U.S. ARMY, The following is an account of the actions taken by Brig. Gen. Norman D. Cota on June 6, 1944–D-Day for the Invasion of Europe," June 16, 1944, 29th Infantry Division Archives, Baltimore, MD, and NARA, College Park, MD; Taylor's Notes.

NOTES

6. War Department, "HEADQUARTERS, 29TH INFANTRY DIVISION, A.P.O. 29, U.S. ARMY, The following is an account of the actions taken by Brig. Gen. Norman D. Cota on June 6, 1944–D-Day for the Invasion of Europe," June 16, 1944, 29th Infantry Division Archives, Baltimore, MD, and NARA, College Park, MD.

7. 2d Information and Historical Service, Headquarters, First U.S. Army, APO #230, Company C, 116th Infantry, 29th Division, U.S. Army Historical Division, Interview with various Company C soldiers, March 25, 1945, pp. 12–14.

8. Oberstleutnant Fritz Ziegelmann, 352d Infantry Division, June 6, 1944, NARA Foreign Military Studies, B-Series (B-0388).

9. Raaen, *Intact*, 54.

10. Taylor's Notes, 94–95.

11. Headquarters, 1st Infantry Division, G-3 Message Journal, First Division Museum, https://www.fdmuseum.org/researchers/digital-archives (hereafter cited as G-3 Message Journal).

12. Memo to Lieutenant Colonel Charles H. Taylor from Lieutenant Jack Shea, 2d Informational and Historical Service, Headquarters, First U.S. Army, APO #230, "Summary of D-Day Material," April 2, 1945.

13. Taylor's Notes, 95–97.

14. Mehlo, *The Lost Ranger*, 301.

15. Shea, 29d-21.

16. Lieutenant Colonel S. L. A. Marshall, "Operations, 29th Infantry Division Group Critique Notes, HQ Company of 2d Battalion, 116th RCT, Maj. Chas. R. Cawthorn, Battalion Commander Who Was HQ CO on D-Day and Chaplain Charles D. Reed," War Department, 1944.

17. G-3 Message Journal.

18. After Action Report, 5th Ranger Infantry Battalion, Flamanville, France, prepared June 30, 1944, NARA INBN-5-0.8, D-Day, June 6, 1944.

19. "Interview with Various Company C Soldiers, 116th Infantry, 29th Division," U.S. Army Historical Division, March 25, 1945.

20. 1st Sergeant Avery Thornhill, 5th Ranger Infantry Battalion, Company B Questionnaire, Mahn Center for Archives and Special Collections, Alden Library, Ohio University, Athens, Cornelius Ryan Collection, Box 10, Folder 55.

21. Ching, Medal of Honor testimony.

22. Taylor's Notes, 97–98.

23. G-3 Message Journal.

24. Shea, 29d-22.

25. Major General John C. Raaen Jr., USA (Ret.), personal correspondence to Cota Medal of Honor Research Team.

26. 121st Engineer Combat Battalion After Action Report, 29th Infantry Division—June 1944—Battle of Normandy.

27. 121st Engineer Combat Battalion After Action Report, 29th Infantry Division—June 1944—Battle of Normandy.

28. Balkoski, *Omaha Beach*, 277.

29. USS *Thompson* War Diary, NARA Catalog ID 4697018, Microfilm No. 77344.

30. USS *McCook* War Diary, NARA Catalog ID 4697018, Microfilm No. 79463.

31. USS *Texas* War Diary, NARA Catalog ID 4697018, Microfilm No. 80974.
32. USS *Texas* War Diary, NARA Catalog ID 4697018, Microfilm No. 80974.
33. United States Navy, *Operational Experience of Fast Battleships: World War II, Korea, Vietnam* (Washington, DC: Naval Historical Center, 1989), http://ibiblio.org/hyperwar/NHC/OpExpFastBBs/OpExpFastBBs.htm.
34. "Naval Weapons of the World: From 1880 to Today," Nathan Okun, NavWeaps, http://www.navweaps.com/Weapons/index_weapons.php.
35. The Geneva International Centre for Humanitarian Demining (GICHD); CHARACTERISATION OF EXPLOSIVE WEAPONS; EXPLOSIVE WEAPON EFFECTS OVERVIEW EXPLOSIVE WEAPON EFFECTS FINAL REPORT; February 2017; ISBN: 978-2-940369-61-4; Areas of harm; Understanding explosive weapons with wide area effects; PAX means peace; October 2016; ISBN 978-94-92487-05-6/NUR 689.
36. United States Army, *Tactics, Techniques, and Procedures for Observed Fire* (FM 6-30) (Washington, DC: Department of the Army, 1991), chap. 8, sect. 3, "Naval Gunfire."
37. United States Marine Corps (USMC), *Close Air Support* (MCWP 3-23.1—PCN 143 000055 00) (Washington, DC: USMC, 1998).
38. War Department, "HEADQUARTERS, 29TH INFANTRY DIVISION, A.P.O. 29, U.S. ARMY, The following is an account of the actions taken by Brig. Gen. Norman D. Cota on June 6, 1944–D-Day for the Invasion of Europe," June 16, 1944, 29th Infantry Division Archives, Baltimore, MD, and NARA, College Park, MD.
39. Memo to Lieutenant Colonel Taylor from Lieutenant Shea.
40. Headquarters, 29th Infantry Division, APO 29, U.S. Army, "ACTIONS OF CP GROUP, CT 116 FROM D-DAY TO 2400 7 JUNE (D+1) 1944."
41. Headquarters, 121st Engineer Combat Battalion, APO 29, U.S. Army, After Action Report for the Month of June 1944, July 20, 1944.
42. 1st Lieutenant John F. MacAllister, correspondence to General Robert R. Ploger in March 2000, later given to Joe Balkoski, 29th Infantry Division Archives, Baltimore, MD.
43. Shea, 29d-2.
44. 1st Lieutenant John F. MacAllister, "Silver Star Citation," 29th Infantry Division Archives, Baltimore, MD.
45. 1st Lieutenant (Infantry) John T. Shea, "Silver Star Citation," 29th Infantry Division Archives, Baltimore, MD.
46. Major Allan F. Olson, "Silver Star Citation," 29th Infantry Division Archives, Baltimore, MD.
47. Shea, 29d-23.
48. Lieutenant Colonel S. L. A. Marshall, "Operations, 29th Infantry Division Group Critique Notes, 116-D," War Department, 1944.

Chapter 9. Seventeen Miles
1. War Department, Historical Division, *Omaha Beachhead*, 95.
2. G-3 Message Journal, June 6, 1944, 1131 hours.
3. War Department, Historical Division, *Omaha Beachhead*, 101.
4. G-3 Message Journal, June 6, 1944, 1328 hours.

5. 1944 07 10 1st Infantry Division (ID) G-3 Report of Operations [NARA 223325 301-3], First Division Museum, https://www.fdmuseum.org/researchers/digital-archives.

6. Operation Neptune Operations Overlay, Annex 1 of Field Order # 35, Ike Skelton Combined Arms Research Library Digital Library. Call No. N7375, http://cgsc.content dm.oclc.org/cdm.

7. War Department, "Combat Narrative of 1st Lt Jack Shea."

8. Kershaw, *Bedford Boys*, 155.

9. Harold Baumgarten, *D-Day Survivor: An Autobiography* (Gretna, LA: Pelican Publishing Company, 1981), chap. 10.

10. 743d TN BN Journal, June 6, 1944, "743rd TN BN S3 Journal 6 Jun–1 Oct," Ike Skelton Combined Arms Research Library Digital Library, Call No. 3519, October 1, 1944, http://cgsc.contentdm.oclc.org/cdm.

11. Kershaw, *Bedford Boys*, 160.

12. War Department, "Combat Narrative of 1st Lt Jack Shea."

13. Shea, 29d-25.

14. Headquarters, 121st Engineer Combat Battalion, APO 29, U.S. Army, "After Action Report for Month of June; HEADQUARTERS; 121st Engineer Combat Battalion; APO 29, U.S. Army, Summary of Operations; Landing and Assault of Beach," July 20, 1944.

15. 5th ESB AAR. Record Group 498, Roll MP63-9_0016, File No. 120, Engineers, 5th Special Brigade, June 6, 1944, fold3.com/image/287188460.

16. 121st Engineer Combat Battalion, "Unit Report No 1—June 5–8," June 8, 1944.

17. Shea, 29d-25.

18. Combat Interview with Major Bratton Asst G-2 116th RCT (002) [2-15-20], 29th Infantry Division: Assault on Omaha Beach, Major Wm. [William] S. Bratton, Assistant G-2, June 17, 1944.

19. War Department, Historical Division, *Omaha Beachhead*, 95–96.

20. War Department, "HEADQUARTERS, 29TH INFANTRY DIVISION; A.P.O. 29, U.S. ARMY, The following is an account of the actions taken by Brig. Gen. Norman D. Cota on June 6, 1944–D-Day for the Invasion of Europe," June 16, 1944, 29th Infantry Division Archives, Baltimore, MD, and NARA, College Park, MD.

21. Jonathan Gawne, *Spearheading D-Day: American Special Units in Normandy* (Paris: Historie & Collections, 2001), 168.

22. Shea, 29d-26.

23. G-3 Message Journal.

24. War Department, Historical Division, *Omaha Beachhead*, 97.

25. 29th Infantry Division: Assault on Omaha Beach, Maj. Wm. [William] S. Bratton, Assistant G-2, June 17, 1944.

26. Shea, 29d-29.

27. G-3 Message Journal.

28. Ewing, *29 Let's GO!*, 47–48.

29. Ewing, *29 Let's GO!*, 49.

30. Ewing, *29 Let's GO!*, 48.

31. Shea, 29d-26–28.

32. Shea, 29d-28–29.

33. Shea, 29d-30–31.

34. War Department, Military Intelligence Division, *The Exploitation of German Documents* (Washington, DC: War Department, 1944).

35. Shea, 29d-34.

36. G-3 Message Journal; Headquarters, 58th Armored Field Artillery Battalion, APO 230, U.S. Army, After Action Report against Enemy for Month of June 1944, First Division Museum, https://www.fdmuseum.org/researchers/digital-archives.

37. Colonel John P. Cooper Jr., Maryland National Guard, *The History of the 110th Field Artillery with Sketches of Related Units* (Baltimore: War Records Division Maryland Historical Society, 1953).

38. 110th Field Artillery Battalion After Action Report, 29th Infantry Division—June 1944—Battle of Normandy.

39. Shea, 29d-35.

40. Combat Interview with Major Bratton Asst G-2 116th RCT (002) [2-15-20], 29th Infantry Division: Assault on Omaha Beach, Major Wm. [William] S. Bratton, Assistant G-2, June 17, 1944.

41. Combat Interview with Major William S. Bratton, Assistant G-2, 29th Infantry Division, June 17, 1944.

42. Shea, 29d-36.

43. Shea, 29d-39–40.

44. Based on 1980s interview between Joe Balkoski, 29th ID Command Historian, and Lieutenant Colonel John Purley Cooper, CO, 110th FA-Bn, Housed at 29th ID Archives, Baltimore, MD; Balkoski, *Omaha Beach*, 155–56.

45. Shea, 29d-45.

46. Shea, 29d-49–50.

47. Oberstleutnant Fritz Ziegelmann, 352d Infantry Division, June 6, 1944, NARA Foreign Military Studies, B-Series (B-0388).

48. Mehlo, *The Lost Ranger*, 268.

49. Caddick-Adams, *Sand and Steel*, 600–601.

50. President Franklin D. Roosevelt, "FDR D-Day Prayer," radio broadcast transcript, Franklin D. Roosevelt Presidential Library and Museum, NARA, June 6, 1944, https://fdr.blogs.archives.gov/2019/06/05/fdrs-d-day-prayer.

Chapter 10. Beyond Intrepidity

1. Frank Oberle, "General Cota Remembered," *The Twenty-Niner*, October 1971.

2. Shea, 29d-2.

3. Major General Norman D. Cota, USA (Ret.), Military Personnel Record File (MPRF), NARA, St. Louis, MO.

4. Cota, MPRF.

5. Cota, MPRF.

6. War Department, "HEADQUARTERS, 29TH INFANTRY DIVISION; A.P.O. 29, U.S. ARMY; 16 June 1944; Lt Jack Shea; The following is an account of the actions taken by Brig. Gen. Norman D. Cota on June 6, 1944–D-Day for the Invasion of

Europe," June 16, 1944, 29th Infantry Division Archives, Baltimore, MD, and NARA, College Park, MD.

7. War Department, "HEADQUARTERS, 29TH INFANTRY DIVISION; A.P.O. 29, U.S. ARMY; 16 June 1944; Lt Jack Shea; The following is an account of the actions taken by Brig. Gen. Norman D. Cota on June 6, 1944–D-Day for the Invasion of Europe," June 16, 1944, 29th Infantry Division Archives, Baltimore, MD, and NARA, College Park, MD.

8. Omar Bradley and Clay Blair, *A General's Life: An Autobiography by General of the Army Omar N. Bradley* (New York: Simon & Schuster, 1983), 249.

9. Bradley and Blair, *A General's Life*, 249–52.

10. Bradley, *A Soldier's Story*, 270–72.

11. General Dwight D. Eisenhower, *Report by the Supreme Commander to the Combined Chiefs of Staff on the Operations in Europe of the Allied Expeditionary Force, 6 June 1944 to 8 May 1945* (CMH Pub 70-58) (1946; rpt. Washington, DC: Center of Military History, United States Army, 1994).

12. 1st Lieutenant Jack Shea, "HQ 2nd Information and Historical Service—Shea Memo to Maj Jerimiah O'Sullivan RE 29th ID History," September 26, 1944, 29th Infantry Division Archives, Baltimore, MD.

13. Hall of Valor: The Military Medals Database, https://valor.militarytimes.com. (Search by service member name) (hereafter cited as Hall of Valor).

14. Hall of Valor.

15. Hall of Valor.

16. Hall of Valor.

17. Hall of Valor.

18. Hall of Valor.

19. Hall of Valor.

20. Marcia Moen and Margo Heinen, *Reflections of Courage on D-Day and the Days That Followed: A Personal Account of Ranger Ace Parker* (Rogers, MN: DeForest Press, 1999).

21. Hall of Valor.

22. War Department, Historical Division, *Omaha Beachhead*, 95–96.

23. Hall of Valor.

24. Hall of Valor.

25. War Department, Historical Division, *Omaha Beachhead*, 52.

26. Shea, 29d-38.

27. Hall of Valor.

28. Hall of Valor.

29. Cota, MPRF.

30. Headquarters, 29th Infantry Division, APO 29, U.S. Army; Recommendation for Award of Distinguished Service Medal, Oak-Leaf Cluster, Cota, Norman D., for period 12 Oct 43 to 13 Aug 44, dated 6 December 1945 by Charles H. Gerhardt, Major General, Division Commander, 29th Infantry Division.

31. Don Whitehead, "All's Well with the 29th If General Cota Is Singing," Associated Press, July 29, 1944.

32. Ewing, *29 Let's GO!*, 82–83.

33. David Irving, *The War between the Generals* (Sussex, UK: Parforce UK, Ltd, 1981), 152.

34. 115 Cong. Rec. S17418–17423 (daily ed. June 25, 1969) (statement of Sen. William B. Spong, Jr., VA), govinfo.gov, https://www.govinfo.gov/content/pkg/GPO-CRECB -1969-pt13/pdf/GPO-CRECB-1969-pt13-4-3.pdf.

35. Earll, Medal of Honor testimony.

Chapter 11. A Dream Realized

1. Bradley and Blair, *A General's Life*, 249.

2. Balkoski, *Omaha Beach*, 359–61.

3. Ching, Medal of Honor testimony.

4. John C. Raaen Jr., personal correspondence with author, 2018.

5. Major General Carroll D. Childers, ARNG (Ret), personal correspondence with author, 2019.

6. Brigadier General Theodore G. Shuey, ARNG (Ret), *Omaha Beach Field Guide* (Saint-Martin-des-Entrées, France: Heimdal, 2014), 79.

7. Holbrook Bradley, "Bradley Describes 29th Division Landing on Normandy Beachhead," *Baltimore Sun*, June 13, 1944.

Bibliography

Altieri, James. *The Spearheaders*. New York: The Popular Library, 1960.

Ambrose, Stephen E. *D-Day: June 6, 1944: The Climatic Battle of World War II*. New York: Simon & Schuster, 1994.

———. *The Victors: The Men of World War II*. New York: Pocket Books, 1998.

Badsey, Stephen. *D-Day: From the Normandy Beaches to the Liberation of France*. Godalming, Surrey, UK: Colour Library Books Ltd., 1993.

———. *Normandy, 1944: Allied Landings and Breakout*. Campaign Series 1. Oxford: Osprey Publishing, 1990.

Balkoski, Joseph. *Beyond the Beachhead: The 29th Infantry Division in Normandy*. Mechanicsburg, PA: Stackpole Books, 1989.

———. *Omaha Beach: D-Day, June 6, 1944*. Mechanicsburg, PA: Stackpole Books, 2004.

Bates, Charles C., Lt. Col., USAF (Ret.). "Sea, Swell and Surf Forecasting for D-Day and Beyond: The Anglo-American Effort, 1943–1945." Unpublished manuscript, 2010.

Baumgarten, Harold. *D-Day Survivor: An Autobiography*. Gretna, LA: Pelican Publishing Company, 1981.

Beevor, Anthony. *D-Day: The Battle for Normandy*. New York: Penguin Books, 2009.

Bernage, Georges. *Omaha Beach*. Saint-Martin-des-Entrées, France: Heimdal, 2002.

Black, Robert W. *The Battalion: The Dramatic Story of the 2nd Ranger Battalion in WWII*. Mechanicsburg, PA: Stackpole Books, 2006.

———. *The Ranger Force: Darby's Rangers in World War II*. Mechanicsburg, PA: Stackpole Books, 2009.

———. *Rangers in World War II*. New York: Ballantine, Presidio Press, an imprint of the Random House Publishing Group, 1992.

Bliven, Bruce, Jr. *Invasion: The Story of D-Day*. New York: Flying Point Press, 1956.

Bradley, Omar. *A Soldier's Story*. New York: Holt, 1951.

Bradley, Omar, and Clay Blair. *A General's Life: An Autobiography by General of the Army Omar N. Bradley*. New York: Simon & Schuster, 1983.

Brown, James D., and Michael Green. *War Stories of D-Day: Operation Overlord: June 6, 1944*. Minneapolis: Zenith Press, 2009.

Bull, Stephen, Dr. *World War II Infantry Tactics: Company and Battalion*. Elite Book 122. Oxford: Osprey Publishing, 2005.

———. *World War II Infantry Tactics: Squad and Platoon*. Elite Book 105. Oxford: Osprey Publishing, 2004.

Caddick-Adams, Peter. *Sand and Steel: The D-Day Invasions and the Liberation of France.* New York: Oxford University Press, 2019.

Coughlin, Fran, and Lou Lisko. "5th Ranger D-Day Mission in Normandy, Col. Max Schneider, Commanding." Unpublished manuscript. Ranger Battalions Association of World War II.

Cutchins, John A., Lt. Col., and Lt. Col. George S. Stewart Jr. *History of the Twenty-Ninth Division "Blue and Gray," 1917–1919.* Philadelphia: Press of MacCalla & Co., 1921.

Delaforce, Patrick. *Smashing the Atlantic Wall: The Destruction of Hitler's Coastal Fortresses.* South Yorkshire, UK: Pen & Sword Books, 2005.

Department of Defense (DoD). *DoD Manual 1348.33.* Vol. 1: *Manual of Military Decorations and Awards: Medal of Honor (MOH).* Washington, DC: U.S. Government, 2016.

Dwyer, John Barry. *Scouts and Raiders: The Navy's First Special Warfare Commandos.* Westport, CT: Praeger, 1993.

Ewing, Joseph H. *29 Let's GO! A History of the 29th Infantry Division in World War II.* Washington, DC: Infantry Journal Press, 1948.

Forty, George. *Fortress Europe: Hitler's Atlantic Wall.* Hersham, Surrey, UK: Ian Allan Printing Ltd., 2002.

François, Dominique. *Normandy: Breaching the Atlantic Wall From D-Day to the Breakout and Liberation.* Minneapolis: Zenith Press, 2008.

Gawne, Jonathan. *Finding Your Father's War: A Practical Guide to Researching and Understanding Service in the World War II US Army.* Drexel Hill, PA: Casemate, 2006.

———. *Spearheading D-Day: American Special Units in Normandy.* Paris: Historie & Collections, 2001.

Glassman, Henry S. *"Lead the Way, Rangers": History of the Fifth Ranger Battalion.* Markt Grafing, Bavaria: U.S. Army—Buchdruckerei Hauser, 1945.

Going, Chris, and Alun Jones. *Above the Battle: D-Day: The Lost Evidence.* Manchester, UK: C'recy Publishing Limited, 2004.

Graves, Garry M. *Bloody Omaha: My Remembrances of That Day by James Robert Copeland, S/Sgt.—Company B, 5th Ranger Infantry Battalion.* N.p.: GGA Publishing, 2010.

Green, Michael, and James D. Brown. *War Stories of D-Day: Operation Overlord: June 6, 1944.* Minneapolis: Zenith Press, 2009.

Hatfield, Thomas M. *Rudder: From Leader to Legend.* College Station: Texas A&M University Press, 2011.

Hathaway, Richard N., Jr. *Training for Bloody Omaha: Activation, Training and Combat of the 5th Ranger Infantry Battalion through 8 June 1944.* New York: Vantage Press, 2002.

Isby, David C., ed. *Fighting in Normandy: The German Army from D-Day to Villers-Bocage.* London: Greenhill Books, 2001.

———. *The German Army at D-Day: Fighting the Invasion.* London: Greenhill Books, 2004.

Kaufmann, J. E., and H. W. Kaufmann. *The American GI in Europe in World War II: The March to D-Day*. Mechanicsburg, PA: Stackpole Books, 2009.

———. *The American GI in Europe in World War II: D-Day: Storming Ashore*. Mechanicsburg, PA: Stackpole Books, 2009.

Kershaw, Alex. *The Bedford Boys: One American Town's Ultimate D-Day Sacrifice*. New York: Da Capo Press, 2004.

Kershaw, Robert J. *D-Day: Piercing the Atlantic Wall*. Annapolis, MD: Naval Institute Press, 1994.

King, Michael J., Dr. *Rangers: Selected Combat Operations in World War II*. Leavenworth Papers No. 11. Fort Leavenworth, KS: Combat Studies Institute, U.S. Army Command and General Staff College, 1985.

Kingseed, Cole. *From Omaha Beach to Dawson's Ridge: The Combat Journal of Captain Joe Dawson*. Annapolis, MD: Naval Institute Press, 2013.

Lane, Ronald L. *Rudder's Rangers: The True Story of the 2nd United States Ranger Battalion's D-Day Combat Action*. Longwood, FL: Ranger Associates, 1979.

Mehlo, Noel F., Jr. *The Lost Ranger: A Soldier's Story*. Miami: YourOnlinePublicist, 2019.

Milano, Vince, and Bruce Conner. *NORMANDIEFRONT: D-Day to Saint-Lo through German Eyes*. Stroud, Gloucestershire, UK: History Press, 2011.

Miller, Edward G. *Nothing Less Than Full Victory, Americans at War in Europe, 1944–1945*. Annapolis, MD: Naval Institute Press, 2007.

Miller, Robert A. *Division Commander: A Biography of Major General Norman D. Cota*. Spartanburg, SC: Reprint Company Publishers, 1989.

Morrison, Samuel Elliot. *History of United States Naval Operations in World War II*. Vol. 2: *The Invasion of France and Germany, 1944–1945*. Champaign: University of Illinois Press, 1957.

Nixon, James C., Capt., USA. "Combined Special Operations in World War II." Unpublished manuscript, Auburn University, Fort Leavenworth, KS, 1982.

O'Donnell, Patrick K. *Beyond Valor: World War II's Rangers and Airborne Veterans Reveal the Heart of Combat*. N.p.: Gale Group, 2001.

Prince, Morris, Pfc. "Co A, 2nd Ranger BN, Overseas, Then Over the Top." Unpublished manuscript, United States Army, Command and General Staff College Library, 1948.

Raaen, John C., Jr. *Intact: A First-Hand Account of the D-Day Invasion from a 5th Rangers Company Commander*. St. Louis: Reedy Press, LLC, 2012.

———. "The Rangers Have Landed Intact: A Story of D-Day and of the 5th Rangers." Unpublished manuscript, U.S. Army Military History Institute, Carlisle Barracks, PA, 1981.

Rommel, Erwin. *The Rommel Papers*. Edited by B. H. Liddell-Hart. New York: Da Capo Press, 1982.

Rottman, Gordon L. *German Field Fortifications 1939–45 (Fortress 023)*. Oxford: Osprey Publishing, 2004.

Ryan, Cornelius. *The Longest Day*. New York: Simon & Schuster, 1959.

Schneider, James F. *My Father's War: The Story of Max Ferguson Schneider, a Ranger Commander.* Boise: Lulu, 2012.

Shuey, Theodore G., Brig. Gen., ARNG (Ret.). *Omaha Beach Field Guide.* Saint-Martin-des-Entrées, France: Heimdal, 2014.

Sinton, S., and R. Hargis. *World War II Medal of Honor Recipients (2): Army and Air Corps.* Elite Book 95. Oxford: Osprey Publishing, 2003.

Slaughter, John Robert. *Omaha Beach and Beyond: The Long March of Sergeant Bob Slaughter.* Stillwater, MN: Voyageur Press, 2009.

———. "Wartime Memories of J. Robert Slaughter and Selected Men of the 116th Infantry, 29th Division, 1941–1945." Unpublished manuscript, 1988.

Sterne, Gary. *The Cover-Up at Omaha Beach: D-Day, the US Rangers, and the Untold Story of Maisy Battery.* New York: Skyhorse Publishing, 2014.

United States Army. *The Administrative and Logistical History of the ETO.* Part VI: *NEPTUNE: Training, Mounting, the Artificial Ports* (by Lt. Clifford L. Jones). Washington, DC: Historical Division, United States Army Forces, March 1946.

———. *The Amphibious Training Center* (by Capt. Marshall O. Becker). Study No. 22. Washington, DC: Army Ground Forces, Historical Section, 1946.

———. *The Army Ground Forces: The Organization of Ground Combat Troops* (by Kent Roberts Greenfield, Robert R. Palmer, and Bell I. Wiley). The United States Army in World War II. Washington, DC: Department of the Army, Historical Division, 1947.

———. *The Mediterranean Theater of Operations, Sicily, and the Surrender of Italy* (by Col. Albert N. Garland, Howard McGaw Smyth, and Martin Blumenson). The United States Army in World War II. Washington, DC: Office of the Chief of Military History, Department of the Army, 1965.

———. *Pictorial Record: The War against Germany and Italy: Mediterranean and Adjacent Areas* (by Kent Roberts Greenfield). The United States Army in World War II. Washington, DC: Department of the Army, Historical Division, 1951.

———. *Tactics, Techniques, and Procedures for Observed Fire (FM 6-30).* Washington, DC: Department of the Army, 1991.

———. *U.S. Army Historical Section Headquarters, European Theater of Operations, War Department Notes* (by Lt. Col. Charles H. Taylor). Vols. 1 and 2. Washington, DC: War Department, 1944.

United States Army, Center of Military History. *The Corps of Engineers: The War against Germany* (CMH Pub 10-22) (by Alfred M. Beck, Abe Bortz, Charles W. Lynch, Lida Mayo, and Ralph F. Weld). United States Army in World War II: The Technical Services. Washington, DC: U.S. Army, 1985.

———. *Cross Channel Attack* (CMH Pub 7-4-1) (by Gordon A. Harrison). United States Army in World War II: The European Theater of Operations. Washington, DC: US Army, 1951.

———. *Logistical Support of the Armies: May 1941–September 1944* (CMH Pub 7-2-1) (by Ronald G. Ruppenthal). U.S. Army in World War II: European Theater of Operations. Washington, DC: US Army, 1995.

———. *Pictorial Record: The War Against Germany: Europe and Adjacent Areas* (CMH 12-3). United States Army in World War II. Washington, DC: War Department, 1989.

———. *The Procurement and Training of Ground Combat Troops* (CMH 2-2). United States Army in World War II. Washington, DC: Department of the Army, 1991.

———. *The Supreme Command* (CMH 7-1) (by Forrest C. Pogue). United States Army in World War II: The European Theater of Operations. Washington, DC: Department of the Army, 1989.

———. *The Transportation Corps: Movements, Training, and Supply* (CMH Pub 10-20) (by Chesler Wardlow). United States Army in World War II: The Technical Services. Washington, DC: War Department, 1956.

———. *The U.S. Army Campaigns of World War II: Tunisia* (CMH Pub 72-12) (by Charles R. Anderson). Washington, DC: Department of the Army, 1996.

———. *The U.S. Army GHQ Maneuvers of 1941* (CMH Pub 70-41-1) (by Christopher R. Gabel). Washington, DC: Department of the Army, 1992.

United States Army, Office of the Theater Historian. *Order of Battle of the United States Army, World War II, European Theater of Operations, Divisions.* Paris: War Department, 1946.

United States Marine Corps (USMC). *Close Air Support* (MCWP 3-23.1—PCN 143 000055 00). Washington, DC: USMC, 1998.

United States Navy. *Operational Experience of Fast Battleships: World War II, Korea, Vietnam.* Washington, DC: Naval Historical Center, 1989.

War Department. *Basic Field Manual: Advanced Map and Aerial Photograph Reading* (FM 21-26). Washington, DC: GPO, 1941.

———. *Basic Field Manual: Conventional Signs, Military Symbols and Abbreviations* (FM 21-30). Washington, DC: GPO, 1941.

———. *Basic Field Manual: Elementary Map and Aerial Photograph Reading* (FM 21-25). Washington, DC: GPO, 1941.

———. *Basic Field Manual: Military Training* (FM 21-5). Washington, DC: GPO, 1941.

———. *Handbook on German Military Forces* (TM-E 30-451). Washington, DC: GPO, 1945.

———. *Heavy Weapons Company, Rifle Regiment* (FM 7-15). Washington, DC: GPO, 1942.

———. *Infantry Battalion* (FM 7-20). Washington, DC: GPO, 1944.

———. *Infantry Field Manual, Headquarters Company, Intelligence and Signal Communication, Rifle Regiment* (FM 7-25). Washington, DC: GPO, 1942.

———. *Infantry Field Manual, Organization and Tactics of Infantry, the Rifle Battalion* (FM 7-5). Washington, DC: GPO, 1940.

———. *Infantry Field Manual; Rifle Regiment* (FM 7-40). Washington, DC: GPO, 1942.

———. *Land Mines and Booby Traps* (FM 5-31). Washington, DC: GPO, 1943.

———. *Military Occupational Classification of Enlisted Personnel* (TM 12-427). Washington, DC: GPO, 1944.

————. *Supply and Evacuation; the Infantry Regiment; Service Company and Medical Detachment* (FM 7-30). Washington, DC: GPO, 1944.

War Department, Chief of Combined Operations. "Combined Operations Pamphlet No 24: Cliff Assaults." United Kingdom: U.S. Army, August 1944.

————. "The Combined Operations Staff Notebook, BR 1293." United Kingdom: U.S. Army, 1944.

War Department, Commanding General ETOUSA. *Preparation for Overseas Movement (Short Sea Voyage)*. European Theater of Operations, United States Army. Washington, DC: U.S. Army, 1944.

War Department, Historical Division. *Omaha Beachhead (6 June–13 June 1944)* (CMH Pub 100-11-1). American Forces in Action Series. Washington, DC: GPO, 1945.

War Department, Military Intelligence Division. *The Exploitation of German Documents*. Washington, DC: War Department, 1944.

War Department, Military Intelligence Service. *German Coastal Defenses*. Special Series No. 15, MIS 461. Washington, DC: U.S. Army Military History Institute, 1943.

Wood, James A. *Army of the West: The Weekly Reports of German Army Group B from Normandy to the West Wall*. Mechanicsburg, PA: Stackpole Books, 2007.

ACKNOWLEDGMENTS

The family and friends of Major General Norman Daniel "Dutch" Cota are so very, very grateful to

Senator Pat Roberts, Gilda Lintz, Lauren Stockwell, and their outstanding colleagues

Generals John Raaen, Carroll Childers, Daniel Long, Grant Hayden, Charles Whittington, Blake Ortner, and H. Steven Blum

Ranger Randall Ching and his daughter Bonnie Louie and family

Denise, Christian, Maggie, and Katie Mehlo, Patricia Hartsough (editor, teacher, and librarian), and Raymond Hartsough (attorney)

Joseph Balkoski and Michael White

Scott, Lisa, and Joey Ritchie

Mike and Betsy Sweeney, Scott and Matt Stewart, Jeff and Jettie Zoller, Mike and Diane Harmon, Leon and Becky Steiner, Mike Zinn, Alan and Kathy Hoffman, Jim and Barbara Musgrove, Emerson Shields

As the author and contributors, we wish to thank and acknowledge several individuals:

The French people—let freedom ever ring upon your shores

Mr. Richard T. Bass, USATC historian, United Kingdom

INDEX

116th Infantry, viii, 35, 69, 70–71, 72,
    75, 135, 137, 141, 142, 151, 153,
    155–58, 160–61, 166–69, 174,
    175–76, 177, 179–80, 181, 183,
    185, 194–95, 211–12, 229, 235,
    239, 248, 250, 256, 273, 282, 287,
    289, 291, 297, 299–300, 305–6, 321
116th Regimental Combat Team
    (RCT), 86, 93, 152–53, 157, 158,
    160, 164, 173, 181, 199, 201, 203,
    204–5, 207, 208, 210, 214, 216,
    230, 233–34, 235, 238–39, 247,
    253–54, 257, 259–60, 272, 282,
    287, 299
121st Engineer Combat Battalion, 82,
    181, 216, 225, 227, 238, 240–41,
    243, 244
146th Special Underwater Demolition
    Battalion, 164
175th Infantry (Regiment), 72, 75, 254,
    264, 270
352d Infantry Division (Wehrmacht),
    112, 113, 114, 116, 117, 118, 120,
    132–33, 138, 140, 144, 182, 192,
    198, 203, 207, 249, 260, 272, 286,
    289, 305
389th Infantry (Regiment), 25–26
503d Parachute Regiment, 38
709th Infantry Division (German), 92,
    133
716th Infantry Division (German), 92,
    112, 115–16, 133, 286
726th Infantry Regiment (German), 112,
    117, 120–21, 124, 139, 207, 213
743d Tank Battalion, 141, 144, 151, 154,
    166, 170, 172, 173, 236, 238

American Expeditionary Forces, 12, 70
Army Group B (German), 111

Army Group G (German), 111
Army-Navy Joint Board, 31

Bastard Brigade, 93, 160
Big Red One. *See* 1st Infantry Division
British No. 4 Commando, 73
British No. 6 Commando, 51, 73

Center Task Force, 38, 39
Combined Operations Headquarters
    (COHQ), 49, 51–52, 53, 78–79,
    82, 84, 197, 278
Combined Operations Liaison Section,
    46, 59
Company A, 116th RCT, 142–45, 147,
    153, 154, 230, 231, 282
Company B, 116th RCT, 145, 149, 151,
    238
Company C, 116th RCT, 151, 158, 174,
    180, 181, 201, 203, 204, 207, 211,
    212–13, 214, 216, 235
Company D, 116th RCT, 149, 150, 199,
    214
Company E, 116th RCT, 152, 279
Company F, 116th RCT, 142, 153–55,
    156, 158, 208, 298
Company G, 116th RCT, 142, 153–55,
    156, 158
Company H, 116th RCT, 155–56,
    157–58, 175, 194, 256, 306

Eastern Task Force, 38
European Theater of Operations, USA
    (ETO, ETOUSA), 46, 49, 50, 52,
    53, 55, 59, 66–67, 68, 73, 74, 79,
    81, 84, 183, 307–8, 312, 326

First Division. *See* 1st Infantry Division
First Joint Training Force, 35

About the Author

Noel F. Mehlo Jr. is a former army counterintelligence agent with an interest in World War II history. He currently serves as an environmental specialist, working as a soil scientist, biologist, and wetland scientist, providing him valuable skills in scientific research. He has worked in cultural resources and has taught how to conduct historical research as well as a myriad of other topics in the transportation industry. Most of his professional written work includes reports and technical guidance. His research of the 5th Ranger Infantry Battalion took off in 2012 when he inherited his grandfather's World War II uniform. His research led to a book titled *The Lost Ranger: A Soldier's Story*.

Mehlo lives in Columbus, Ohio, with his family.